1 YEAR UPGRADE

BUYER PROTECTION PLAN

Developing
Web Services with
Java APIs
for XML Using WSDP

Jerry Foster

Mick Porter

Dreamtech Software, Inc.

Natalie Wear

Bob Hablutzel Technical Editor

KEY	SERIAL NUMBER
001	945T5GHD4T
002	MPET4AKRT4
003	3VN54NMER6
004	B39UNGD3S4
005	U6N7VH8U8M
006	NTE4NFMG4R
007	TBR46TWBVH
008	565M2PRB9R
009	R4BA3N58MS
010	2ZFCG6YTH2

PUBLISHED BY
Syngress Publishing, Inc.
800 Hingham Street
Rockland, MA 02370

Developing Web Services with Java APIs for XML Using WSDP

Printed in the United States of America

1 2 3 4 5 6 7 8 9 0

ISBN: 1-928994-85-7

Technical Editor: Bob Hablutzel
Technical Reviewer: Alex Ceponkus
Acquisitions Editor: Jonathan Babcock
Indexer: Jennifer Coker

Cover Designer: Michael Kavish
Page Layout and Art by: Shannon Tozier
Copy Editor: Mike McGee and Jesse Corbeil

Distributed by Publishers Group West in the United States and Jaguar Book Group in Canada.

Acknowledgments

We would like to acknowledge the following people for their kindness and support in making this book possible.

Ralph Troupe, Rhonda St. John, Emlyn Rhodes, and the team at Callisma for their invaluable insight into the challenges of designing, deploying and supporting world-class enterprise networks.

Karen Cross, Lance Tilford, Meaghan Cunningham, Kim Wylie, Harry Kirchner, Kevin Votel, Kent Anderson, Frida Yara, Jon Mayes, John Mesjak, Peg O'Donnell, Sandra Patterson, Betty Redmond, Roy Remer, Ron Shapiro, Patricia Kelly, Andrea Tetrick, Jennifer Pascal, Doug Reil, David Dahl, Janis Carpenter, and Susan Fryer of Publishers Group West for sharing their incredible marketing experience and expertise.

Jacquie Shanahan, AnnHelen Lindeholm, David Burton, Febea Marinetti, and Rosie Moss of Elsevier Science for making certain that our vision remains worldwide in scope.

Annabel Dent and Paul Barry of Elsevier Science/Harcourt Australia for all their help.

David Buckland, Wendi Wong, Marie Chieng, Lucy Chong, Leslie Lim, Audrey Gan, and Joseph Chan of Transquest Publishers for the enthusiasm with which they receive our books. And welcome back to Daniel Loh—glad to have you back Daniel!

Kwon Sung June at Acorn Publishing for his support.

Ethan Atkin at Cranbury International for his help in expanding the Syngress program.

Jackie Gross, Gayle Voycey, Alexia Penny, Anik Robitaille, Craig Siddall, Darlene Morrow, Iolanda Miller, Jane Mackay, and Marie Skelly at Jackie Gross & Associates for all their help and enthusiasm representing our product in Canada.

Lois Fraser, Connie McMenemy, Shannon Russell, and the rest of the great folks at Jaguar Book Group for their help with distribution of Syngress books in Canada.

Contributors

Jay Foster has been an IT professional since 1989. His areas of expertise include object-oriented design and modeling, software engineering, Web based application design/development, extranet/intranet security, and N-tier application development. He has extensive experience in the following technologies: Java Servlets, Enterprise JavaBeans (EJB), Java Server Pages (JSP), Java Database Connectivity (JDBC), Remote Method Invocation (RMI), Java Foundation Classes (JFC), Swing, OOA/OOD/OOP using the Unified Modeling Language (UML), CORBA, Web Services, .NET Framework, C#, ASP.NET, Web Security and Enterprise Application Integration. Jay has been developing object-oriented systems in Java since 1996 and is a Sun Certified Java Programmer. Jay has authored several books on various Java programming topics.

Mick Porter (SSJCP, MCP) is a Senior Technical Architect for Logica, a global systems integrator. Mick specializes in the design and implementation of wireless and mobile commerce systems. With 15 years of experience in the IT industry, Mick has worked on an enormous variety of systems and projects, and over the last few years, he has delivered a number of major e-commerce systems. Mick holds a bachelor's degree in Computer Science, and became a Sun Certified Java Programmer five years ago, as well as having passed eight Microsoft Certified Professional exams. Mick lives in Sydney, Australia, with his wife, Andrea, and children, Holly and Anthony.

Jonothon Ortiz is Vice President of Xnext, Inc. in Winter Haven, FL. Xnext, Inc. is a small, privately owned company that develops Web sites and applications for prestigious companies such as the *New York Times*. He has been a professional developer for over nine years now and has been exposed to a wide range of programming languages and styles. He uses JSP extensively to perform transformations of XML data in conjunction with other languages. Jonothon lives with his wife, Carla, in Lakeland, FL.

Dreamtech Software India Inc. is a software solution and service provider that provides a broad range of services and offers a dynamic blend of consultancy and system integration to help corporations build and implement innovative e-business strategies. A futuristic vision motivates the globally acclaimed software products of Dreamtech Software. Dreamtech has already distinguished itself with an excellent track record of publishing books on advanced technologies including XML and XSLT, WAP, Bluetooth, 3G , peer-to-peer networking, C#, and Java. The success of Dreamtech's endeavors to provide world-class software products can be gauged by the fact that its clientele includes some of the most distinguished names in IT-related publishing and solutions.

Natalie S. Wear is a Senior Java Developer and Systems Engineer at Telecommunications Services, Inc. in Tampa, FL. She creates code designs, provides architecture recommendations, and writes software for the Java applications used within her department. Such applications are primarily centered on back-end integration using XML and wireless industry-standard APIs. Her specialties include e-commerce, CORBA implementation, back-end system integration, and internet/intranet development. Natalie's background includes positions as Senior Java Engineer at Verizon Wireless and as an instructor of Vitria at PriceWaterhouseCoopers, LLP. She also teaches an undergraduate course on Java at the University of South Florida. Natalie holds a bachelor's degree in Political Science and another bachelor's degree in Management Information Systems (MIS) from the University of South Florida. She holds a master's degree in Business Administration (MBA) from the University of South Florida.

Greg Bylenok is a Software Engineer with iConverse. In his role at iConverse, Greg is involved in the design and development of products for the mobile industry. He has been using Java, J2EE, and XML technologies in his daily work for over three years.

Technical Editor and Contributor

Bob Hablutzel is a Senior Consultant with 20 years experience in enterprise-scale software systems. He is currently a Founding Partner in InflexionPoint, a consultancy whose practice spans the full cycle of a software product, from business needs analysis through architecture, development, debugging, and deployment. Bob is particularly interested in the efficiency and accuracy of large systems and has advised numerous projects on the identification and elimination of bottlenecks and errors. His background also includes time as CTO and Principle Architect of various startup companies. Bob's Web Services experience includes being a founding member of the XAML (XML-based business transactions) working group and implementing high-availability and clustering for the Bowstreet XML-based application server. His Java experience includes implementation of Java bytecode compilers and contributing to the book *Sun Certified Programmer for Java 2*. Bob lives in New Hampshire with his wife, Trish, and daughters, Anna and Katie.

Contents

Answers to You Frequently asked Questions

Q: What is the JWSDP?

A: The JWSDP is a collection of libraries, tools, and standard interfaces designed to ease the development of XML-based Web services in the Java programming language.

ix

Selecting a SAX Parser

The *newInstance()* method searches the target environment at runtime for a suitable SAX engine. It searches the following places in order:

1. System property space

2. JAXP properties file

3. JAR metafile

NOTE

The ParsingXML servlet uses the *GET* method (in which the servlet receives data in the form of a query string) for the request. However, the ParsingXML servlet does not read any data using the *HTTPServletRequest* object, since data is being read from a file-based source. Thus, the use of *doGet()* or *doPost()* is figurative and not practically relevant to this particular servlet.

**JAX-P and Underlying
XSL Engines**

- JAX-P is not an
XSL/XSLT engine; it is
actually a layer that
allows a developer to
use JAX-P regardless of
the XSL/XSLT engine
that lies beneath.

- Current popular
XSL/XSLT engines
include SAXON and
Xalan.

- Since JAX-P has to
provide a proper layer
over all available
XSL/XSLT engines it can
only support common
functionality.

Chapter 5 Using JSTL (JSP Standard Tag Library)   159

XML Support Tags

- All expressions in the XML Tag Library use XPath expressions.

- JSTL provides XML transformation capabilities via the *x:transform* action.

- By using the *x:transformer* action you can define a transformer instance that is reusable against multiple XML documents within the same page.

The Components of a SOAP Message

Unboxing

Unboxing is the act of converting an object back into a value type. The syntax for this process looks very similar to explicit casting in Java, as the following C# code demonstrates:

```
int x = 29;
object xObj = x; //
    Boxing
int x1 = (int)xObj; //
    Unboxing
```

ProviderConnections

ProviderConnection
objects essentially perform
three different tasks:

1. Allow information
   (meta data) about the
   Provider to be queried.

2. Provide
   MessageFactory objects
   that can produce
   messages specific to a
   certain profile.

3. Pass messages to the
   Provider to be sent
   asynchronously.

NOTE

WSDL supports four basic types of operations. These are:

- **One-way**, in which the service receives a message.

- **Request-Response**, in which the service receives a message and sends a response.

- **Solicit-Response**, in which the service (not the client) initiates communication by sending a message and receives a response.

- **Notification**, in which the service sends a message and seeks no response.

Answers to You Frequently asked Questions

Q: What version of SSL does JSSE support?

A: JSSE 1.0.2 supports SSL version 3.

Q: Can JSSE perform RSA encryption?

A: Yes, JSSE 1.0.2 performs RSA encryption.

Limitations

JWSDP does not support the following messages within the Registry Server:

- add_publisher Assertions

- delete_publisher Assertions

- get_assertionStatus Report

- get_publisherAssertions

- find_relatedBusiness

Foreword

It should come as no surprise to someone reading this foreword that two of the most influential forces in information systems over the last few years have been Java and XML. Java provides a stable, industrial-strength language that runs on a variety of platforms, while XML offers a simple format for the exchange of information across a variety of platforms. Together, they showcase tools for developing numerous applications: from reaching back into legacy computer systems, to reaching out to users and partners on the World Wide Web.

Lately, it has become popular to combine these two technologies in a highly-distributed architectural technique called *Web services*. Broadly speaking, a Web service is the exposure of a business process over a network. The connotation is generally that XML-based traffic is being moved on a public network (the Internet) via the HTTP protocol. However, Web services can also be useful internally to an organization, as a mechanism for encapsulating and exposing the business logic inherent in legacy systems. New applications can then utilize this Web service interface to leverage the complex business logic that has been refined, sometimes for decades, in these legacy systems. This allows for the reuse of systems at the logical level, without regard to physical configuration.

There is nothing specific to Java in Web services. In fact, the whole point of Web services is that any language, and any platform, can be used. I've written Web services in languages as varied as Java, C++, C#, and Perl, but the features that make Java attractive for general server programming (rich libraries, straightforward execution model, and portability) are the same ones that make Java attractive when writing new Web-service-based systems as well.

Until recently, Java programmers wanting to use XML-based Web services have been faced with a variety of libraries, each presenting a slightly different API and functionality. Web service standards such as SOAP, UDDI, and ebXML appeared (being key for next-generation Web-based applications), but had no direct support in Java.

This recently changed with the introduction of the *Java Web Services Developer Pack (JWSDP)*. The JWSDP was designed to create or endorse standard interfaces for the Java processing of XML. The name is somewhat misleading in that the JWSDP can be used for applications that have nothing to do with Web services. However, it does focus on the presentation of business logic over a network: Web services.

JWSDP is a rich collection of existing interfaces and libraries that Java endorsed, new standards developed under the Java Community Process, and code that Sun developed internally to support Web services. At the time this book was written, the most recent release was the EA2 (Early Access 2) version, which is the version focused on in these pages. As updates become available, check the Syngress Web site for amendments to this book.

The first chapter is intended to introduce you to the components of the JWSDP. It introduces the history of the JWSDP, and the components that make up the package. It's a good idea to read chapter one before skipping to any of the other chapters, just to get an overview of how the parts interoperate.

Since processing XML is key to Web services, the next three chapters take an in-depth look at processing XML in Java, each covering a different aspect of the process. Chapter 2 tackles parsing XML using SAX—the Simple API for XML. Chapter 3 covers parsing again, but this time for the Document Object Model. SAX and DOM are the two dominant mechanisms for processing XML in Java, and after reading these chapters you'll be able to decide which best fits your application needs.

Chapter 4 explores XML processing using XSL, a powerful system for transforming XML data, while Chapter 5 concentrates on the new APIs contained in the JWSDP. After reading Chapter 4, you'll be set to begin applying your XSL stylesheets to the XML you parsed in Chapters 2 and 3.

While XML is the core of a Web-services-based system, you need to be able to present those services externally. Its frequently the case that these services need to be presented directly to end users, and in J2EE that often means JSP. Chapter 5 also introduces the JSP Standard Tab Library, a component of the JWSDP designed to facilitate the development of complex JSPs.

Next, Chapters 6 and 7 turn to computer-to-computer communication, each discussing the SOAP (Simple Object Access Protocol) support built into JWSDP. Chapter 6 concentrates on writing SOAP clients—requesting a remote service (perhaps one of those wrapped legacy systems) perform some business logic, while Chapter 7 explores the flip side: writing SOAP servers to provide encapsulated business logic to remote clients. These chapters also introduce the concepts of SOAP *providers*, which can supply reliable routing of SOAP messages, and/or simplify the development of systems that rely on higher-level, SOAP-based protocols such as ebXML.

While message passing works well for many Web service systems, there are times where you want to be able to encapsulate the functionality of a remote service and present it as an object in your local application. This technique, known as *remote procedure calls*, is nothing new—Unix systems have provided this functionality for years, as have middleware tools such as COM and CORBA. However, with XML-based RPC, the remote system can be wildly different from the local machine—and doesn't even have to run a specific middleware tool. Chapter 8 investigates the XML-based RPC systems, and shows how you can develop applications that act as clients or servers.

Chapter 9 addresses the issue of finding and describing Web services. It covers the JWSDP interfaces to UDDI and ebXML registries, which are the dominant mechanisms for describing Web services. Registries were originally conceived as a global resource—a mechanism for finding an electronic business partner on the Internet—but the advent of low-cost registries such as the JWSDP Registry tool and jUDDI have made it practical for organizations to deploy registries for internal systems as well. After reading Chapter 9, you will be ready to dynamically describe and locate Web service descriptions a variety of ways.

For applications that do communicate with external partners, security is always a concern. Chapter 10 addresses the JSSE (Java Secure Sockets Extension). JSSE introduces a portable (and exportable) API for securing the point-to-point transfer of information. Using JSSE ensures that the messages you send are not intercepted or viewed by unintended audiences.

Finally, Chapter 11 addresses some of the miscellaneous tools included in the JWSDP. These tools, including Tomcat, Ant, and the JWSDP Registry, are designed to provide a development environment for building and testing Web-service-based applications. Again, these tools are complex, and could easily be a book topic on their own. Chapter 11 strives to introduce just enough of them for you to use them in conjunction with the JWSDP.

Writing a book, like an enterprise-class application, is an exercise in changing priorities, requirements, and scope. This is particularly true when writing about emerging technologies such as the JWSDP. The contributing authors and I have striven to produce a book that is as current as possible without being speculative, and useful in the real-world application of the JWSDP libraries. We hope that this book serves as both an introduction and a reference when writing Web-service-based systems in Java.

I want to give thanks to my editor, Jonathan Babcock, who made my first technical editing job easier than I expected. On a personal note, I want to thank my ever-supportive wife, Trish, and my daughters, Anna and Katie. Without Anna and Katie, larger portions of the book would have been done in daylight hours, but the laughter they bring more than makes up for any lost sleep. And without Trish, there would be no laughter or daylight at all.

—Bob Hablutzel, Technical Editor and Contributor
Sun Certified Java Architect
Consultant and Founding Partner, InflexionPoint

Chapter 1

Introduction to the JWSDP

Solutions in this chapter:

- **JWSDP History**

- **JAXP**

- **JAXM**

- **JAX-RPC**

- **JAXR**

- **JSSE**

- **JSTL**

- **Ant and Tomcat**

☑ **Summary**

☑ **Solutions Fast Track**

☑ **Frequently Asked Questions**

1

Introduction

The Java Web Services Developer Pack (JWSDP) is a collection of tools and libraries designed to make the development of Web services in Java as painless as possible. First introduced in January 2002 as an Early Access (EA) release, the JWSDP brings together XML parsers, SOAP support, service containers, and build tools that can be used to create and consume widely distributed services based on XML protocols.

At the time of this writing, the current release is EA2, which contains the following components:

- The JAXP XML processing libraries
- The JAXM XML messaging libraries
- The JAX-RPC XML Remote Procedure Call libraries
- The JAXR libraries for accessing XML registries
- The Java Secure Sockets (JSSE) library
- JSP Standard Tag Libraries
- The Apache/Jakarta Ant build tool
- The Apache/Jakarta Tomcat servlet container
- A simple UDDI registry (WSDP Registry tool)
- The Web Application Deployment tool

You probably noticed that parts of the JWSDP were not written by Sun. In fact, the JWSDP is mostly a collection of existing products; the JWSDP acts to package these tools in a form convenient to download and install. Also, with the JWSDP you know you have versions of the tools that work together, saving a lot of frustration when trying to get some code working.

This book covers the components of the JWSDP in detail. However, in order to make the book something you can actually lift without heavy machinery, some background information has been excluded. Specifically, this book won't teach you how to program Java (it's assumed you already know that). It won't teach you details about XML, SOAP, or other related protocols, although there will be some coverage of those topics in order to make points clear.

This book is focused on the libraries and tools that come with the JWSDP, and using these tools for real-world applications. After reading this book, you should be ready to begin writing and using Web services and XML documents in Java.

JWSDP History

As just mentioned, the JWSDP is a collection of existing tools, and is, in some sense, a marketing response to Microsoft's .Net initiative, gathering and highlighting existing technologies, and giving them a common name.

In most cases, this works to the benefit of the user. You no longer have to worry about what APIs are going to survive in the long run; the APIs in the JWSDP have Sun's blessing and are good choices to standardize on. You also don't have to wonder about version compatibility between different libraries; so long as the libraries all come with the JWSDP, you shouldn't have compatibility problems.

There are a few places where the gathering of libraries results in some oddities. In particular, the JAXM, JAXP, and JAX-RPC libraries were developed as separate initiatives by the Apache XML project and the Java Community Process. Because they were developed separately, there are places where the APIs overlap—for instance, some functionalities in the JAXM is also provided in JAXP. These places are pointed out in the text. It remains unclear if future versions of the JWSDP will address these issues.

The other aspect that can be confusing about the JWSDP is that some parts of it are available in different forms on the Web. For example, the JAXP libraries are shipped as a part of the JDK 1.4 release. JWSDP includes these libraries for capability with older versions of the JDK, especially as it will take some time for vendors to migrate to supporting the newer JDK releases.

Having said all that, it's worth looking at the individual components of the JWDSP.

JAXP

The Java API for XML Processing (JAXP) provides standardized interfaces for parsing and transforming XML documents. JAXP is designed to fill a hole in the XML standard interfaces: there are standard interfaces for transforming and parsing XML, but no standard interfaces for obtaining the transformers and parsers.

When XML first started gaining popularity, there were no standards for processing it. As time went on, standards developed for processing XML, but these standards were all interface-based—they did not contain any required classes. Libraries meeting the standards did so by implementing the standard interfaces and adding their own proprietary mechanisms for creating instances of those implementing classes. So, while your XML processing code, based in the interfaces, might be portable, the small bits of code used to create those objects were not. This meant XML libraries could not be swapped in and out without making small changes to the application code.

JAXP provides a standard set of interfaces, and more importantly classes, that allow for the creation of these implementation objects. JAXP does not redefine XML standards; instead, it leverages those standards (DOM, SAX, XSLT) that already have wide acceptance. JAXP ensures that code utilizing the standards will not have to be changed if the XML library supporting the standard interfaces is changed.

Because JAXP does not define XML interfaces on its own, you will find that some interfaces exposed in JAXP are not in the *java* or *javax* packages. Instead, Sun chose to adopt those standards already in wide use. This means that modifying code to use JAXP will hopefully be limited to those sections of code that create the parsers and transformers.

The next three chapters of the book cover the three aspects of JAXP: parsing using SAX and DOM parsers, and processing XML through XSLT transforms.

JAXM

The Java API for XML messaging addresses a similar problem: when the SOAP (Simple Object Access Protocol) standard was proposed, it did not have a standard set of libraries for Java. Not particularly surprising, given Microsoft's involvement in the creation of the standard, but still a problem for Java programmers. JAXM addresses this issue by providing a standard interface for SOAP 1.1 and the SOAP with Attachments, so that Java programmers can easily send and receive SOAP messages.

JAXM provides a number of features above just the implementation of the SOAP standards. It gives vendors a mechanism for supporting reliable delivery of messages, and for partial population of SOAP messages for specific SOAP-based protocols (such as ebXML).

It was earlier mentioned that some areas of the JWSDP overlap. JAXM is one example of this. Parts of JAXM provide a simple implementation for manipulating XML documents—an example of what JAXP provides in greater detail, and with standard interfaces. Ideally, JAXM would just leverage the interfaces provided by JAXP, but it doesn't.

This is because JAXM and JAXP were developed in parallel, by separate Java Community Process teams. It's unfortunate and confusing, however, and makes the processing of XML documents with both JAXM and JAXP harder. If you have to receive a message via SOAP, and process it further (for example, with XSLT transforms), you have to transform the document from one representation to another.

Sun has not, to my knowledge, publicly discussed this issue. However, one can hope that future JAXM releases will fix this problem.

JAXM is discussed in detail in Chapters 6 and 7 of this book.

JAX-RPC

The Java API for XML-based Remote Procedure Calls (JAX-RPC) provides a mechanism for making what appear to be object calls across a network via SOAP-based messages. JAX-RPC allows for the implementation of Web services described by WSDL (Web Service Definition Language) documents—the apparent standard for describing Web services.

With JAX-RPC, the implementation of what appears to be a Java object can, in reality, be hosted on a machine across a network (including the Internet), in any language that supports SOAP. This gives a powerful mechanism for decoupling business systems. Unlike other distributed systems (COM, CORBA), XML-based RPC can span architectures without requiring a large investment in common support software. All that is required is you process XML documents at each end. The mechanism for processing them, and the underlying system, are completely unimportant.

JAX-RPC acts much like RMI in that stub objects are created for use in invoking remote objects. Conceptually, you use the two systems identically. What differs between JAX-RPC and RMI is the format of the data transferred between the two machines. RMI uses low-level, Java-specific protocols (or CORBA IIOP), while JAX-RPC uses XML. Because of this, RMI may be faster—since the protocols are more efficient—but it is important to remember that JAX-RPC isn't about performance, it's about interoperability.

JAX-RPC, like JAXM, was a Java Community Process project, and was developed in parallel. However, JAX-RPC does a better job of hiding the implementation details. It does not need to expose the underlying XML structures as much as JAXM did. The current reference implementation does not appear to use JAXP, but implementations from other vendors could (as could the reference implementation in future releases). Again, this is a legacy from when JAX-RPC might have been downloaded without downloading JAXP—a problem the JWSDP (and JDK 1.4) eliminates.

JAX-RPC is covered in Chapter 8 of this book.

JAXR

Once Web services have been defined via WSDL, there needs to be a mechanism for finding them. WSDL documents are often published in *registries*, which provide a mechanism for the storage and retrieval of service descriptions. Registries allow users to search for services that will fulfill their needs, and download the specifications for those services.

The most common registry interfaces right now are the Universal Description Discovery and Integration (UDDI) and the ebXML (Electronic Business using XML) Registry and Repository. JAXR, the Java API for XML Registries, provides an abstract interface for querying registries; JAXR can be used to isolate the user from having to know the specifics of either UDDI or ebXML RegRep.

Registries provide rich, complex mechanisms for categorizing services. A large part of the JAXR API is targeted toward providing a standardized view of these categories. This is the main reason JAXR was created as a separate library, rather than extending JNDI (Java Naming and Directory Interface, which provides a similar functionality). The categories used by JAXR would be meaningless to most JNDI users, so it did not make sense to include them in the JNDI package. On the other hand, it isn't possible to use WSDL registries without these categories, therefore JAXR is a package that stands on its own.

JAXR, like packages discussed previously, was developed in parallel. However, the JAXR committee did a good job of watching the other Java Community Process efforts, and has come up with a specification that can be implemented using JAX-RPC, JAXM, and JAXP.

JAXR is covered in Chapter 9 of this book.

JSSE

At this point, you might have the impression that the JWSDP is nothing but XML processing. That isn't really true. JWSDP is closely related to the Java XML pack, which is limited to those packages discussed earlier. However, the JWSDP includes additional packages useful for creating Web-based applications.

The Java Secure Socket Extension (JSSE) is a good example of this. JSSE provides a mechanism for communicating over encrypted network connections and managing the keys associated with that encryption.

JSSE provides a royalty free implementation of SSL (Secure Sockets Layer) v3 and TLS (Transport Layer Security) 1.0 support. More importantly, the JSSE implementation may be exported from the United States, dramatically easing the adoption of secure communication in worldwide organizations.

In addition to providing low-level socket support for encryption, JSSE provides additional URL handlers, so that the *java.net.URL* class can understand and process HTTP URLs. This means that Web services, which require transport-level security, can be easily implemented in Java.

The JSSE is discussed in Chapter 10.

JSTL

Just as Web services are not only about XML, they are not only about business processing. There needs to be a mechanism for presenting functionality to end users, as well as to remote machines. It's common to use Java Server Pages (JSPs) to encapsulate the user interface of an application; this provides a simpler interface than coding servlets by hand.

However, JSPs have traditionally had to include either direct Java code or custom-written tag libraries in order to access the underlying business functionality. The JSP Standard Tag Library (JSTL) is designed to help ease this burden. JSTL provides a standard set of tags for common JSP tasks, such as iterating over a collection of objects, making database queries, and internationalizing text.

JSTL also provides for *expression languages*, which allow the user to directly access business objects with a simple expression. JSTL currently provides support for not one but a number of expression languages. This allows the user to choose the language that best suits their needs, but more importantly, protects the user from an upcoming JSP standard that should directly include expression languages.

JSTL comes directly from an Apache Jakarta project of the same name, which later came under the Java Community Process. JSTL is covered in Chapter 5.

Ant and Tomcat

Like JSTL, Ant comes from Apache Jakarta. Ant isn't a Java library—rather, it's a build tool. It's included with the JWSDP simply because it makes writing and bundling Java applications easy to do. Ant comes with built-in tasks for creating WAR (Web Application aRchive), which are the default packing for Java Web Services. Ant is an open-source project, whose sources can be found on www.apache.org

Similarly, Apache Jakarta's Tomcat is a reference implementation of the JSP and servlet standards. As such, it allows for the development hosting of servlet-based

Web services, such as JAXM supports. Unlike Ant, you likely will not use Tomcat for production deployments; it does not support failover, reliable message delivery, EJBs, or a host of other production features. However, it is free, fast, and lightweight to install; you can easily run Tomcat as a test server on your development machine. Like Ant, Tomcat is open-source and available at www.jakarta.apache.org/ant.

Along with Ant and Tomcat, JWSDP includes the WSDP (Web Services Developer Package) Registry server. This is a simple UDDI server, again for development and testing use. Unlike Ant and Tomcat, WSDP is a Sun project and is not open-source.

Ant, Tomcat, and WSDP Registry are covered in Chapter 11.

Summary

The JWSDP provides a collection of libraries and tools designed to give you everything you need to begin developing and testing Web services. In addition to the standard interface libraries, reference implementations for each library are provided. In some cases (JAXP), these reference implementations are production quality; in other cases (JAXM), they are sufficient for development. In all cases, the interfaces are designed to allow for the replacement of the reference implementations with alternative versions.

JWSDP also provides some tools to ease the development of Web services. They may not replace production servers (such as IBM WebSphere or BEA WebLogic) and other tools, but they will allow you to begin developing Web services.

Once you download the JWSDP, you have everything you need to develop Web services. The following chapters will walk you through all the pieces in detail, explaining how they work and how to use them. After finishing this book, you will be able to quickly develop high-quality Web services in Java.

Solutions Fast Track

JWSDP History

☑ The JWSDP is a collection of existing tools.

☑ JWSDP is, in some sense, a marketing response to Microsoft's .Net initiative—it gathers and highlights existing technologies, and gives them a common name.

☑ The JAXM, JAXP, and JAX-RPC libraries were developed as separate initiatives by the Apache Jakarta project and the Java Community Process. Because they were developed separately, there are places where the APIs overlap.

JAXP

☑ The Java API for XML Processing (JAXP) provides standardized interfaces for parsing and transforming XML documents.

☑ Because JAXP does not define XML interfaces on its own, you will find that some interfaces exposed in JAXP are not in the Java or javax packages. Instead, Sun chose to adopt standards already widely used. This means that modifying code to use JAXP will hopefully be limited to those sections of code that create the parsers and transformers.

JAXM

☑ JAXM provides a standard interface for SOAP 1.1 and SOAP with Attachments, so that Java programmers can easily send and receive SOAP messages.

☑ JAXM gives vendors a mechanism for supporting the reliable delivery of messages, and for partial population of SOAP messages for specific SOAP-based protocols (such as ebXML).

JAX-RPC

☑ The Java API for XML-based Remote Procedure Calls (JAX-RPC) provides a mechanism for making what appear to be object calls across a network via SOAP-based messages.

☑ With JAX-RPC, the implementation of what appears to be a Java object can, in reality, be hosted on a machine across a network (including the Internet), in any language that supports SOAP.

☑ JAX-RPC acts much like RMI in that stub objects are created to invoke remote objects. Conceptually, you use the two systems identically. What differs between JAX-RPC and RMI is the format of the data transferred between the two machines. RMI uses low-level, Java-specific protocols (or CORBA IIOP), while JAX-RPC uses XML.

JAXR

☑ JAXR, the Java API for XML Registries, provides an abstract interface for querying registries; JAXR can be used to isolate the user from having to know the specifics of either UDDI or ebXML RegRep.

☑ The JAXR committee did a good job of watching the other Java Community Process efforts, and has come up with a specification that can be implemented using JAX-RPC, JAXM, and JAXP.

JSSE

- ☑ JSSE provides a mechanism for communicating over encrypted network connections and managing the keys associated with that encryption.

- ☑ JSSE provides a royalty-free implementation of SSL (Secure Sockets Layer) v3 and TLS (Transport Layer Security) 1.0 support.

- ☑ In addition to providing low-level socket support for encryption, JSSE provides additional URL handlers, so that the *java.net.URL* class can understand and process HTTP URLs.

JSTL

- ☑ JSTL provides a standard set of tags for common JSP tasks, such as iterating over a collection of objects, making database queries, and internationalizing text.

- ☑ JSTL also provides for *expression languages*, which allow the user to directly access business objects with a simple expression.

- ☑ JSTL currently provides support for not one but a number of expression languages. This allows the user to choose the language that best suits their needs, but more importantly, protects the user from an upcoming JSP standard that should directly include expression languages.

Ant and Tomcat

- ☑ Ant is an open-source build tool that comes with built in tasks for creating WAR (Web Application aRchives), which are the default packing for Java Web Services.

- ☑ Tomcat is a reference implementation of the JSP and servlet standards. As such, it allows for the development hosting of servlet-based Web services, such as those JAXM supports.

- ☑ JWSDP also includes the WSDP (Web Services Developer Package) Registry server. This is a simple UDDI server, used for development and testing.

Frequently Asked Questions

The following Frequently Asked Questions, answered by the authors of this book, are designed to both measure your understanding of the concepts presented in this chapter and to assist you with real-life implementation of these concepts. To have your questions about this chapter answered by the author, browse to **www.syngress.com/solutions** and click on the **"Ask the Author"** form.

Q: What is the JWSDP?

A: The JWSDP is a collection of libraries, tools, and standard interfaces designed to ease the development of XML-based Web services in the Java programming language.

Q: How do I obtain JWSDP?

A: The JWSDP can be obtained from the following Web site: http://java.sun.com/Webservices/Webservicespack.html.

Q: What version of the JWSDP does this book cover?

A: At the time this book was written, the current version of the JWSDP was the EA2 release. That release is the one covered here.

Q: Is JWSDP new technology?

A: No, in most cases the JWSDP is a consistent packaging of existing technologies. Some portions, such as the WSDP registry, are unique to the JWSDP.

Q: Is JWSDP Sun's answer to .Net?

A: JWSDP is one aspect of the overall Java programming environment. It provides some features that compete with features in the .Net platform. Other parts of the Java programming environment, especially the J2EE specification, are equally important to consider when compared against .Net.

Q: Is there a charge for JWSDP?

A: No, JWSDP can be downloaded free from the site listed earlier in these questions.

Chapter 2

Processing XML Documents with SAX

Introduction

JAXP provides wrappers around two different mechanisms for processing XML data. The first is the Simple API for XML or SAX, and is covered in this chapter. The second, the Document Object Model (DOM), is covered in the next.

In the SAX model, XML documents are provided to the application as a series of events, with each event representing one transition in the XML document. For example, the beginning of a new element counts as an event, as does the appearance of text inside that element. A SAX parser reads through the XML document one time, reporting each event to the application exactly once in the order it appears in the document.

Event-based parsing has strengths and weaknesses. Very large documents can be processed with events; there is no need to read the entire document into memory at once. However, working with sections of an XML document (a record made up of many elements, for example) can become complicated because the application developer has to track all the events for a given section.

SAX is a widely used standard, but is not controlled by any industry group. Rather, it is a *de facto* standard that was originally developed by a single developer (David Megginson) and by others in the XML community and is now supported by an open source project (http://www.saxproject.org).

The SAX wrapper provided by JAXP allows for plugging in different SAX parsers without concern for the underlying implementation. This feature is somewhat moot because there aren't that many SAX parsers in widespread use today. However, it does provide for safeguards against changes in future versions.

Understanding Event-Based XML Parsing

One benefit of using XML is its inherent readability. You can take an XML document, print it out on paper, and show it to someone, who'll likely make some sense of its contents. Most XML documents provide some amount of context. You can probably discern a document of product inventory levels from a document of account balances just by looking at the tag names.

Although it helps in sharing information, sometimes all those tag names just get in the way. This is especially true within the confines of some programs. For example, your program may involve reading a document of account balances, and you may already have business objects defined for Accounts and Customers. In Java, you may find it easier to work directly with objects rather than raw tags and text. This is where a parser can assist you. A parser takes the raw text and converts it into something directly useable by a program.

The SAX Event Model

Most XML parsers fall into one of two main categories: tree-based or event-based. Each kind of parser represents XML information slightly differently. A tree-based parser converts an XML document into a tree of objects (You will learn more about tree-based parsers in the next chapter). An event-based parser presents a document as a series of events, each representing a transition in the document. Taken together, these events provide your program with a complete picture of the document.

Overview of Event Processing

Imagine again that we have printed out an XML document. How would you begin to read the document? You would probably begin at the top of the page and continue line by line, left to right. Since you are familiar with XML, you know that the tags have specific meanings. You would likely take notice of where one element ends and another begins; and with each new element you would gain a better understanding of the complete document.

Event-based parsers work in much the same way. An event-based parser scans through a document from top to bottom. As it scans, the parser takes notice of interesting points in the document. For example, it would notice where one element ends and another begins. The parser then alerts your program, giving it the opportunity to respond to the transition. In parser terminology, the alert is called an *event* and your program's response is a *callback*. A complete document parse may consist of hundreds or even thousands of events in series. Each event provides further information about the document.

Handling hundreds or thousands of events sounds overwhelming, and there's no doubt that it can get complicated. Event-based parsing suits some situations better than others. The simpler the DTD associated with a document is, the easier it will be to use event-based processing. Oftentimes these documents contain repeating groups of elements, where each group is to be processed the same way. Poor candidate documents are much the opposite. They are loosely-structured or contain deep and complex hierarchies. You may also want to avoid documents where elements are reused throughout multiple levels of a hierarchy. For these types of documents, consider the tree-based parsers discussed elsewhere in this book.

If you are interested in using an event-based parser, then you will need to learn the SAX API. Luckily, the S in SAX stands for "Simple." The SAX API defines a simple means for interacting with event-based parsers. SAX is a standard part of the JAXP package; so all JAXP parsers follow the SAX API. The rest of this chapter describes the SAX API in more detail.

History of SAX

SAX was one of the first XML technologies for Java. It has evolved only slightly since it was first released, and it has certainly proven itself a stable foundation for building XML applications in Java. Part of its success lies in how it was developed. It was conceived by an early group of XML users in an open, collaborative forum.

XML's creators addressed a common problem: systems from one vendor could not easily communicate with systems from another. XML breaks down those barriers by introducing a standard way to represent data. Once the standard was in place, early XML users began to focus on the problem of reading and incorporating XML into their applications.

It soon became clear that there was room for more than one parser, and quite a few companies developed their own implementations. Some of these parsers adopted the same basic approach, relying on an event-based model to parse documents. Although early parsers read XML documents just fine, they each presented results in a proprietary manner, and it became difficult to compare the various parsers one-on-one, especially for conformance with the XML spec. More importantly, users needed to learn new APIs for each parser. Suddenly, a technology created for interoperability was under threat of fragmentation by proprietary implementations.

Parser developers agreed that interoperability was a good idea for parsers, too. One early parser implementer, David Megginson, proposed a scheme for standardizing the interface to all event-based parsers. He solicited input from other interested members of the XML community, and then demonstrated the new scheme in his own early parser, *Ælfred*. The scheme was donated to the XML developer community as the Simple API for XML Processing.

SAX was primarily the work of one driving individual and several interested contributors. It was released without the backing of a formal sponsor or standards body. It found success, however, because it addressed a clear need in the XML community. Parser developers could write to one half of the API, and parser users could write to the other half. This leveled the playing field for parser implementers and parser users alike. Furthermore, SAX was simple to understand and to implement. It made learning the technologies less confusing and encouraged further adoption of XML.

SAX caught on and is now maintained by an open-source community, which can be found at http://www.saxproject.org. The community's job is to evolve the standard as XML itself evolves. For example, after the initial release, it soon became clear that XML namespaces would take an important role in XML's future. The SAX community responded by publishing SAX Version 2.0 with better support for namespaces. Since then, little has changed in the core of SAX except minor clarifications and bug fixes. Over time, it has proven to be a complete and stable package.

Basic SAX Events

The XML language allows us to build very complex documents while learning only a few simple rules. For example, all XML documents must start with one root element. Elements in turn may contain more elements, attributes, and text in any number of combinations. There are only a handful of other concepts – namely entities, namespaces, and Document Type Definitions. These latter concepts are indeed important, but they are secondary to understanding and using XML. Elements, attributes, and text remain the foundation of any XML document.

SAX includes at least one event for each of the basic XML structures, and since there are only a handful of basic XML structures, there are only a handful of SAX events. This is part of what makes SAX simple to learn and use; a real world XML document may be large and complex, but it can still be broken down into the basic events outlined below.

Here are the basic SAX events:

Document Events

Document events notify your program of the beginning and end of an XML document. A SAX parse always begins with a *start document* event and ends with an *end document* event. The end document event is particularly useful because it's the SAX parser's signal that the parse is complete.

Element Events

Element events notify your program of the beginning and end of each element. The SAX parser creates a *start element* event for each opening tag in the document. Likewise, it will create an *end element* event for each closing tag it finds.

Empty elements, or those without content, may not have distinct start and end tags. However, the SAX parser will still create both a start and end event for any empty element.

Character Events

Character events notify your program of any character data found between elements. Character data includes any text, entities, and CDATA sections.

SAX includes a few other events that are useful in special situations. These advanced events cover some of XML's advanced concepts, including:

- namespaces

- entities and entity declarations

- ignorable whitespace

- processing instructions

We will cover the advanced events in greater depth further in this chapter.

Example Parse Events

Figure 2.1 shows a clearer picture of how events fit together. It illustrates an example XML document and the event sequence created by the SAX parser. As you can see, even a simple XML document results in quite a number of events.

Figure 2.1 Example XML with Associated Parse Events

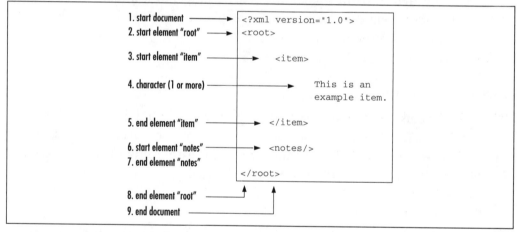

Understanding Event Handlers

Events by themselves aren't very interesting, especially if nothing listens for the events. When the parser creates an event, however, your program has the opportunity to respond. It's up to you as the programmer to supply the logic to handle the events. You provide that logic by writing an *event handler*.

Overview of Handlers

The SAX parser and the event handler work in unison to parse an XML document. First, the SAX parser notifies the event handler of every event it creates.

The event handler then services the event before passing control back to the parser. In servicing the event, your event handler can interpret the event in whatever manner you see fit. Parsing an XML document thus shifts back and forth between the parser and the event handler.

ContentHandler

The *ContentHandler* is the core interface of any SAX parser. It defines the most frequently used callbacks in the SAX API. Once you have a class that implements the *ContentHandler* interface, you are ready to begin using SAX in your programs. *ContentHandler* defines ten distinct callbacks, so you would need to write ten distinct methods to implement your own *Content Handler*.

DefaultHandler

You can easily create a class to implement all the SAX callbacks, but there's an even easier way to get started. The SAX package includes the *DefaultHandler* class to get you up and running quickly. You have already learned that SAX includes both frequently used events and less frequently used events. The *DefaultHandler* class allows you to concentrate on the frequently used events that are most interesting for your purposes.

The *DefaultHandler* serves as a concrete implementation of the *ContentHandler* interface, and defines simple callbacks for every event. However, the callbacks do nothing more than consume the events, making it an extremely basic implementation.

To create a more interesting event handler for your program, extend the *DefaultHandler* with your own subclass. You can provide your own implementation for only those callbacks that interest you most and ignore the other, less frequently used callbacks. If you do not implement a callback for a particular event, then the *DefaultHandler's* callback will take care of it.

Basic SAX Callbacks

You have already learned about the basic SAX events; here we describe the basic SAX callbacks. Each SAX event requires its own corresponding callback. When the SAX parser creates a particular event, the parser will call the appropriate callback method, as outlined below.

Document Callbacks

Document callbacks handle the corresponding document events that occur at the beginning and end of an XML document. The SAX parser begins every parse with a call to the *startDocument()* callback method. The *startDocument()* callback is an excellent place to perform any necessary initialization before continuing with the parse.

```
public void startDocument() throws SAXException;
```

```
public void endDocument() throws SAXException;
```

Likewise, the parser ends with a call to *endDocument()*. This is the final event provided by the SAX parser, and signals that the parse is complete.

Element Callbacks

The element callbacks execute at the beginning and end of each element. The element callbacks are much more interesting than the document callbacks because the SAX parser includes information parsed right out of the XML document. This information includes the element's name, namespace URI, and attributes.

```
public void startElement(String uri, String localName,
                         String qName, Attributes atts)
                         throws SAXException
```

```
public void endElement(String uri, String localName,
                       String qName) throws SAXException
```

The element's name is probably of most immediate interest. It gives some sense of the parser's progress through the document. You find the name of the parsed element in one of two parameters: the *localName* or the *qName*, which are each used in slightly different situations. The *localName* is interesting only while processing namespaces. Since namespace processing is disabled by default, we'll ignore the *localName* for now. Instead, look for the element name in the *qName* parameter. We'll discuss the differences between the *localName* and *qName* when we explore namespace processing later in this chapter.

A typical callback method will begin by interpreting the current element's name. Different elements may require different actions, so the callback must choose an action based on the element's name. Here is a simple example:

```
public void startElement(String uri, String localName,
                         String qName, Attributes atts)
                         throws SAXException
{
    if (qName.equals("order"))
    {
```

```
        //code to handle <order> element

    }

    else if (qName.equals("orderItem"))

    {

        //code to handle <orderItem> element

    }

}
```

If the element includes any attributes, the event will provide an *Attributes* object. The *Attributes* object contains the names and values of any element attributes. To find the value of an attribute, simply refer to a specific attribute by name. For example:

```
String value = atts.getValue("id"); // return the value of
                                     // the "id" attribute
```

Characters Callback

The characters callback handles any character events from the parser. As it scans the document, the SAX parser reads characters into an array. This includes text, entities, and CDATA sections. The parser then passes the array to the *characters()* callback method.

Importantly, the SAX parser may reuse the array between calls, so it may contain more than just the characters for the most recent event. The *start* and *length* parameters help you find the valid characters. The *start* parameter provides the offset into the array, while the *length* parameter provides the number of characters for the most recent event.

```
public void characters(char[] ch, int start,
                int length) throws SAXException
```

Unlike other events, it's difficult to predict just when or how many character events will occur. For any group of characters, the SAX parser is free to decide how many events to create. You cannot assume the parser will report a group of characters with one event; it may choose to report the characters with one event per line, or even one event per character. The SAX standard provides a lot of freedom here for parser implementations, so we cannot expect all parsers to behave identically. The example below describes a technique for dealing with this.

Example Event Handler

To get a better idea of how the callbacks fit together, we'll implement a basic SAX event handler and associated callbacks. However, before we can even begin to design an event handler, we must first understand the structure of the XML document to be parsed. In this example, we will be building part of an application to help manage a company's inventory. Here is an typical XML document containing information about the example company's wares and its inventory:

```
<?xml version="1.0" encoding="UTF-8"?>
<INVENTORY>
    <ITEM>
        <SKU>3956</SKU>
        <DESCRIPTION>widget</DESCRIPTION>
        <QUANTITY>108</QUANTITY>
    </ITEM>
    <ITEM>
        <SKU>5783</SKU>
        <DESCRIPTION>gadget</DESCRIPTION>
        <QUANTITY>32</QUANTITY>
    </ITEM>
    <ITEM>
        <SKU>6583</SKU>
        <DESCRIPTION>sprocket</DESCRIPTION>
        <QUANTITY>7</QUANTITY>
    </ITEM>
</INVENTORY>
```

Our example handler will read the XML document above and convert it into something more useful. In this example, we'll construct an object representation of the items in the company's inventory. Our business objects (of type "Item") simply hold the values from the XML document. After parsing, the business objects may then be manipulated further by the client application. Converting XML into objects is a very common application of SAX, so you may find these techniques useful for your own programs.

Here is the example event handler with its callbacks:

```
import org.xml.sax.helpers.DefaultHandler;
import org.xml.sax.SAXException;
import org.xml.sax.Attributes;
```

```java
/**
 *  This class implements a SAX event handler for parsing
 *  item inventory levels from an XML document.
 */
public class InventoryHandler extends DefaultHandler
{
    private Item currentItem;      //item model object
    private ItemCollection items; //parse results holder

    private StringBuffer characters; //buffer for element content

    /**
     * SAX callback to handle character events
     */
    public void characters(char[] ch, int start, int length)
                        throws SAXException
    {
        characters.append(ch,start,length);
    }

    /**
     * SAX callback to handle start of document
     */
    public void startDocument() throws SAXException
    {
        // Initialize before parsing this document
        characters = new StringBuffer();
        items = new ItemCollection();
    }

    /**
     * SAX callback to handle start of each element.
     */
    public void startElement(String uri, String localName,
                            String qName, Attributes aAttribs)
                            throws SAXException
```

```java
    {
        if (qName.equals("ITEM"))
        {
            //Create a new Item object to hold Item data
            currentItem = new Item();
        }

        //Prepare character buffer for element content
        characters = new StringBuffer();
    }

    /**
     * SAX callback to handle end of each element.
     */
    public void endElement(String uri, String localName,
                            String qName) throws SAXException
    {
        //read element contents from buffer
        String content = characters.toString();

        if (qName.equals("SKU"))
        {
            //We have just parsed a SKU
            currentItem.setSKU(content);
        }
        else if (qName.equals("QUANTITY"))
        {
            //We have just parsed a QUANTITY
            currentItem.setQuantity(content);
        }
        else if (qName.equals("ITEM"))
        {
            //We have finished parsing one item. Save in
            //collection before we parse another.
            items.add(currentItem);
        }
    }
}
```

The event handler code may be difficult to follow until you consider the original XML document. The XML document itself drives the sequence of events created by the parser. With each event, the parser will call the appropriate callback method. Each callback in turn processes a small portion of the document. To better understand the order of execution, it helps to envision the parser as it scans the XML document. Consider the parser's progress through the example document:

1. **Document start** The parser triggers the *startDocument* callback. We begin by initializing any data structures needed for the parse.

2. **<INVENTORY> element** The parser triggers its first *startElement* callback. The inventory element doesn't tell us anything useful, so we move on without performing any special processing.

3. **<ITEM> element** The parser triggers a second *startElement* callback. We are now parsing information about a particular item. This is our opportunity to create a new data structure to hold information about the coming item.

4. **<SKU> element** The parser triggers yet another *startElement* callback. We are about to read information about the SKU, but we must wait for a subsequent *character* event for the SKU itself.

5. **Element content** The parser passes in the SKU data itself through one or more calls to the *characters* callback. Remember, the element content may all appear in one callback, or it may be broken up into multiple callbacks. Thus, we collect the character data in a buffer.

6. **</SKU> end element** The parser triggers its first *endElement* callback, letting us know that we have finished reading in the element content. We interpret the content as a SKU and add it to our model object.

7. **<QUANTITY/> and <DESCRIPTION/> elements** The parser handles these in much the same way as the *<SKU/>* element, repeating steps 4 through 6 for each element. For this particular example, our code ignores the *<DESCRIPTION/>* element completely. This is one of the key benefits of event-based parsing. SAX allows us to save some parts of the document while filtering out others completely.

8. **</ITEM>** With the *endElement* callback, we have completely read one item. We add the completed item to a collection to be retrieved later.

9. **<ITEM/>** If the document contains additional items, then steps 3 through 8 will be repeated until all items have been read.

10. **</INVENTORY>** The parser triggers one last *endElement* callback.

11. Finally, the parser terminates with an *endDocument* callback. We defer to the *DefaultHandler's* implementation since our handler does not provide its own implementation. The *DefaultHandler* simply consumes the event.

When the parse is complete, the *InventoryHandler* will have created a complete object representation of the original XML document. Running this *InventoryHandler* against an XML document requires a few more pieces, however. It must be combined with a SAX parser and a source of XML data. We'll pick up this example in later sections, adding the other components to complete the picture.

Creating a SAX Parser

The SAX parser does much of the heavy lifting in reading an XML document, while you only need to provide a simple event handler. In this section, you'll learn how to instantiate the parser itself.

SAX Interfaces and SAX Implementations

Interoperability among parsers was one of the original design goals of SAX. The SAX creators wanted to make it easy for developers to swap in one parser for another. This is accomplished through heavy use of interfaces, which are an excellent way to shield developers from underlying implementations. In SAX, this shield works two ways: It protects both the SAX user and the parser.

We've already seen how this works with the event handler interface described in the previous section. As a SAX user, you implement the *ContentHandler* interface yourself. Whenever the parser needs to communicate with your application, it does so only through the narrowly defined *ContentHandler* interface. The SAX parser never concerns itself with the specifics of your implementation; it simply creates events and passes them through the *ContentHandler* interface.

SAX defines another interface specifically for SAX parser implementers. Here the roles are reversed: The SAX parser implements the *XMLReader* interface, through which you communicate with the parser. The *XMLReader* is the main SAX interface to the underlying parse engine: it defines every action you can perform with the parser, such as providing it with an XML document or initiating a parse.

With these two interfaces, the parser and the event handler remain virtually decoupled. They can each proceed without ever acknowledging one another's concrete implementation, which is an excellent quality because it allows you to write applications that are independent of the underlying SAX engine. In fact, you can write an entire SAX application without ever referring to a specific SAX parser.

JAXP and Underlying SAX Engines

So far we've talked a lot about SAX but not a lot about JAXP. The reason for this is simple: SAX is very much complete and usable in and of itself. That being said, JAXP adds some important refinements that merit discussion.

Introducing the JAXP Package

JAXP essentially bundles a number of existing XML technologies into one convenient and unified framework. Most of these technologies—including SAX—predate JAXP itself. Further, existing applications may be using SAX independently of JAXP, so JAXP strives to ensure backwards compatibility. One result is that under JAXP, existing XML classes maintain their original naming conventions. This can be rather confusing at first, so it helps to understand how things are organized.

First, the core SAX classes are located in their original SAX packages. These are found in the following packages:

```
org.xml.sax.*
org.xml.sax.helpers.*
```

JAXP introduces several new classes in several new packages. The classes for working with SAX parsers are located here:

```
javax.xml.parsers.*
```

The new JAXP classes add a "plugability layer" over the existing SAX interfaces. With JAXP, you can plug a SAX engine into the Java runtime and then refer back to it through the JAXP API. Here, we'll see how to use this plugability layer to create applications that are portable across SAX engines.

Using the *SAXParserFactory*

The core SAX API merely provides an interface to the underlying SAX parser. If you've worked with interfaces before, you know that you can't create an object instance directly from an interface. However, you could always instantiate a SAX parser by name if you knew about the underlying implementation and its constructors. This latter approach would make your code dependent on a specific SAX parser.

Fortunately, JAXP allows us to construct parsers in a manner that is completely portable. It provides an abstract factory mechanism for constructing parsers irrespective of the underlying implementation. Use the abstract factory class, called *SAXParserFactory*, to construct an instance of a parser. It is actually a two-step process: You first, obtain an instance of the concrete factory, and then you obtain a concrete parser from the concrete factory:

```
SAXParserFactory factory = SAXParserFactory.newInstance();
SAXParser parser = factory.newSAXParser();
```

By applying the factory, we avoid referencing any specific SAX engine by name, which helps to keep things portable. The JAXP factory's *newInstance()* method ends up returning a concrete SAX factory for a specific SAX engine, but we never concern ourselves with the concrete implementation's details. In the next section, you'll learn how the *newInstance()* method makes its selection.

With the concrete factory in hand, we can begin to build concrete instances of the parser. The *newSAXParser()* factory method creates instances of JAXP's *SAXParser* class. The *SAXParser* class is just a simple wrapper over the SAX's standard *XMLReader* parser class. It also provides a few convenience methods for interacting with the underlying parser.

NOTE

Although SAX originally included its own parser factory, only the new JAXP factories provide for plugability. Use JAXP's SAXParserFactory to instantiate a parser, and ignore SAX's older XMLReaderFactory.

Selecting a SAX Parser with the Plugability Interface

The JAXP plugability layer always provides a valid SAX engine, but how do we know exactly which engine it provides? The answer lies within *SAXParserFactory's* *newInstance()* method. The *newInstance()* method searches the target environment at runtime for a suitable SAX engine. It searches the following places in order:

1. System property space
2. JAXP properties file

3. JAR metafile

4. Platform default

System Property Space

JAXP begins its search by querying for a system property named *javax.xml .parsers.SAXParserFactory*. To force JAXP to use a particular engine, simply set the property to the name of a specific SAX implementation. You can set this at runtime through the command line. For example, starting Java as follows will force JAXP to use the Xerces XML parser:

```
java -Djavax.xml.parsers.SAXParserFactory=
org.apache.xerces.jaxp.SAXParserFactoryImpl   <your main class>
```

JAXP Properties File

If you choose not to set the system property, JAXP will look in a specific properties file for the information. The properties file, called jaxp.properties, must be installed as a Java extension. Simply create a properties file with the same key and value as above and save it to your Java runtime environment's JRE/lib directory. This is convenient because you only need to go through this once; there's no need to set system properties everytime you run.

JAR Metafile

JAXP provides a third method that is more complicated but more powerful than the first two methods. This is where JAXP will most likely find its parser, so it is important to understand how it works. Basically, JAXP looks for a preferred SAX engine within each JAR file in the classpath. The name of the preferred SAX engine is tucked away in a metafile within the JAR file itself. Conveniently, most JAXP parsers already contain this metafile. Thus, the simple act of adding your parser's JAR file to the classpath is all that's needed to access this functionality. If you'd like to introduce a new parser, simply place it somewhere forward in the classpath and JAXP will automatically configure itself to use the parser, without forcing you to explicitly set any properties.

Platform Default

Finally, some Java environments offer a default SAX engine. This is the case with Sun's new Java Development Kit version 1.4, which bundles a number of XML technologies. When all else fails, JAXP will use the platform's default SAX engine.

Developing & Deploying…

Parser Proliferation

If XML continues to grow in popularity, XML parsers may eventually become ubiquitous. Already, XML is an integral part of many products. These products may bundle their own XML parsers; if these are Java products, then chances are the XML parsers use SAX. For example, if you are using a modern Integrated Development Environment, it likely includes a SAX parser, soyou may already have a SAX-compliant parser in your possession without even realizing it.

As you begin to work with XML, here are some of the parsers you will likely encounter:

- **Xerces 1** Xerces 1 is the workhorse of modern parsers. It is SAX 2.0 compliant but does not support the JAXP plugability layer. Even so, many XML tools, development environments, and application servers still depend on the Xerces parser. If you are developing for a server-side environment, check to see if your application server requires you to use Xerces.

- **Crimson** Sun originally developed this parser as a technology demonstration, then donated it to the open-source community. Now it has found its way back into Sun's product fold. Crimson is the standard parser in JAXP 1.1, and it is the standard parser bundled with Sun's Java Development Kit version 1.4.

- **Xerces 2** Xerces 2 is a next-generation, high performance XML parser. Xerces 2 is the standard parser included with JAXP 1.2, which makes it a sign of things to come. Eventually, it should replace both Xerces 1 and Crimson in Sun's lineup.

As XML standards continue to evolve, we can expect XML parsers to evolve with the standards. Newer parsers may offer extra features, like schema-based validation in the Xerces parser. JAXP insulates you from these changes without preventing you from using them to full effect.

JAXP plugability can simplify the task of distributing SAX applications, because you don't necessarily need to bundle a SAX parser. As long as your code follows the SAX standard, you can be reasonably confident it will work with whatever SAX engine is available. Of course, it is always best to test your application thoroughly with each parser. If you notice any difference, you can always bundle a SAX parser with your application and configure JAXP to use your preferred parser.

Parsing Data with a SAX Parser

Parsing with SAX requires three things: an event handler, a parser instance, and an XML document to be parsed. You've already learned how to write an event handler and how to create a parser instance; this section describes how to combine an event handler and parser along with an XML document itself.

Input Sources

XML documents may be static or dynamic. Static documents may be stored in a file system or document repository, whereas dynamic documents may be assembled on the fly from databases or other enterprise systems. Either may be transmitted electronically through any number of networking protocols. Whatever its source, you can find a way to parse the document with SAX.

InputSource

Use the SAX *InputSource* class to pass the XML document to a parser. The *InputSource* object allows the parser to locate the XML data.

URI-based Sources

If you know the XML document's exact location, you can create an *InputSource* directly from a Uniform Resource Identifier (URI). This method works particularly well for reading in static documents from your local file system. You can also read documents over the Internet using the HTTP protocol:

```
InputSource fromFile = new InputSource("file:///"+aFilename);
InputSource fromWeb  = new InputSource("http://www…");
```

Stream-based Sources

Many applications may not deal with static XML documents on a physical disk. This is particularly true of web services, where XML messages may be constructed on the fly and passed electronically. For these types of sources, you may construct an *InputSource* directly from a stream:

```
InputSource byteSource = new InputSource( someInputStream );
InputSource charSource = new InputSource( someReader );
```

Stream-based sources provide a lot of flexibility, but they also come with some additional responsibility. With stream-based sources, you may need to provide additional information to help the parser correctly interpret the source. For example, when working with byte streams, the parser must convert the bytes into characters. It then becomes important to tell the parser how the characters are encoded. If you've set the character encoding within the document's XML declaration, then the parser should be able make the conversion on its own. However, if you've failed to set the encoding within the document, you should set it on the *InputSource* itself. For example, to set the stream's encoding to UTF-8, use the following method:

```
byteSource.setEncoding("UTF-8");
```

Character encodings can get quite complex and SAX parsers are not required to support all encodings known to man. Generally, parsers support at least the common encodings, including US-ASCII, ISO-Latin-1, and UTF-8. If you are working with international content, make sure that your XML parser can understand the encoding for your content.

An Example Servlet

You've just about learned everything needed to begin building SAX applications. You've learned how to construct a parser, create an event handler, and locate an input source. Now we will demonstrate how to put these pieces together into a complete application. The example application is part of a fictitious company's inventory management system.

Earlier in this chapter, we created an event handler to read information about the company's inventory. This example picks up where the first example left off: it adds a source of XML data and a parser instance to the original event handler. The three pieces are combined within a servlet, providing web-based access to the company's inventory.

In continuing this example, we've made some slight alterations to the original event handler. Most importantly, we've added a method to retrieve the parsed results from the event handler. The servlet itself calls this method after completing the parse. Secondly, the event handler no longer skips anything from the example XML document. It now reads all information for each inventory item, including its full description. Figure 2.2 shows the servlet's complete output.

Figure 2.2 Example Servlet Output

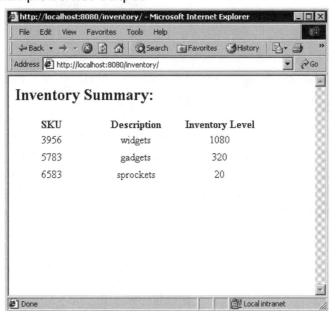

Below you'll find the code for the servlet that produced the output in Figure 2.2. When examining the code, begin with the servlet's *init()* method. If you are familiar with servlets, you know that the *init()* method is a good place to perform any initialization work. In our case, it's a perfect place to instantiate a parser factory from JAXP's abstract factory. The *init()* method is only called once, so we save the factory within a member variable.

After initialization, the servlet waits for any user requests. Each request to the servlet invokes the servlet's *get()* method. The *get()* method is where the servlet constructs an event handler, a parser, and an input source. After running the parser, the servlet obtains the results of the parse from within the event handler. Finally, it iterates through the parsed results and displays them in a simple table.

```
import java.util.Iterator;
import java.io.IOException;

import javax.servlet.ServletException;
import javax.servlet.ServletOutputStream;
import javax.servlet.http.HttpServlet;
import javax.servlet.http.HttpServletRequest;
import javax.servlet.http.HttpServletResponse;
```

```java
import javax.xml.parsers.SAXParserFactory;
import javax.xml.parsers.SAXParser;
import javax.xml.parsers.ParserConfigurationException;

import org.xml.sax.InputSource;
import org.xml.sax.SAXException;

public class InventoryServlet extends HttpServlet
{
    //share one instance of the parser factory
    private SAXParserFactory parserFactory;

    /**
     * Initializes the servlet. The servlet container
     * will only call this method once!
     */
    public void init() throws ServletException
    {
        //instantiate a concrete factory
        parserFactory = SAXParserFactory.newInstance();
    }


    /**
     * Handles a GET request to this servlet.
     */
    public void doGet(HttpServletRequest request,
                      HttpServletResponse response)
                      throws IOException, ServletException
    {
        //contruct custom event handler
        InventoryHandler eventHandler = new InventoryHandler();

        //obtain SAX parser instance
        SAXParser parser = null;
        try
        {
```

```
                parser = parserFactory.newSAXParser();
        }
        catch (ParserConfigurationException pce)
        {
                throw new ServletException("Error constructing parser.", pce);
        }
        catch (SAXException se)
        {
                throw new ServletException("Error constructing parser.", se);
        }


        try
        {
                //provide XML document
                String uri =
                            "file:///C:/samples/inventory.xml";
                InputSource sourceDoc = new InputSource(uri);

                //initiate the parse
                parser.parse(sourceDoc,eventHandler);
        }
        catch (SAXException se)
        {
                throw new ServletException("Error parsing inventory.", se);
        }


        //retrieve and print results
        ItemCollection items = eventHandler.getParseResults();
        printItems( items, response.getOutputStream() );
}


/**
 * Prints output as HTML.
 */
private void printItems(ItemCollection items,
                        ServletOutputStream out)
                        throws IOException
```

```
    {
        Iterator iter = items.iterator();

        //set up the HTML
        out.println("<HTML><BODY><H2>Inventory Summary:</H2>");
        out.println("<TABLE><TR ALIGN='CENTER'>");
        out.println("<TH WIDTH='30%'>SKU</TH>");
        out.println("<TH WIDTH='40%'>Description</TH>");
        out.println("<TH WIDTH='30%'>Inventory Level</TH></TR>");

        //print a table row for each item
        while (iter.hasNext())
        {
            Item currentItem = (Item) iter.next();

            out.println("<TR ALIGN='CENTER'>");
            out.println("<TD>"+currentItem.getSKU()+"</TD>");
            out.println("<TD>"+currentItem.getDescription()+"</TD>");
            out.println("<TD>"+currentItem.getQuantity()+"</TD>");
            out.println("<TR>");
        }

        //close out the HTML
        out.println("</TABLE></HTML>");
        out.flush();
    }
}
```

Servlets and Multithreading

Servlet-based applications are multithreaded by nature so it is important to keep multithreading in mind when working with servlets. The example servlet demonstrates how to apply SAX within a multithreaded environment. The most important thing to remember is that SAX parsers are not thread safe. Although you may reuse one parser to parse several documents, you can't reuse it to parse several documents at the same time. Our servlet's *get()* method therefore constructs a new parser with each user request, allowing the servlet to handle multiple users simultaneously.

Parser instances cannot be shared between threads, but the *SAXParserFactory* can be shared under certain circumstances. The example servlet maintains only one instance of the factory, and it refers back to that instance over and over again within the servlet's *get()* method. This works fine in a multithreaded environment because the *SAXParserFactory's newSAXParser()* method is declared to be thread safe. Consequently, we can safely use the factory object in many threads at once.

Debugging…

Using Locators to Aid Debugging

XML applications are often data-driven, and this can make them especially difficult to debug. Your program's execution depends not only on the correctness of your code, but also the that of every XML document processed. If your event handler is not doing what you expect, start by getting a better understanding of the event sequence. Once you understand the parser's progress through the XML document, you can begin to diagnose the problem.

Traces are a basic technique for understanding the event sequence. Within your event handler, create a trace routine that prints out messages to the screen or to a log file. Then, call the trace routine at the start of every event callback. The trace output should give you a clearer picture of the event sequence, much like that shown in Figure 2.1.

While tracing is useful for debugging small documents, it can quickly become unwieldy; a large document may produce thousands of events, so following the event trace may be overly tedious. For complex documents, correlating the trace with the original document may still pose challenges. Fortunately, SAX includes a mechanism to help you make better sense of your trace output.

Use the *Locator* mechanism to make tracing even more effective. The *Locator* object provides the parser's exact location as it scans through the XML document. It will help you zero in on the position of events within the document. To begin using the *Locator* within your event handler, first implement the *setDocumentLocator()* method to save a reference to the Locator itself. (The SAX parser calls this method to hand you the *Locator*.) During the parse, query the Locator whenever you need to know the parser's position:

Continued

```
     private void traceEvent(String eventMessage)
     {
          System.out.print("Event:"+eventMessage);

          // if locator is set, print line and column
          if (this.locator != null)
          {
             int line = this.locator.getLineNumber();
             int column = this.locator.getColumnNumber();
             System.out.println(" at line: "+line+
                                 " and column: "+column);
          }
     }
```

Officially, the *Locator* mechanism is an optional part of SAX. As with any optional feature in SAX, it's a good idea to check that the parser supports it. Thus, the code above first checks for the Locator's presence. You will find that most common parsers supply a Locator, simply because it's so useful.

Configuring the Parser

Real world XML documents are rarely as simple as those demonstrated in Figure 2.2. This is especially true in web services, where XML documents often partake in complex exchanges. Web services present a couple of challenges: First, the XML documents must conform to an agreed-upon structure. Second, the meaning of each tag must not be misinterpreted.

Two XML features help deal with each of these challenges. First, Document Type Definitions (DTD) allow you to validate a document's structure. Second, namespaces allow you to associate elements with specific XML grammars. These features are used prominently in web services. Together, they help keep communications running smoothly.

All SAX-compliant parsers include support for both DTDs and namespaces, whereas specific SAX parsers may provide other special capabilities as well. This section describes how to enable these features and use them in your applications.

Enabling Validation

If your XML document refers to a DTD, you may want to enable DTD validation. With DTD validation, the SAX parser will check the structure of the document against the DTD as it parses; if the document's structure does not match the DTD, the parser responds with an error.

Use JAXP's *SAXParserFactory* class to enable validation. Once enabled, the validating option will apply until it is changed. Any new parsers created through the factory will perform DTD validation. Try the following code to create one or more validating parsers:

```
SAXParserFactory factory = SAXParserFactory.newInstance();
factory.setValidating(true);
SAXParser validatingParser = factory.newSAXParser();
```

SAX provides a couple of other mechanisms that work hand-in-hand with DTD validation. When using validation, you may want to specify a *DTDHandler* and an *ErrorHandler* in along with your usual event handler. The *DTDHandler* assists in parsing the DTD itself, while the *ErrorHandler* can deal with any validation errors. Neither of these is necessary to use DTD validation, but we'll get back to these in the next section.

Finally, you should understand that validation incurs a performance penalty because validating a document is simply extra work for the parser. If performance is a critical part of your application, you may want to reconsider using any validation. As a tradeoff, consider turning on validation during testing and turning it off during production.

Enabling Namespaces

SAX includes support for processing XML namespaces. Like DTD validation, namespace processing is a special feature that must be explicitly enabled. Use JAXP's *SAXParserFactory* class to enable namespace processing. Once enabled, any new parsers created through the factory will read and interpret any namespace declarations and namespace prefixes used in the document. Try the following code to create a namespace-aware parser:

```
SAXParserFactory factory = SAXParserFactory.newInstance();
factory.setNamespaceAware(true);
SAXParser validatingParser = factory.newSAXParser()
```

> **NOTE**
>
> JAXP disables namespace processing by default. This is in slight contrast with the stand-alone SAX package, where namespace processing *is* enabled.

Namespaces and Events

Namespace processing makes SAX parsing a little more complicated. Namespaces are an extra piece of information to juggle, both for you and for the parser. With namespaces enabled, the SAX parser reads any namespace declarations from the document and locates the corresponding namespace for each and every element in the document. Finally, it interprets the namespace prefixes with each element or attribute. The SAX parser provides all this information to you through standard SAX callbacks, and its up to you to make sense of it all.

Here is how namespaces influence the SAX callbacks:

Element Callbacks

We've already discussed the element callbacks earlier in the chapter, but we now have a chance to explore them in depth. Here is the element callback once again:

```
public void startElement(String uri, String localName,
                    String qName, Attributes atts)
                    throws SAXException
```

The element callback provides several pieces of information about each element. These include the element's URI, its *localName*, and its *qName*. When we originally discussed the element callback, we focused mostly on the *qName*, But now that we are processing namespaces, the other two parameters take on new significance.

The *URI* parameter is simply the namespace URI of the current element. The URI is important because it uniquely identifies the element's namespace. If your document contains more than one namespace, you may want to break your callback logic into parts, where each part handles processing for one particular namespace.

The *localName* and *qName* each provide the name of the current element. The two are similar, but the *localName* omits the namespace prefix provided in the *qName.* This is actually a good thing, because the namespace prefix usually just gets in the way; you already know the particular namespace's URI, which does a much better job at uniquely identifying the namespace. The local name will be most frequently used, but the *qName* can be used for clarificiation when embedded namespaces have identically named elements.

It does little harm to enable namespace processing, even if your document contains no namespaces. You may continue to use the *localName* parameter as long as namespace processing is enabled. For any elements without a namespace, simply expect the URI parameter to be empty.

Prefix Mapping Callbacks

For documents that contain more than one namespace definition, it may be important to track where one namespace begins and another ends. SAX includes another callback specifically for this purpose. When namespace processing is enabled, the SAX parser will automatically recognize any change in namespace. It then notifies your event handler via a special namespace event. You can add the following callbacks to your event handler to pick up these events:

```
public void startPrefixMapping(String prefix, String uri) ;
public void endPrefixMapping(String prefix);
```

If an element declares a namespace, the namespace takes effect for that element as well as any child elements. As it scans the document, the parser will move in and out of different namespaces. Use the prefix mapping callbacks to keep track of where one namespace begins and another ends.

Enabling Other Features

The SAX creators tried to keep the SAX standard as simple as possible by limiting the standard to a core of common features that would be useful to a wide audience. You have already learned about two of these features: namespace processing and validation via DTDs. A parser must offer both of these features to be considered SAX-compliant.

While the SAX standard was kept simple, it was also made flexible. It allows SAX parsers to add their own innovations. Some parsers may very well offer proprietary features that you might find useful for your applications. Though these new capabilities are not mandated by the SAX standard, they are still welcome within SAX applications.

The Xerces parser, included with JAXP 1.2, is a perfect example. In addition to validating from a DTD, the Xerces parser can also validate from an XML

Schema. XML Schemas hold promise because they are more powerful and more flexible than traditional DTDs. For now, however, XML Schemas remain an emerging technology. Until XML Schemas become ubiquitous, we cannot expect all SAX parsers to offer this same innovation.

Features and Properties

SAX organizes parser capabilities into two categories: SAX parser features and SAX parser properties. From a practical standpoint, the differences between these two are minor. There's little sense in getting hung up on terminology, but here are some guidelines to help you understand the difference:

- Use *features* to control parser behavior.
- Use *properties* to control parser state.

SAX defines a few core features and properties for all SAX engines. These are described further in Table 2.1 and Table 2.2. You'll need to refer to your specific parser's documentation to learn about any additional proprietary features and properties that it may offer. Before trying to use any features or properties, make sure they are actually implemented by your particular parser.

Table 2.1 Core SAX Features

Feature Name	Description
http://xml.org/sax/features/namespaces	Turns namespace processing on or off.
http://xml.org/sax/features/namespace-prefixes	Reports namespace prefixes
http://xml.org/sax/features/string-interning	Uses string interning (see java.util.String .intern() for details)
http://xml.org/sax/features/validation	Turns validation on or off.
http://xml.org/sax/features/external-general-entities	Includes or skips external text entities.
http://xml.org/sax/features/external-parameter-entities	Includes or skips external parameter entities.

Table 2.2 Core SAX Properties

Property Name	Description
http://xml.org/sax/properties/dom-node	Retrieves the current DOM node under parse. This is only useful when using SAX over a DOM parser.
http://xml.org/sax/properties/xml-string	Retrieves the raw string of characters responsible for the current event.

Setting Features

SAX offers a standard way to access all of a parser's features, even if the features themselves are proprietary. If a SAX parser supports a particular feature, it will expose the feature through the *SAXParserFactory* object. In JAXP, features are set on the factory rather than on the parser. Once you enable a particular feature, any new parsers created through the factory will exhibit the new behavior.

To turn a feature on or off, you need to know the unique name of the feature. For example, here is how you would enable Xerces' schema-based validation:

```
try {
    parserFactory.setFeature(
        "http://apache.org/xml/features/validation/schema",
        true);
} catch (SAXException e) {
    System.err.println("Implementation does not" +
                        "include schema support.");
}
```

Remember, not all parsers will support a given proprietary feature. The parser factory will throw an exception if it does not support your requested feature.

Setting Properties

SAX properties work in much the same way as SAX features, but there are a couple of slight differences. First and foremost, SAX properties work at the parser level rather than the factory level, which means that your setting is only valid for one particular parser instance. SAX properties are often used to expose the internal state of the parser, so it makes sense to work with one parser instance at a time. Secondly, properties are not limited the simple on/off style logic of SAX features. You can set or retrieve complete objects directly through a SAX property.

Here is an example of SAX property that returns a String value. Query this property during a parse to find the parse event's string literal:

```
try {

    String currentLiteral = parser.getProperty(

        "http://xml.org/sax/properties/xml-string ",

        true);

} catch (SAXException e) {

    System.err.println("Parser does not support "+

                        "literal property.");

}
```

The SAX standard specifies only a couple of SAX properties, but does not require SAX parsers to support any of them. As before, the parser will throw an exception if it does not recognize a particular property. If you expect the property to be available, you'll have to handle any exception accordingly.

Handling Advanced Events

So far, you've learned about some basic SAX events. The basic events covered the basic structures of XML: documents, elements, and characters. However, there's a lot more to XML than these three basic structures. XML documents may contain more advanced structures, such as processing instructions and entity declarations. Eventually, you are bound to run into an XML document that contains one of these advanced structures.

SAX includes additional event handlers for dealing with advanced XML structures. To use these event handlers, follow the same basic pattern as we have been exploring: Create a class that implements the handler, add logic for the handler's callback methods, and register the event handler with the parser.

ContentHandler

In addition to the basic SAX callbacks and namespace callbacks, the *ContentHandler* defines a few more useful callbacks:

```
public void ignorableWhitespace(char[] ch, int start, int length)
                            throws SAXException
```

Use the *ignorableWhitespace()* callback to capture non-essential document whitespace. In normal processing, the parser reports all whitespace characters through the *ContentHandler's* own *characters()* callback. However, if you've added a

DTD to the document, the parser behaves slightly differently: the DTD provides enough semantic information to allow the parser to distinguish significant and insignificant whitespace. The parser always reports significant whitespace through the usual *characters()* callback. While using a DTD, the parser reports any other whitespace through the *ignorableWhitespace()* callback. If you wish to preserve the insignificant whitespace during parsing, be sure to catch the whitespace through the *ignorableWhitespace()* callback:

```
public void processingInstruction(String target,
                                  String data) throws SAXException
```

If your document contains any XML processing instructions, you may need to implement the *processingInstruction()* callback. A processing instruction is a special XML directive intended for the XML parser. The target parameter is simply the name of the processing instruction. The data parameter includes everything after the processing instruction's name. Processing instructions are completely open-ended, so it's up to you to parse and interpret any data as you see fit.

```
public void skippedEntity(String name) throws SAXException
```

Implementing the *skippedEntities()* callback is usually unnecessary. In most cases, the parser will resolve any entities automatically through one of the other *ContentHandler* callbacks. However, the parser may skip over some entities if you explicitly tell it not to resolve references. (See the *http://xml.org/sax/features/external-general-entities* and *http://xml.org/sax/features/external-parameter-entities* properties.) Implement the *skippedEntity()* callback to record any skipped XML entities.

ErrorHandler

Implement the SAX *ErrorHandler* interface to catch and trap different types of XML parsing errors. If a parser has difficulty parsing a document, it will trigger an exception error. Some parsing errors are more serious than others. The *ErrorHandler* allows you to distinguish serious parse errors from less serious ones. For less serious errors, you may wish to record the error and continue on parsing. Each type of error may be handled in its own way. The *ErrorHandler* defines three callbacks for the three different types of parsing errors:

```
public void fatalError(SAXParseException exception) throws SAXException
```

```
public void error(SAXParseException exception) throws SAXException
```

```
public void warning(SAXParseException exception) throws SAXException
```

Fatal errors are the most serious types of parse errors, and unfortunately they are the ones you will encounter most frequently. Fatal errors occur when a parser tries to read an XML document that is not well formed. For example, if your document is missing an end tag or your document contains a syntax error, the parser will respond with a fatal error. The fatal error lets you know that the parser cannot continue.

However, there are situations where you may be able to recover from a parse error and continue parsing. *Errors* are non-fatal parsing situations where the parser cannot determine whether to continue or terminate. For example, if validating, the parser will trigger an error when the document does not match the DTD. In such a scenario, the parser gives you the opportunity to record the error and continue parsing, or re-throw the error and terminate the parse. *Warnings* are non-fatal situations that are less serious than errors.

The *ErrorHandler* interface only includes three methods, so it's a very easy class to implement. However, there is an easier way to get started with the *ErrorHandler*: the *DefaultHandler* class implements the *ErrorHandler* interface as well as the core *ContentHandler* interface. The *DefaultHandler* serves as a very rudimentary *ErrorHandler*. It only reports SAX fatal errors, and it completely consumes SAX errors and warnings. If you want to report all errors, simply override the *DefaultHandler's* methods with your own versions.

You may also prefer to keep your error handling code separate from your event handling code. If so, simply implement the *ErrorHandler* and *DefaultHandler* in completely separate classes. This approach has one downside: registering and using the handlers becomes slightly more involved. JAXP does not allow you to register an *ErrorHandler* directly with a parser, so you'll need to work through the underlying *XMLReader* instance. The following code demonstrates how to register each handler and invoke parsing through the *XMLReader*:

```
//contruct handlers
ErrorHandler errorHandler = new MyErrorHandler();
ContentHandler defaultHandler = new DefaultHandler();

//obtain XMLReader from SAXParser
XMLReader xmlReader = ((SAXParser)parser).getXMLReader();
xmlReader.setContentHandler( defaultHandler );
xmlReader.setErrorHandler( errorHandler);

//invoke parsing
xmlReader.parse (someInputSource);
```

> **NOTE**
>
> If you have implemented a separate *ErrorHandler* class, do not use the *SAXParser.parse()* method provided through JAXP. The *SAXParser.parse()* method automatically resets the *ErrorHandler*, so use the *XMLReader.parser()* method instead.

SAX2 Extensions

Although SAX includes quite a few different event handlers, these handlers are by no means comprehensive. XML documents may contain a variety of structures not covered in the core SAX event handlers. Eventually, you may run up against some of these limitations in your own work. For example, SAX can't help you if you're interested in parsing an XML document's comments. Basic SAX parsers will skip right over comments without triggering any events. Luckily, SAX still gives you some alternatives for handling these cases.

If you've found SAX event handlers too limiting, try making use of *SAX2 Extensions*. The SAX2 Extensions add two new event handlers to the core SAX library. These new event handlers add almost a dozen new SAX events. If your parser supports these extensions, then you'll be able to handle most XML parsing challenges.

The SAX2 Extensions are an optional part of SAX, so not every parser can be expected to support them. However, they are so useful that most common parsers support them anyway. If you're using the standard parsers included in JAXP, then you have everything you need to begin using the SAX2 Extensions.

Here are the new event handlers included with SAX2 Extensions:

LexicalHandler

The *LexicalHandler* provides greater lexical information about an XML document. It defines callbacks for reading XML comments and finding the beginnings and endings of DTD declarations. Additionally, the *LexicalHandler* provides a finer grain of control over XML character events. You may recall that the SAX *ContentHandler* interface includes basic support for character data, but it passes all types of characters through one *character()* callback. It does not allow you to distinguish normal characters from others, like entities and CDATA. The *LexicalHandler* corrects this shortfall. It provides distinct events for entities and CDATA characters.

DeclHandler

If you need to parse a DTD, use the *DeclHandler* interface. It's easy to confuse this class with the *DTDHandler* included in the core of SAX. The *DeclHandler* reports all element, attribute, and entity declarations. The *DTDHandler* only reports notation declarations and unparsed entities. You'll likely need both the *DeclHandler* and *DTDHandler* to fully parse a DTD.

Using the two extension event handlers is much like using core SAX event handlers. First, create a class that implements the appropriate handler interface, then add logic for each callback method. Finally, register the event handler with your parser instance.

Registering an extension event handler is slightly more work than registering a core SAX event handler. The extension handlers are registered through the SAX Property mechanism you learned about earlier. SAX defines two new properties for setting the respective handlers. Simply set the appropriate property, passing in the extension handler as its value:

```
try
{

    //create and register a LexicalHandler
    LexicalHandler lexHandler = new MyLexicalHandler ();
    saxParser.setProperty(
    "http://xml.org/sax/properties/lexical-handler", lexHandler);


    //create and register a DeclHandler
    DeclHandler decHandler = new MyDeclHandler ();
    saxParser.setProperty(
    "http://xml.org/sax/properties/declaration-handler", decHandler);
}
catch (SAXException se)
{
System.err.println("SAX2 Extensions not supported");
}
```

SAX2 Extensions are an optional part of SAX, and not all parsers may support the extensions. The above code simply catches any exceptions in case the extensions are unavailable.

Summary

In the SAX model, XML documents are provided to the application as a series of events. The SAX parser scans an XML document once from beginning to end. As it scans, the parser reports each document transition as an event. With each event, the application has a chance to respond to the change in the document

Event-based parsing has strengths and weaknesses. Very large documents can be processed with events, as there is no need to read the entire document into memory at once. However, working with sections of an XML document can be complicated because the application developer must track all the events for that section. For documents with complex hierarchies, consider using DOM parsing instead.

SAX defines a number of interfaces for interacting with the SAX parser. The event handler interfaces provide callbacks for handling each event. As a convenience, extend the *DefaultHandler* class rather than implementing the full *ContentHandler* interface. Within your class, simply implement those callbacks you find most interesting. You will most likely want to implement the *character* callback, the element callbacks, and possibly the document callbacks.

Once you have created an event handler, combine it with an actual parser. Use JAXP's abstract factory mechanism to create concrete parser instances. The abstract factory allows you to instantiate a parser without referring to any one parser in particular. This keeps your code portable, should parser technology change in the future. If you'd like to try out a new parser, set a system-wide property naming the *SAXParserFactory* implementation class. Alternatively, simply replace your old parser on the classpath with a new parser.

SAX parsers provide additional capabilities beyond basic event handling. SAX parsers are namespace-aware, but namespace processing must be explicitly enabled. Additionally, SAX parsers can validate documents as they parse. Use the *SAXParserFactory* to activate both of these features.

SAX parsers may implement features beyond the original API. Some of these features are strictly optional, like the event handlers provided by the SAX2 Extensions package. Other features are proprietary, like Xerces' validation through XML Schema. All of these features are accessed indirectly because they are not part of the core API. With flexibility built into the standard itself, SAX should remain a part of the XML landscape for years to come.

Solutions Fast Track

Understanding Event–Based XML Parsing

☑ The SAX parser scans an XML document once from beginning to end, creating events for each document transition.

☑ With each event, the SAX parser calls an event handler. The event handler contains callbacks for each type of event.

☑ To quickly create an event handler, simply extend the SAX *DefaultHandler* class. Provide implementations for only those callbacks you find interesting.

Creating a SAX Parser

☑ To keep your applications portable, avoid writing to a specific parser implementation. Instead, work through the SAX interfaces.

☑ Use the abstract factories provided by JAXP rather than SAX to create parser instances. The JAXP factories are preferred because they are more portable.

☑ Follow the JAXP search path to figure out what parser is instantiated.

Parsing Data with a SAX Parser

☑ To parse a document, you need three things: a parser, an event handler, and an XML input source.

☑ Wrap your XML document from a stream or file with an *InputSource* object. If it's not specified within the XML itself, set the character encoding properly.

☑ SAX parsers are not thread-safe. If you are working with servlets or other multithreaded applications, create a new parser for each thread.

Configuring the Parser

☑ Enable DTD validation and namespaces through convenience methods on the JAXP *SAXParserFactory* class

☑ With namespace processing enabled, rework your event handler callbacks to use the element's *localName* and namespace URI.

☑ Enable other SAX features and properties through methods on either the *SAXParserFactory* or *SAXParser* classes, respectively.

Handling Advanced Events

☑ Implement the *ContentHandler* callbacks to detect ignorable whitespace, processing instructions, and skipped entities.

☑ Register an *ErrorHandler* to detect different types of errors. Some errors may be recoverable, so you may be able to continue parsing.

☑ Use the SAX2 Extension interfaces to parse and detect XML comments, DTDs, CDATA, and entities.

Frequently Asked Questions

The following Frequently Asked Questions, answered by the authors of this book, are designed to both measure your understanding of the concepts presented in this chapter and to assist you with real-life implementation of these concepts. To have your questions about this chapter answered by the author, browse to **www.syngress.com/solutions** and click on the **"Ask the Author"** form.

Q: When should I choose SAX parsing over DOM parsing?

A: Use SAX parsing when performance is critical. Also use SAX parsing on very large documents. SAX-based parsing is generally quicker and consumes far less memory than building a DOM tree.

Q: When the SAX parser reads my XML document, some of the characters show up as garbage. Why?

A: Make sure you are setting the document's character encoding properly. This is best done through the XML declaration within the document itself. If you do not specify a character encoding, the XML parser will assume the document uses UTF-8 encoding.

Q: I can open my XML document fine in Internet Explorer, but my SAX parser can't parse it. What's wrong?

A: Internet Explorer does a good job of correcting some minor errors in your document when it does not impact the document meaning. Make sure in particular that your document does not have whitespace before the XML declaration.

Q: My SAX parser is reporting an attribute value that I don't see in the document. Where is it coming from?

A: If your document contains a DTD, the DTD may specify a default value for some attributes. SAX parsers will automatically report any default attributes in the *startElement()* callback.

Q: My XML document references an external DTD, but the SAX parser can't seem to locate the DTD. What can I do?

A: Some SAX parsers will automatically try to read external DTDs. This can be inconvenient, especially when you are off the network and can't reach the DTD. Certain parsers allow you to control loading of DTDs, but this is a proprietary feature of each parser. For the Xerces parser in JAXP 1.2, turn the *http://apache.org/xml/features/nonvalidating/load-external-dtd* feature off.

Q: Where can I find out more about specific SAX parsers?

A: The two parsers discussed in this chapter (Xerces and Crimson), are maintained by the Apache open source community. You can find the project's homepage and a wealth of information at http://xml.apache.org/.

Chapter 3

Processing XML Documents with DOM

Solutions in this chapter:

- The Document Object Model
- JAXP and Underlying DOM Engines
- Creating a DOM Parser
- Parsing XML into a DOM
- Manipulating DOM Objects
- Advanced Topics

☑ Summary

☑ Solutions Fast Track

☑ Frequently Asked Questions

Introduction

In the last chapter we discussed event-based parsing. Event-based parsing has some limitations. For instance, one cannot manipulate entire sections of a document at once. Also, multiple passes over the document data calls for multiple runs through the parser. Often, it would be more efficient if an entire document could be read into the memory and manipulated as an in-memory representation.

This can be achieved using the Document Object Model (DOM), which is by far the most widely used among the various standards proposed for in-memory representation of XML documents. A standard specified by the World Wide Web Consortium (W3C), the DOM specifies an abstract mapping of XML elements into runtime objects. Binding this specification to various languages, including Java, has been implemented by a variety of vendors.

In the DOM, every XML document is represented as a hierarchy of objects. This hierarchy forms a tree structure that mimics the structure of the XML document. Once you are familiar with XML and DOM, translating between the two becomes a simple matter.

One thing the current DOM specification omits is an API for the parsing of an XML document into a DOM. This is left to the individual vendor when writing a DOM parser. The latest DOM specification (DOM 3) seeks to address this issue too, but until it gains in popularity, application developers have to take into account the prospects of modifying their code when moving to a different parser. JAXP solves this problem by presenting a standardized interface for parsing XML data; the result of this parsing is an object that conforms to the standard W3C DOM Document interface.

This chapter presents a discussion on the reading, writing, and simple manipulations of a DOM representation. More complex manipulations, such as those pertaining to stylesheets, will be discussed in the next chapter.

The Document Object Model

The Document Object Model (DOM) is a World Wide Web consortium (W3C) specification that provides a programming interface for both XML and HTML documents. The basic objective of W3C DOM is to provide a standard, cross-platform, that is, cross-language programming interface that can be used in a wide variety of environments and with any programming language. Using a DOM, you can dynamically create or modify the structure or the contents of a document, add or delete its elements and navigate through its structure. The DOM focuses upon the model of a document and not upon the methods, interfaces etc. which may be required only to define and implement a DOM. Consequently, to use DOM in Java or in any other language, the appropriate language binding must be developed. These language bindings would serve as the APIs that can be used to create and manipulate document as per the DOM specifications.

In the DOM, documents have a logical structure that is usually depicted as a tree. The DOM is akin to the traditional object-oriented design concept since it models a document using objects. All these objects have methods and properties associated with them. Let us consider an example to illustrate the concept of DOM.

The DOM Tree

Figure 3.1 is an XML file that contains an objective type question along with two answer options, only one of which is correct. The correct option is marked *Y* while the incorrect option is marked *N*. Such an XML file may be used for, say, dynamically generating questions for an online examination.

Figure 3.1 A Simple XML

```
<ROOT>
  <question>
  <questionid>1</questionid>
  <questiontext>The earth revolves around the sun (State True or False)
      </questiontext>
  <option>False</option>
  <optionno>1</optionno>
  <correct>N</correct>
  <option>True</option>
  <optionno>2</optionno>
  <correct>Y</correct>
  </question>
</ROOT>
```

If we were to represent this XML graphically using the DOM, it would be as shown in Figure 3.2.

In the DOM tree structure, each XML tag (and its value) is viewed as a node object. In Figure 3.2, we have numbered each of these node objects from 1 to 18 for ease of explanation. In an actual DOM document, these nodes will not be numbered.

Figure 3.2 DOM Tree for XML of Figure 3.1

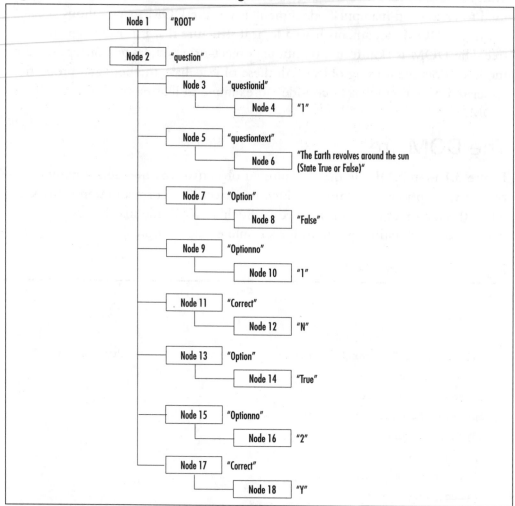

The *<ROOT>* tag (see *Node1* in Figure 3.2) forms the root node of the tree, and is referred to as the first child of the document. The *<question>* tag is a child node for the root node. *<questionid>*, *<questiontext>*, *<option>*, *<optionno>* and *<correct>* are child nodes for the question node. These nodes representing the XML tags are *element* nodes. *Node 1, Node 2, Node 3, Node 5, Node 7, Node 9, Node 11, Node 13, Node 15* and *Node 17* in Figure 3.2 represent *element* nodes. The DOM tree also represents the values of various elements (Corresponding to

CDATA in XML) as nodes, except that these values are represented by *text* nodes (*Node 4, Node 6, Node 8, Node 10, Node 12, Node 14, Node 16* and *Node 18* all represent *text* nodes). This is because in most DOM parsers, *CDATA* nodes are reserved for text that is explicitly marked as CDATA.

NOTE

The text within quotes ("ROOT", "question" etc.) given alongside each node in Figure 3.2, has been given solely to correlate the node with its corresponding XML tag, attribute or value (as the case may be). In actuality, this text is embedded within the DOM tree as node names or node values. For example, the node name for *Node 1* will be "ROOT" while *Node 4* is a text node that represents the value ("1") of the *<questionid>* tag.

The DOM is organized into Levels instead of versions. Level 1 (Core) of the DOM represents the hierarchy of content within a document. Level 2 (Core) improves upon the general structure specified in Level 1 by providing a set of core interfaces and modules that are meant for content-specific models. For example, Level 2 contains specialized interfaces that are dedicated to XML. We shall limit our discussions in this section to Level 1 only.

The Basic Classes

As shown in Figure 3.2, Level 1 of the DOM represents documents in a hierarchical structure of *Node* objects. Each of these nodes (except for *Text* and *CDATA* nodes, which will be covered further later) may have zero or more child nodes of various types and may form a sub-tree under it. If a node has no child nodes under it, it is referred to as a *leaf* node. There are different types of nodes such as an *Element* nodes, a *Text* node, an *Attribute* nodes and so on.

The Java API for XML processing (JAXP) provides various interfaces to process the different types of elements in an XML document. We shall now discuss, in brief, the fundamental JAXP interfaces that are contained in a DOM implementation. However, you should bear in mind that these interfaces are a part of the DOM Level 1 specification as developed and recommended by the World Wide Web Consortium (W3C) and are not specific to JAXP. This is to say that to manipulate DOM documents, JAXP defines interfaces/classes with names same as (or similar to) W3C's standard DOM interfaces. For example, W3C has defined the standard interface *Document* that encompasses a complete document. To make use of the *Document* W3C interface with JAXP's data structures and APIs, JAXP has developed its own interface with the same name. Thus, *Document* is a generic interface that may be supported by various vendors to make it interoperable with their proprietary APIs.

Document

The *Document* interface specifies the top node of the DOM tree and encompasses an entire document (XML or HTML). It provides access to the document's elements and data. Since every other node has to be within the document, this interface contains methods to create other nodes as well as methods for manipulating the document structure and its properties. The *Document* interface extends the *Node* interface inherits various properties and methods from it.

Element

The *Element* interface represents an XML or HTML element. A document's data is contained within its elements. An element may also have attributes providing additional content information. The *Element* interface provides methods to set or retrieve the attributes of an element as an *Attr* (attribute) object or as an attribute value. This interface also inherits from the *Node* interface.

Referring back to the XML in Figure 3.1, each of the tags will be represented by an Element; for instance, *question, questionid, option, optionno* and *correct* will all be elements in a DOM document.

Text

This interface represents the text content (character data in XML) of an element or an attribute value. This interface is also implemented as a node on the DOM tree structure; that is, as a child node of the element containing the text data (Refer to Figure 3.2). The content/text of an element may or may not contain markup. If there is no markup, the *Text* interface implements the text content as a single node object. If any markup is present, it is further broken down into elements, comments. with the markup constituents forming a sub-tree under the text node that represents the original text data. The *Text* interface inherits from both the *Node* interface and the *CharacterData* Interface.

As mentioned during our discussions on the DOM tree in Figure 3.2, the value of an XML value tag or the value of an attribute are represented as *text* nodes and not as *CDATA* nodes. Most DOM parsers reserve *CDATA* nodes for text explicitly marked as CDATA.

Attribute

The *Attribute* object represents the attributes of an element in the document. The Java API defines the *Attr* interface for the attributes of an element. Though the *Attr* interfaces inherit from the *Node* interface, the DOM treats them not as separate entities, but as properties of the element with which they are associated. Thus, attributes are not accessed through the document tree. This also implies that node attributes like *parent node*, *next* or *previous sibling* will have a *null* value for the *Attr* object. This is because attributes do not form child nodes of the element they describe.

An attribute may contain a simple text value or an entity reference (as in XML). However, the DOM does not distinguish between attribute types. It treats all attribute values as strings.

Node

The *Node* interface is central to the DOM tree. *Node* objects form the core structure of a DOM tree. The entire concept of a DOM tree is based on the node object contained in the *Node* interface. Note that all the DOM data types discussed above; *Document*, *Element*, *Text* and *Attribute* are represented in the DOM tree as nodes. While some properties and methods of these nodes are common, others are specific to the specific node's type. For example, the *Text* node does not have child nodes while the Attribute node has no parent or sibling nodes.

The *Node* interface provides methods to retrieve information about a node, such as the node name, the node value, the node attributes, the child nodes associated with a node, and so on. Additionally, it also provides a mechanism for obtaining and manipulating information about a node's child nodes.

NodeList

The *NodeList* interface represents a collection of node objects. This interface provides a mechanism to access a document's node structure as an indexed list of nodes beginning at *0*. This allows for iteration through the nodes collection. Any changes made to a document's structure, say by adding or removing a node, are immediately reflected in the Node list. The Node list is an abstract entity in the sense that it does not consider the implementation of the nodes collection or the types of nodes within the collection. However, it provides a convenient means to gloss over a document's DOM structure and can be especially useful for documents whose structure (number of nodes and their attributes, for instance) are not known.

Interrelationships

In a DOM tree, various nodes are related to one another as child-nodes, parent-nodes, sibling-nodes and so on. The possibility of placing one type of node below the other, . whether or not one type of node can form the child node of another type, for instance, is an area that calls for careful consideration. In this section, we will explore the relationships of elements with other elements, as well as with their own character data and attributes.

Hierarchy Imposed by the *Document/Element/Attribute/Text* Classes

The different objects of a DOM structure are interrelated in a hierarchical pattern. This hierarchy can be represented in its very basic form as shown in Figure 3.3.

Figure 3.3 Hierarchy of DOM Objects

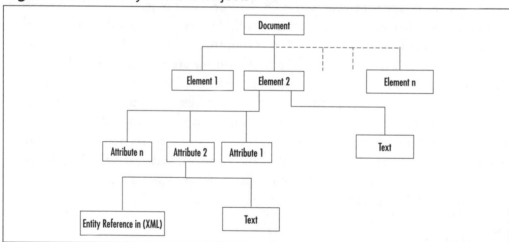

The *Document* object lies at the top of the hierarchy, which is obvious considering that no data or content that lies outside a document is relevant to it. All elements, text data, processing instructions, or comments have to lie within the context of a document. A document is composed of *Element* objects, which provide a structure and meaning to a document by separating the document's content into a readable and logical format. Elements within a document may further be nested to define a document's content structure. Elements that lie directly below another element are called its *child* elements. The upper element forms the *parent* node for the underlying elements. Elements that lie directly under the same parent node are called *siblings*. The actual data or text content of the document is stored as *Text* objects, which may represent either element data or an attribute value. Attributes are used to provide additional information about an element (apart from the data content). Attribute values are also represented as text objects. It is important to note that objects in the DOM structure cannot be placed haphazardly, for example, a document object cannot be placed under an attribute object. The nesting of elements follows a logical and orderly manner that conforms to the DOM specifications.

Let us now consider a modified version of Figure 3.1 for a better understanding of the relationship among elements in a DOM hierarchy.

Relationship between Elements in a DOM Hierarchy

In the XML file given in Figure 3.4, the *questionid* tag has been removed. This tag is now being represented as an attribute of the *question* element. Similarly, *optionno* and *correct* have been made into attributes of the *Option* element.

Figure 3.4 An XML with Attributes

```
<ROOT>
 <question questionid="1">
  <questiontext>The earth revolves around the sun (State True or False)
      </questiontext>
  <option optionno="1" correct="N">False</option>
  <option optionno="2" correct="Y">True</option>
 </question>
</ROOT>
```

The DOM structure for this XML document will follow the hierarchy shown in Figure 3.5

Figure 3.5 clearly shows that *Element 1* is a child element of the *ROOT* element, which is the root element for the document. *Element 2*, *Element 3* and *Element 4* in turn form child elements for *Element 1*. *Element 2*, *Element 3* and *Element 4* are siblings. *Element 1* also has an attribute object under it, named *Attribute 11,* as shown in Figure 3.3. This attribute represents the *questionid* attribute of the *question* element.

Element 2 has a child of type *Text*, named *Text 1* (as seen in Figure 3.3). *Element 3* and *Element 4* represent the two *option* tags and each have two attribute nodes under them. Thus, the DOM maintains the hierarchy as explained in the above section. The following sections clarify concepts of DOM with regard to Java's API for XML parsing, JAXP.

Figure 3.5 DOM Hierarchy for the XML Document

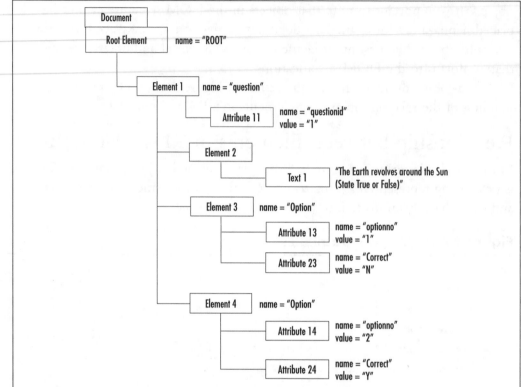

JAXP and Underlying DOM Engines

Sun's Java API for XML Processing (JAXP) provides classes and methods to parse XML documents, irrespective of which XML processing implementation is used. JAXP supports XML processing using SAX, XSLT and DOM, and attempts to provide cohesiveness to the SAX and DOM APIs. While it does not alter any of these, it does add some convenient methods for making the XML APIs easier to use for java developers

JAXP does not redefine DOM and SAX, but ensures that parsers can be accessed in a Java application through a pluggable interface. The principles of using JAXP and DOM are similar to those of SAX. For example, just as we use *SAXParser* and *SAXParserFactory* in SAX, we use *DocumentBuilder* and *DocumentFactoryBuilder* in JAXP. In fact, these two interfaces use the SAX API internally and hence throw the same Exceptions as well. Figure 3.6 illustrates the way the two interfaces work .

Figure 3.6 The JAXP DOM API

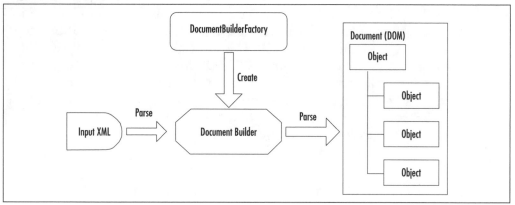

As shown in Figure 3.6, the *DocumentBuilderFactory* class is used to create a document builder. The document builder receives the input XML and parses it to create its DOM Document.

Developing & Deploying…

JWSDP EA2

JWSDP can be downloaded for free from http://java.sun.com/webservices/downloads/webservicespack.html

The Java Web Services Developer Pack (Java WSDP) download will contain the following technologies:

- JavaServer Pages Standard Tag Library (JSTL)

- Java XML Pack, which includes: Java API for XML Messaging (JAXM), Java API for XML Processing (JAXP), Java API for XML Registries (JAXR), and Java API for XML-based RPC (JAX-RPC)

- Tomcat (Java servlet and JavaServer PagesTM container and tools)

- Ant build tool

Continued

■ The deploytool web application deployment utility

■ Registry Server

When the Java WSDP is installed, it automatically sets the JAVA_HOME and CATALINA_HOME environment variables in JWSDP_HOME/bin/setenv.bat (in Windows) to the current locations of the J2SE SDK and the Java WSDP. The start scripts in JWSDP_HOME/ bin call setenv. If you change your J2SE SDK installation, update setenv to reflect the new location if it is different than the previous location. Adding JWSDP_HOME/bin to the front of your path will ensure that the Java WSDP scripts are used instead of any other installations.

Your WSDP pack is now ready to be used.

Let us illustrate the JAXP parser with the help of an example. The sample code is shown in Figure 3.7:

Figure 3.7 Sample Code for a JAXP Parser

```
import java.io.*;

import javax.xml.parsers.*;

import org.xml.sax.*;

import org.xml.sax.helpers.*;

import org.w3c.dom.*;


public class parserDemo
{
 // Step 1: Create an instance of the DocumentBuildefactory class

 DocumentBuilderFactory documentFactory;
 documentFactory = DocumentBuilderFactory.newInstance();


 // Step 2: create a DocumentBuilder that satisfies the
 // constraints specified by the DocumentBuilderFactory
 DocumentBuilder myDocumentBuilder = null;
 try {
  myDocumentBuilder = documentFactory.newDocumentBuilder();
 } catch (ParserConfigurationException pce) {
  System.err.println(pce);
```

Continued

Figure 3.7 Continued

```
 System.exit(1);
}
// Sets the Error Handler..
myDocumentBuilder.setErrorHandler(new MyErrorHandler());

// Step 3: parse the input file
Document parsedDocument = null;
try {
 parsedDocument = myDocumentBuilder.parse(new File(FileName));
} catch (SAXException se) {
 System.err.println(se.getMessage());
 System.exit(1);
} catch (IOException ioe) {
 System.err.println(ioe);
 System.exit(1);
}
}
```

Even a cursory glance over the import statements is enough to make out that the code does not contain any vendor-specific details. Otherwise the code is quite similar to that for any other parser. Note that the parser, though created using JAXP, throws the same *SAXException*. This is because internally JAXP uses many of the classes used by SAX. We may now proceed to discuss the core issues involved in building a practical JAXP parser.

Creating a DOM Parser

To build a document's DOM tree structure, the document should be parsed and nodes corresponding to each element should be placed systematically in the DOM tree. The nesting of elements should conform to the DOM specifications. The Java XML processing API defines the *DocumentBuilderFactory* class to parse XML documents and obtain their DOM tree structure.

The DocumentBuilderFactory Class

The *DocumentBuilderFactory* class defines methods and properties that allow the user to create DOM parsers. An instance of the *DocumentBuilderFactory* class is created,then used to obtain instances of the *DocumentBuilder* class to parse the XML and extract DOM document instances from it.

WARNING

The *DocumentBuilderFactory* class is *not* thread safe. Though an application can use the same instance of the *DocumentBuilderFactory* class to create instances of *DocumentBuilder*, it is incumbent upon the application developer to ensure that the instance of the *DocumentBuilderFactory* class is not used by more than one thread at a time.

The following section goes into the various steps involved in creating a JAXP parser, then integrates these steps to build a practical parser.

Obtaining a New Instance of the *DocumentBuilderFactory*

A *DocumentBuilderFactory* class instance can be obtained by using the *newInstance()* method, which creates a new factory instance.

```
DocumentBuilderFactory dbf = DocumentBuilderFactory.newInstance();
```

The *newInstance()* method is defined as a static method that throws a *FactoryConfigurationError* exception if the factory implementation is not available or cannot be instantiated.

```
public static DocumentBuilderFactory newInstance() throws
    FactoryConfigurationError
```

As mentioned earlier, an application may use the same factory instance to create multiple *DocumentBuilder* instances, or it may create one factory instance per thread. However, in either case it is the responsibility of the application developer to ensure that only one thread uses the factory instance at a time.

Using the *DocumentBuilderFactory* to Create a *DocumentBuilder*

The *DocumentBuilder* class is actually used to obtain the DOM document from a given XML file. Once this class is instantiated, it can be used to parse the XML, which may be available in the form of an input stream, a file, a URL, or other data source (Detailed discussions on various input sources are included later in this chapter). An instance of the *DocumentBuilder* class can be created using the *DocumentBuilderFactory* instance:

```
DocumentBuilder db = null;
try {
 db = dbf.newDocumentBuilder();
} catch (ParserConfigurationException pce) {}
```

Here, *dbf* is the factory instance. If the *DocumentBuilder* cannot be created, a *ParserConfigurationException* exception is thrown. As in the case of a factory instance, the same *DocumentBuilder* instance should not be concurrently used by two threads. An application developer should either create one *DocumentBuilder* instance per thread or ensure that two threads do not use the same *DocumentBuilder* instance at the same time. It would be worthwhile to mention here that several classes from the SAX API are reused by the *DocumentBuilder* class. However, this does not necessitate the use of a SAX parser to parse the XML for which the DOM implementation is being implemented.

Setting Parser Attributes

The *DocumentBuilderFactory* instance can be used to configure the parser by setting its attributes. These attributes define what the parser considers and what it ignores while traversing through an XML file. Here, we'll discuss the major parser attributes that can be set using the factory instance. Take note that to be effective, these properties need to be set before a document builder is requisitioned. Say, if the properties are set after a document builder (*db1,* for instance) has been instantiated, then the document builder will not be automatically updated; instead, it will parse XML documents using the default property values for any properties that had not been explicitly set when it was created. However, subsequent builder instances will use the property values set by the factory class.

Coalescing

This attribute specifies whether or not the parser will convert character data (CDATA) into *Text* nodes. If this attribute is set to *true*, the parser converts each *CDATA* node to a *Text* node and appends it to an adjacent text node, if one exists. The following line of code may be used to set the coalescing property to true:

```
dbf.setCoalescing(true);
```

In this code line, *dbf* is the factory instance. The coalescing property is set to *false* by default.

ExpandEntityReferences

This property, if set to true, instructs the parser to expand entity reference nodes. The following line of code configures the parser to expand entity reference nodes:

```
dbf.setExpandEntityReferences(true);
```

Though we assume that readers would be aware of the concept of entities in XML, we are repeating it to explain the *ExpandEntityReferences* property's functionality. An entity in an XML file may refer either to a certain piece of text or to an entire document. For example, we define an entity as follows:

```
<!ENTITY JAXPentity "Java API for XML Processing, JAXP">
```

We now call this entity in an XML tag as follows:

```
<info>Welcome to &JAXPentity; - manipulating DOM objects the Java way
</info>
```

When this text is retrieved from the *<info>* tag, the *JAXPentity* entity gets expanded and the tag value is read as "Welcome to Java API for XML Processing, JAXP – manipulating DOM objects the Java way."

If we set *ExpandEntityReferences* to *true* while parsing the XML, the document builder expands (replaces with its defined value) *JAXPentity* in the *<info>* tag above. The concept of expanding entity references will become clearer later in the chapter when we discuss *EntityResolvers* in the Input Source Types section (See the examples in Figure 3.11 and Figure 3.12).

IgnoreComments

This property specifies whether or not the parser should ignore comments given in an XML. This property may be set using the following line of code:

```
dbf.setIgnoringComments(true);
```

IgnoreElementContentWhitespace

The *IgnoreElementContentWhitespace* property applies to the insignificant white spaces in an XML file, while ignoring the significant white spaces such as spaces internal to a text block. When this property is set, the parser eliminates ignorable white spaces in the XML. The following line of code sets this property:

```
dbf.setIgnoringElementContentWhitespace(true);
```

NamespaceAware

The *NamespaceAware* property specifies whether or not the parser is namespace aware. The factory instance can be used to make the parser namespace aware:

```
dbf.setNamespaceAware(true);
```

Any parsers created by the factory after setting this property will support name spaces in the XML.

Validating

This property is set to *true* for configuring the parser such that it validates the XML file while parsing it. The following line sets this property to true:

```
dbf.setValidating(true);
```

We now integrate the methods and properties listed above to configure JAX-P to be validating, coalescing, and namespace-aware.

Creating a Coalescing, Validating, Namespace Aware DOM Parser

To perform a validating parse, we choose an XML file with a *DOCTYPE* declaration to check whether the parser validates the XML. The file TempDTD.xml is used as the source XML. The XML in file TempDTD.xml, is listed in Figure 3.8.

Figure 3.8 An XML with a DTD

```
<?xml version='1.0' encoding="ISO-8859-1" standalone="yes"?>
<!DOCTYPE ROOT [
    <!ELEMENT ROOT (questionid)>
    <!ELEMENT questionid (#PCDATA)>
    ]>
<ROOT>
<questionid>9</questionid>
</ROOT>
```

We call our parser class *Example1* whose code is listed in Figure 3.9.

Figure 3.9 The Parser Class

```
import java.io.*;
import javax.xml.parsers.*;
```

Continued

Figure 3.9 Continued

```
import org.xml.sax.*;

import org.xml.sax.helpers.*;

import org.w3c.dom.*;


public class Example1

{

 String  result = new String();


 String filename = new String();

 // Constructor..

 // 1. File Name of the File To Be Parsed


 Example1(String filename)

 {


  this.filename = filename;

  // Step 1: create a DocumentBuilderFactory and configure it

  DocumentBuilderFactory documentFactory;

  documentFactory = DocumentBuilderFactory.newInstance();


  // Optional: set various configuration options

  documentFactory.setValidating(true);

  documentFactory.setIgnoringComments(true);

  documentFactory.setIgnoringElementContentWhitespace(true);

  documentFactory.setNamespaceAware(true);

  // The opposite of creating entity ref nodes is expanding them inline

  documentFactory.setExpandEntityReferences(true);


  //At this point the DocumentBuilderFactory instance can be saved

  //and reused to create any number of DocumentBuilder instances

  //with the same configuration options.


  //Step 2:create a DocumentBuilder that satisfies the constraints

  //specified by the DocumentBuilderFactory

  DocumentBuilder myDocumentBuilder = null;

  try {
```

Continued

Figure 3.9 Continued

```
  myDocumentBuilder = documentFactory.newDocumentBuilder();
 } catch (ParserConfigurationException pce) {
 System.err.println(pce);
 System.exit(1);
 }
 // Sets the Error Handler..
 myDocumentBuilder.setErrorHandler(new MyErrorHandler());

 // Step 3: parse the input file
 Document parsedDocument = null;
 try {
 parsedDocument = myDocumentBuilder.parse(new File(filename));
 } catch (SAXException se) {
 System.err.println(se.getMessage());
 System.exit(1);
 } catch (IOException ioe) {
 System.err.println(ioe);
 System.exit(1);
 }
 // Store the DOM tree in a String Object
  storeResult(parsedDocument);
}

void storeResult(Node node)
{
 // The function is responsible for Traversing the DOM Tree and
 // storing the result in the Object of the Class String

}

String returnResult()
{
 // This function is responsible for returning the result to
 // the calling program.
}
```

Continued

Figure 3.9 Continued

```
// Error Handler Implementation....
private static class MyErrorHandler implements ErrorHandler
{
  /**
   * Returns a string describing parse exception details
   */
  private String getParseExceptionInfo(SAXParseException spe)     {
    String systemid = spe.getSystemId();
    if (systemid == null) {
     systemid = "null";
    }
    String info = "URI=" + systemid +
                   " Line=" + spe.getLineNumber() +
                   ": " + spe.getMessage();
    return info;
  }


  // The following methods are standard SAX ErrorHandler methods.
  // See SAX documentation for more info.

  public void warning(SAXParseException spe) throws SAXException {
    System.out.println("Warning: " + getParseExceptionInfo(spe));
  }


  public void error(SAXParseException spe) throws SAXException {
    String message = "Error: " + getParseExceptionInfo(spe);
    throw new SAXException(message);
  }


  public void fatalError(SAXParseException spe) throws SAXException {
    String message = "Fatal Error: " + getParseExceptionInfo(spe);
    throw new SAXException(message);
  }
}
```

Continued

Figure 3.9 Continued

```
public static void main(String args[])
{
  // Main Program...
}


}
```

The *MyErrorHandler* class takes care of the XML validation. It contains the *getParseExceptionInfo()* method that prints out the URI for the source that caused the exception, the description of the exception and the line number within the source that caused the exception to be thrown. The *warning(), error()* and *fatalError()* methods are used for the respective types of error. The *storeResult()* method is called for each node in the DOM tree, and the corresponding node name and value are appended to the *result* string variable. The *storeResult()* method will be discussed later when we build a complete working parser (See *XMLParser.java* class of Figure 3.16).

Parsing XML into a DOM

Before we commence our discussion on how an XML file can be parsed into a DOM tree, we discuss the various possible input sources for the XML file to be parsed. JAXP handles each of the input source types differently..

Input Source Types

An input source refers to the resource (a URL, a string, a file and so on) that provides a parser with the XML to be parsed. The source XML can be made available to a parser from various types of sources. These sources include an XML file (for example, myXML.xml) that needs to be read by the parser, a string (One method calls a parsing function and passes the source XML to it as a string parameter value), an input stream (The XML is being read from a remote source using a socket), an entity (when the entity within an XML refers to another complete XML document) and so on. In this section we focus on how JAXP can be used to read/receive XML from various sources.

InputSource

This class encompasses input from a single source object; for example, a byte stream or a character stream. This input source is passed on to the parser's *parse()* method. How the JAXP parser reads the XML depends upon the input stream. For example, if the input source is a character stream, it will be read directly. Otherwise, the parser will try to read it using a byte stream. If the input is neither a byte stream nor a character stream, the parser will try to open a URL connection to the identified resource. Note that this is also true in the case of SAX parsers. As mentioned earlier, this is because the JAXP parsers build the DOM based on SAX events.

The class uses the method *getByteStream()* if the input is in the form of a byte stream, the method *getCharacterStream()* if the input is a character stream, else, it uses the *getSystemId()* method to read from the input source.

File-based Source

If the XML is in the form of a file (say myfile.xml), the file can be directly passed to the the JAXP parser's *parse()* method in the following form:

```
parserObject.parse(new File("myfile.xml"))
```

This command's return value will be a *Document* object containing the parsed XML's DOM tree.

InputStream-based Sources

In *InputStream*-based sources, a connection is opened to an XML source and the input stream associated with the XML source is obtained. This *InputStream* is passed to the parser class. For example, if the XML file is named Temp.xml, we obtain the input stream using the following code:

```
String urlName = "http://localhost:8080/examples/Temp.xml";
URL url = new URL(urlName);
URLConnection connection = url.openConnection();
InputStream XMLStream  = connection.getInputStream();
```

We pass this input stream to the *parse()* method as follows:

```
parserObject.parse(XMLStream);
```

The *parse()* method now uses *XMLStream* to parse the XML.

String

If a piece of XML code is assigned to a *String* variable, this variable can straight-away be passed to the *parse()* method for parsing. For example, if the XML is assigned to the *XMLString* variable, the following line of code will cause the parser class to parse the XML and return its *Document* object:

```
parserObject.parse(XMLString);
```

EntityResolvers

An XML document may contain a reference to an external entity. When parsed, this entity is resolved and loaded in the original document. Figure 3.10 shows XML in that contains reference to an external entity.

Figure 3.10 An XML file with an External Entity

```
<!-- Sample2.xml -->
<!DOCTYPE poem [
<!ENTITY ext1 SYSTEM "Sample2.xml">
]>
<poem>
<verse>Take Care To Get What You Like.</verse>
<verse>OtherWise you'll be Forced to like what you Get.</verse>
&ext1;
<verse>Don't worry about pressure..</verse>
<verse>Remember it is the pressure that makes diamond out of coal.</verse>
</poem>
```

Ext1 contains the reference to the external entity that is an XML file named *Sample2.xml*. Sample2.xml contains the code given in Figure 3.11.

Figure 3.11 File Sample2.xml

```
<!-- Sample2.xml (Sample2.xml) -->
<verse>May Lord Almighty be with you Always.</verse>
<verse>May Lord Almighty help in Difficult times.</verse>
```

When the first XML file is run, the entity ext1 is resolved and the output is as shown in Figure 3.12.

Figure 3.12 The XML Output with a Resolved External Entity

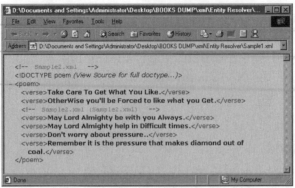

Note that the output reflects the XML from file *Sample2.xml*. If an application needs to handle any external entities, it must implement the *EntityResolver* interface and register with the SAX driver. Only then will the XML reader allow the class to implement customized handling for these entities (For example an external DTD subset). This is typically required when the XML is being generated from a database or the input is from specialized sources such as URI types other than URLs. For example, if you need to generate an XML entity at runtime as per a specific DTD and you wish to define your own customized handler for this entity, then you need to implement the *EntityResolver* interface. If, however, you do not require any customized handling for the entities and thus decide not to implement the *EntityResolver*, then the parser will use the default entity resolving mechanism.

The class uses the *resolveEntity()* method to resolve external entities. This method returns an *InputSource* associated with the entity.

```
public InputSource resolveEntity(String publicId, String systemId) throws
SAXException, IOException
```

If the entity cannot be resolved, a *SAXException* is thrown. If the designated entity cannot be reached, an *IOException* is thrown.

An important facet however, is that JAXP SAX wrappers do not resolve external entity references. The same applies to non-validating parsers. When a parser cannot resolve an entity, it may simply skip it or generate an error. If an entity is skipped, a callback is issued that gives the name of the skipped entity. This enables another parser with the required resolving features to resolve the entity.

The *skippedEntity()* method can be used to retrieve the name of the skipped entity.

```
public void skippedEntity(String name) throws SAXException
```

The *name* parameter contains the name of the skipped entity.

> **NOTE**
>
> Established parsers like Apache Xerces, even if they are non-validating, will not skip entities. Instead they will expand entity references and include them in the parsed results. However, be careful when using another parse engine. Also take care that the parameter passed to the *skippedEntity()* method does not contain the leading ampersand and the trailing semicolon that are used to denote an entity. (For example, "&ext1;" in Figure 3.10 would be passed as "ext1")

Manipulating DOM Objects

Once an XML file has been parsed and its DOM tree constructed, simple functions can be created to traverse through the DOM tree. The *Node* interface provides ample methods and properties to separately obtain each node object in the DOM tree and its respective text values, its attributes and its child nodes. Each of the nodes can be processed further down until the leaf nodes (those with nothing below them) are reached. In the following sections, we shall discuss how this is done.

Walking a DOM Constellation

To create a DOM tree, we first need to parse an XML file and create the *Document* object. Readers may recall that the document object is representative of the complete parsed XML file, with all the XML elements and data contained within it. Assuming that the XML source is a file, the following code will create a *Document* from the XML:

```
Document doc = null;
try {
  doc = db.parse(new File(filename));
} catch (SAXException se) {}
} catch (IOException ioe) {}
```

Here, *db* is the *DocumentBuilder* object created from the instance of the *DocumentBuilderFactory* class. Note that a *SAXException* is thrown if the XML cannot be parsed and an *IOException* is thrown if the XML file cannot be read.

We now list an *echo()* function that accepts the document object, *doc*, as a parameter.

```
private void echo(Node n) {
  int type = n.getNodeType();
  switch (type) {
   case Node.ATTRIBUTE_NODE:
    // Check if the node represents an attribute
    System.out.println("Attribute Node");
    break;
   case Node.CDATA_SECTION_NODE:
    // Check if the node represents a CDATA section
    System.out.println("CDATA Section Node");
    break;
   case Node.COMMENT_NODE:
    // Check if the node represents a Comment
    System.out.println("Comment Node");
    break;
   case Node.DOCUMENT_FRAGMENT_NODE:
    // Check if the node represents a Document Fragment
    System.out.println("Document Fragment Node");
    break;
   case Node.DOCUMENT_NODE:
    // Check if the node represents a Document Node
    System.out.println("Document Node");
    break;
   case Node.DOCUMENT_TYPE_NODE:
    // Check if the node represents a node that defines the type
    // of document
    System.out.println("Document Type Node");

    // If the node defines the document type, obtain its NodeMap
    NamedNodeMap nodeMap = ((DocumentType)n).getEntities();
    indent += 2;
    for (int i = 0; i < nodeMap.getLength(); i++) {
     Entity entity = (Entity)nodeMap.item(i);
     echo(entity);
```

```
  }
  break;
case Node.ELEMENT_NODE:
  // Check if the node represents an element
  System.out.println("Element Node");
  // If the node represents an element, obtain its attributes
  // using its NodeMap
  NamedNodeMap atts = n.getAttributes();
  for (int i = 0; i < atts.getLength(); i++) {
   Node att = atts.item(i);
    echo(att);
  }
  break;
case Node.ENTITY_NODE:
  // Check if the node represents an Entity
  System.out.println("Entity Node");
  break;
case Node.ENTITY_REFERENCE_NODE:
  // Check if the node represents an Entity Reference
  System.out.println("Entity Reference Node");
  break;
case Node.PROCESSING_INSTRUCTION_NODE:
  // Check if the node represents a Processing Instruction
  System.out.println("Processing Instruction Node");
  break;
case Node.TEXT_NODE:
  // Check if the node represents a Text Node
  System.out.println("Text Node");
  break;
default:
  // Check if the node type is not recognised
  System.out.println("Unrecognised Node Type");
  break;
  }

// Run a for loop to obtain the children if any for the node
// passed a Parameter to the echo() method
```

```
for (Node child = n.getFirstChild(); child != null;
 child = child.getNextSibling()) {
 echo(child);
 }
}
```

Note that *doc* is being passed to the *echo()* method as a *Node* object. This is because the *Document* object is treated as a node in the DOM tree. (Refer to the discussions in the previous sections for clarification.)

We quote snippets from the *echo()* method to analyze how the DOM tree is traversed.

Obtaining the Document Root

Notice the code line:

```
case Node.DOCUMENT_NODE:
```

This line retrieves the document node when it is encountered. This document node is the root node of the document from where further processing down the DOM tree begins. The document node will be the first node encountered when the document object (*doc*), is first passed to the *echo()* method.

Walking the Hierarchy

The *echo()* method uses the *in-order* technique to traverse the DOM tree. In the in-order technique, when a node (Node A, for example) is encountered, the processing sequence follows the path under that node until the leaf nodes are reached, and then the processing resumes at the node's next sibling. We redraw part of Figure 3.2 as Figure 3.13 to explain the sequence in which the DOM tree is traversed.

Root Element is the first one to be obtained. The program then goes to *Element 1* and retrieves its attribute as given by *Attribute 11*. *Element 2* is fetched next, followed by its text value, *Text 1*. The next in sequence is *Element 3*. Its attributes, *Attribute 13* and *Attribute 23*, are obtained and the program goes to *Element 4* and so on. The *Path* arrows in Figure 3.13 have been numbered to represent the path followed.

Since the focus in this chapter is on JAXP rather than on DOM, other traversal techniques like left-to-right (LTR) are not being explained. Interested readers may refer to relevant material when using a parser that uses a different traversal technique.

Figure 3.13 Traversing the DOM Tree

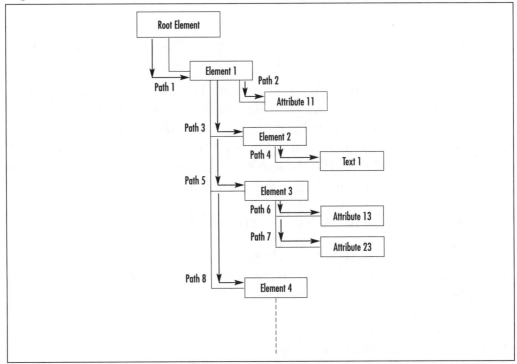

Finding sibling and child nodes

Consider the following *for* loop of the *echo()* method

```
for (Node child = n.getFirstChild(); child != null;
            child = child.getNextSibling()) {
            echo(child);
        }
    }
```

When the document object is passed to the *echo()* method, the first execution of the loop returns *Root Element* (See Figure 3.6) as the first child of the *doc* object,. The *echo()* function is recalled, except that this time the node object being passed to *echo()* is *Root Element*. The next pass through this *for* loop returns *Element 1* as the child element of *Root Element* and passes it as a parameter to the *echo()* method. Since *Element 1* is an *Element* node, the *case* statement, *case*

Node.ELEMENT_NODE:, causes the *NamedNodeMap* of *Element 1's* attributes to be created through the following code:

```
NamedNodeMap atts = n.getAttributes();
for (int i = 0; i < atts.getLength(); i++) {
 Node att = atts.item(i);
  echo(att);
}
```

The first pass through the main *for* loop invokes this code against *Element 1*. The next pass through the *for* loop returns *Element 2* as the child for *Element 1*. Again, the *echo()* method is called and *Element 's 2* attributes are retrieved. The next pass through the *for* loop returns *Element 3* as the next sibling of *Element 2*. The processing thus follows the in-order sequence discussed above.

The following discussion clarifies the concept of walking the DOM tree.

A Servlet to Write Out Name/Value Pairs from Example Schema

First of all, Figure 3.14 lists the XML that is being parsed. Note that we shall be using the same XML for further examples, so Figure 3.14 will be referenced in future discussions.

Figure 3.14 XML Code for Parsing

```
<?xml version='1.0'?><ROOT>
<question>
<questionid>1</questionid>
<questiontext>Type Any Question Here ?</questiontext>
<option>Option 1</option>
<optionno>1</optionno>
<correct>N</correct>
<option>Option 2</option>
<optionno>2</optionno>
<correct>Y</correct>
<option>Option 3</option>
<optionno>3</optionno>
<correct>N</correct>
<option>Option 4</option>
<optionno>4</optionno>
```

Continued

Figure 3.14 Continued

```
<correct>N</correct>
</question>
</ROOT>
```

Assuming that this XML is available as a file named Temp.xml, we now create the ParsingXML.java servlet (Figure 3.15), to open a connection to the Temp.xml file using Java's *URLConnection* object. We also assume that Temp.xml lies within the examples folder in the servlet's document root.

Figure 3.15 The ParsingXML.java Servlet

```
import java.io.*;
import java.net.*;
import javax.servlet.*;
import javax.servlet.http.*;


public class  ParsingXML extends HttpServlet
{
 InputStream xmlStream;
 public void doGet(HttpServletRequest request,
                   HttpServletResponse response)
           throws ServletException, IOException
 {
  PrintWriter outputWriter = response.getWriter();
  response.setContentType("text/html");

  // Providing the urlName of the XML File..

  String urlname = "http://localhost:8080/examples/Temp.xml";
  URL url = new URL(urlname);
  URLConnection connection = url.openConnection();
  xmlStream  = connection.getInputStream();

  // Calling the Class XMLParser with the Stream of the XML File,
  // to parse the XML File.
```

Continued

Figure 3.15 Continued

```
XMLParser myParser = new XMLParser(xmlStream);


// Obtaining the result from the Class.


String returnValue = myParser.returnResult();


outputWriter.println("<center><h1>Result of Parsing</center>");
outputWriter.println("<h4> "+returnValue);
outputWriter.close();
xmlStream.close();
 }

}
```

The ParsingXML servlet extends the HTTPServlet used for the HTTP protocol. The ParsingXML servlet calls the *XMLParser* class within its *doGet()*
method. The servlet passes the contents of the Temp.xml file to the parser class
using the data stream stored in the *xmlstream* variable.

NOTE

The ParsingXML servlet uses the *GET* method (in which the servlet
receives data in the form of a query string) for the request. However, the
ParsingXML servlet does not read any data using the *HTTPServletRequest*
object, since data is being read from a file-based source. Thus, the use of
doGet() or *doPost()* is figurative and not practically relevant to this particular servlet.

The *XMLParser* class is responsible for creating instances of the
DocumentBuilderFactory class and *DocumentBuilder* class to create the XML's
DOM tree. The code for the *XMLParser* class is listed in Figure 3.16:

Figure 3.16 The XMLParser.java Class

```
import java.io.*;
import javax.xml.parsers.*;
import org.xml.sax.*;
```

Continued

Figure 3.16 Continued

```
import org.xml.sax.helpers.*;
import org.w3c.dom.*;

public class XMLParser
{
 String  result = new String();

 // Constructor..
 // 1. InputStream of the File to be parsed..

 XMLParser(InputStream xmlStream)
 {

  // Step 1: create a DocumentBuilderFactory and configure it
  DocumentBuilderFactory documentFactory;
  documentFactory = DocumentBuilderFactory.newInstance();

  // Optional: set various configuration options
  documentFactory.setValidating(false);
  documentFactory.setIgnoringComments(true);
  documentFactory.setIgnoringElementContentWhitespace(true);
  documentFactory.setCoalescing(true);
  // The opposite of creating entity ref nodes is expanding them inline
  documentFactory.setExpandEntityReferences(true);

  // At this point the DocumentBuilderFactory instance can be saved and
  //reused to create any number of DocumentBuilder instances with the
  // same configuration options.
  // Step 2: create a DocumentBuilder that satisfies the constraints
  // specified by the DocumentBuilderFactory
  DocumentBuilder myDocumentBuilder = null;
  try {
   myDocumentBuilder = documentFactory.newDocumentBuilder();
  } catch (ParserConfigurationException pce) {
   System.err.println(pce);
```

Continued

Figure 3.16 Continued

```
    System.exit(1);
  }


    // Step 3: parse the input file
    Document parsedDocument = null;
    try {
     parsedDocument = myDocumentBuilder.parse(xmlStream);
    } catch (SAXException se) {
     System.err.println(se.getMessage());
     System.exit(1);
    } catch (IOException ioe) {
     System.err.println(ioe);
     System.exit(1);
    }


    // Store the DOM tree in a String Object
    storeResult(parsedDocument);
  }


// The function is responsible for Traversing the DOM Tree and storing
// the result in the Object of the Class String (result). During the
// Traversal special HTML tags as also added along with the Node
// Name/Value to as to facilitate understanding.


void storeResult(Node node)
{
  String val = node.getNodeValue();
  if (val == null)
  {
    result += "<Font color = \"//ff0000\">Name :</Font> "+
              node.getNodeName();
    result += "<BR>";
  }
  else if (val.trim().equals(""))
```

Continued

Figure 3.16 Continued

```
  {
    // Simple Ignore...
  }
  else
  {
   result += "<Font color = \"//ff0000\">Name :</Font> "+
              node.getNodeName();
   result += "<Font color = \"//0000FF\">   Value :" +
              "</Font>" + val+ "<BR>";
  }


  for (Node child = node.getFirstChild(); child != null;
            child = child.getNextSibling())
    storeResult(child);
  }


// This function is responsible for returning the result to the
//Calling program.

 String returnResult()
 {
  return(result);
 }
}
```

The constructor of the *XMLParser* class accepts the servlet's input stream. The constructor instantiates the *DocumentBuilderFactory* class and uses this instance to create a document builder object. Note the parser attributes: it is non-validating (*documentfactory.setValidating(false);*), ignores comments (*documentfactory.setIgnoringComments(true);*), ignores white spaces (*documentfactory.setIgnoringElementContentWhitespace(true);*), is a coalescing parser (*documentfactory.setCoalescing(true);*) and expands entity references (*documentfactory.setExpandEntityReferences(true);*).

The document builder's *parse()* method parses the XML stream and creates a document from it as shown by the following code line:

```
parseddocument = mydocumentbuilder.parse(xmlstream);
```

In the above line *parseddocument* is a *Document* object that contains the DOM structure for the XML given by *xmlstream*.

The *storeResult()* method accepts a node object and obtains the node name (*node.getNodeName();*) and the node value (*node.getNodeValue();*). If the node value is null, only the node name is appended to the *result* string. Otherwise, both the node's name and value are appended to *result*. The HTML <Font> and <BR> tags are being used to present the node names and values in a readable format and hold no other significance for the parsing result.

NOTE

The *storeResult()* method accepts a *Node* object as parameter. However, the *XMLParser* class' constructor makes the first call to *storeResult()* by passing a *Document* object to it (Note the code line "storeResult(parsed-document);"). Recollect from our discussion on the *Document* interface ("The Basic Classes" sub-section under "The Document Object Model") that *Document* extends the *Node* interface. This is equivalent to saying that the *Document* object is also a *Node* object. Therefore, the call to *storeResult()* with a *Document* object as parameter is perfectly valid.

We now examine the following *for* loop within the *storeResult()* method:

```
for (Node child = node.getFirstChild(); child != null;
        child = child.getNextSibling())
   storeResult(child);
```

The first node returned by the loop will be the node representing the <ROOT> tag, which happens to be the first child for the *Document* object given by *parseddocument*. This node (*ROOT*) is passed to the *storeResult()* method. This means that during the second execution, the *for* loop will return the first child of the *ROOT* node (the node that represents <questionid>). The third execution returns the node that represents the tag <questiontext> and is a sibling of the questioned node and so on. Thus, the *for* loop executes until all nodes within the *Document* are covered.

The *returnString()*method returns the string variable to the calling servlet (ParsingXML).

The output of the *ParsingXML* class is shown in Figure 3.17.

Figure 3.17 Output from ParsingXML.java

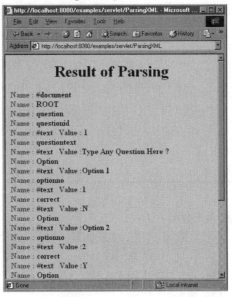

Finding Lists of Nodes

The DOM tree can be searched for specific nodes by supplying the node name. The *Node* interface provides the *getNodeName()* and *getNodeValue()* methods to obtain the name and value of a node, respectively. These node names andvalues may then be compared against a specified name/value to be searched. A loop can be run to iterate through nodes with matching names/values.

Figure 3.18 illustrates searching a DOM tree for nodes that contain a specified value. We shall use the DOM tree from Figure 3.1for our example. First of all, we create an HTML form with an input field in which to type the value for which we'll search. Let us call it searchForm.html (see Figure 3.18)

Figure 3.18 Code for searchForm.html:

```
<html>
 <head>
  <title>Untitled Document</title>
  <meta http-equiv="Content-Type" content="text/html; charset=iso-8859-1">
```

Continued

Figure 3.18 Continued

```
  </head>
  <body bgcolor="//FFFFFF" text="#000000">
   <form name="form1" method="get"
         action="http://localhost:8080/examples/servlet/SearchInXML">
    Enter the Search Criteria Here...
    <input type="Text" name="NodeToSearch" size = "20"><br><br>
    <center>
     <input type="submit" name="Submit" value="Click to Find The Node">
    </center>
   </form>
  </body>
</html>
```

Figure 3.19 The Search Form

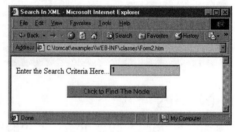

The form of searchForm.html appears in the browser as shown in Figure 3.19.

Finding a List of Nodes that Match a Particular Criteria

We now create a class that accepts two parameters: a search word and an XML input stream that is to be searched for the search word. This class, *DOMXML,* uses the *DocumentBuilder* class to parse the XML and build its DOM tree. It then searches the resulting DOM tree for the specified search value (see Figure 3.20).

Figure 3.20 Code for DomXML.java

```
import java.io.*;
import javax.xml.parsers.*;
import org.xml.sax.*;
import org.xml.sax.helpers.*;
import org.w3c.dom.*;
```

Continued

Figure 3.20 Continued

```
public class DOMXML
{
 String result = new String();
 String searchCriteria = new String();
 boolean found = false;
 int valueNo = 1;

 // Constructor..
 //  1. InputStream of the File to be parsed..
 //  2. Node Value to be searched.

 DOMXML(InputStream xmlStream, String searchCriteria)
 {
  this.searchCriteria = searchCriteria;
  // Step 1: create a DocumentBuilderFactory and configure it
  DocumentBuilderFactory documentFactory;
  DocumentFactory = DocumentBuilderFactory.newInstance();

  // Optional: set various configuration options
  documentFactory.setValidating(false);
  documentFactory.setIgnoringComments(true);
  documentFactory.setIgnoringElementContentWhitespace(true);
  documentFactory.setCoalescing(true);
  // The opposite of creating entity ref nodes is expanding them inline
  documentFactory.setExpandEntityReferences(true);

  // At this point the DocumentBuilderFactory instance can be saved and
  //reused to create any number of DocumentBuilder instances with the
  //same configuration options.

  // Step 2: create a DocumentBuilder that satisfies the constraints
  //specified by the DocumentBuilderFactory
  DocumentBuilder myDocumentBuilder = null;
  try {
```

Continued

Figure 3.20 Continued

```
    myDocumentBuilder = documentFactory.newDocumentBuilder();
  } catch (ParserConfigurationException pce) {
    System.err.println(pce);
    System.exit(1);
  }


  // Step 3: parse the input file
  Document parsedDocument = null;
  try {
    parsedDocument = myDocumentBuilder.parse(xmlStream);
  } catch (SAXException se) {
    System.err.println(se.getMessage());
    System.exit(1);
  } catch (IOException ioe) {
    System.err.println(ioe);
    System.exit(1);
  }


  // Store the DOM tree in a String Object
  storeResult(parsedDocument);
}


// The function is responsible for Traversing the DOM Tree and storing
//the result in the Object of the Class String (result). During the
//Traversal special HTML tags as also added along with the Node
//Name/Value to as to facilitate understanding.

void storeResult(Node node)
{
  String val = node.getNodeValue();
  if (val != null)
  {
    val = val.trim();
    if (val.equalsIgnoreCase(searchCriteria))
    {
      found = true;
```

Continued

Figure 3.20 Continued

```
    result += valueno+".   " +node.getParentNode().getNodeName()+"<br>";
    valueNo++;
  }
 }
 for (Node child = node.getFirstChild(); child != null;
          child = child.getNextSibling())
   storeResult(child);

}


// This function is responsible for returning the result to the Calling
//program.If the Flag found is false that is no name for a specific value
// is found then the String Object (result) is assigned a value "Empty".

String returnResult()
{
 if (!found)
   result = "Empty";
 return(result);
 }
}
```

The name of the node whose value matches the search criterion is appended to the *result* output String variable. The *storeResult()* method is repeatedly called for all nodes in the DOM tree to check for those with matching value entries. If no match is found, the *Empty* string is assigned to the *result* variable.

Now we create a servlet to read the search value from the HTML form and pass it to the *DomXML* class for searching. The servlet will also print out the search results it receives from the *DomXML* class. We call this servlet *SearchInXML*. SearchInXML's code displayed in Figure 3.21.

Servlet to Write Out All Node Names that Contain a Specific Value

The SearchInXML servlet opens a connection to the Temp.xml file, which contains the XML to be searched. It also reads the search word from searchForm.html using the *getParameter()* method. The servlet then passes the XML stream and the search word to a *DomXML* object (Figure 3.21).

Figure 3.21 The SearchInXML Servlet

```
import java.io.*;

import java.net.*;

import java.util.*;

import javax.servlet.*;

import javax.servlet.http.*;


public class  SearchInXML extends HttpServlet
{
 InputStream xmlStream;
 String searchCriteria = new String();
 public void doGet(HttpServletRequest request,
                   HttpServletResponse response)
          throws ServletException, IOException
 {
  PrintWriter outputWriter = response.getWriter();
  response.setContentType("text/html");
  //  Storing the parameter passed to the servlet in a string variable.
  searchCriteria = request.getParameter("NodeToSearch");

  // Providing the urlName of the XML File..
  String urlName = "http://localhost:8080/examples/Temp.xml";
  URL url = new URL(urlName);
  URLConnection connection = url.openConnection();
  xmlStream  = connection.getInputStream();

  // Calling the Class DomXML with the Stream of the XML File and a
  //particular search criteria to search in the XML File.

  DOMXML  myParser = new DOMXML( xmlStream, searchCriteria);

  // Obtaining the result from the Class.
  String returnValue = myParser.returnResult();
  outputWriter.println("<center><h1>Result of Searching</center>");
```

Continued

Figure 3.21 Continued

```
// Displaying the result in appropriate format.
if (returnvalue.equals("Empty"))
  outputWriter.println("<h4> <font color=\"#FF0000\" align=\"left\">"
                        + "<b> Search Yielded 0 result(s). </font> ");
else
{
  StringTokenizer tokens = new StringTokenizer(returnValue, "<br>");
  int numberOfTokens = tokens.countTokens();
  outputWriter.println("<h4> <font color=\"#FF0000\" align=\"left\">"
      + "<b> Search Yielded "+ numberOfTokens + " result(s). </font> ");
  outputWriter.print("<h4> "+returnValue);
}


  outputWriter.close();
  xmlStream.close();
}
}
```

If *returnValue* contains "Empty," it outputs the message "Search Yielded 0 result(s)." Otherwise, *returnValue* is split using the HTML <BR> tag that was appended after each matching entry by the *DomXML* class. Assuming that the user entered the value "1" into searchForm.html's input field (See Figure 3.21), the node names satisfying the search criterion are displayed as shown in Figure 3.22.

Figure 3.22 Node Names that Match the Search Criterion

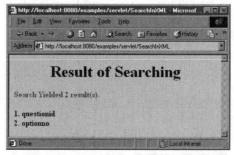

Changing the Contents of a Node

The DOM tree can be used not only to read node names or their values, but also to modify an XML file. This modification could take the form of appending nodes, changing node values or deleting nodes. Once again, the various methods provided by the *Node* interface come into play while modifying the DOM tree.

We start by creating a single user interface in the form of an HTML form that accepts a node name and the corresponding node value in input fields and provides two buttons, one to empty the DOM tree (by removing all nodes in the tree) and the other to modify the node value or to append a new node. We call this file modifyForm.html. Figure 3.23 shows the code for this file:

Figure 3.23 The modifyForm.html Code

```
<html>
<head>
<title>Untitled Document</title>
<meta http-equiv="Content-Type" content="text/html; charset=iso-8859-1">
</head>
<body bgcolor="#FFFFFF" text="#000000">
<form name="form1" method="get" action="http://localhost:8080/examples/
    servlet/AdditionInXML">
  Enter the Node Name Here..<input type="Text" name="NodeToAdd" size =
      "20"><br>
  Enter the Node Value Here..<input type="Text" name="ValueToAdd" size =
      "20"> <br><br>
  <center><input type="submit" name="Submit" value="Click to Add/Change
      Node in The XML">
  </center>
</form>
<form name="form1" method="post" action="http://localhost:8080/examples
    /servlet/EmptyXML">
  <input type="submit" name="Submit" value="Empty the Entire DOM">
</form>
</body>
</html>
```

Consider the form displayed in Figure 3.24, where we have assumed that the user has added *Option* as the name of the new node and *New Option* as the value of the node after opening the modifyForm.html file in the browser.

Figure 3.24 The Form for Modifying the DOM Tree

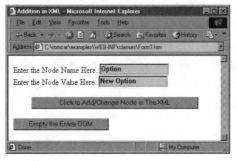

Creating and Updating Elements and Text Nodes

We create a single class, *ModifyXML.java,* that matches the node name passed to its constructor with all the nodes in the DOM tree. If the node name is found, its value is updated using the node value passed as another parameter to the constructor function. If the node is not found, a new node with the given name and value is appended to the root of the DOM tree. Code for *ModifyXML.java* is shown in Figure 3.25.

Figure 3.25 The *ModifyXML.java* Class

```
import java.io.*;

import javax.xml.parsers.*;

import org.xml.sax.*;

import org.xml.sax.helpers.*;

import org.w3c.dom.*;


public class ModifyXML
{
 String result = new String();
 String nodeName = new String();
 String nodeValue = new String();
 int empty = 0;


 boolean found = false;
```

Continued

Figure 3.25 Continued

```
boolean addedAtEnd = false;


int valueNo = 1;


// Constructor..
// 1. InputStream of the File to be parsed..
// 2. Node name which is to be affected.
// 3. New Node value of the Node name which is to be affected.
// 4. Flag empty which is used to Empty out the entire DOM Tree..



ModifyXML(InputStream xmlStream, String nodeName,
          String nodeValue, int empty)
{
 this.nodeName = nodeName;
 this.nodeValue = nodeValue;
 // Step 1: create a DocumentBuilderFactory and configure it
 DocumentBuilderFactory documentFactory;
 DocumentFactory = DocumentBuilderFactory.newInstance();

 // Optional: set various configuration options
 documentFactory.setValidating(false);
 documentFactory.setIgnoringComments(true);
 documentFactory.setIgnoringElementContentWhitespace(true);
 documentFactory.setCoalescing(true);
 // The opposite of creating entity ref nodes is expanding them inline
 documentFactory.setExpandEntityReferences(true);

 // At this point the DocumentBuilderFactory instance can be saved and
 //reused to create any number of DocumentBuilder instances with the
 //same configuration options.

 // Step 2: create a DocumentBuilder that satisfies the constraints
 // specified by the DocumentBuilderFactory
 DocumentBuilder myDocumentBuilder = null;
 try {
```

Continued

Figure 3.25 Continued

```
   myDocumentBuilder = documentFactory.newDocumentBuilder();
} catch (ParserConfigurationException pce) {
 System.err.println(pce);
 System.exit(1);
}

// Step 3: parse the input file
Document parsedDocument = null;
try {
 parsedDocument = myDocumentBuilder.parse(xmlStream);
} catch (SAXException se) {
 System.err.println(se.getMessage());
 System.exit(1);
} catch (IOException ioe) {
 System.err.println(ioe);
 System.exit(1);
}

if (empty == 1)
{
 Document emptyDocument = null;
 parsedDocument = emptyDocument;
 showResult(parsedDocument);
}
else
{
 storeResult(parsedDocument);
 //  If a node of a particular name is not found then call
 //  the Function "AddNewNode" to create a new Node at the End.
 if (!found)
 {
  addedAtEnd = true;
  Element newNode  = parsedDocument.createElement(nodeName);
  Text textNode = parsedDocument.createTextNode(nodeValue);
```

Continued

Figure 3.25 Continued

```
      parsedDocument = addNewNode(parsedDocument,newNode,textNode);
   }


   // Store the DOM tree in a String Object
   showResult(parsedDocument);
 }
}


// The function is responsible for Traversing the DOM Tree and checking
// whether a Node of a particular name is present or not. If it is
// present then the value of the node is replaced buy the new Value
// and a flag "Found" is set to be true.

void storeResult(Node node)
{
 String val = node.getNodeName();
 val = val.trim();
 if (val.equalsIgnoreCase(nodeName))
 {
  found = true;
  Node childNode = node.getFirstChild();
  childNode.setNodeValue(nodeValue);
 }
 for (Node child = node.getFirstChild(); child != null;
         child = child.getNextSibling())
  storeResult(child);
 }


 // The function is responsible for Traversing the DOM Tree and storing
 // the result in the Object of the Class String (result). During the
 // Traversal special HTML tags as also added along with the Node
 // Name/Value to as to facilitate understanding.

 void showResult(Node node)
 {
```

Continued

Figure 3.25 Continued

```
if (node == null)
{
 result = "Empty";
}
else
{
 String val = node.getNodeValue();
 if (val == null)
 {
  result += "<Font color = \"#ff0000\">Name :</Font> "+
           node.getNodeName();
  result += "<BR>";
 }
 else if (val.trim().equals(""))
 {
  // Simple Ignore...
 }
 else if(val.equalsIgnoreCase(nodeValue))
 {
  if (addedAtEnd)
  {
   result += "<Font color = \"#FF0000\">Name :</Font>"+
            node.getNodeName();
   result += "<Font color = \"#008000\">   " +
            "Value : "+ val + "</Font><BR>";
  }
  else
  {
   result += "<Font color = \"#FF0000\">Name :</Font> "+
            node.getNodeName();
   result += "<Font color = \"#FF00FF\">   " +
            "Value : "+ val+"</Font><BR>";
  }
 }
 else
```

Continued

Figure 3.25 Continued

```
        {
     result += "<Font color = \"#ff0000\">Name :</Font> "+
                node.getNodeName();
     result += "<Font color = \"#0000FF\">   " +
                "Value : </Font>" + val+"<BR>";
     }

    for (Node child = node.getFirstChild(); child != null;
            child = child.getNextSibling())
      showResult(child);
    }
}


// This function is responsible for returning the result to the Calling
//program.

String returnResult()
{
 return(result);
}


// This function "AddNewNode" is responsible for adding a new Node to
// theDOM Tree it takes as parameter three Objects of the Type Node..
// 1. The original Dom Tree..
// 2. The Name of the Node to be added..
// 3. The value of the Node to be added..
// The return type of this function is the updated DOM Document.



Document addNewNode(Node original, Node nodeElement, Node nodeText)
{
 Node position = original.getLastChild();

 if (position.getNodeType() != Node.TEXT_NODE)
 {
```

Continued

Figure 3.25 Continued

```
     position.appendChild(nodeElement);
     position.appendChild(nodeText);
  }
  else
   while(position.getNodeType() == Node.TEXT_NODE)
   {
     for (Node child = position.getFirstChild(); child != null;
              child = child.getNextSibling())
     if (child.getNodeType() != Node.TEXT_NODE)
     {
       child = child.appendChild(nodeelement);
       child = child.appendChild(nodetext);
       original.appendChild(child);
       break;
     }
   }
  return((Document)original);
  }
}
```

The code iterates through the *storeResult()* method to check if the node name given by the *nodeName* variable exists in the DOM tree. If it does, the *setNodeValue()* method is called to set its value to that passed to the constructor as the *nodeValue* variable. If the node is not found, the *addNewNode()* method is called to append the node to the end of the DOM tree.

If the value of the integer being passed to the constructor is 1, the *ModifyXML* class sets the value of the parsed document objectto *null*. This automatically removes all the nodes in the document.

AdditionInXML Servlet to Modify Nodes in the DOM Tree

We now list the servlet (AdditionInXML), that reads the node name and the value entered by the user and calls the *ModifyXML* class to change the value of the node if it exists, or to append the node name and value if the node does not exist. The code for *AdditionInXML* is shown in Figure 3.26.

Figure 3.26 The AdditionInXML Servlet

```
import java.io.*;

import java.net.*;

import java.util.*;

import javax.servlet.*;

import javax.servlet.http.*;


public class AdditionInXML extends HttpServlet
{
 InputStream xmlStream;
 String nodeName = new String();
 String nodeValue = new String();


 public void doGet(HttpServletRequest request,
                    HttpServletResponse response)
           throws ServletException, IOException
 {
  PrintWriter outputWriter = response.getWriter();
  response.setContentType("text/html");
  //  Storing the parameters passed to the servlet in  string variables.
  nodeName = request.getParameter("NodeToAdd");
  nodeValue = request.getParameter("ValueToAdd");


  // Providing the urlName of the XML File..
  String urlname = "http://localhost:8080/examples/Temp.xml";
  URL url = new URL(urlname);
  URLConnection connection = url.openConnection();
  xmlStream = connection.getInputStream();


  // Calling the Class ModifyXML with the Stream of the XML File, nodeName
  //and nodeValue of the node to be replaced/appended.
  ModifyXML myParser = new ModifyXML(xmlStream, nodeName, nodeValue, 0);


  // Obtaining the result from the Class.
  String returnValue = myParser.returnResult();
  outputWriter.println("<center><h1>Result of Modification</center>");
```

Continued

Figure 3.26 Continued

```
outputWriter.print("<h4> "+returnvalue);
outputWriter.close();
xmlStream.close();
}
}
```

The servlet uses the *HTTPServletRequest* object to read the values of the form (Figure 3.23) fields in its *doGet()* method. Note that the form named *Form1* in Figure 3.23 specifies "get" as the value of its *method* attribute.

> **WARNING**
>
> The AdditionInXML servlet uses the *doGet()* method to obtain information entered by the user, in the form of query string variables. Since the information being passed in this example is not sensitive in nature, the *get* method is acceptable. If, however, you are accepting confidential information from the user, say, a user name and password pair, then use the HTTPServlet's *doPost()* method instead. This will also require changing the *method* attribute of *Form1* in Figure 3.23 to "post." In case you wish to only use the *doGet()* method, be sure to encode the values being passed in the query string.

Assuming that the user puts the *option* string in the node-name input field and the *New Option* string in the node-value input field, the output from AdditionInXML will be as shown in Figure 3.27.

Observe that the value of all the existing nodes named "option" in the DOM tree has been changed to "*New Option.*"

Now, if the user enters a node name, say "New Node," that does not exist in the DOM tree, the new node and its value will be appended to the end of the document root as shown in Figure 3.28.

The EmptyXML.java servlet is called when the user clicks on the *Empty the Entire DOM* button in modifyForm.html (See the *action* attribute of *Form1* in Figure 3.23). The servlet contains the code in Figure 3.29.

Figure 3.27 Modifying the Value of an Existing Node

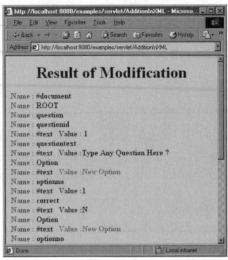

Figure 3.28 Adding a New Node to the DOM Tree

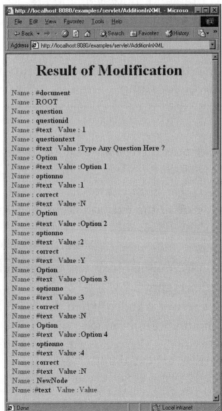

Figure 3.29 The EmptyXML Servlet

```
import java.io.*;

import java.net.*;

import java.util.*;

import javax.servlet.*;

import javax.servlet.http.*;


public class EmptyXML extends HttpServlet
{
 InputStream xmlStream;
 String nodeName = new String();
 String nodeValue = new String();

 public void doGet(HttpServletRequest request,
                   HttpServletResponse response)
          throws ServletException, IOException
 {
  PrintWriter outputWriter = response.getWriter();
  response.setContentType("text/html");
  nodeName = request.getParameter("NodeToAdd");
  nodeValue = request.getParameter("ValueToAdd");

  // Providing the urlName of the XML File..
  String urlname = "http://localhost:8080/examples/Temp.xml";
  URL url = new URL(urlname);
  URLConnection connection = url.openConnection();
  xmlStream  = connection.getInputStream();

  // Calling the Class ModifyXML with the Stream of the XML File, and last
  // parameter 1 indicating that DomTree is to be emptied.
  ModifyXML myParser = new ModifyXML(xmlStream, nodeName, nodeValue, 1);

  // Obtaining the result from the Class.

  String returnValue = myParser.returnResult();
  outputWriter.println("<center><h1>DOM TREE DESTROYED</center>");
```

Continued

Figure 3.29 Continued

```
outputWriter.close();

xmlStream.close();

}

}
```

This servlet calls the *ModifyXML* class; however, it passes the value *1* to the integer parameter, *empty*. The output from this servlet is a single line saying "DOM TREE DESTROYED" as shown in Figure 3.30.

Figure 3.30 Destroying the DOM Tree

Advanced Topics

This completes our discussion on using JAXP to create, modify and manipulate XML documents based on the DOM model. We will now briefly discuss certain advanced topics relevant to developing and deploying JAXP applications practically.

Multi-threaded Applications

As mentioned in the previous discussions, the *DocumentBuilderFactory* class is not thread-safe. Practical applications, however, are likely to be multi-threaded with various threads requesting the *DocumentBuilderFactory* class simultaneously. In all of this chapter's examples, the object of the parsing class is being created in the servlet's *doGet()* method (See Figure 3.15). Since the *doGet()* method is called for each request to the servlet, this ensures that each thread creates and uses its own instance of the *DocumetnBuilderFactory* class, which makes these examples thread-safe.

```
public void doGet(HttpServletRequest request , HttpServletResponse
     response) throws ServletException, IOException
 {
     ....................................................... .

     ....................................................... .
```

```
XMLParser  myparser = new XMLParser(xmlstream);
```

```
.............................................................. .

.............................................................. .

}
```

Another way of developing thread-safe applications would be to create only one object of the *DocumentBuilderFactory* class per application and ensure that only one thread at a time can use the instance. We explain this concept with an example.

Safe Routines

Let us instantiate the parsing class in the servlet's *init()* method. Since the *init()* method is called only once (when the servlet is loaded or called for the first time), only one instance of the *DocumentBuilderFactory* is created and will be used by every subsequent call to the *service()* method. The handling of parsing functions by a single thread at any instance is implemented via the *synchronized()* method as shown in the ThreadSafe.java servlet example (Figure 3.31).

Figure 3.31 The ThreadSafe Servlet

```
import java.io.*;

import java.util.*;

import java.net.*;

import javax.servlet.*;

import javax.servlet.http.*;


public class ThreadUnsafe extends HttpServlet
{
 UnsafeParser myParser;
 PrintWriter   outputWriter;
 InputStream   xmlStream;
 String returnValue;

 public void init()
 {
  myParser   = new UnsafeParser();
 }
```

Continued

Figure 3.31 Continued

```
public void doGet(HttpServletRequest request,
                    HttpServletResponse response)
            throws IOException, ServletException
{
  outputWriter = response.getWriter();
  response.setContentType(" text/html ");

  String urlname = "http://localhost:8080/examples/Temp.xml";
  URL url = new URL(urlname);
  URLConnection connection = url.openConnection();
  xmlStream   = connection.getInputStream();
  synchronized(this)
  {
   myParser.parseNow(xmlStream);
   returnValue = myParser.returnResult();
  }
  outputWriter.println("<center><h1>Result of Parsing</center>");
  outputWriter.println("<h4> "+returnvalue);
  outputWriter.close();
  xmlStream.close();
 }
}
```

We list the *UnsafeParser* class before moving on to the explanation. The change made to the parsing code is that the *DocumentBuilder* class is being instantiated in a new method called *parseNow()*. This prevents the constructor of the *UnsafeParser* class from being called for every request, thereby ensuring that the *DocumentBuilderFactory* class is instantiated only once (when the constructor of *UnsafeParser* class is created during servlet initialization). Remember that we are using this code just to explain how the threading issues can be addressed. This may not necessarily be code that you should use for practical applications (see Figure 3.32).

UnsafeParser is an odd name in a section on thread safety. You can alternately call it "UnsychronizedParser" or something similar that implies that it is assuming the externalization of synchronization policy.

Figure 3.32 The UnsafeParser.java Class

```
import java.io.*;

import javax.xml.parsers.*;

import org.xml.sax.*;

import org.xml.sax.helpers.*;

import org.w3c.dom.*;


public class UnsafeParser

{

 String result = new String();

 DocumentBuilderFactory documentFactory;

 DocumentBuilder myDocumentBuilder = null;

 Document parsedDocument = null;


 // Constructor..


 UnsafeParser()

 {

  documentFactory = DocumentBuilderFactory.newInstance();


  // Optional: set various configuration options

  documentFactory.setValidating(false);

  documentFactory.setIgnoringComments(true);

  documentFactory.setIgnoringElementContentWhitespace(true);

  documentFactory.setCoalescing(true);

  // The opposite of creating entity ref nodes is expanding them inline

  documentFactory.setExpandEntityReferences(true);



 }


 void parseNow(InputStream xmlStream)

 {

  try {

   myDocumentBuilder = documentFactory.newDocumentBuilder();

  } catch (ParserConfigurationException pce) {
```

Continued

Figure 3.32 Continued

```
    System.err.println(pce);

    System.exit(1);

  }


  try {

    parsedDocument = myDocumentBuilder.parse(xmlStream);

  } catch (SAXException se) {

    System.err.println(se.getMessage());

    System.exit(1);

  } catch (IOException ioe) {

    System.err.println(ioe);

    System.exit(1);

  }


  // Store the DOM tree in a String Object

  storeResult(parsedDocument);

}


// The function is responsible for Traversing the DOM Tree and storing

// the result in the Object of the Class String (result). During the

// Traversal special HTML tags as also added along with the Node

// Name/Value to as to facilitate understanding.


void storeResult(Node node)

{

 String val = node.getNodeValue();

 if (val == null)

 {

  result += "<Font color = \"#ff0000\">Name :</Font> "+

            node.getNodeName();

  result += "<BR>";

 }

 else if (val.trim().equals(""))

 {
```

Continued

Figure 3.32 Continued

```
  // Simple Ignore...
 }
 else
 {
  result += "<Font color = \"#ff0000\">Name :</Font> " +
          node.getNodeName();
  result += "<Font color = \"#0000FF\">   Value " +
          ":</Font>" + val+"<BR>";
 }


 for (Node child = node.getFirstChild(); child != null;
        child = child.getNextSibling())
  storeResult(child);


}


// This function is responsible for returning the result to the Calling
//program.

String returnResult()
{
 return(result);
}
}
```

The parsing class, *UnsafeParser* (we call it "unsafe" because this class in itself does not address the issue of threading. The ThreadSafe servlet calls it in a thread-safe manner) is instantiated by the servlet's *init()* method.

```
public void init()
 {
 myparser  = new UnsafeParser();
 }
```

Since the *init()* method is called only once, the *UnsafeParser* class's constructor is likewise invoked once. This in turn means that only one instance of the

DocumentBuilderFactory class (created when the constructor of *UnsafeParser* class is called), is being created as shown in the code snippet below:

```
UnsafeParser()
{
            documentfactory = DocumentBuilderFactory.newInstance();
            .................................................... .
            .................................................... .


}
```

Note that the servlet's *doGet()* method uses this instance using a *synchronized()* block:

```
synchronized(this)
{
 myParser.parseNow(xmlstream);
 returnValue = myParser.returnResult();
}
```

The *synchronized()* block ensures that only one thread at a time executes the code given within it. Thus, even if multiple threads are needed to use the parser, they are forced to do so in a thread-safe manner.

Unsafe Routines

In Figure 3.31 if we do not enclose the call to the *parseNow()* method within a *synchronized()* block, it is possible that more than one thread will try to use the *myParser* object simultaneously. Since there is only one instance of the *DocumentBuilderFactory* class (*DocumentFactory*), the parser's *parseNow()* method tries to use this instance for creating more instances of the *DocumentBuilder* class:

```
void parseNow(InputStream xmlStream)
{
 try {
  myDocumentBuilder = documentFactory.newDocumentBuilder();
 }
            .................................................... .
            .................................................... .
```

Since the *DocumentBuilderFactory* class in itself is not thread–safe, the code may behave erratically or exceptions/errors may be thrown.

Parser Attributes

SAX parsers are configured by setting their features and properties. A feature has a *Boolean* value (*true* or *false*), while a property has an object value. The *XMLReader* interface provides the *getFeature()* and *setFeature()* methods respectively to obtain and to set the value of a feature:

```
public void setFeature(String name, boolean value) throws
    SAXNotRecognizedException, SAXNotSupportedException
public Boolean getFeature(String name) throws SAXNotRecognizedException,
    SAXNotSupportedException
```

Standard feature names begin with http://xml.org/sax/features/. For example, the following code sets the validating feature to *true*:

```
parserObject.setFeature("http://xml.org/sax/features/validation", true);
```

If the parser cannot recognize a feature, the *SAXNotRecognizedException* is thrown. If the parser is not equipped to support the feature, a *SAXNotSupportedException* is thrown.

SAX parsers do not have any of the properties required. However, the *XMLReader* interface provides two methods, *setProperty()* and *getProperty()*, to set and to retrieve the parser properties:

```
public void setProperty(String name, Object value) throws
    SAXNotRecognizedException, SAXNotSupportedException
public Object getProperty(String name) throws SAXNotRecognizedException,
    SAXNotSupportedException
```

For example, to set the schema location for elements that are not in any namespace of http://www.propertyexample.com/schema.xsd, the following code may be used:

```
parserObject.setProperty(http://apache.org/xml/properties/schema +
    "external-noNamespaceSchemaLocation", "http://www.propertyexample.com
    /schema.xsd");
```

As against the SAX parsers discussed above, the parsers used in the various examples in this chapter set validation, namespace-awareness, and so on as parser attributes and not as parser properties or features. However, these are not attributes in the XML sense. Attributes, as defined in XML, are name-value pairs providing additional content information. The parser attributes, however, are boolean values that can be turned on or off.

Unlike the SAX parsers, JAXP-aware parsers do not have a standardized set of features. Instead, they support various custom and vendor-specific features. For example, Xerces, has a *http://apache.org/xml/features/dom/create-entity-ref-nodes* feature that lets you choose whether or not to include entity reference nodes in the DOM tree. This is different from deciding whether or not to expand entity references, which determines whether or not the entity nodes that are placed in the tree have children representing their replacement text.

JAXP allows you to get and set these custom features as objects of the appropriate type using the following two methods:

```
public Object getAttribute(String name) throws IllegalArgumentException
public void setAttribute(String name, Object value) throws
    IllegalArgumentException
```

Suppose you are using Xerces and you do not want to include entity reference nodes. Since they are included by default, you need to set *http://apache.org/xml/features/dom/create-entity-ref-nodes* to *false*. You may use *setAttribute()* on the *DocumentBuilderFactory,* as in the following:

```
DocumentBuilderFactory factory;
factory = DocumentBuilderFactory.newInstance();
factory.setAttribute(
  "http://apache.org/xml/features/dom/create-entity-ref-nodes",
  new Boolean(false)
);
```

The naming conventions for both attribute names and values depend on the underlying parser. Xerces uses URI strings like SAX feature names. Other parsers may do something different. JAXP 1.2 will add a couple of standard attributes related to schema validation.

Selecting a DOM Parser with the Plugability Interface

JAXP is reasonably parser-independent. The parser that a JAXP program uses depends on which parsers are installed in your class path and how certain system properties are set. The default is to use the class named by the *javax.xml.parsers .DocumentBuilderFactory* system property. For example, if you want to make sure that Xerces is used to parse documents, then you would run Example1.java as per the following code:

```
D:\books\XMLJAVA>java-Djavax.xml.parsers.DocumentBuilderFactory=org.apache.
    xerces.jaxp.DocumentBuilderFactoryImpl Example1
```

If you want to consistently use a certain DOM parser, *gnu.xml.dom*
.JAXPFactory for instance, place the following line in the META-INF.mf file of
the JAXP package:

```
javax.xml.parsers.DocumentBuilderFactory=gnu.xml.dom.JAXPFactory
```

If this fails to locate a parser, JAXP looks for a META-INF/services/
javax.xml.parsers.DocumentBuilderFactory file in all JAR files available at runtime to find the name of the concrete *DocumentBuilderFactory* subclass.

If that also fails, the *DocumentBuilderFactory.newInstance()* returns a default class,
generally the parser from the vendor who provided the JAXP classes. For example,
the JDK JAXP classes pick *org.apache.crimson.jaxp.DocumentBuilderFactoryImpl* by
default. Thus, JAXP implementation provides parsers with sufficient plugability
options.

DOM Parser Search Path

When the *DocumentBuilderFactory* class is instantiated, it checks the *Classpath* variable to locate the XML parser implementation. If the *Classpath* has not been
updated to point to the XML parser implementation, or if no parser implementation is provided, an instance of the *DocumentBuilderFactory* class cannot be created.
Trying to do so throws a *FactoryConfigurationException* Exception:

```
public class FactoryConfigurationException extends Error{
public FactoryConfigurationError();
public FactoryConfigurationError(String msg);
public FactoryConfigurationError(Exception e);
public FactoryConfigurationError(Exception e, String msg);
public Exception getException();
}
```

The *FactoryConfigurationError()* method is used to handle the exception.

As already discussed, the object of the *DocumentBuilderFactory* class is used to
set the parser's attributes. If the parser cannot be constructed with the validation
and namespace-awareness settings as specified by the parser code, a
ParserConfigurationException exception is thrown.

```
public class ParserConfigurationException extends Exception{
public ParserConfigurationException();
```

```
public ParserConfigurationException(String msg);
}
```

ParserConfigurationException may be thrown if the XML parser implementation specifies contrary configurations settings.

Error Handling

The readers were introduced to error handling in Figure 3.9. The *Example1.java* class, which is a validating DOM parser, contains the *MyErrorHandler* class that implements the *ErrorHandler* interface. The *ErrorHandler* interface is implemented for customized error handling. Refer to the following line of code in The *Example1.java* class (Figure 3.9)

```
MyDocumentBuilder.setErrorHandler(new MyErrorHandler());
```

This line sets the Error handler by registering its instance with the XML reader.

WARNING

If the instance of Error handler is not registered with the XML reader, XML parsing errors will go unreported and the program code may behave unpredictably.

Registration of the error handler's instance with the XML reader enables the SAX driver to report parsing errors, warnings and fatal errors through this interface instead of throwing exceptions. The three methods *error()*, *warning()* and *fatalError()* call the error handler class to report errors, receive a *SAXParseException* object. The *error()* method is used for notification of recoverable errors, the *warning()* method reports warnings and the *fatalError()* method reports non-recoverable errors.

Summary

In this chapter we introduced the concept of DOM structures for XML documents. We showed how a DOM tree is built from an XML file, using relevant examples. We then discussed the basic interfaces given in W3C's specification for the DOM model. This was followed by traversing the hierarchy imposed by the objects of DOM interfaces and exploring the interrelationship among various DOM objects, again with relevant examples. After sufficient information on DOM was provided, we moved on to discuss DOM in the context of JAXP. In this section, we discussed the JAXP DOM API and its deployment. We followed this up with examples on how to use JAXP classes such as *DocumentBuilderFactory*, *DocumentBuilder* and so on, to build DOM parsers and to set the parser attributes. We then delved into the issue of handling various XML input sources (files, streams and so on) using JAXP. Thereafter, we walked down a DOM constellation to see what its constituents (the root document, the elements, the attributes, attribute values and so on) are and how they can be obtained.

The chapter contains complete working program codes for: building a DOM parser, searching the DOM tree for specific nodes, modifying the DOM tree nodes/node values, and so on. We critically examined and explained these codes to enumerate the code execution and to show the ease with which DOM documents can be manipulated. In the end of the chapter, we addressed issues of multi-threading and how the thread-unsafe *DocumentBuilderFactory* class can be used to build thread-safe parsers, configuring SAX parsers using the *XMLReader* class, configuring the *Classpath* to ensure that the proper XML parser implementation is used by JAXP classes, and error handling in JAXP parsers. After going through this chapter, you should be in a position to build customized DOM parsers using JAXP to handle the processing requirements of XML documents.

Solutions Fast Track

The Document Object Model

☑ The Document Object Model (DOM) is a World Wide Web consortium (W3C) specification that provides a programming interface for both XML and HTML documents.

☑ DOM provides a cross-language, cross-platform object-based model for documents that can be used in a wide variety of environments and with any programming language.

☑ The Tree-based model is easy to navigate, modify and update.

☑ The DOM is efficient for repeated use of a single XML file.

JAXP and Underlying DOM Engines

☑ JAXP supports XML processing using DOM and provides some convenient methods to make the XML APIs easier to use for java developers.

☑ The *DocumentBuilderFactory* and *DocumentBuilder* interfaces are available for creating DOM parsers using JAXP.

Creating a DOM Parser

☑ The *newInstance()* method creates an instance of the *DocumentBuilderFactory* class; this instance can then be used with the *newDocumentBuilder()* method to create a document builder.

☑ Various methods such as *setIgnoringComments()*, *setExpandEntityReferences(), setCoalescing()* and so on can be used to set the attributes for a JAXP parser.

☑ An XML can be parsed using the *DocumentBuilder* class' *parse()* method to create a DOM document.

Parsing XML into a DOM

☑ The *parse()* method of JAXP's *DocumentBuilder* class accepts different type of parameters, for example strings, input streams, files and so on to accept XML input from different types of sources.

☑ The *DocumentBuilder* class' *parse()* method converts the XML into a DOM tree.

Manipulating DOM Objects

- ☑ The node object provides methods such as *getNodeName()*, *getNodeValue()*, *getFirstChild()* and so on that can be used to navigate through the DOM constellation.

- ☑ The *nodeName* and *nodeValue* properties are used to add new nodes or to modify existing node values in a DOM tree.

- ☑ The DOM tree can be destroyed by setting the document object value to *EmptyDocument*.

Advanced Topics

- ☑ In a multi-threaded environment, the thread-unsafe *DocumentBuilderFactory* class can be used in a thread-safe manner by calling the parser within a *synchronized()* block.

- ☑ An error handler can be set using the *setErrorHandler()* method of the *DocumentBuilder* class for customized error handling.

Frequently Asked Questions

The following Frequently Asked Questions, answered by the authors of this book, are designed to both measure your understanding of the concepts presented in this chapter and to assist you with real-life implementation of these concepts. To have your questions about this chapter answered by the author, browse to **www.syngress.com/solutions** and click on the **"Ask the Author"** form.

Q: Why should I use the DOM?

A: The DOM model provides a standardized view of a document's contents. By implementing the DOM API, the data from one program can be manipulated by other routines. Additionally, these manipulations can be reused with other DOMs. This interoperability justifies the use of DOM implementations.

Q: How is JAXP different from DOM and SAX?

A: DOM and SAX represent two standard approaches to handling XML documents: in-memory and event-driven. Both DOM and SAX omit a definition of how to create a compliant parser; JAX-P provides this standard factory interface.

Q: Where do I find JAXP?

A: JAXP can be downloaded free of cost from the official Java website at http://java.sun.com/jaxp/.

Q: Can I append a node to any other node in an existing DOM tree?

A: Yes, you can append a node to any other existing node, except to a *Text* node. Trying to do so will result in a *DOMException* being raised.

Q: What happens if a parser's *setValidating* attribute is set to *true*, but no error handling mechanism is defined in the parser?

A: The code executes normally in such a case. However, the XML parser generates a warning that the default error handling mechanism will be used, since one has not been defined by the developer.

Chapter 4

XML Transformations

Solutions in this chapter:

- Reviewing XSL and XSLT
- JAXP and Underlying XSL Engines
- Using JAXP Classes
- Miscellaneous JAXP for XSL Issues

☑ Summary

☑ Solutions Fast Track

☑ Frequently Asked Questions

Introduction

In the previous two chapters, we discussed the parsing of XML data, as well as some simple XML manipulations. The final component of JAXP encapsulates more complicated XML manipulations. Specifically, it is designed to provide an interface to XSLT and stylesheets.

XSLT and stylesheets provide a mechanism for automating the transformation of XML from one form to another. While most frequently used to transform XML into HTML, it can also be used to transform equivalent XML data between schemas, or to output data in other browser formats (such as VoiceXML).

XSLT and stylesheets are often associated with client-side browsers, not server-side programming. However, nothing in their design limits them to client-side. There are often good reasons to perform these manipulations on the server: to support browsers that do not support XSLT, or to transform XML between schemas.

JAXP provides a very thin layer over XSL engines. The Transformation classes in JAXP aren't really designed to be general-purpose XML transformation classes, so writing your own Transformer subclass can be a bit tricky.

Reviewing XSL and XSLT

XML, as you may have noticed, requires a lot of work for it to be properly parsed through and then displayed accurately on an HTML page. Proper code needs to be written to make sure that the values display the correct color scheme, proper spacing between areas, and the correct information displayed row-by-row or even table-by-table. XSL provides a mechanism for encapsulating the transformation of XML into HTML in a language specifically designed for this task, and moving this task out of the Java code can make the system easier to maintain and understand. (We won't go into a full review of XSLT/XPath since it's outside the scope of this book.)

XSL is the actual recommendation from the WC 3, and consists of two parts: XSLT and XSLFO. XSLFO stands for XSL Formatting Objects, which are an XSL specification used to control the formatting of printed documents. XSLT, or XSL for Transformations, is what we'll primarily deal with here.

There is another recommendation which comes into play with XSL as well: XPath. XPath is the recommendation used within XSL to locate the tags, elements, and attributes within an XML document.

Let's take a small XML file and transform it through XSLT. Figure 4.1 shows our XML file.

Figure 4.1 text.XML

```
01:  <?xml version="1.0" encoding="ISO-8859-1"?>
02:  <article>
03:   <title>Top Story</title>
04:   <author>Lydia Gonzalez</author>
05:   <text>
06:    Many children today in Churches
07:    may say the verse "I am the Son
08:    of God" out loud without reading
09:    because they are unable to read.
10:
11:    In tomorrow's edition: see why this
12:    Church has began an outreach program
13:    to parents in low income areas to
14:    provide their children with reading
15:    assistance.
16:   </text>
17:  </article>
```

Let's take a look at how our XML file appears on a browser without XSL applied to it (Figure 4.2).

Figure 4.2 text.XML without XSL/XSLT

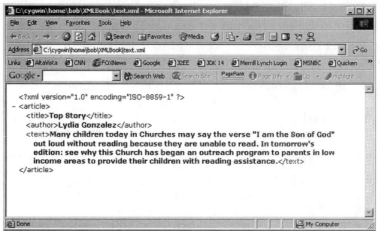

Pretty much like your normal XML file in Explorer, right? Now let's take a look at it via XSL in Figure 4.3.

Figure 4.3 text.XML with XSL/XSLT

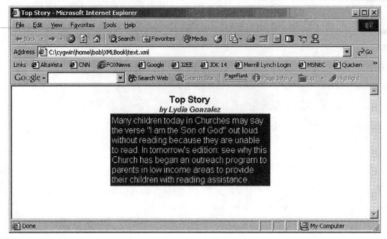

Pretty neat huh? We've taken a lifeless XML file, added a reference to the XSL/XSLT file, and voilà—we get something that, while not perfect, isn't as much of an eyesore. Only one line was added to the XML file. Let's take a look at the revised header:

```
<?xml version="1.0" encoding="ISO-8859-1"?>
<?xml-stylesheet type="text/xsl" href="demo.xsl"?>
```

If you've seen CSS/DHTML code before, you may notice a similarity between the xml-stylesheet tag and the src tag. In both cases, the main file is calling a stylesheet to transform tags or, in this case, transform the page completely to another output. In case you're curious, Figure 4.4 has the XSL/XSLT code used to display Figure 4.3.

Figure 4.4 demo.xsl

```
00: <?xml version="1.0" encoding="ISO-8859-1"?>
01: <xsl:stylesheet version="1.0"
02:       xmlns:xsl="http://www.w3.org/1999/XSL/Transform">
03:   <xsl:template match="/">
04:     <html>
05:       <head>
06:         <title>
```

Continued

Figure 4.4 Continued

```
07:        <xsl:value-of select="article/title"/>
08:       </title>
09:     </head>
10:     <body>
11:      <center>
12:       <b>
13:        <font face="Arial" size="3">
14:         <xsl:value-of select="article/title"/>
15:        </font>
16:       </b>
17:       <br/>
18:       <b>
19:        <i>
20:         <font face="Arial" size="2" color="#FF0000">
21:          by <xsl:value-of select="article/author"/>
22:         </font>
23:        </i>
24:       </b>
25:       <table bgcolor="#003366" width="300">
26:        <tr>
27:         <td>
28:          <font face="Arial" size="3" color="#FFFFFF">
29:           <xsl:value-of select="article/text"/>
30:          </font>
31:         </td>
32:        </tr>
33:       </table>
34:      </center>
35:     </body>
36:    </html>
37:   </xsl:template>
38: </xsl:stylesheet>
```

Take a quick look at lines 06, 14, 21, and 29 in the previous figure. You may have noticed that these lines don't contain anything that may fit with either

HTML or even XML, but sound like they are "matching" something. They are, in fact, XPath expressions used with XSL/XSLT to locate the items in the XML file that will be displayed, and fall under the Procedural XSL category.

XPath and XSLT

Before we look at just how XSLT works, we need to first understand what XSLT uses to find its information. XPath is a W3C recommendation made specifically for locating nodes, attributes, and their values within an XML file for an XSLT processor to transform. XPath uses notation similar to a directory structure notation in order to locate nodes.

An XPath picks out a set of target nodes by specifying how to match nodes down the XML hierarchy. Each successive level of the hierarchy is specified by one part of the XPath, much like directories and subdirectories are specified in Unix. Similar to Unix, the root of the XML file is defined as a single forward slash (/). Each successive level of the hierarchy is separated by another forward slash. The complete specification is referred to as a *location path*, and serves to identify the XML nodes to use in the transformation.

XPath requires that the name of the root node of the XML file be defined when used within XSLT. Back in Figure 4.4 in line 03 we defined the root node as "/" within our XSLT; this allowed us to use the root as a relative path in lines 06, 14, 21, and 29.

Using the XML in Figure 4.1 as our example XML, we can think of the "/" root as pointing to the overall XML document. Therefore, lines 06, 14, 21, and 29 pointed to various specific areas within the XML. Table 4.1 has a listing of the referenced nodes and what they point to.

Table 4.1 XPath Node Reference

Line	Complete XPath	Points to:
06	/article/title	Line 03 of Figure 4.1
14	/article/title	Line 03 of Figure 4.1
21	/article/author	Line 04 of Figure 4.1
29	/article/text	Lines 05 through 09 of Figure 4.1

We can also use a double forward slash (//) to indicate multiple matches. For example, "//text" would locate all text elements anywhere below the *article* node. The wildcard symbol (*) can be used within XPath. Assuming we had a second-level to the XML in Figure 4.1 we could also match all the nodes named "text" within the XML by using /articles/*/text.

You may be wondering right about now what the difference is between using "//" and the "*" character. The "//" will match all nodes that match the search criteria, while the "*" will match all nodes based on the proceeding path. So, if you wanted to locate all of the nodes within an XML file you can't just do "//" or "/*" you would have to do "//*", which would match all elements with all names. XPath is able to do all this thanks to its use of axes.

Axes and Locations

In the simplest sense, an *axis* is a symbolic link to the parent node that it is currently selected, and contains all the immediate child nodes. Based on this one axis, several other axes can be determined. Table 4.2 displays the list of axes that are exposed.

Table 4.2 Exposed Axes

Axis	Description
Ancestor	All the parents of the current node up to and including the root of the topmost parent node; it will display any grandparents, and so on. The "//" is an alias for ancestor.
Ancestor-or-self	The parents of the current node but also includes its position relative to the root node; it will display any grandparents, and so on.
Attribute	An XML attribute of the current node, if any. "@" is an alias for attribute.
Child	An immediate child of the current node. Child is the default and can be omitted.
Descendant	All nodes descending from the current node; does not include namespace or attributes.
Descendant-or-self	All nodes descending from the current node; does not include namespace or attributes. Always includes the current node.
Following	All nodes after the current node in the document, in the order the nodes appear in the source document. Does not include descendant, namespace, or attribute nodes.
Following-sibling	Same as *following* but only on nodes with same immediate parent as current node. Does not include namespace or attribute nodes.

Continued

Table 4.2 Continued

Axis	Description
Namespace	Any namespace child nodes within current node.
Parent	Immediate parent of the current node if it's available. Returns a single-parent only. The ".." character is an alias for parent.
Preceding	All preceding nodes listed, including root, excluding attribute and namespace nodes, in the order they appear in the source document.
Preceding-sibling	All preceding nodes of the current node that share the same parent. Namespace and attribute nodes are excluded.
Self	The current node. The "." character is an alias for self.

A *location step*, a construct to select a node based on the information from the axis, is then used to do the actual node selection behind the scenes. A complete location step contains the axis, two colons, the node-test and a set of predicates within brackets. The predicates act as a filter within the location step. Think of a node-test as a conditional statement. A location step can also use certain functions allowed by XPath. We won't be going into long detail about XPath functions and how they work since it's outside the scope of this book. You can find more information about them at www.w3.org/TR/xpath#section-Function-Calls. We will, however, go through the more common functions as we work through XSL before looking at JAX-P.

Procedural XSLT

Now that we have a better idea of how XPath works, we can start to view how XSLT works with XPath. XPath, as we noticed in the XSLT example, usually is called from an XSLT procedure. Remember, XSLT works as a procedure, executing transformations when called.

<xsl:template>

<xsl:template> is perhaps the procedure you'll most often work with. It allows you to define a template to match node items directly. You always use *<xsl:template>* to define the template applied with *<xsl:apply-template>*.

   <xsl:template> can take the following attributes:

- **match** This can be any node or location path. An example might be: *<xsl:template match="node">* where "node" is where you want the match to take place. For example, *<xsl:template match="/">* starts the match from the root of the document.

- **mode** *mode* is used with match to allow multiple matches that require different implementation. An example might be: *<xsl:template match= "node" mode="mode">*. Modes are used to match *xsl:templates* to *xsl:apply-templates*, allowing you to control which templates are used for a given element. For example, a mode could be *"set1"*, which would mean that the template would apply its values to elements that have the mode *"set1"*.

- **name** *name* is used to define a called template and is used in conjunction with *<xsl:with-param>* and *<xsl:call-template>*. An example might be: *<xsl:template name="demoTemplate">*.

- **priority** *priority* is rarely used. Its main purpose is to give a template a higher priority and is only truly useful when working with multiple XSL stylesheets that happen to have similar matches or names. Generally speaking, however, whenever you work with multiple stylesheets you will *always* want to avoid conflicting matches. This can also be used for single stylesheets but I think we all agree that conflicting matches on purpose are a bad thing. An example might be: *<xsl:template priority= "10">*.

<xsl:apply-template>

This is the procedure used to apply the template defined by *<xsl:template>*. It can also use the *mode* attribute.

- **select** Declares which XML pattern will be matched; can use any location path combination. An example might be *<xsl:apply-template select="/">*, which states that the template should be applied to the root of the XML tree. This is often used with XML, that generates HTML to replace the entire output tree into HTML format.

- **mode** Matches the mode given in the xsl:template that is being applied.

<xsl:for-each>

As the name implies, this XSL procedure handles a standard for-each loop. It uses the same *select* attribute that *<xsl:apply-template>* has.

The basic syntax is:

```
<xsl:for-each select="node or location path">
..transformation here
</xsl:for-each>
```

Looking back at Figure 4.1, we can see that if our XML contained multiple authors, the XSL would not work. We'd need to use a *<xsl:for-each>* loop to generate individual tables for each item. Let's modify the XSL in Figure 4.4 to include a *<xsl:for-each>* loop. Figure 4.5 has our modified XSL code and Figure 4.6 contains a new XML, displaying a new root element "articles" with each news item listed as an "article".

Figure 4.5 demo2.xsl

```
01: <?xml version="1.0" encoding="ISO-8859-1"?>
02: <xsl:stylesheet version="1.0"
03:     xmlns:xsl="http://www.w3.org/1999/XSL/Transform">
04:   <xsl:template match="/">
05:    <html>
06:     <head>
07:      <title>Articles</title>
08:     </head>
09:     <body>
10:      <center>
11:       <xsl:for-each select="articles/article">
12:        <table border="0">
13:         <tr>
14:          <b>
15:           <font face="Arial" size="3">
16:            <xsl:value-of select="title"/>
17:           </font>
18:          </b>
19:          <br/>
20:          <b>
21:           <i>
```

Continued

Figure 4.5 Continued

```
22:            <font face="Arial" size="2" color="#FF0000">
23:             by <xsl:value-of select="author"/>
24:            </font>
25:           </i>
26:          </b>
27:         </tr>
28:        </table>
29:        <table bgcolor="#003366" width="300">
30:         <tr>
31:          <td>
32:           <font face="Arial" size="3" color="#FFFFFF">
33:            <xsl:value-of select="text"/>
34:           </font>
35:          </td>
36:         </tr>
37:        </table>
38:       </xsl:for-each>
39:      </center>
40:     </body>
41:    </html>
42:   </xsl:template>
43: </xsl:stylesheet>
```

Figure 4.6 text2.xml

```
01: <?xml version="1.0" encoding="ISO-8859-1"?>
02: <?xml-stylesheet type="text/xsl" href="demo2.xsl" ?>
03: <articles>
04:  <article>
05:   <title>Top Story</title>
06:   <author>Lydia Gonzalez</author>
07:   <text>
08:    Many children today in Churches
09:   may say the verse "I am the Son
10:    of God" out loud without reading
```

Continued

Figure 4.6 Continued

```
11:      because they are unable to read.

12:

13:      See why this Church has began

14:      an outreach program to parents in

15:      low income areas to provide their

16:      children with reading assistance in

17:      tomorrow's edition.

18:    </text>

19:   </article>

20:   <article>

21:    <title>Another Idea</title>

22:    <author>Luis Gonazalez Sr.</author>

23:    <text>

24:     We will continue to explore the

25:     findings at this Church as the

26:     story continues to develop.

27:    </text>

28:   </article>

29: </articles>
```

The resulting HTML displayed is shown in Figure 4.7.

<xsl:if>

This XSL procedure handles a standard if-then test. *<xsl:if>* only has one
attribute, *test*, which specifies the value to test against, and is then converted to a
true-false value. Often, the value of a node is checked and then the necessary
changes or effects applied. The syntax for *<xsl:if>* is the following:

```
<xsl:if test="test procedure>"
           .. transformation here
</xsl:if>
```

Here's an example. Let's assume the XML in Figure 4.1 had multiple news
items, with one written by the editor. Because of this, you'd probably want to see
the editor's title in a different color below the name. To get this effect, all we'd
have to do is modify the code in lines 22 and 23. We'll use the same XML shown
previously in Figure 4.6. Figure 4.8, meanwhile, shows the modified xsl file.

Figure 4.7 HTML Resulting from Code in Figure 4.6

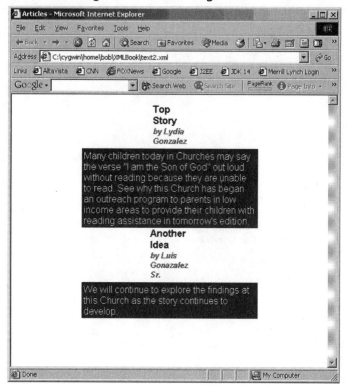

Figure 4.8 demo-if.xsl

```
01:  <?xml version="1.0" encoding="ISO-8859-1"?>
02:  <xsl:stylesheet version="1.0"
03:      xmlns:xsl="http://www.w3.org/1999/XSL/Transform">
04:   <xsl:template match="/">
05:    <html>
06:     <head>
07:      <title>Articles</title>
08:     </head>
09:     <body>
10:      <center>
11:       <xsl:for-each select="articles/article">
12:        <table border="0">
13:         <tr>
14:          <b>
```

Continued

Figure 4.8 Continued

```
15:              <font face="Arial" size="3">
16:                <xsl:value-of select="title"/>
17:              </font>
18:             </b>
19:             <br/>
20:             <b>
21:              <i>
22:               <font face="Arial" size="2" color="#FF0000">
23:                by <xsl:value-of select="author"/>
24:                <xsl:if test="author='Luis Gonazalez Sr.'">
25:                  <br/>
26:                  <b>News Editor</b>
27:                </xsl:if>
28:               </font>
29:              </i>
30:             </b>
31:            </tr>
32:           </table>
33:           <table bgcolor="#003366" width="300">
34:            <tr>
35:             <td>
36:              <font face="Arial" size="3" color="#FFFFFF">
37:               <xsl:value-of select="text"/>
38:              </font>
39:             </td>
40:            </tr>
41:           </table>
42:          </xsl:for-each>
43:         </center>
44:       </body>
45:      </html>
46:    </xsl:template>
47: </xsl:stylesheet>
```

Figure 4.9 shows how the document would now be displayed.

Figure 4.9 Result of Adding the xsl:if Clause to Our XSL

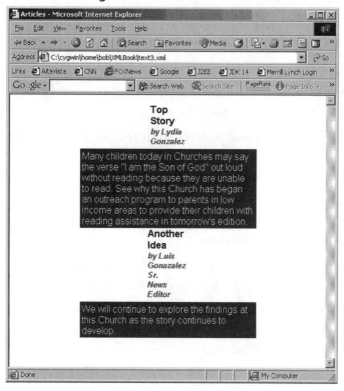

<xsl:choose>, <xsl:when>, <xsl:otherwise>

These three procedures work together to form a multitest conditional statement. These statements are similar to the switch statement in Java, as shown in the following example:

```
<xsl:choose>
    <xsl:when test="test"
    .. transformation
    </xsl:when>
    <xsl:otherwise
      .. transformation
    </xsl:otherwise>
</xsl:choose>
```

You can have multiple *<xsl:when>* within the choose. Meanwhile, the *<xsl:otherwise>* handles any cases that don't match.

<xsl:sort>

<xsl:sort> allows a simple sort to be run on the XML file, and can take the following attributes:

- **select** Declares which XML pattern will be matched; can use any location path combination. An example might be: *<xsl:apply-template select="node or location path">*.

- **lang** This is a language declaration for use in multilanguage sorts and uses the same values defined in RFC 1766 (www.ietf.org/rfc/rfc1766.txt).

- **data-type** This defines the data type we are sorting for. It can be text, number, or qname (see www.w3.org/TR/xslt#qname for more information). The default is text.

- **order** Defines the order in which the sort is displayed; can be either ascending or descending. Default is descending.

- **case-order** Defines which case type takes priority when working with text. *upper-first* gives priority to uppercase letters and *lower-first* gives priority to lower case letters.

Here is an example:

```
<xsl:sort select="article/author"
        lang = "en-us" data-type="text"
        order="descending" case-order="uppercase" />
```

Note that *<xsl:sort>* is a standalone procedure.

<xsl:value-of>

<xsl:value-of> allows us to query a particular element and retrieve its value. Back in Figure 4.4, we used it to display the values of the title, author, and text elements.

XSLT supports various output types called *output trees*. Technically, this is just the method you chose within your XSLT code that the XML is output as. You can choose from HTML, XML, TEXT, or QName. You can then define the output tree type within XSL using the *<xsl:output>* procedure. This is a top-level procedure so you have to have it at the beginning of your XMSLT file, preferably before the *<xsl:template match="/">* line.

Here is an example of the output:

```
<xsl:output
        method = "HTML"
        version = "4.0"
        encoding="ISO-8859-1"
        standalone="yes" />
```

<xsl:output> supports the following attributes:

- **method** Sets which type of file to output to; can be HTML, XML, TEXT, or Qname.

- **version** Sets which version of the selected method to use.

- **encoding** Sets which language encoding to display.

- **omit-xml-declaration** Determines whether or not an XML declaration should be output; can be yes or no.

- **standalone** Determines whether or not a standalone document declaration should be output; can be yes or no.

- **doctype-public** Sets the public identifier to be used in the dtd.

- **doctype-system** Sets the system identifier to be used in the dtd.

- **cdata-section-elements** Specifies qnames that need to be output as CDATA sections.

- **indent** Determines whether or not additional whitespace is included when outputting the file. Can be yes or no.

- **media-type** Defines the MIME content type of the output data.

Now that we are done with our review of basic XSLT concepts, we can turn our attention to the matter at hand: the JAXP interfaces for Java.

JAXP and Underlying XSL Engines

While the XSL language is standardized, the XSL engines for Java are not. Engines like SAXON and Xalan have a lot of functionality, but do so with proprietary interfaces. Java developers need an API that is compatible with Java but can work with pre-existing engines that already have widespread support and usage within the Java community. JAX-P, the Java API for XML Processing, was built with this type of interface in mind. JAXP itself originates from a previous project named TrAX that was incorporated into JAX-P.

As in the parsing capabilities of JAX-P, the XSLT capabilities are a series of interfaces that wrap an underlying engine. The engine provides the functionality, while the APIs provide a regular mechanism for accessing this functionality. This allows code to be written that leverages an XSLT engine, without becoming dependant on its proprietary APIs.

In order for XSLT engines to be swapped in and out, JAXP introduces a transformer factory class. The factory class returns an instance of a class specific to an XSLT implementation; this class acts as the bridge between the underlying functionality and the generic API.

The plugability interfaces will be discussed more later. In general, however, you don't have to worry about them, so long as you have a JAX-P-compliant library available. The library will automatically configure the system to use its own implementation classes. It's only if you have multiple XSLT libraries available, or if you want to try to mix and match XSLT and parsing capabilities across libraries, that you have to worry about plugability. These cases are discussed next.

Using JAXP Classes

The JAXP classes for transformation are almost all contained in the *java.xml .transform* package, which provides the basic functionality for XSLT transformations. Three additional packages, *javax.xml.transform.dom, javax.xml.transform.sax*, and *javax.xml.transform.stream* provide some additional classes for specifying how the XSLT engine should read input and write output.

This section will cover the basic JAXP XSLT classes: the *javax.xml.transform* package. Later, we'll discuss the supporting packages for input and output, and show a complete example program.

Creating a Transformer

A transformation is the process of applying an XSL file to an XML file and then producing the output. In order to isolate the application from the specifics of creating transformation-supporting code in a specific XSLT engine, JAXP uses the TransformerFactory class. TransformerFactorys are used to create Tranformer and Template instances (more about these in the following) from classes the engines implement.

The first thing you have to do for any XSLT transformation using JAXP is obtain a TransformerFactory. TransformerFactory is an abstract class provided by the JAXP library, and has two purposes. A static method of this class is used to obtain an instance of a concrete subclass provided by an XSLT engine. Once this concrete instance is obtained, methods defined by the abstract class and implemented by the concrete can be used to create the Transformers and Templates used to handle the transformations.

Sound confusing? It really isn't, once you see an example. The following program (shown in Figure 4.10) obtains a TransformerFactory, and then uses it to create a new Transformer. The Transformer would then be used to process an XSL stylesheet, but that isn't included in this example.

Figure 4.10 Our first JAX-P/XSL Example Program

```
package com.syngress.jwsdp.xsl;

import javax.xml.transform.*;

public class Example1
{
 public static void main( String args[] )
 {
  try
  {
   // Obtain a new TransformerFactory
   TransformerFactory factory;
   factory = TransformerFactory.newInstance();

   // Use it to create a new transformer
   Transformer transformer;
   transformer = factory.newTransformer();
  }
  catch (TransformerFactoryConfigurationError tfce)
  {
   System.out.println( "Could not obtain factory" );
   tfce.printStackTrace();
  }
  catch (TransformerConfigurationException tce)
```

Continued

Figure 4.10 Continued

```
    {
      System.out.println( "Could not create transformer" );
      tce.printStackTrace();
    }
  }
}
```

You'll note in the preceding code that we had to catch two exceptions. The first, TransformationFactoryConfigurationException, is thrown if the *concrete factory* class can't be found or instantiated. This will generally be due to not having a XSLT library in the classpath, but could potentially have other causes as well. The second, *TransformerConfigurationException*, will generally be because you have requested the factory (via the following methods) to create a *Transformer* with specific properties, but those properties are not supported.

NOTE

The *newTransformer()* method that follows actually returns a default Transformer object that just copies XML from one place to another. This is not generally a useful transformation, but since we are just trying to illustrate the use of the TransformerFactory in this example, it's a handy simplification.

Table 4.3 describes the list of methods available to *TransformerFactory*.

Table 4.3 TransformerFactory Methods

Methods	Description
getAssociatedStylesheet(Source, String, String, String)	Gets stylesheet that matches the xml-stylesheet processing tag.
getAttribute(String)	Gets the attributes of the implementation in use.
getErrorListener()	Returns the error event handler.
GetFeature(String)	Returns the value of the feature.

Continued

Table 4.3 Continued

Methods	Description
getURIResolver()	Returns the default object used to resolve a URI found in *<xsl:import>*, *<xsl:include>*, or *document()*.
newInstance()	Creates a new *TransformerFactory* instance.
newTemplates(Source)	Returns a new Template associated with the given source.
newTransformer()	Creates a new *Transformer* instance.
newTransformer(Source)	Creates a new *Transformer* instance for a given source.
setAttribute(String, Object)	Defines attributes in the underlying implementation.
setErrorListener(ErrorListener)	Used in conjunction with class *ErrorListener*; sets the error event listener for a *TransformerFactory* object.
setURIResolver(URIResolver)	Sets the *URIResolver* object to be used with the current *TransformerFactory*.

Note that *newInstance* was already introduced earlier in the chapter. The *newTemplates* and *newTransformer* methods are used to create Templates and Transformers, respectively, and are discussed later in this chapter.

The *getAssociatedStylesheet* method is used to scan through an XSL document that contains multiple embedded stylesheets. It attempts to find the best match for the given criteria, which can specify the media, title, and character set. Using getAssociatedStylesheet allows you to maintain a collection of stylesheets which have the same purpose (but for different environments) in a single master document.

The *getAttribute* and *setAttribute* methods should be used with caution. They give you access to setting attributes of the underlying implementation, and as such, bind your code to that implementation. If you switch to a different implementation that does not support that attribute, an *IllegalArgumentException* will be thrown. Since this may happen long after you decide to use *get/setAttribute*, and only at the point in time that you change XSLT libraries, you may confuse this with errors in the underlying XSLT engine. Proceed with caution with these methods, and document the code that uses them carefully.

Similarly, *getFeature* can be used to query the underlying XSLT engine. The *getFeature* method accepts a string representing a URI, and returns a Boolean result. While the URI passed in could be any valid URI, there are a few predefined ones. For example, in the *javax.xml.transform.dom.DOMSource* class, a public static variable *Feature* is defined. This can be used to query the underlying XSLT engine to ensure that DOM-based sources are supported. If they are, the method will return True, otherwise it will return False.

The *getErrorListener* and *setErrorListener* methods manipulate the *ErrorListener* objects associated with the factory. *ErrorListeners* are discussed in further detail later, but to summarize them briefly they provide a mechanism for responding to errors encountered while performing the XSL processing. *getErrorListener* returns the *ErrorListener* currently in use, while *setErrorListener* changes to a new one. The error listeners on the factory should not be confused with the error listeners associated with Transformers or Templates; the *error listener* associated with the *factory* is used when processing transformation instructions, not while processing the transformation itself.

The *getURIResolver* and *setURIResolver* methods manipulate *URIResolver* objects associated with the factory. These objects are used when processing XSL constructs that reference external stylesheets (the xsl:import and xsl:include tags, and the *document()* method). URIResolvers have the chance to perform custom code to resolve the location of these entities. Unlike *ErrorListeners*, the *URIResolver* associated with the factory does effect the Transformers and Templates created by a factory; the *URIResolver* associated with a factory will be the default *URIResolver* for all Templates/Transformers that are created after the call to *setURIResolver*.

Source and Result

Before we can talk about the Transformer and Templates classes (which perform the actual XSL processing), we should discuss how the input and output of the processing are communicated to the underlying engine. The *Source* class and *Result* class handle exactly what their name suggests—the source XML file or transformation instructions, and the result of the transformation, respectively.

The Source and Result interfaces are little more than markers, allowing for the setting and getting of a system ID (a unique identifier associated with the location of the data), but nothing else. You won't ever create an instance of Source or Result directly; rather you will create an instance of *DOMSource*, *DOMResult*, *SAXSource*, *SAXResult*, *StreamSource*, or *StreamResult*. These classes provide the mechanisms for wrapping DOM-based data, SAX-based data, and Stream-based data, respectively. They do this by accepting an instance of the data they are wrapping in their constructors. For example, DOMSource takes a *org.w3c.dom.Node* object in its constructor, while *StreamResult* can take an instance of *OutputStream*.

DOMSource and *DOMResult* are members of the *javax.xml.transform.dom* package. *SAXSource* and *SAXResult* are members of *javax.xml.transform.sax*, while *StreamSource* and *StreamResult* are members of *javax.xml.transform.stream*. XSLT engines are not required to support all these data types, but most will.

Data types can be freely mixed and matched (so long as they are supported). For example, you can specify a DOMSource and a StreamResult. The XSLT engine would then read data from a DOM in memory, and write data to an OutputStream.

You might be tempted to ask about creating your own *Result* and *Source* classes to support some other data type. Unfortunately, you can't. The XSLT engine will actually check the *Source/Result* object via the *instanceof* operator, comparing it to the well-known implementing classes. If it isn't one of those classes, the engine will not know what to do. Generally, however, you can use the *StreamSource* and *StreamResult* classes for most types of data—for example, you can specify URL-based data (with the stream return from *URL.openStream*), file-based data (with a *FileInputStream* or *FileOutputStream*), and so forth.

Transformer

Now that we've looked at how to create a factory, and how to specify the source and result locations, we need to look at the actual classes used for performing transformations. The first of these is the *Transformer* class; we will look at this class first and defer discussing the other class (*Templates*) for just a bit.

Transformer defines a class for performing XSL transformations. The Transformer class itself is abstract; the actual object you get back from the *TransformerFactory* is a concrete implementation class specific to the XSLT engine. However, you don't have to worry about that; you can just use the object through the public interface of Transformer.

The main method of Transformer is the *transform* method. The *transform* method accepts a source object (the input XML document) and a result object (the resulting XML document). The XSL stylesheet associated with the transformation is inherent in the *Transformer* object; when you create a Transformer with a *TransformerFactory*, you specify a *Source* object that represents the XSL stylesheet to use.

This means you can use the same Transformer multiple times to transform multiple sources. However, as we'll see in just a moment, there are some serious limitations when doing this. Shortly, we'll introduce the *Templates* class, which is more useful for repeated transformations.

As we've mentioned, the *transform* method is the one you will use most often with the *Transformer* class. However, there are some other methods of interest.

The *getParameter, setParameter*, and *clearParameters* methods are used to get, set, and clear all parameters, respectively. These routines allow you to specify values for *xsl:param* tags in your templates; specifying values for parameters allows you to pass values into the stylesheet.

Like *TransformerFactory*, you can use *setErrorListener* and *getErrorListener*, as well as *setURIResolver* and *getURIResolver*. The URI resolver methods act as you might expect; they override the default URI resolvers set at the factory level with Transformer-specific instances. The error listener methods do the same, but you have to remember that the error listener set at the factory level is not the default for the Transformer; it only applies to the factory itself. So if you need URI resolvers for your Transformers, you can set a default at the factory level and be done. However, if you need an error listener for your Transformers, you have to set it explicitly for each Transformer you create.

The remaining methods of Transformer manipulate the output properties set for the stylesheet. These properties, initially defined in an xsl:output tag, specify how the output is to be rendered. (See the earlier section on *xsl:output*.) You can use *getOutputProperty* to retrieve a specific property, or *getOutputProperties* to retrieve all the properties currently defined. To change the properties (which overrides the defaults set in the stylesheet), you can use *setOutputProperty* to set a specific property, or *setOutputProperties* to change them all at once.

Table 4.4 summarizes the Transformer methods.

Table 4.4 Transformer Methods

Methods	Description
clearParameters()	Flushes parameters that have been set with *setParameters()*.
getErrorListener	Sets the error listener object
getParameter(String)	Gets the value of a parameter.
getOutputProperties()	Returns a copy of output properties.

Continued

Table 4.4 Continued

Methods	Description
getOutputProperty(String)	Returns one output property.
getURIResolver()	Returns the object used to resolve a URI found in *<xsl:import>*, *<xsl:include>*, or *document()*.
setErrorListener(ErrorListener)	Sets the error listener for a *Transformer* object.
setOutputProperties(Properties)	Sets the output properties.
setOutputProperty(String, String)	Sets one output property.
setParameter(String, Object)	Sets the value of a parameter.
setURIResolver(URIResolver)	Sets the *URIResolver* object that will be used with the current Transformer.
transform(Source, Result)	Actual transformation using the current source tree in the *Source* object to output to the *Result* object.

Now we will look at an example program that creates a Transformer based on the demo.xsl file we introduced earlier. The code looks similar to the preceding example program, except for some additional imports, until about line 18. At that point, instead of creating the default Transformer object, we create a Transformer that is associated with the *demo.xsl* file.

We do this by first creating a *FileInputStream* associated with the file, and then wrapping that in a *StreamSource*. As mentioned previously, *StreamSource* allows you to pass the source for a document into the XSL transform engine via an input stream. Once we've wrapped the XSL file stream in a *StreamSource*, we use the factory *newTransformer* method to obtain a Transformer that is based on that XSL stylesheet.

On lines 24 through 26, we do something similar for the file output stream that specifies the result: we wrap it in a *StreamResult* object so we can pass it into the XSL engine. Lines 28 through 30 wrap the source XML, and we are ready to invoke the transform. We do this on line 32, by using the *transform* method of the Transformer class.

You'll also note that we added some additional exception handling. Lines 45 through 54 are there to handle exceptions thrown by the java.io libraries, or the stream wrappers. (See Figure 4.11.)

Figure 4.11 A Working JAX-P/XSL Example

```
01: package com.syngress.jwsdp.xsl;
02:
03: import java.io.*;
04: import javax.xml.transform.*;
05: import javax.xml.transform.stream.*;
06:
07: public class Example2
08: {
09:   public static void main( String args[] )
10:   {
11:    try
12:    {
13:     // Obtain a new TransformerFactory
14:     TransformerFactory factory;
15:     factory = TransformerFactory.newInstance();
16:
17:     // Use it to create a new transformer
18:     Transformer transformer;
19:     InputStream xslInput;
20:     xslInput = new FileInputStream( "demo.xsl" );
21:     Source xslSource = new StreamSource( xslInput );
22:     transformer = factory.newTransformer( xslSource );
23:
24:     OutputStream resultStream;
25:     resultStream = new FileOutputStream( "result.html" );
26:     Result result = new StreamResult( resultStream );
27:
28:     InputStream sourceStream;
29:     sourceStream = new FileInputStream( "text.xml" );
30:     Source source = new StreamSource( sourceStream );
31:
32:     transformer.transform( source, result );
33:
34:    }
35:    catch (TransformerFactoryConfigurationError tfce)
```

Continued

Figure 4.11 Continued

```
36:    {
37:      System.out.println( "Could not obtain factory" );
38:      tfce.printStackTrace();
39:    }
40:    catch (TransformerConfigurationException tce)
41:    {
42:      System.out.println( "Could not create transformer" );
43:      tce.printStackTrace();
44:    }
45:    catch (FileNotFoundException fnf)
46:    {
47:      System.out.println( "File not found" );
48:      fnf.printStackTrace();
49:    }
50:    catch (TransformerException te)
51:    {
52:      System.out.println( "Transformer exception" );
53:      te.printStackTrace();
54:    }
55:  }
56: }
```

Templates

It isn't practical to use Transformers alone in high volume, multithreaded applications. For one thing, the *TransformerFactory.newTransformer* method parses the XSL source each time, which can be a significant overhead. More to the point, Transformers aren't thread-safe, so in a multi-threaded application you either have to manage the thread safety yourself, or use Templates.

Templates are designed to solve many of the problems that Transformers have. They parse the XSL one time, and keep a parsed copy of it internally. From that internal copy, they can create multiple Transformers—in a thread-safe manner. So, you can create a single Template object and use it to create multiple Transformers, one for each thread. This can result in significant performance improvements in a heavily-used application.

Using Templates is pretty straightforward. You basically have a single extra set in our code from using Transformers directly. Instead of calling the *new Transformer* method of TransformerFactory, you call *new Templates* with the same arguments. This returns a Templates object. Once you have this object, you can call *new Transformer* on it (which takes no arguments) to obtain a Transformer object you can use.

The only other method on the Templates interface is the *getOutputProperties* method, which can be used to retrieve the output properties defined in an xsl:output tag in the stylesheet associated with Templates.

The code that follows (Figure 4.12) shows the example program modified to use Templates. Of course, in the real world you would only do this for a multi-threaded application; there isn't any benefit to using Templates in a single-threaded one. Also, you would probably want to synchronize the creation of the *Templates* object, so it's only created by one thread.

Figure 4.12 Using Templates in JAX-P

```
01: package com.syngress.jwsdp.xsl;
02:
03: import java.io.*;
04: import javax.xml.transform.*;
05: import javax.xml.transform.stream.*;
06:
07: public class Example3
08: {
09:   public static void main( String args[] )
10:   {
11:     try
12:     {
13:       // Obtain a new TransformerFactory
14:       TransformerFactory factory;
15:       factory = TransformerFactory.newInstance();
16:
17:       // Use it to create a new transformer
18:       Templates templates;
19:       Transformer transformer;
20:       InputStream xslInput;
21:       xslInput = new FileInputStream( "demo.xsl" );
22:       Source xslSource = new StreamSource( xslInput );
```

Continued

Figure 4.12 Continued

```
23:    templates = factory.newTemplates( xslSource );
24:
25:    OutputStream resultStream;
26:    resultStream = new FileOutputStream( "result.html" );
27:    Result result = new StreamResult( resultStream );
28:
29:    InputStream sourceStream;
30:    sourceStream = new FileInputStream( "text.xml" );
31:    Source source = new StreamSource( sourceStream );
32:
33:    transformer = templates.newTransformer();
34:    transformer.transform( source, result );
35:
36:    }
37:    catch (TransformerFactoryConfigurationError tfce)
38:    {
39:     System.out.println( "Could not obtain factory" );
40:     tfce.printStackTrace();
41:    }
42:    catch (TransformerConfigurationException tce)
43:    {
44:     System.out.println( "Could not create transformer" );
45:     tce.printStackTrace();
46:    }
47:    catch (FileNotFoundException fnf)
48:    {
49:     System.out.println( "File not found" );
50:     fnf.printStackTrace();
51:    }
52:    catch (TransformerException te)
53:    {
54:     System.out.println( "Transformer exception" );
55:     te.printStackTrace();
56:    }
57:   }
58: }
```

The main changes to the application from Figure 4.11 are on lines 23, and 33 through 34. On line 23, I create a Templates object rather than a Transformer object. On lines 33 and 34, I use the Templates object to create a Transformer, and then use the Transformer to perform the transformation. I moved the creation of the Transformer close to the usage in order to emphasize how you will generally use Templates: you will create the Template object first, then create the Transformer object on the fly from it as necessary.

Miscellaneous JAXP for XSL Issues

Our exploration of JAXP is almost complete. There are only a few things left to cover, including error handling, resolving URIs, thread safety, and the plugability interface. We'll discuss error handling first.

Error Handling

In JAX-P, error handling is carried out by the *ErrorListener* and *SourceLocator* classes. *ErrorListener* provides a way to output all errors while *SourceLocator* is used to locate errors within an XSL source.

ErrorListener

In JAX-P, error messages are typically reported to System.err, which is fine when you are working from the command line. When you do need to redirect the error messages to a more agreeable output, you can use *ErrorListener*. In order to use ErrorListener, you need to implement an *ErrorListener* object and pass it to the *setErrorListener* method in Transformer. Table 4.5 displays the methods for *ErrorListener*.

Table 4.5 ErrorListener Methods

Methods	Description
error(TransformerException)	Used to report an error.
fatalError(TransformerException)	Used to report a fatal error.
warning(TransformerException)	Used to report a warning.

If you choose, you can throw the exceptions that are passed in to you—or any other exception, for that matter. If you do nothing, the XSL engine will continue to process, with one caveat: The engine is not required to continue to process after fatal errors are reported (even though it may anyway).

SourceLocator

SourceLocators are used in conjunction with the *TransformerException* class. SourceLocators may be provided by the underlying XSL engine to report the location of the error—the file, line, and column number that the XSL engine had trouble understanding. These locations will be approximate—they may be off by a line or two—but can be very useful in determining how to respond to errors.

You will never create SourceLocator objects yourself (unless you write an XSL engine). SourceLocators are created for you, and obtained through a TransformerException. Table 4.6 lists the SourceLocator methods.

Table 4.6 SourceLocator Methods

Methods	Description
getSystemId()	Returns the system ID for the document.
GetPublicId	Gets the public ID for the document.
getColumnNumber()	Returns the first character of the area where the error was found.
GetLineNumber	Returns the line number where the error was found.

URIResolver

URIResolver allows developers to create a custom implementation of how URI references in XSLT stylesheets are resolved. URIResolver has only one method: *resolve*. The *resolve* method expects two string items to be passed to it; the first one is href (URI) and the second one is a base. The base may sound a bit complicated, but it just refers to the domain (location) that the href (URI) needs to be checked against. For example:

```
<!- - and - ->
<xsl:variable name="item" select="document('test.xml')"/>
```

This snippet of XSLT code basically states that the document is named test.xml, but doesn't state how this document should be found. By default, it is found relative to the URI used to locate the original document; so if the original document and the included document are not in the same location, problems can arise.

The *URIResolver* class is given both the document requested (the href parameter) and the current base URI (the base parameter). It returns a fully-qualified

URI for locating the document. The following example *resolve* method resolves all documents to a directory in the Syngress Web site. Note that it ignores the base URI passed in.

```
public Source resolve(String href, String base)
{
    String URI = "http://www.syngress.com/xsl/" + href;
    return new StreamSource( URI );
}
```

URIResolvers can be very useful when the XSL stylesheets for your application are stored somewhere other than the default working directory. In this case, it is not a problem to find the main XSL; you just create a *FileInputStream* with the full path name to the XSL file, and wrap that in a *StreamSource*. However, if you include other XSLs from that main XSL, you have two options: you can code the entire path in the *xsl:include* tag (which severely reduces the portability of your application), or provide a *URIResolver*. The *URIResolver* would then add the path for the XSL directory to the file name provided, and use that to create a *FileInputStream* (and then a *StreamSource*).

URIResolver has only a single method, *resolve(String, String)*. This method is called by the processor when it finds an *xsl:include*, *xsl:import*, or *document()* function and defines how the processor should behave.

Thread Safety

We've mentioned thread safety a few times. It is important to understand the threading limitations of the JAXP interfaces, since understanding what threading JAXP allows for can make your application more stable and perform better.

The TransformerFactory class is never thread-safe. You will always have to synchronize usage of TransformerFactory instances, or create a new instance for each thread.

Transformer classes are not thread-safe either. You will generally want to create a separate Transformer instance for each thread—generally through use of a Templates object.

Templates objects are thread-safe. The Transformers they create are not, of course, so you will generally use them to create a new Transformer each time.

Plugability

In general, all you will have to do to use JAXP is make sure a JAX-P-compliant library is in your classpath. However, there are times when you want to change which XSL engine is used, or ensure that a particular one is used regardless of classpath order.

In these cases, you can use the plugability features of JAX-P. Plugability allows you to specify a particular XSL engine to use, and is actually the mechanism used by XSL libraries to announce themselves to the *TransformerFactory* class.

The key to the plugability interface is the system property *javax.xml.transform.TransformerFactory*. This shouldn't be confused with the class of the same name. The name of the property was intentionally chosen to be the name of the class in order to minimize changes of collision with existing properties.

The property *javax.xml.transform.TransformerFactory* contains the fully-qualified class name of the XSL engine's implementation of the *javax.xml.transform.TransformerFactory* abstract class. If you have a specific XSL engine you want to use, you can explicitly set this property (either through a System.setProperty call, or through the *-D* command-line option).

If the system property is not set, then the system will look for a file jaxp.properties, located in the lib subdirectory of the active JRE home. If this file exists, it is expected to be a properties file containing at least one property: the *javax.xml.transform.TransformerFactory* (along with the class name you want associated with it).

If this file can't be found, then the Services API is used to find any files named javax.xml.transform. *TransformerFactory* in the services subdirectory under META-INF for all jar files in the class path. (Technically, it's the effective class path for the object that is making the call, but that's beyond the scope of this book.) If this file is found, it should again contain a single line: the name of the fully-qualified class name for the *TransformerFactory* implementation.

And should all else fail, there is a platform-dependent default TranformerFactory class that is used. For the JWSDP EA2 release, this is the Xalan class *org.apache.xalan.processor.TransformerFactoryImpl*. For other releases, this default value could change.

Summary

JAXP has come a long way since its conception as TrAX. Many changes have been applied and many more are sure to come as more users begin to use JAXP for their XML/XSLT needs.

What Sun is doing now is basically creating an item to fill the void within the XML community. While there are a number of XSL processors available to Java programmers, they all come with a proprietary interface, which makes the code dependent on a specific library. This makes it hard to change processors if the need arises.

JAXP circumvents this problem by providing a standardized interface. This interface, while somewhat less powerful than the native XSL library interfaces, provides the basic functionality needed to transform XML documents with XSL. Using the JAXP interfaces protects your code from future library API changes.

Solutions Fast Track

Reviewing XSL and XSLT

☑ XSL is a specification made up of three different recommendations: XSLT, XSL-FO, and XPath.

☑ XSLT handles the actual transformation sequence that takes places with an XSL stylesheet and an XML file. XSLT procedures are also used within the XSL stylesheet.

☑ XSL-FO deals with transformation XML data to print formats, such as PDF.

☑ XPath is the recommendation that controls how XML data is located and queried through XSL/XSLT.

JAXP and Underlying XSL Engines

☑ JAXP is not an XSL/XSLT engine. It is actually a layer that allows a developer to use JAXP regardless of the XSL/XSLT engine that lies beneath.

☑ Current popular XSL/XSLT engines include SAXON and Xalan.

☑ Since JAXP has to provide a proper layer over all available XSL/XSLT engines, it can only support common functionality.

Using JAXP Classes

☑ Basic transformations can be done through Transformers created by a *TransformerFactory*. Transformer instances implicitly contain the source XSL, and receive the Source XML and a result to output the transformed file.

☑ *TransformerFactory* may cause data corruption in high-load situations due to its poor threading ability. In these cases, it is best to use Templates, which creates a copy of the output from *TransformerFactory* and can be threaded into separate Transformer instances.

Miscellaneous JAXP for XSL Issues

☑ *ErrorListener* can be set to gracefully handle error messages that the servlet/java may throw while running the transformation.

☑ *SourceLocator* is used to pass the location of the error as part of a *TransformerException*.

☑ *URIResolver* allows developers to create a custom implementation of how URI references in XSLT stylesheets are resolved.

☑ Multithreaded applications should consider using Templates because Templates are thread-safe.

☑ *TransformerFactory* packages are currently not developed to be thread-safe, and should not be used in threading situations.

☑ Plugability allows you to specify a particular XSL engine to use, and is actually the mechanism used by XSL libraries to announce themselves to the *TransformerFactory* class.

Frequently Asked Questions

The following Frequently Asked Questions, answered by the authors of this book, are designed to both measure your understanding of the concepts presented in this chapter and to assist you with real-life implementation of these concepts. To have your questions about this chapter answered by the author, browse to **www.syngress.com/solutions** and click on the **"Ask the Author"** form.

Q: Why are some parts of JAXP unable to properly thread?

A: Unfortunately, due to some construct issues when dealing with the plugability layer, the TransformerFactory packages can't be made thread-safe. However, both of these items can be properly implemented so they are thread-safe. TransformerFactory often doesn't need to be used several times, and can instead be used in conjunction with a Template, which is thread-safe and can be used to store the output from TransformerFactory. You would want to then access Templates to retrieve the information.

Q: Why does JAXP only provide basic support for the underlying parser?

A: Every parser has its own level of support. By restricting the support to just the basics, JAXP can ensure developers that an interface that will not only abide by W3Cspecifications but also be flexible enough to not be locked in a specific parser.

Q: Which is the best default parser for JAX-P?

A: This question is asked quite a bit and people have always felt the need to promote their favorite. However, JAXP was not created to be a layer that operates best with a specific parser but to be the best layer for any parser. The easiest way to decide whether you need JAXP is to optimize your machine for the parser of your choice.

Q: Is JAXP still in beta?

A: No. However, JAXP can be considered a work in progress, even though it is not still in beta. Issues have been raised regarding how JAXP should behave and what functionality it should have. Expect more changes throughout the year as additional user input is generated. (JAXP saw two releases within three months!)

Chapter 5

Using JSTL
(JSP Standard
Tag Library)

Solutions in this chapter:

- **Expression Languages**

- **Core Tags**

- **SQL Query Tags**

- **Internationalization Tags**

- **XML Support Tags**

☑ **Summary**

☑ **Solutions Fast Track**

☑ **Frequently Asked Questions**

Introduction

The JSP Standard Tag Library (JSTL) provides a standard tag library (actually several of them) that can be used by JSP writers to handle certain frequent tasks. The JSTL, like much of the WSDP, comes out of the Apache Jakata project; earlier releases of JSTL were available through Apache before it became part of the JCP (and from there, the WSDP).

JSTL is still in its early stages, and is likely to change in the future. If you read this book and are dealing with a later version of JSTL, you may want to check the Syngress website for the latest information and updates.

In particular, the support of *expression languages* within JSTL is slated to change. Expression languages give JSP developers a mechanism for embedding expressions to be evaluated in the place of constants and are scheduled to be added to the JSP specification itself. JSTL's designers have added a temporary mechanism for using expression languages within JSTL, but have also committed to supporting the JSP standard once it is established.

JSTL consists four libraries—and if you get down to it, it's really eight. The four libraries provide XML support, structured language support, SQL support, and internationalization (i18n). Each of these provides a regular and an expression language version, for a total of eight libraries.

Expression Languages

Before we delve into the tag libraries that comprise the JSTL, it behooves us to go over one of the JSTL's most important new features, Expression Languages (EL). Since expression language support is pervasive across all of the tag libraries it makes sense to understand them before proceeding into the tag libraries themselves.

JavaServer Pages (JSP) came into existence to alleviate the problem of creating Java Servlets that generated more than a small amount of presentation code. Those of you who have had to "escape sequence" what seemed like hundreds of quotation marks in a Java Servlet will know exactly what I mean. With JSPs, you could define a web page (for example) using what resembles regular HTML. The JSP is then converted to a Java Servlet in Java code and compiled.

It has long been considered a good design practice to separate out the logic of a presentation into the three components: Model, View and Controller. This paradigm, abbreviated as MVC, is the cornerstone of many current-day web applications. To extend this paradigm into the Java realm, the servlet would act as the controller, the JSP as the view and the various JavaBeans as the model.

Why Expression Languages?

Now that the parts of a presentation have been separated into their respective model, view and controller components, there remains the issue of communicating among them. The issue of communication between the controller/business logic and the view, represented as a JSP, is of particular importance. Typically, the division of reasonability in a web development effort has different teams working on the controller/business logic and the views, and there is no guarantee that the view team is as familiar with programming languages as the business logic development team. How then to facilitate the communication between these components?

In the past there have been two methods used to achieve this communication: the first has been the use of scriptlet code. This scriptlet code is pure Java code embedded directly into the JSP file. While serving the purpose of communication between components, this method did assume a certain level of knowledge on the syntax and use of the Java language on the developer's part. The second method was the use of a custom tag library. This custom tag library would facilitate the communication in the form of tags that resemble HTML. This approach, while cleaner in its implementation, was not standardized; and each implementation could be vastly different than another.

Expression languages use scoped attributes of JSPs to convey information from the underlying business logic (such as JavaBeans) to the presentation layer, in this case JavaServer Pages. This offers the distinct advantage of being able to access that business logic from JSPs without having to resort to confusing scriptlet code or expression statements.

Supported Expression Languages

All indicators point to future versions of the JavaServer Page Specification being standardized on one expression language. With this first release of the JSTL, however, there is built-in support for a number of expression languages, including SPEL, ECMAScript, and JXPath.

Simplest Possible Expression Language (SPEL)

The Simplest Possible Expression Language (SPEL) is just that. It was designed and developed to serve as an expression language with the minimum number of features needed to be useful in that capacity. Its biggest appeal is its simplicity, which makes it easy to learn and to use.

A SPEL notation can take the form of a value or an expression. A value is evaluated literally and an expression is evaluated according to the rules of the SPEL specification.

Each attribute is accessible by a name. Each attribute's properties are referenced with the "." operator and may be nested as appropriate. These attributes may also be scoped. The allowable scope values are:

- **page** This puts or retrieves the attribute from the *Page* scope and is thus available during the lifecycle of the currently executing JavaServer Page. The *Page* scope is analogous to calling the *PageContext.getAttribute()* and *PageContext.setAttribute()* methods.

- **request** This puts or retrieves the attribute from the *Request* scope and is thus available during the lifecycle of the current HTTP request, possibly spanning multiple JavaServer Pages and Servlets. This Request scope is analogous to calling the *ServletRequest.getAttribute()* and *ServletRequest.setAttribute()* methods.

- **session** This puts or retrieves the attribute from the *Session* scope and is thus available during the current user browser session's lifecycle. This scope is analogous to calling the *HttpSession.getAttribute()* and *HttpSession.setAttribute()* methods.

- **app** This puts or retrieves the attribute from the *Application* scope and is thus available during the lifecycle of the application as a whole. Every session and servlet will have access to these attributes. This scope is analogous to calling the *ServletContext.getAttribute()* and *ServletContext.setAttribute()* methods.

- **header** This retrieves the attribute from the header information that is part of the current HTTP request. The *Header* scope is analogous to calling the *HttpServletRequest.getHeader()* method.

- **param** This retrieves the attribute from the *Request* scope as a submitted parameter of that request. The *Param* scope is analogous to calling the *ServletRequest.getParameter()* method.

- **paramvalues** This retrieves the attributes from the *Request* scope as submitted parameters of that request. The *ParamValues* scope is analogous to calling the *ServletRequest.getParameterValues()* method.

If no scope is specified, the attribute is located according to the rules governing the search for an attribute as defined by the *PageContext.findAttribute()* method. This essentially means that the *findAttribute()* method will search for the named attribute in the following context order: *Page, Request, Session* and *Application*. As soon as it finds an attribute with the specified name, the search stops. Therefore if you have two different attributes with the same name but different contexts, and you attempt to retrieve their values without specifying the appropriate context, the value of the one that's stored in the broader scope will always be used. The following example will echo out the request parameter named *username* with the value that was entered in the submitting form.

```
<c:out value="${param:username}"/>
```

Note the use of the *param* scope notation to alert the JSP that the *username* attribute can be found as a request parameter. The next example shows how you can use the *app* scope to set applicable attributes across the entire web application.

```
<c:set var="log"
        value="${app:config.logfile}"
        scope="page"/>
```

In this case we are pulling an attribute that refers to an instance for logging, and assigning it to a *var* visible for the currently executing JSP's lifecycle.

Using Literals

You can use literal values (as opposed to expression values) in your JSTL attributes. Anything in the attribute of a JSTL tag that is not encapsulated by the *${...}* characters is treated as a literal notation. To use the dollar *$* sign as a literal value you escape it with the backslash "\" character.

```
<c:set var="amount" value="\$1,000,000"/>
```

ECMAScript

ECMAScript was borne out of the chaos that was (and some would say still is) the confusion of browser support for JavaScript. ECMAScript is a standardized scripting language that has its roots in JavaScript version 1.2. The JWSDP framework supports, and expects, expression languages to be in ECMAScript unless specified otherwise.

JXPath

JXPath is a powerful and feature-rich scripting technology that provides support for XPath expressions. It provides graph traversal to retrieve property values by name or map elements by a key. By specifying an index or search criterion you can retrieve elements from a collection as well. JXPath also provides support for logical, arithmetic, character and collection manipulation.

Selecting an Expression Languge

The choice of an expression language depends on your particular needs. Once determined, there are two methods of denoting which expression language to use when evaluating the attributes of JSTL tags. These two methods are *Application-Wide* and *Code Section Explicit*.

Application-Wide

As mentioned earlier the default expression language is ECMAScript. To use an expression language other than this, you have to set the appropriate context parameter in your web application's *web.xml* deployment descriptor.

The following example will set up your application to use the JXPath expression language evaluator.

```
<context-param>
<param-name>
    javax.servlet.jsp.jstl.temp.ExpressionEvaluatorClass
</param-name>
<param-value>
    org.apache.taglibs.standard.lang.jxpath.JXPathExressionEvaluator
</param-value>
</context-param>
```

NOTE

Support for the *web.xml* deployment descriptor became mandatory with the Java Servlet Specification version 2.2. Web servers that do not support this version of the specification will not be able to execute JavaServer Pages with tag libraries.

Code Section Explicit

It is conceivable that you will wish to override the expression language evaluator for certain parts of your application. JSTL does provide a means to accomplish this.

c:expressionLanguage

The expression language can also be explicitly set at the code level. This involves the use of the *expressionLanguage* action from the core tag Library. If, for example, you wanted to override the application-wide setting for a particular code block in order to use JXPath as the expression language you would use the following notation:

```
<c:expressionLanguageclass="org.apache.taglibs.standard.lang.jxpath.
JXPathExressionEvaluator">


</c:expressionLanguage>
```

If SPEL was your expression language choice, you would set it using the following notation:

```
<c:expressionLanguage class="org.apache.taglibs.standard.lang.spel.
ExpressionEvaluatorClass">


</c:expressionLanguage>
```

And finally if ECMAScript was the desired EL then you would set it as follows:

```
<c:expressionLanguage class="org.apache.taglibs.standard.lang.javascript.
JavascriptExpressionEvaluator">


</c:expressionLanguage>
```

The *expressionLanguage* action's child tags will inherit the evaluator class that was specified during the evaluation of any expressions encountered during page rendering.

> **NOTE**
>
> Be advised that if JSTL does standardize on a single expression language, support for this action will most likely disappear.

Expression Languages and Tag Library Selection

The JWSDP comes with both the EL support and non-EL support versions of the four tag libraries. The non-EL tag libraries will have an "-rt" suffix in the filename. The EL support tag libraries will have no such suffix.

The non-EL tag libraries function the same way as you have come to expect tag libraries to function, according to the JavaServer Page Specification version 1.1. The runtime expressions of the tag attributes are evaluated in the JSP scripting language. You may elect to use the non-EL tag libraries should the expression language support not contain the necessary functionality you need to implement your application.

If you do choose to use the EL support tag libraries you will not be allowed to use the JSP scripting language to derive attribute values.

Future Compatibility with Expression Languages

As mentioned earlier, the specifications that make up the JWSDP are still in a state of flux. As a result, the support for expression languages will no doubt undergo modifications. However, there have been assurances from the group responsible for the JWSDP that future versions will be backwards compatible.

Developing & Deploying...

Configuring Your Web Application to use the JSTL

JSTL comes as a optional tool for the JWSDP. The class packages and supporting TLD files are located at <JWSDP_HOME>/tools/jstl. To use some or all of the tag libraries defined there you must do three things: First you must copy the two JAR files, jstl.jar and standard.jar, to your web application's /WEB-INF/lib directory. Second, you must copy the TLD files for the tag libraries you wish to use to the /WEB-INF directory. Last, you must add a reference to each of the TLD files copied to your *web.xml* deployment descriptor as separate *<taglib>* elements.

Core Tags

Now that we have an understanding of the syntax and use of expression languages we can go over the meat of the JSTL, the tag libraries themselves.

The core tag library of JSTL represents the basic functionality used in the development of JavaServer pages. This basic functionality can be broken down into three groups: expression language, flow control, and importing.

NOTE

The subsequent sections in this chapter provide examples of the actions available from the four tag libraries that comprise the JSTL. We show these examples using the standard naming conventions as used in the specification itself. As a result the core tag library is assigned a *c:* prefix , the SQL tag library is assigned an *sql:* prefix of, the internationalization tag library is assigned an *fmt*: prefix and finally the XML tag library is assigned an *x:* prefix of. Using these prefixes keeps the examples in this chapter consistent with the specification.

Expression Language

The JSTL core tag library offers support for the evaluation and manipulation of expressions. The validation of expressions is governed by the rules mandated by the expression evaluator specified in either the deployment descriptor or explicitly within the JSP using the *expressionLanguage* action.

The values of the attributes in the expression can be retrieved from any of a web application's associated valid scopes. Scoped attributes can be set in the *web.xml* deployment descriptor and retrieved using the *app* scope notation. They can be set in a request as *form* parameters. If you use JavaBeans in your JSP files then you can reference the properties of those beans using expression language.

In a nutshell, the expression language is used to retrieve and set an application's attributes using a simple notation to denote the name and scope of the desired attribute. This removes the necessity of putting scriptlet code that might be confusing to follow into your JSP. An example of this would be to access the properties of a bean. Consider a JavaBean with the following semantics:

```
import java.beans.*;
```

```java
public class Person extends java.lang.Object
        implements java.io.Serializable
{
    private String fn;
    private String ln;
    private String mi;

    public String getFN()
    {
        return this.fn;
    }

    public void setFN( String value )
    {
        this.fn = value;
    }

    public String getLN()
    {
        return this.ln;
    }

    public void setLN( String value )
    {
        this.ln = value;
    }

    public String getMI()
    {
        return this.mi;
    }

    public void setMI( String value )
    {
        this.mi = value;
    }
}
```

Using the traditional JSP scripting language to access these bean properties, a JSP page that uses this bean might look like the following example:

```
<%@ page contentType="text/html" %>
<%@ taglib uri="/jstl-c" prefix="c" %>

<html>
<head><title>Show Person</title></head>
<body>

<jsp:useBean id="person" class="Person" scope="session"/>

Welcome <%= person.getFN(); %>
</body>
</html>
```

With the introduction of expression languages, the effort to access and use attributes such as the JavaBean to which we have been referring, become much simpler to develop and follow.

```
<%@ page contentType="text/html" %>
<%@ taglib uri="/jstl-c" prefix="c" %>

<html>
<head><title>Show Person</title></head>
<body>

<jsp:useBean id="person" class="Person" scope="session"/>

Welcome <c:out value="${session:person.fn}"/>
</body>
</html>
```

Expression languages have provided a means of defining the values of tag attributes as scoped JSP attributes, greatly simplifying the notation.

c:out

The *out* action takes the expression specified in its *value* attribute and evaluates it. The result of the evaluation is sent to the *JspWriter* object of the currently executing JSP.

```
<%@ page contentType="text/html" %>
<%@ page errorPage="error.jsp" %>
<%@ taglib uri="/jstl-c" prefix="c" %>

<html>
<head>
    <title>c:out</title>
    <link rel="stylesheet" type="text/css" href="stylesheet.css">
</head>
<body>
<h2>c:out (cont)</h2>
<p>The following parameters were retrieved from PARAM scoped attributes
    via the <span class="code">c:out</span> tag.</p>
<ul>
<li>street = <c:out value="${param:street}"/></li>
<li>city = <c:out value="${param:city}"/></li>
<li>zipCode = <c:out value="${param:zipCode}"/></li>
</ul>
</body>
</html>
```

c:set

The *set* action sets the value of an attribute. The name of the attribute is denoted by the *id* attribute. The optional *scope* attribute is used to set the scope visibility of the attribute. To specify the value of the attribute you can either use the value attribute or the body of the *set* action.

```
<%@ page contentType="text/html" %>
<%@ page errorPage="error.jsp" %>
<%@ taglib uri="/jstl-c" prefix="c" %>

<html>
<head>
    <title>c:set example</title>
    <link rel="stylesheet" type="text/css" href="stylesheet.css">
</head>
<body>
```

```
<h2>c:set</h2>
<p></p>
<hr/>
<c:set var="requri" scope="page">
    <%= request.getRequestURI() %>
</c:set>
<h3>The RequestURI was parsed from the request object and set to the var
"requri". The value found is "<c:out value="${requri}"/>".
</body>
</html>
```

Iterations

The capability to loop or iterate through a collection of object is offered by *Iterations*. JSTL's core tag library provides two actions to support such iterations: *forEach* and *forTokens*.

c:forEach

The *forEach* action allows a developer to iterate over a collection of objects within the JSP. The *items* attribute (which refers to the collection to iterate over), can be one of the following data types.

- Arrays of either primitive or object types. Primitive arrays are automatically converted into their respective wrapper class instances.

- An instance of a class that is defined as implementing one of the following interfaces: *java.util.Collection, java.util.Iterator, java.util.Enumeration* or *java.util.Map*.

- A *java.lang.String* instance containing comma delimited fields.

```
<%@ page contentType="text/html" %>
<%@ page errorPage="error.jsp" %>
<%@ page import="CompanyBean" %>
<%@ taglib uri="/jstl-c" prefix="c" %>

<html>
<head>
    <title>c:forEach example</title>
```

```
        <link rel="stylesheet" type="text/css" href="stylesheet.css">
</head>
<body>
<h2>c:forEach</h2>
<p></p>
<hr/>
<jsp:useBean id="company" class="CompanyBean" scope="page"/>
<c:set var="departments" value="${page:company.departments}"/>

<table>
    <tr><th>Department</th></tr>
<c:forEach var="dept" items="${departments}">
    <tr><td><c:out value="${dept}"/></td><?tr>
</c:forEach>
</table>
</body>
</html>
```

c:forTokens

The *forTokens* action allows a developer to iterate over a set of tokens using a specified delimiter. The difference between this action and the *forEach* action is that the *forTokens* action will allow you to define a delimited collection using one or more delimiters of your choice.

```
<%@ page contentType="text/html" %>
<%@ page errorPage="error.jsp" %>
<%@ page import="CompanyBean" %>
<%@ taglib uri="/jstl-c" prefix="c" %>

<html>
<head>
    <title>c:forTokens example</title>
    <link rel="stylesheet" type="text/css" href="stylesheet.css">
</head>
<body>
<h2>c:forTokens</h2>
<p></p>
```

```
<hr/>

<c:set var="tokens" value="Welcome,About Us,Services,Opportunities"/>

<h3>Menu Items</h3>
<ol>
<c:forTokens items="${tokens}" delims="," var="menuItem">
    <li><c:out value="${menuItem}"/>
</c:forTokens>
</ol>
</body>
</html>
```

Conditional Expressions

Conditional expressions are a means to conditionally execute blocks of code depending upon the result of an expression evaluation. JSTL's core tag libraries contains two sets of conditional expressions: *if* and *choose/when/otherwise*.

c:if

The *if* action provides conditional execution support within the JSP. The body of the *<if>* tag is evaluated if the condition denoted by the *test* attribute evaluates to *true*.

```
<c:if test="${session:sessionData.loggedIn == true}">
    <%-- Perform some conditional action --%>
</c:if>
```

c:choose

The *choose* action encapsulates a series of nested *when* actions. The *choose* action is therefore analogous to the *switch* statement in Java.

c:when

The *when* action is a child tag of a *choose* action. Each *when* action has a *test* attribute that when evaluated as *true* executes its body.

c:otherwise

The *otherwise* action is the last child element of a *choose* action. This action only executes its body content if all proceeding *when* actions evaluated as *false*.

The following is an example of how to use these tags to personalize an order processing JSP according to the customer's age.

```
<%@ page contentType="text/html" %>
<%@ page errorPage="error.jsp" %>
<%@ taglib uri="/jstl-c" prefix="c" %>

<html>
<body>
<h2>Order Status</h2>
<c:choose>
    <c:when test="${session:personBean.age < 18}">
      You must get parental permission to complete the purchase process.
    </c:when>
    <c:when test="${session:personBean.age > 65}">
        You are entitled to a senior discount on your purchase.
    <c:otherwise>
        Thank you for your order. Please shop with us again.
    </c:otherwise>
</c:choose>
</body>
</html>
```

Importing External Resources

JSTL's core tag library extends the inherent capability of the JSP to incorporate external resources into the currently executing JSP.

c:import

The *import* action is used to combine the output from an external resource into the currently executing JSP. This resource can be accessible from either a relative or an absolute URL. The contents of this external resource can be stored in a variable denoted by a *var* attribute, a reader object denoted by a *varReader* attribute, or simply to the page itself.

The key difference between this JSTL action and the standard JSP script action *jsp:include* is that the latter can't reference a URL that is external to the currently executing web application. Use of JSTL's *import* action also does not involve the buffering inherent in the traditional *jsp:import* action.

The following is an example of using the JSTL *import* action.

```
<table>
<tr><th>Your Weather</th></tr>
<tr><td>
<c:import url="/portlet-weather.jsp" >
    <c:param name="zipcode" value="${session:person.zipCode}/>
</c:import>
</td></tr>
</table>
```

c:param

The *param* action works as a nested tag of the *import* action. These nested *param* actions allow you to set additional parameters to which the external resource can have access. Each *param* action will add one more parameter to the URL of the request, in the same manner as the *get* request. The following example shows how this *param* action could be used:

```
<c:import url="/orderform.jsp>
    <c:param name="shippingZipCode"
             value="34050-1010"/>
</c:import>
```

In this example, the invoked URL would be modified from */orderform.jsp* to */orderform.jsp?shippingZipCode=34050-1010*.

URL Manipulation

JSTL offers the ability to encode a string to be used as a URL.

c:urlEncode

The *urlEncode* action takes a value as represented by its *value* attribute and encodes it as *x*-www-form-urlencoded. The following is an example of the usage of this action:

```
<a href="<c:urlEncode value="http:/myserver.com/servlet1?name=
    John Doe&address=123 Main Street, Suite 17"/>">Add User</a>
```

When executed, the resultant HTML will contain an anchor tag (*<a>*) that looks like the following:

```
<a href="http:/myserver.com/servlet1?name=John Doe&address=
    123%20Main Street,%20Suite%2017">Add User</a>
```

This is useful when programmatically constructing a URL for constructs requiring one, for example an anchor tag.

c:redirect

The *redirect* action sends an HTTP redirect command to the client. As with the *import* action, you may specify optional *param* actions to add embedded parameters to the URL. This action's behavior is analogous to the *HttpServletResponse.sendRedirect()* method.

SQL Query Tags

JSTL provides support for simplistic database interaction from within a JSP using the SQL Tag Library package. Support for SQL commands in JSTL was not intended to replace the proper placement of database interactions in business objects like JavaBeans and Enterprise JavaBeans. Rather the SQL Tag Library was provided to allow for quick prototyping of database-enabled applications. If the business application is simple enough these SQL actions may suffice. It is up to the developer's discretion to decide if this approach is prudent. Recklessly inserting database interaction logic into a JSP tends to complicate the JSP and make it harder to follow. The addition of SQL statements in the JSP also tends to deviate from the desired MVC architecture in web application design.

Setting up a Driver

JSTL allows the driver being used for SQL database interaction to be defined in a couple different ways. The data source to be used can also be specified in the *web.xml* deployment descriptor in a *resource-ref* element, as shown in the following example:

```
<resource-ref>
    <res-ref-name>jdbc/LibraryDB</res-ref-name>
    <res-type>javax.sql.DataSource</res-type>
```

```
        <res-auth>Container</res-auth>
</resource-ref>
```

Your application code will then take this data source and place it in the *javax.servlet.jsp.jstl.sql.dataSource* scoped attribute.

sql:driver

The *driver* action is provided to set up a data source from with the JSP. It is important to note here that this scheme should only be used for prototyping; there are more appropriate places to establish a data source, such as creating a data source from within servlet initialization and placing the data source with the application context for multiple sources to use.

> **NOTE**
>
> It is not recommended to use the *<driver>* tag in a production environment.

Executing Queries

JSTL provides functionality to query a database and return the results. This is primarily used with simple query statements like the *SELECT* command. Results from the query are returned via an instance of the *javax.servlet.jsp.jstl.sql.Result* interface.

sql:query

The *query* action executes an SQL query statement as specified in the *sql* attribute or in the body of the *query* action itself.

sql:param

The *param* action supplies parameters to be used in an enclosing *query* action.

```
<sql:query var="results" dataSource="${app:pool.dataSource}">
    SELECT * FROM EMPLOYEES WHERE SSN = ?
    <sql:param value="${param:ssn}" />
</sql:query>
```

The result set from a query can be stored within a JSP scoped variable as specified in the *query* action's *var* attribute. In the above example the results from the query against the EMPLOYEE table will be stored in the *results* instance. The *Result* class has a *getRows* method, which will return a *Row* array. Each *Row* instance has a *getColumns* method that returns a *Column* array. The actual value of that *Column* instance can be acquired using the *getValue* method.

Using the SPEL as our expression language evaluator we can create queries and display the results in a JSP:

```
<%@ page contentType="text/html" %>
<%@ page errorPage="error.jsp" %>
<%@ taglib uri="/jstl-c" prefix="c" %>
<%@ taglib uri="/jstl-sql" prefix="sql" %>

<html>
<head>
    <title>c:query example</title>
    <link rel="stylesheet" type="text/css" href="stylesheet.css">
</head>
<body>
<h2>c:query</h2>
<p></p>
<hr/>

<sql:driver var="ds"
            driver="sun.jdbc.odbc.JdbcOdbcDriver"
            url="//localhost/db">
    <sql:query datasource="ds" var="result">
        SELECT * FROM EMPOYEES
    </sql:query>
</sql:driver>

<h3>Employee List</h3>
<table>
<c:forEach var="employee" items="${result.rows}">
    <tr><td><c:out value="${employee.lastName}"/>,
            <c:out value="${employee.firstName}"/></td></tr>
```

```
</c:forEach>
</table>
</body>
</html>
```

In this example, the JSP first establishes a JDBC driver using the *driver* action. A nested *query* action performs the *SELECT* query as specified, storing the results in a result instance held in the *var* named *result*. The next group of tags takes that result collection and iterates through it to create a table with each row containing one row of the result.

Executing Updates

The JSTL provides the functionality to update databases. This is primarily for use with simple update statements like the *UPDATE* command, although any SQL command that does not return results can be used in this action.

sql:update

The *update* action essentially allows you to execute an SQL command that returns no data. The most common SQL commands used in this context are *INSERT*, *UPDATE* and *DELETE*. As it is with the *query* action the *update* action can also contain nested *param* actions that affect the behavior of the SQL command.

```
<%@ page contentType="text/html" %>
<%@ page errorPage="error.jsp" %>
<%@ taglib uri="/jstl-c" prefix="c" %>
<%@ taglib uri="/jstl-sql" prefix="sql" %>

<html>
<head>
    <title>sql:update example</title>
    <link rel="stylesheet" type="text/css" href="stylesheet.css">
</head>
<body>
<h2>sql:update</h2>
<p></p>
<hr/>

<c:set var="tableName" value="$param:tableName"/>
```

```
<sql:driver var="ds"
            driver="sun.jdbc.odbc.JdbcOdbcDriver"
            url="//localhost/db">
    <sql:update datasource="ds">
        DROP <c:out value="$tableName"/>
    </sql:update>
</sql:driver>


Table <c:out value="$tableName"/> has been dropped.
</body>
</html>
```

In the preceding example the JSP reads the *tableName* attribute, which exists as a request parameter, submitted in the current request. Once the attribute has been retrieved, the *driver* action creates a data source. Nested within this action is the *update* action that executes the *DROP* command, effectively erasing the table from the database. Upon successful completion of the table drop the user is presented with a message stating that the operation was successful.

Denoting Transactional Boundaries

It is often desirable to execute several database functions within the context of a single transaction. An example of this would be a bank funds transfer: an amount would be withdrawn from one account in the first database function, and the same amount would be added to another account in a second database function. The success of both functions is critical if the transfer is to be completed successfully. If the amount was withdrawn from the first account but an exception occurred while depositing that amount into the recipient account, then the transfer should fail and the amount be credited back to the first account.

sql:transaction

The *transaction* action is used to nest database actions within the boundaries of a single transaction.

```
<%@ page contentType="text/html" %>
<%@ page errorPage="error.jsp" %>
<%@ taglib uri="/jstl-c" prefix="c" %>
<%@ taglib uri="/jstl-sql" prefix="sql" %>
```

```
<html>
<head>
    <title>c:transaction example</title>
    <link rel="stylesheet" type="text/css" href="stylesheet.css">
</head>
<body>
<h2>c: transaction</h2>
<p></p>
<hr/>

<c:set var="checkAmount" value="${param:checkAmount}"/>
<c:set var="fromAccount" value="${param:fromAccount}"/>
<c:set var="toAccount" value="${param:toAccount}"/>

<sql:driver var="ds"
            driver="sun.jdbc.odbc.JdbcOdbcDriver"
            url="//localhost/db">
    <sql:transaction datasource="ds">
        <sql:update datasource="ds">
            UPDATE bankAccounts SET currentBalance = currentBalance - ?
            WHERE account = ?
            <sql:param value="${checkAmount}"/>
            <sql:param value="${fromAccount}"/>
        </sql:update>
        <sql:update datasource="ds">
            UPDATE bankAccounts SET currentBalance = currentBalance + ?
            WHERE account = ?
            <sql:param value="${checkAmount}"/>
            <sql:param value="${toAccount}"/>
        </sql:update>
    </sql:transaction>
</sql:driver>

Transaction Completed
</body>
</html>
```

The preceding example illustrates how a *transaction* action can group related and interdependent SQL commands so that the sequence of commands is treated as one event. In this example (a variant of the previous banking example), we have a JSP that receives a request from some other source. This request contains three parameters of interest: the number of the checking account withdrawing the amount, the number of the checking account depositing the amount, and the amount of the transaction itself. Once this data has been retrieved the *driver* action establishes a data source, presumably the database holding the account information. An encapsulating transaction action is used to hold the two *UPDATE* commands that remove the amount from one checking account and deposit it into the other account. Failure of either *UPDATE* will result in a rollback of the entire transaction.

Internationalization Tags

When web-based application development was in its infancy (circa 1995) developers did not have to concern themselves with support for multiple languages and locales. Typically the scope and reach of an application was limited to a certain group communicating in a common language. This is no longer the case; nowadays these same developers must be cognizant of the implications of deploying an internationalized application that is capable of supporting multiple languages and locales. One approach is to port an application developed in one language such that multiple copies of the application exist, each catering to the specific needs of a particular language or area. Needless to say, this approach is extremely costly, both in terms of development and maintenance.

NOTE

The process of enabling an application to work with multiple locales is known as Internationalization (I18N). When you insert the various formatting actions into the JSP files you are performing I18N. The process of actually creating the content specific to each locale is known as Localization (L10N). When you create a resource bundle you are performing L10N.

Fortunately the JSTL provides a mechanism to support multiple languages and locales from within the same code base. This mechanism allows the developer to remove all textual messages, formatting, and layout instructions and place them into a *resource bundle*. The resource bundle is where the developer places custom tags designed to specify a locale and to retrieve certain information or perform certain tasks based on the value of the locale that was either received from the client's browser or calculated internally in the web application itself.

Defining the Locale

There are two methods by which a locale can be specified: The first is by the client's browser, and the second is by the web application itself. The first method is more common as the support for specifying a desired language is built into the browser software and frees the developer from the burden of implementing language preference functionality. The second method is used less frequently; some web applications will let a user select a language, typically from a list of languages that have been implemented in the form of resource bundles, and store the selection. This storage is either session-based or persisted to a datastore.

Browser Specified

Web browsers allow the user to compile a list of their preferred languages and store that information locally on the user's computer. When the browser makes an HTTP request, it passes the preferred language settings within the headers of that request to the web server. During the course of execution, JSP files that invoke any of the custom tag actions from the *fmt.tld* tag library descriptor will use a locale derived from that header information as the basis for the resource bundle lookup.

Figure 5.1 is a screen capture of the language selection dialog from Internet Explorer.

Figure 5.1 Browser Language Selection

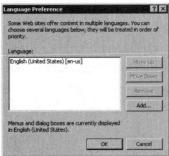

You may enter multiple languages in this dialog and arrange them into the order of precedence that you wish.

JSP Specified

The JSP files do have the capability to explicitly set the locale to use when looking up internationalized messages.

fmt:locale

This *locale* action sets the locale to use when attempting to discover the best resource bundle match or when using the various *formatXXXX* or *parseXXXX* actions as discussed later.

```
<fmt:locale value="de-DE" variant="EURO"/>
```

In this example we are setting the locale of the currently executing JSP to the German language with a variant of EURO.

Defining the Timezone

The JSTL uses the *javax.servlet.jsp.jstl.i18n.timeZone* scoped JSP attribute to denote the time zone with which to format data representing a date and time. This attribute can be set either by the application (using a formula), through user selection, or it can be explicitly stated within the JSP itself using the *<timeZone>* tag.

fmt:timeZone

To explicitly set the time zone from within the JSP you would use the *timeZone* action as seen in the following example. This example would set the time zone to Eastern Standard Time.

```
<fmt:timeZone value="GMT-5:00">
     ... other date and time formatting tags ...
</fmt:timeZone>
```

If you set the time zone by this method, there are several different types of values you could use in the *value* parameter. These value types are:

- **Abbreviation** As shown in the example above, you could use the standard abbreviation for the time zone. Examples include PST, MDT and EDT. The official Java documentation discourages the use of such abbreviations in lieu of the *Full Name*.

- **Full Name** This is the full name of the time zone.

- **Custom** You can specify a custom time zone by denoting the delta from GMT. Examples of this include GMT-5:00, GMT+2:00, etc.

If you are interested in seeing all of the Time Zones that are defined in Java you can run the following program:

```
import java.util.*;
public class ListTimeZones extends java.lang.Object
{
    public static void main( String[] args )
    {
        String[] ids = TimeZone.getAvailableIDs();
        for( int i = 0; i < ids.length; i++ )
        {
            String id = ids[i];
            System.out.print( "id="+id );
            TimeZone tz = TimeZone.getTimeZone( id );
            System.out.println( ", timezone="+
                                tz.getDisplayName() );
        }
    }
}
```

Specifying a Resource Bundle

There are two ways to set the base name of the resource bundle you wish to use when localizing messages, dates and times. The first way is to set it at the application level through a context parameter in the *web.xml* deployment descriptor.

```
<context-param>
    <param-name>
        javax.servlet.jsp.jstl.i18n.basename
    </param-name>
    <param-value>
        i18n.Messages
    </param-value>
</context-param>
```

The other way is to use the *<bundle>* tag from the core library.

fmt:bundle

The *bundle* action allows you to explicitly load a particular resource bundle. This bundle is then valid for the remaining parts (after the *bundle* action) of the currently executing JSP.

```
<fmt:bundle basename="Application"/>
```

Locating the Resource Bundle

A resource bundle contains thelocalization information that defines the specific messages and the formatting of those messages, based upon a specific locale. When an application is asked to display internationalized information it must first locate the resource bundle in which that information is contained.

A resource bundle may take the form of a class file or a properties file. The names of these files must follow a defined pattern if the application is to find the correct one. There are four parts to a resource bundle's filename. These parts are:

- **Base Name** An arbitrary identifier selected bythe web application's developer, and which is commonly used to communicate the contents or consumer of the resource bundle. Examples of this are *ErrorMessages* or *OrderProcessing*.

- **Language** A twolower-case letter language code. This code must be ISO-639-compliant.

- **Country** A two upper-case letter code that denotes the country. This code must be ISO-3166-compliant.

- **Variant** This code consists of one or more underscore-separated tokens that are specific to a particular vendor or browser.

When put all four parts together, the resource bundle filename will look like:

```
<<basename>>_<<languageCode>>_<<countryCode>>_<<variant>>
```

A search for a resource bundle always starts with the base name. The search mechanism will take the list of desired locales (as supplied by the client's browser) or the explicitly defined locale (as set programmatically by the application) and search for the best possible match against all available resource bundles. The best possible match refers to how closely the available resource bundles' filenames pair up with the desired resource bundle file name as calculated from the base name and the specified locale.

As defined by the specification, the JVM will search for a resource bundle by looking for names in the following order. When a match is found the search stops.

- basename+"_"+languageCode+"_"+countryCode+"_"+variant

- basename+"_"+languageCode+"_"+countryCode+"_"+variant+ ".properties"

- basename+"_"+languageCode+"_"+countryCode

- basename+"_"+languageCode+"_"+countryCode+".properties"

- basename+"_"+languageCode

- basename+"_"+languageCode +".properties"

As the list suggests, *ResourceBundles* will take precedence over *PropertyResourceBundles* of the same name. An example of a resource bundle created to hold localized messages for Germany might look like so:

```
ElectronicsSales_de_DE_EURO
```

In this example, the *ElectronicSales* is the base name. All resource bundles will start with this name. The lowercase *de* is the language identifier for German. The uppercase *DE* is the country identifier for Germany. The variant in this case is denoted by *EURO*.

Using Internationalized Messages

The use of internationalized messages within a web application is realized by the two sets of tags provided by JSTL for that purpose. These two sets are *<Messaging>* and *<Formatting>*. These tags are defined within the *fmt.tld* tag library descriptor (with EL support) and the *fmt-rt.tld* tag library descriptor (with no EL support).

Obtaining Simple Internationalized Messages

Once a resource bundle has been created and placed where the web application can locate it in the CLASSPATH, it is a simple matter to access the internationalized messages contained therein.

fmt:message

The *message* action is the easiest means with which you can access internationalized messages. The following code shows how you will use this page directive to enable the use of the I18N tags.

```
<%@ taglib uri="/jstl-fmt prefix="fmt" %>
```

As mentioned earlier, internationalized messages are stored in resource bundles. Before initiating lookups of internationalized messages you must specify which resource bundle contains the messages you want. If you did not specify a basename as a context parameter in your *web.xml* deployment descriptor you must include a reference to the desired bundle within the JSP itself using the *fmt:bundle …* action.

Now, somewhere else in your JSP you will want to place the actual *<message>* tag with a specified key to substitute with the internationalized message. Using this key, the *<message>* tag will lookup the following:

```
<span class="page.message">
    <fmt:message key="greeting"/>
</span>
```

Performing Parameter Substitution

There are instances where simple message replacement will not suffice. Consider the problem of rendering complete phrases or sentences containing proper names. These proper names appear in vastly different positions depending on the locale in which the sentence is being rendered. The JSTL provides a means with which to perform this. It is called parameter substitution, and is accomplished using the *<messageFormat>* tag with one or more child *<messageArg>* tags.

fmt:messageFormat

The *messageFormat* action provides the web application developer with a means of defining how a message is formatted when key elements of the message are arranged differently, depending upon the locale in which the message is rendered. This action takes parameters which it them substitutes within a pattern string. This pattern string is obtained from the *value* attribute of the action or, if missing, from the body of the action itself.

fmt:messageArg

The *messageArg* action is used to specify the argument of a parent *message* or *messageFormat* action. For each variable in the parent action there must be a corresponding *messageArg* action. Substitution occurs in the order that the *messageArg* actions are specified.

An example of how all this works together might look as follows. Assuming that you have a Resource Bundle named *Messages* that had an entry of:

```
welcome=Welcome {0} {1} from {2} to our corporate web site.
```

You could use the following JSP to display a custom welcome message using data submitted with the request:

```
<%@ page contentType="text/html" %>
<%@ page errorPage="error.jsp" %>
<%@ taglib uri="/jstl-fmt" prefix="fmt" %>

<html>
<head>
    <title>fmt:message</title>
    <link rel="stylesheet" type="text/css" href="stylesheet.css">
</head>
<body>
<h2>fmt:message</h2>
<h2>fmt:messageArg</h2>

<fmt:bundle basename="Messages" var="i18n"/>

<fmt:message key="welcome" bundle="${i18n}">
    <fmt:messageArg value="${param:fn}"/>
    <fmt:messageArg value="${param:ln}"/>
    <fmt:messageArg value="${param:state}"/>
</fmt:message>
</body>
</html>
```

In this example we wish to welcome a person to a web site with a customized greeting. The *bundle* action sets the basename of the resource bundle we use to lookup localized messages. The subsequent *message* action retrieves the desired localized message, passing substitution variables in the form of nested *messageArg* actions.

Exception Localization

The custom exception classes that derive from the *java.lang.Exception* class come with built-in support for the localization of exception messages. The localization of exceptions is accomplished by overriding the *getLocalizedMessage* method of the *java.lang.Throwable* class. The default behavior of this method is to call the *getMessage* method of the same class. So out of the box the two methods return the same result. The *getLocalizedMessage* method can be overridden in your custom exception class to perform a lookup against a resource bundle:

```
import java.util.ResourceBundle;
import java.util.MissingResourceException;
public class LocalizedException extends java.lang.Exception
{
    private String messageKey;
    /**
     * Constructor
     * Creates a new <code>LocalizedException</code>
     * without a detail message.
     * @param msg The detailed message for this exception.
     */
    public LocalizedException( String key )
    {
        super();
        this.messageKey = key;
    }

    /**
     * Overrides the getLocalizedMessage of the parent
     * java.lang.Throwable class.
     */
    public String getLocalizedMessage()
    {
        try
        {
```

```
            ResourceBundle rb = ResourceBundle.getBundle(
                                    "i18n.ErrorMessages" );

            String message = rb.getString( messageKey );

            return message;

        }

        catch( MissingResourceException mre )

        {

            mre.printStackTrace();

            return this.messageKey;

        }

    }

}
```

In the example, the constructor of this exception takes a single *String* argument. This *String* argument represents the key to use when performing a lookup against a resource bundle. The constructor takes this key, performs the lookup and stores, in a private member variable, the internationalized message to associate with this instance.

When an *Exception* class is designed in this manner and used in conjunction with a JSP Error page it becomes possible to display an internationalized error message, generated by the exception and stored within a resource bundle.

```
<%@ page contentType="text/html" %>
<%@ page isErrorPage="true" %>


<html>
<head><title>Error Page</title></head>
<body>
<span class="error.message">
    <% exception.getLocalizedMessage() %>
</span>
</body>
</html>
```

Here we have set up a JSP to serve as an error page using the *isErrorPage* directive. Using this directive affords us access to the *exception* implicit object within the JSP. In this example we call the *getLocalizedMessage* method on that exception instance to return a localized error message.

Remember that the default behavior of the *getLocalizedMessage* method is to return the same value as *getMessage*, so if this error page gets called with an exception that is not an instance of our *LocalizedException* class (or a derived class thereof) then the usual message will appear in place of of an internationalized one.

fmt:exception

The JSTL provides additional support for the localization of exception messages. The *exception* action is designed to display an exception in a localized form as denoted by its *value* attribute.

```
<fmt:exception value="{request:exception}"/>
```

Even if value attribute is missing, the *exception* action can still be used in a JSP that has been slated as an error page by using the *isErrorPage* directive. Under these circumstances the *exception* action will display the localized value of the implicit exception variable.

```
<%@ page contentType="text/html" %>
<%@ page isErrorPage="true" %>
<%@ taglib uri="/jstl-fmt" prefix="fmt" %>


<html>
<head><title>Error</title></head>
<body>
<h2 class="errorTitle">An error has occured</h2>
<h3 class="errorMessage"><fmt:exception/></h3>
</body>
</html>
```

Parsing and Formatting

The JSTL provides actions that parse data and format strings. These actions include *formatNumber*, *parseNumber*, *formatDate* and *parseDate*. With these actions you can localize numerical values such as currencies and date-time notations.

fmt:formatNumber

The *formatNumber* action is used to localize the formatting of numbers.

```
<%@ page contentType="text/html" %>
<%@ page errorPage="error.jsp" %>
<%@ page import="CompanyBean" %>
```

```
<%@ taglib uri="/jstl-c" prefix="c" %>
<%@ taglib uri="/jstl-fmt" prefix="fmt" %>


<html>
<head>
    <title>c:formatNumber example</title>
    <link rel="stylesheet" type="text/css" href="stylesheet.css">
</head>
<body>
<h2>c:formatNumber</h2>
<p></p>
<hr/>


<c:set var="number" value="1250000.50"/>


Examples of the <span class="code">>c:formatNumber</span> action used
on the numerical value of <c:out value="${number}"/>
<table>
<tr>
    <th>Locale</th>
    <th>Formatted Number</th>
</tr>
<tr>
    <td>en_US</td>
    <td><fmt:formatNumber value="${number}"
                          type="currency"
                          parseLocale="en_US"/>
    </td>
</tr>
<tr>
    <td>de_DE</td>
    <td><fmt:formatNumber value="${number}"
                          type="currency"
                          parseLocale="de_DE"/></td>
</tr>
<tr>
    <td>es_MX</td>
```

```
    <td><fmt:formatNumber value="${number}"
                        type="currency"
                        parseLocale="es_MX"/></td>
</tr>
<tr>
    <td>ja</td>
    <td><fmt:formatNumber value="${number}"
                        type="currency"
                        parseLocale="ja"/></td>
</tr>
</table>
</body>
</html>
```

Allowable values for the type attribute are *number*, *currency* and *percentage*.

fmt:parseNumber

The *parseNumber* action takes a string value from the *value* attribute and parses it as a number, currency or a percentage, however denoted in the *type* attribute.

```
<fmt:parseNumber value="100.00" type="currency" var="cost" scope="page"/>
```

fmt:formatDate

The *formatDate* action formats a date (or time). The style and pattern attributes dictate the final format of the date (or time).

```
<%@ page contentType="text/html" %>
<%@ page errorPage="error.jsp" %>
<%@ page import="CompanyBean" %>
<%@ taglib uri="/jstl-c" prefix="c" %>
<%@ taglib uri="/jstl-fmt" prefix="fmt" %>

<html>
<head>
    <title>c:formatDate example</title>
    <link rel="stylesheet" type="text/css" href="stylesheet.css">
</head>
<body>
<h2>c:formatDate</h2>
```

```
<p></p>
<hr/>

Current Date/Time in Helsinki:<p>
<fmt:timeZone value="Europe/Helsinki">
    <fmt:formatDate timeStyle="long" dateStyle="long"/>
</fmt:timeZone>
</body>
</html>
```

fmt:parseDate

The *parseDate* action performs in a similar fashion to the *parseNumber* action in that it takes a string and parses it for a *Date* object.

XML Support Tags

XML support tags provide a means to easily access and manipulate the contents of an XML document. JSTL XML tags use XPath expressions to perform their functions.

Parsing and Searching

JSTL provides actions that allow you to parse XML documents and perform a search for data meeting specified criteria. These actions include *parse* and *expr*.

x:parse

The *parse* action retrieves the content from an XML document. This XML document can be specified by either the *source* attribute or from the body of the *<parse>* tag itself. A *var* attribute specifies the JSP scoped attribute in which to save the result.

```
<x:parse var="library">
    <library>
        <book checkedout="true">
            <title>Book Title 1</title>
            <isbn>0130894680</isbn>
            <type>Fiction</type>
        </book>
        <book checkedout="false">
```

```
                <title>Book Title 2</title>
                <isbn>0210504683</isbn>
                <type>Non-Fiction</type>
            </book>
         <book checkedout="false">
                <title>Book Title 3</title>
                <isbn>0140911380</isbn>
                <type>Non-Fiction</type>
            </book>
      </library>
</x:parse>
```

x:out

The *out* action enables the developer to denote XPath expressions when working with XML documents. The expression specified is applied to the current node and the result is sent to the current *JspWriter* object.

```
<x:out select="${library/book/title}"/>
```

x:set

The *set* action also evaluates a XPath expression on the current node. In this case the result is assigned to a JSP scoped attribute as denoted by the *var* attribute.

```
<x:set var="isbns" select="${library/book/isbn}"/>
```

Iteration

JSTL provides functionality for iterating over a collection of XML elements. The tag for this XML element iteration is the *forEach* action.

x:forEach

The *forEach* action allows you to iterate over a collection of XML elements. The set of XML elements to use is specified by the *select* attribute. This *select* attribute contains a valid XSL statement with which to filter the XML document.

```
<h2>Library Contents</h2>
<x:forEach select="${library/book}">
    Title: <x:valueof select="title"/>
```

```
        ISBN: <x:valueof select="isbn"/>
</x:forEach>
```

Flow Control

JSTL provides functionality to conditionally branch execution of the current JSP document based upon an XPath expression. The action provided by the XML Tag Library includes the *if* action and the *choose/when/otherwise* actions.

x:if

The *if* action is a conditional operator that executes its body only if the XPath expression denoted by the *select* attribute evaluates to *true*.

```
<x:forEach select="${library/book}">
    <x:if select="[@checkedout='false']">
        <x:valueof select="$title"/> is available for checkout
    </x:if>
</x:forEach>
```

x:choose

The *choose* action encapsulates a series of nested <when> tags. The *choose* action therefore acts like the *switch* statement in Java. This tag functions identically to the action of the same name in the core package.

x:when

The *when* action is a child tag of a *choose* action. Each *when* action has a *select* attribute containing an XPath expression that, when evaluated to *true*, executes its body.

x:otherwise

The *otherwise* action is the last of the *choose* action's child elements. This action only executes its body content if all proceeding *when* actions evaluated to *false*.

```
<x:forEach select="${library/book}">
    <x:choose>
        <x:when test="$[type='Fiction']">
            <x:valueof select="$title"/> is in the Fiction section.
        </x:when>
```

```
        <x:when test="$[type='Non-Fiction']">
            <x:valueof select="$title"/> is in the Non-Fiction section.
        </x:when>
        <x:otherwise>
            I do not know where <x:valueof select="$title"/> is.
        </x:otherwise>
    </x:choose>
</x:forEach>
```

In our example we have an XML document holding data representing books in a library. The *forEach* action will iterate over each book, the location of which is specified in the *select* attribute. For each book element found the type is compared to expected values, in this case a type equal to *Fiction* or *Non-Fiction*, and an appropriate message is displayed. Failure to identify the type will result in an error message from the JSP.

Translation and XSLT

JSTL provides actions that perform translations of XML documents. This gives you the ability to modify XML that is structured according to one schema into a new XML document conforming to a different schema.

x:transform

The *transform* action applies a transformation to an XML document. The *xslt* attribute points to the XSL template to use for defining the transformation. The XML document itself can be specified either in the *source* attribute or within the body of the *transform* action itself.

```
<x:transform source="library.xml" xslt="showCheckedOut.xsl"/>
```

The result can end up in one of three places.; in lieu of any explicit destination notation, the output goes directly to the page content. If the *result* attribute is present in the action, the output gets stored as a *javax.xml.transform.Result* instance named with the value of the *result* attribute. Finally, the output can be saved as an instance of *org.w3c.dom.Document* when the *var* and *scope* attributes are specified.

x:param

The *param* action is used to pass parameters to the *Transformer* object of a *<transform>* tag.

Summary

The Java Standard Tag Library (JSTL) represents a major step forward in the standardization of JSP tag library functionality. JSTL provides ready-made, commonly used functionality to a web application; including collection iteration, flow control, attribute manipulation, XML parsing and searching, and basic database support using SQL and internationalization and localization. Using JSTL will facilitate a wider deployment of your application across web servers that support the JSTL specification.

The support for Expression Languages (EL) further de-couples the presentation logic from the business logic. By providing access to business methods and scoped data from an expression we lessen the need to resort to scriptlet code and proprietary custom tag libraries. The use of expression languages is by no means mandatory, however. For every EL-supporting tag library provided, there is a twin tag library that supports attribute expression evaluation using the standard JSP scripting language.

Again, it is important to remember that these specifications are still largely being formed. Modifications to the number, type and attributes of tags may change by the time of the final release. Therefore, care must be taken to not deploy applications that rely too heavily on JSTL at this time.

Solutions Fast Track

Expression Languages

☑ Expression Languages (EL) facilitate communication between business logic and JSPs through scoped JSP attributes.

☑ Although the initial release of the JWSDP supports several different Expression Languages, the direction is to eventually standardize on a single EL.

☑ Each of the four tag libraries that make up JSTL come in both EL and non-EL versions. The non-EL versions possess an "-rt" suffix on their tag library descriptors.

Core Tags

☑ JSTL's core tag library provides the *c:out* and *c:set* actions to manipulate JSP scoped attributes using expressions.

☑ The *c:forEach* action is used to iterate over collections of objects.

☑ The *c:forTokens* action is used to iterate over a series of tokens using a specified delimiter.

☑ Conditional expressions are realized by the *c:if*, *c:choose*, *c:when* and *c:otherwise* actions.

☑ The *c:choose* body is only executed if all preceding *c:when* actions evaluate their expressions to *false*.

☑ The *c:import* and *c:param* actions are used to incorporate external resources into the current JSP document.

☑ The *c:encodeURL* action will encode a string according to the *www-form-urlencoded* format.

SQL Query Tags

☑ The *<driver>* tag should not be used in production. Instead, create your data source within some business logic and store it within the appropriate context.

☑ The *<transaction>* tag is used to bundle consecutive SQL statements within the same transactional context.

☑ The SQL Tag Library contains *<query>* and *<update>* tags to perform those respective functions.

Internationalization Tags

☑ Internationalized messages and formatting instructions are stored in resource bundles.

☑ The resource bundle filename follows a naming convention that is used during a search for the best possible match.

☑ The best possible match for a resource bundle will not necessarily be an exact match. The best match is based upon the available resource bundles.

☑ The *<message>* and *<messageFormat>* tags are used to retrieve and format internationalized messages, respectively.

☑ The messages associated with classes that are derived from *java.lang.Throwable* can be internationalized by overriding the *getLocalizedMessage* method.

XML Support Tags

☑ All expressions in the XML Tag Library use XPath expressions.

☑ JSTL provides XML transformation capabilities via the *x:transform* action.

☑ By using the *x:transformer* action you can define a transformer instance that is reusable against multiple XML documents within the same page.

Frequently Asked Questions

The following Frequently Asked Questions, answered by the authors of this book, are designed to both measure your understanding of the concepts presented in this chapter and to assist you with real-life implementation of these concepts. To have your questions about this chapter answered by the author, browse to **www.syngress.com/solutions** and click on the **"Ask the Author"** form.

Q: How do I define the expression language evaluator that I wish to use within my application?

A: You can either add a context parameter in the *web.xml* deployment descriptor called *javax.servlet.jsp.jstl.temp.ExpressionEvaluatorClass* and give it a value equal to the full package name of the appropriate evaluation class, or you can specify it at the page level using the *c:expressionLanguage* action.

Q: How do I set the basename of the resource bundle I want to use when localizing messages?

A: You can either add a context parameter in the *web.xml* deployment descriptor called *javax.servlet.jsp.jstl.i18n.basename* and give it a value equal to the base name of the desired resource bundle or you can specify it at the page level using the *fmt:bundle* action.

Q: How can I reuse an XSLT for multiple XML documents?

A: Define a Transformer (XSLT) using the *fmt:transformer* action.

Q: Do I need to use expression languages to programmatically set the attributes of JSTL actions?

A: No, you can use JSTL without enabling EL support by using those tag libraries that have an "-rt" suffix in their filename.

Q: Does the use of XPath expressions in the XML tag library actions conflict with my choice of a global expression language?

A: The only attribute of the XML Tag Library actions to use the XPath expression language is the *select* attribute. You cannot mix expression languages in this attribute, whichavoids any conflict regarding EL evaluation.

Q: How can I set a default data source for all JSP files in my web application, with the option to override locally?

A: Somewhere in your application code, set the *javax.servlet.jsp.jstl.sql.dataSource* scoped attribute to point to the desired *DataSource* object.

Chapter 6

Writing SOAP Clients

Solutions in this chapter:

- **Understanding SOAP**

- **SOAPElement and JAXM DOM**

- **JAXM SOAP Elements**

- **Creating a SOAP Message**

- **Bringing it all Together—A Complete SOAP Client**

- ☑ **Summary**

- ☑ **Solutions Fast Track**

- ☑ **Frequently Asked Questions**

Introduction

For the next few chapter, we will explore the development of SOAP communications using the Java Web Services Developers Pack. This chapter will provide a brief introduction to SOAP, which is an XML-based protocol for communicating between distributed systems and can be extended with attachments containing essentially any media type.

The Java API for XML Messaging (JAXM) provides an API and specification for supporting services that enable developers to implement SOAP communications in Java. This chapter will cover the implementation of SOAP clients using JAXM (that is, consumers of web services), and the next chapter will cover the implementation of SOAP servers (that is, providers of web services).

Unlike most of the scenarios covered in this book, it is possible to implement synchronous communications (that is, request/reply) without the aid of a servlet or EJB container, and this chapter will fully describe an example of such a standalone Java application that functions as a SOAP client.

Understanding SOAP

The Simple Object Access Protocol (SOAP) is an XML-based protocol that is designed to be a lightweight method for exchanging information between distributed systems. It is very much a cross-platform and cross-vendor technology, and has the backing of a very wide range of companies. We will discuss two flavors of SOAP documents: plain SOAP, which is a pure XML message, and SOAP with Attachments, which allows for many types of data to be transmitted with a SOAP message.

SOAP is a fairly unique technology for use in distributed computing; it has some things in common with other mechanisms such as RMI, but it also has a number of differentiating features. These differences stem largely from the fact that SOAP is designed as a *simple* protocol—it has been deliberately designed to be lightweight, and for this reason it does not support such features as passing objects by reference.

SOAP is also designed to be extensible, and these goals of simplicity and extensibility have meant that the use of SOAP does not imply any particular programming models; a given implementation's semantics are extremely flexible. There are a number of possible models for exchanging messages, as well as mechanisms for exchanging data of application-defined types and for performing remote procedure calls and responses.

SOAP messages do not need to be bound to a particular protocol; HTTP is an obvious choice for many situations (and will be used for the examples in this chapter and the next), but there are many other possibilities. Likewise the model for exchanging messages is essentially a one-way transmission between two peers; the sender sends a message to the receiver. However this model can be extended—"request-response" is an obvious possibility, as are one-to-many transmissions and asynchronous transmission or reception via some form of queuing mechanism.

A complete study of the SOAP specifications is well beyond the scope of this book. We would recommend the following documents for more detailed information:

- **Simple Object Access Protocol (SOAP) 1.1** www.w3.org/TR/SOAP

- **SOAP Messages with Attachments** www.w3.org/TR/SOAP-attachments

Additionally, there are a number of tutorials and books available. The soaprpc.com site is a good place to look for information; it contains a list of links to SOAP tutorials at www.soaprpc.com/tutorials/.

Envelopes

Although SOAP Messages with Attachments can contain attachments of various content types, a simple SOAP message is an XML document that contains the elements displayed in Figure 6.1.

The SOAP Envelope is the top element of the XML document; as such, it must be present in every SOAP message. If present, the Header will exist as an element within the Envelope; the Body will also be present as an element within the Envelope. An empty envelope would look as follows:

```
<soap-env:Envelope xmlns:soap-
env="http://schemas.xmlsoap.org/soap/envelope/">

</soap-env:Envelope>
```

Because it doesn't contain a Body element, this envelope would not be a valid SOAP message, but it illustrates an important point about namespaces in SOAP messages: The SOAP namespace is defined by this envelope as having a URI of *"http://schemas.xmlsoap.org/soap/envelope/"* and a prefix of *"soap-env"*. This is because the SOAP specification states that all of the elements in a SOAP message must be qualified by this very namespace—an element named *"Header"* that was either locally-named or qualified by a different namespace would not be recognized as a SOAP Header element.

Figure 6.1 The Components of a SOAP Message

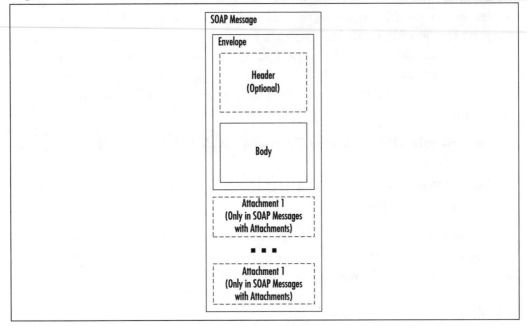

Headers

The *Header* is an optional element that may exist in the envelope. *Header* elements are used to transmit additional information along with a message, such as authentication or transaction information. Header elements can also contain certain attributes. One of these is the *mustUnderstand* attribute, which can be used to specify that the recipient of the message must be able to process that header element. If the *mustUnderstand* attribute is not set, or contains a value of 0 rather than 1, it implies that the recipient of the message is free to ignore the header element if it does not know how to process it.

An envelope that contains a header specifying an ignorable authentication ID could look like this:

```
<soap-env:Envelope xmlns:soap-
env="http://schemas.xmlsoap.org/soap/envelope/">

    <soap-env:Header>

        <auth:AuthID xmlns:auth="my-URI">

        Admin
```

```
        </auth:AuthID>
    </soap-env:Header>
</soap-env:Envelope>
```

In this example, you can see the use of the *soap-env* namespace prefix against the *Header* element, allowing it to be recognized as a SOAP header. Within the header is an additional element defining a new namespace with a prefix *"auth"* and a URI of *"my-URI"*. Such a namespace can be defined by anybody. The main thing is that, though it is preferable that the namespace will be globally unique, it must at least be unique within the environment in which it will be used. For this reason, our example code will make use of a namespace URI *"www.syngress.com/JWSDP/soap-example"*—this can be relied on as being globally unique as long as someone within the Syngress organization ensures that it is locally unique.

The actual element name used in this example (*AuthID*) indicates that it contains authentication information. If the message's receiver understands what the *AuthID* element means (within the defined namespace), it should process the element, in this case by checking that *Admin* is an authorized account name. If the receiver of this message does not know how to process the element, it can be ignored.

Bodies

The Body element must exist in a SOAP message (as an immediate child element of the Envelope), and can contain various kinds of information such as information being requested or returned, or error information. If error information is being transmitted in a SOAP message, it is carried using an optional entry within the Body element known as a SOAP *Fault*.

An envelope containing a simple *Body* element containing the time may look like this:

```
<soap-env:Envelope xmlns:soap-
env="http://schemas.xmlsoap.org/soap/envelope/">
    <soap-env:Body>
        <x:CurrentTime xmlns:x="my-URI">
        23:12:17
        </x:CurrentTime>
    </soap-env:Body>
</soap-env:Envelope>
```

Attachments

SOAP Messages with Attachments extend SOAP's basic model of a single XML document by adding one or more attachments, each of which can contain content that is not restricted to being XML.

You may wonder why it is so important for a message to contain attachments. The answer lies in the fact that a standard SOAP message must contain only XML, and that sometimes it may be desirable for a message to contain another form of data.

As an example, consider a web service that provides information on the surf conditions for beaches local to a particular city. You can readily imagine SOAP being employed to allow people to send a message that requested the conditions at a particular beach; the response could very easily contain a textual description along the lines of "Comfortable water temperature, waves up to 3 feet, no wind" or "Treacherous conditions—BEACH CLOSED."

Imagine then if this very useful web service was to be upgraded; Maybe the town council installed digital cameras at each of the beaches. The web service would then provide not only a textual description of the surfing conditions, but a snapshot photograph of the beach as well, transmitted as a JPEG binary. That's all well and good, but how do you transmit a JPEG within a SOAP message? Obviously there's no problem sending such photographs over HTTP using MIME encoding, but the XML-only nature of the SOAP standard doesn't allow for it.

The answer is the optional use of attachments. If a message can be transmitted as a pure SOAP message containing only XML, then the *SOAPMessage* will contain just the SOAP content. However, if the message is to also contain attachments, the *SOAPMessage* will actually be a MIME-encoded message containing the SOAP content and one or more attachments of any type. So SOAP messages effectively fall into two distinct categories:

- Messages that contain only XML content and are not MIME-encoded.
- Messages that are MIME-encoded, and that contain an initial XML payload as well as any number of attachments. These attachments could each contain any kind of data; it may be text data, it may be images, it may be audio, video—anything.

SOAPElement and JAXM DOM

As soon as you start working with JAXM's DOM implementation you will notice some similarities and some very obvious differences between it and the W3C DOM implementation as used by JAXP. It seems perhaps unnecessary to have this additional DOM implementation when a W3C DOM implementation will most likely will be available along with any JAXM implementation. The reason for this is purely historical; the JAXM work was performed as a JCP effort in parallel to the JAXP work. However, until such time as the JAXM API supports JAXP more closely you will have to learn this additional specification if you intend to program with JAXM.

SOAPElement

The *java.xml.soap.SOAPElement* interface is a key interface in the JAXM DOM API. *SOAPElement* has a lot in common with the *org.w3c.dom.Element* interface that was covered in the chapter on JAXP. As mentioned, however, there are a number of differences.

When you first look at the two interfaces side by side, some differences become immediately obvious. These include differences in the names of methods (*addAttribute* in *SOAPElement* versus *setAttribute* in *Element*). Another difference is that the *org.w3c.dom.Element* interface contains a number of near-duplicate methods (those with the "NS" suffixes) for supporting operations involving namespace-qualified names rather than local names; the *SOAPElement* approach is to use a single method for each operation and to use a *Name* parameter to represent either a local name or a namespace-qualified name (although there is some inconsistency in this, as there are overloaded variants of the *addChildElement* method for specifying local names or namespace-qualified names). The *Name* interface will be examined below.

SOAPElement is the direct superinterface for most of the SOAP objects in the JAXM API. We have already seen that a SOAP message contains such components as an envelope, a header (perhaps), and a body; we will shortly see that the JAXM API represents these with interfaces named *SOAPEnvelope*, *SOAPHeader*, *SOAPBody* and the like. Each of these interfaces is a subinterface of *SOAPElement* and therefore most of the work you do in manipulating and reading from these components will be done via methods of the *SOAPElement* interface.

Attributes

The *SOAPElement* interface provides several methods for adding, retrieving and removing attributes of an element—Table 6.1 lists these methods.

Table 6.1 SOAPElement Methods for Adding, Retrieving and Removing Attributes

Method	Description
SOAPElement addAttribute(Name name, java.lang.String value)	Add a new attribute to an element. As already mentioned, the *name* parameter allows either a local name or a namespace-qualified name to be specified.
java.util.Iterator getAllAttributes()	Retrieves the list of all attributes of an element by returning an iterator over the names of those attributes. For each of those names, *getAttributeValue* can be used to retrieve the values individually. Each element returned by the iterator will be an object of type *Name*.
java.lang.String getAttributeValue(Name name)	Retrieves the value of an attribute by local or namespace-qualified name.
boolean removeAttribute(Name name)	Deletes an attribute by local or namespace-qualified name.

Child Elements

The JAXM DOM implementation also provides a set of methods for adding, retrieving and removing child elements of an *SOAPElement*, as listed in Table 6.2.

Table 6.2 SOAPElement Methods for Adding, Retrieving and Removing Child Elements

Method	Description
SOAPElement addChildElement(Name name)	Adds a new child element to an *SOAPElement* with either a local name or a namespace-qualified name.
SOAPElement addChildElement(SOAPElement element)	Takes an already-created *SOAPElement* object and adds it as a child element.
SOAPElement addChildElement(java.lang.String localName)	Adds a new child element to an *SOAPElement* with a local name.
SOAPElement addChildElement(java.lang.String localName, java.lang.String prefix)	Adds a new child element to an *SOAPElement* with a local name and namespace prefix.
SOAPElement addChildElement(java.lang.String localName, java.lang.String prefix, java.lang.String uri)	Adds a new child element to an *SOAPElement* with a namespace-qualified name.
java.util.Iterator getChildElements()	Gets all of the child elements of an *SOAPElement* by returning an iterator over the elements.
java.util.Iterator getChildElements(Name name)	Gets all of the child elements of an *SOAPElement* that match a certain name (local or namespace-qualified) by returning an iterator over the matching elements.
void detachNode()	Inherited from the *javax.xml.soap.Node* interface (which is the direct superinterface of *SOAPElement*), allows an element to be deleted from the tree.
void recycleNode()	Also inherited from *Node*, this method should *only* be called after calling *detachNode*, and notifies the JAXM implementation that the object is no longer being

Continued

Table 6.2 Continued

Method	Description
	used and can be re-used for elements that may be created in the future.
void setParentElement(SOAPElement parent)	By setting the parent element of a child element, it is possible to move a child element around within the tree.

As an example, the following code can be used to remove from a SOAP Body all of the child elements that have the local name *"category"*:

```
// soapMsg is an SOAPMessage object
SOAPPart part = soapMsg.getSOAPPart();
SOAPEnvelope env = part.getEnvelope();
SOAPBody body = env.getBody();
Name nm = env.createName("category");
Iterator it = body.getChildElements(nm);
while (it.hasNext()) {
    SOAPElement child = (SOAPElement)it.next();
    child.detachNode();
    child.recycleNode();
}
```

Text Nodes

Text nodes are another area where the JAXM DOM implementation differs from that of JAXP. A text node is added to a *SOAPElement* by calling the *addTextNode* method and passing in the text data as the parameter. The data can be read out of a text node by calling the *getValue* method. As an example, the following code adds a child element with a local name of *"bodytype"* and a text node of *"saloon"*.

```
// body is an SOAPBody object
SOAPElement child;
child = body.addChildElement("bodytype");
child.addTextNode("saloon");
```

After this code has been executed, the *child* object will represent the following XML:

```
<bodytype>saloon</bodytype>
```

Likewise, to read the data back from this text node, you would call *getValue* against the immediate parent element of the text node, in this case the *child* object as follows:

```
String textVal = child.getValue();
```

The *getValue* method will only return data if the immediate child element is a text node, otherwise it will return *null*.

Name

Name objects represent XML names, which may be either local names , or namespace-qualified. As mentioned above, the use of the *Name* interface in the JAXM API simplifies the DOM implementation(especially in terms of the number of methods required for the *SOAPElement* interface).

Name objects need to be created using a *SOAPEnvelope* object, which will be described below. The *SOAPEnvelope* object represents the *Envelope* in a SOAP message; whether you are building a SOAP message to transmit or are parsing a received SOAP message you will always have access to a *SOAPEnvelope* object. The following code can be used to create both local and namespace-qualified *Name* objects:

```
// soapMsg is an SOAPMessage
SOAPPart part = soapMsg.getSOAPPart();
SOAPEnvelope env = part.getEnvelope();


Name localName = env.createName("model");


Name nsName = env.createName(
    "RequestMakeAndModel",
    "mkt",
    "http://www.mydomain.com/market");
```

In the example above, the *localName* object will represent the local name *"model"*. The *nsName* object, on the other hand, will represent a namespace-qualified name with a local name of *"RequestMakeAndModel"*, a prefix of *"mkt"*, and a URI of *"http://www.mydomain.com/market"*. This would be represented in XML as:

```
<mkt:RequestMakeAndModel xmlns:mkt="http://www.mydomain.com/market">
```

Text

The *Text* interface models text nodes; the *Text* object is created when a text node is added to an element via the *addTextNode* method. It is also possible for a *Text* object to represent a comment; the *isComment* method is available to determine whether this is the case.

JAXM SOAP Elements

The SOAP specification defines a very clear structure of elements: *Envelope, Header, Body, Fault,* and the like; the specification for SOAP Messages with Attachments extends this structure. In this section we will cover the JAXM API's representation of all of these elements as Java types, and we will also see that JAXM provides a few additional elements that do not map exactly to elements within the SOAP specification but which are used to enable messages, both with and without attachments, to be represented in a unified object structure.

SOAPMessage

The *javax.xml.soap.SOAPMessage* class is the root class for all JAXM SOAP messages. The *SOAPMessage* class is slightly different to the majority of the JAXM SOAP classes in that it doesn't map directly to the SOAP standard hierarchy—in fact, it represents a layer on top of the SOAP standard with one specific purpose: to allow a message to contain attachments, conforming to the *SOAP Messages with Attachments* specification.

Figure 6.2 shows an example of the first kind of message—it contains SOAP content as XML and is not MIME encoded.

Figure 6.2 SOAPMessage Containing Only SOAP Content

Figure 6.3 shows the second kind of message. The message is MIME encoded and contains SOAP content followed by at least one attachment of any multi-media type.

Figure 6.3 SOAPMessage Containing One or More Attachments

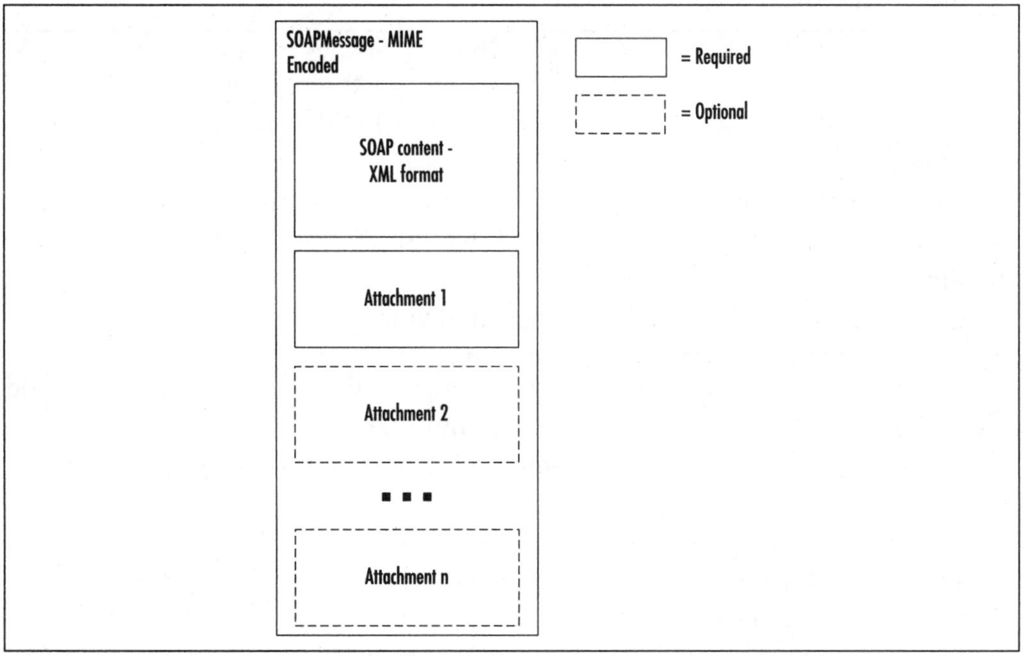

MIME encoding

Multi-purpose Internet Mail Extensions (MIME) is a set of specifications with the purpose of transferring text using different character sets, as well as transfer-ring multi-media data between computers.

As its name implies, MIME was originally designed to facilitate the transfer of data via e-mail; it is MIME that allows all kinds of multimedia e-mail attachments to be transmitted. However, MIME is also very useful for the interchange of data via other means, from the downloading of various types of data to web browsers through to such uses as transmitting various attachments with SOAP messages.

If you examine a MIME-encoded message, you will see that MIME is really a way of labeling parts of a message so that they can be handled in the correct way. For example, if a web browser sees MIME content marked as *image/jpeg*, it knows that the content is to be displayed as a binary JPEG image.

One of the great features of MIME encoding is that various parts of a mes-sage can be labeled as having different content types, and it is this feature that allows multiple attachments of varying content types to co-exist in a SOAP message. Some of the many possible content types are listed in Table 6.3.

Table 6.3 Examples of MIME Content Types

Content Type/Subtype	Description
text/xml	XML text. This will always be the content type for the SOAP part of the message; it is also a valid type for attachments.
text/plain	Plain text.
application/octet-stream	A stream of bytes representing raw binary data; serves as a default type for binary data.
image/gif	GIF image data.
video/mpeg	MPEG-encoded video.

If we create an *SOAPMessage* and populate it with very simple data, then add some kind of attachment, the message will immediately be MIME-encoded: the SOAP part will be marked with a content type of *text/xml*, while the attachment will be marked with its appropriate type.

Note that within a multipart MIME-encoded message, there can be several different types of MIME headers: the *Content-Type* header defines the MIME type, while the *Content-ID* header allows the part to be referenced by other MIME parts, whereas the *Content-Location* header can be used to enable a MIME part to be referenced by HTML MIME parts. For this reason, *SOAPPart* contains methods for manipulating the *Content-ID* and *Content-Location* headers, but does not provide for manipulation of the *Content-Type* header since the MIME type is fixed to *text/xml*.

The following output shows the content of a sample message. There are clearly two parts to this message; the first is obviously the SOAP content itself (in this case with some added formatting for clarity) and the second part is marked as plain text and carries the *Sample attachment content* data:

```
------=_Part_0_7615385.1014026663603
Content-Type: text/xml

<soap-env:Envelope xmlns:soap-env="http://schemas.xmlsoap.org/soap/
        envelope/">
    <soap-env:Header/>
    <soap-env:Body>
```

```
        <sample:SimpleExample xmlns:sample="http://my.domain/myuri/">
            <name>example</name>
        </sample:SimpleExample>
    </soap-env:Body>
</soap-env:Envelope>
------=_Part_0_7615385.1014026663603
Content-Type: text/plain

Sample attachment content
------=_Part_0_7615385.1014026663603--
```

In contrast to the above message, a message with no attachments will actually contain no MIME information at all, as shown in this sample content:

```
<soap-env:Envelope xmlns:soap-
env="http://schemas.xmlsoap.org/soap/envelope/">
    <soap-env:Header/>
    <soap-env:Body>
        <sample:SimpleExample xmlns:sample="http://my.domain/myuri/">
            <name>example</name>
        </sample:SimpleExample>
    </soap-env:Body>
</soap-env:Envelope>
```

NOTE

The above examples demonstrate messages that can clearly be sent as text. However, what happens if we need to add an attachment that clearly does not contain text data (such as a JPEG image)? The answer is that the data will be *Base64*-encoded; Base 64 is a scheme that uses four characters to encode each group of three bytes, thus enabling binary data to be represented by all variants of ASCII and EBCDIC text encoding.

SOAPPart

The *javax.xml.soap.SOAPPart* class is very similar to the *SOAPMessage* class in that it does not map directly to an element within the SOAP specification.

Instead, *SOAPPart* represents the part of a message carrying the SOAP payload, as opposed to any attachments that may be carried by the message.

Every SOAP Message must contain a *SOAPPart*. Furthermore, since the SOAP component of a message must be in XML format, the *SOAPPart* will always contain a *Content-Type* MIME header with a value of "text/xml." Note that you do not need to explicitly create the *SOAPPart*; once an *SOAPMessage* is created, you can simply retrieve the *SOAPPart* from it.

The *SOAPPart* interface, as well as extending the *SOAPElement* interface described above, defines the methods listed in Table 6.4. Note also that, in common with the *SOAPMessage* class, *SOAPPart* is an abstract class; you should always obtain a *SOAPPart* object from a corresponding *SOAPMessage* object.

Table 6.4 SOAPPart Methods

Method	Description
void addMimeHeader(java.lang.String name, java.lang.String value)	Creates a new *MimeHeader* object and adds it to the *SOAPPart*.
Java.util.Iterator getAllMimeHeaders()	Returns an iterator over all of the *MimeHeader* objects attached to this *SOAPPart*.
Source getContent()	Returns the *SOAPEnvelope* content as a *javax.xml.transform.Source* object, as covered in the chapter on JAXP.
java.lang.String getContentId()	Retrieves the value of a specific MIME Header—that with the name "Content-Id"
java.lang.String getContentLocation()	Retrieves the value of a specific MIME Header—that with the name "Content-Location"
SOAPEnvelope getEnvelope()	Returns the SOAPEnvelope object.
java.util.Iterator getMatchingMimeHeaders (java.lang.String[] names)	Returns an iterator over all of the *MimeHeader* objects that match one of the names in the array.
java.lang.String[] getMimeHeader(java.lang.String name)	Returns an array of values for MIME Headers that match the name.
java.util.Iterator getNonMatchingMimeHeaders (java.lang.String[] names)	Returns an iterator over all of the *MimeHeader* objects that do *not* match one of the names in the array.

Continued

Table 6.4 Continued

Method	Description
Void removeAllMimeHeaders()	Removes all of the *MimeHeader* objects from the *SOAPPart*.
void removeMimeHeader (java.lang.String header)	Remove any MimeHeader objects that match the name.
Void setContent(Source source) Envelope from a JAXP Source object.	Populates the content of the SOAP
void setContentId(java.lang.String contentId)	Sets the value of a specific MIME Header—that with the name "Content-Id"
void setContentLocation (java.lang.String contentLocation)	Sets the value of a specific MIME Header—that with the name "Content-Location"
void setMimeHeader(java.lang.String name, java.lang.String value)	Sets the value of the first matching existing MIME Header matching a certain name to a certain value. If no matching header exists, a new one will be created and added.

SOAPEnvelope

Unlike *SOAPMessage* and *SOAPPart*, both of which do not strictly map to the SOAP specification, the interface *javax.xml.soap.SOAPEnvelope* maps to the specification exactly—a *SOAPEnvelope* object is a representation of a SOAP Envelope.

Just as the SOAP specification states that an Envelope may contain a header and must contain a body, a *SOAPEnvelope* can contain objects representing the header and body. A newly-created message's default behavior is that it will contain a *SOAPEnvelope* that in turn will contain an empty header and body. In the following chapter we will show that Profiles can be used to generate messages that adhere to higher-level protocols (such as ebXML), and that such messages may be generated with additional elements specific to that protocol.

The *SOAPEnvelope* is a subtype of *SOAPElement* and therefore inherits the DOM functionality of that interface. Additionally, an *SOAPEnvelope* object will implement the methods listed in Table 6.5.

Table 6.5 SOAPEnvelope Methods

Method	Description
SOAPBody addBody()	Adds a new Body to the Envelope if none already exists, otherwise throws an exception. You would not normally need to call this explicitly as the Envelope should contain a Body by default after creation.
SOAPHeader addHeader()	Adds a new Header to the Envelope if none already exists, otherwise throws an exception. You would not normally need to call this explicitly as the Envelope should contain a Header by default after creation.
Name createName (java.lang.String localName)	As described above, the Name object can represent a local or a namespace-qualified name. This method will create a local name.
Name createName (java.lang.String localName, java.lang.String prefix, java.lang.String uri)	Creates a namespace-qualified name.
SOAPBody getBody()	Provides access to the Body element.
SOAPHeader getHeader()	Provides access to the Header element.

SOAPHeader and *SOAPHeaderElement*

The *javax.xml.soap.SOAPHeader* interface is designed to represent a SOAP Header, and accordingly, the *javax.xml.soap.SOAPHeaderElement* interface represents elements within that Header.

SOAPHeader, in common with all of the SOAP element interfaces, is a subtype of *SOAPElement*, but in addition it defines a number of methods that are described in Table 6.6.

Table 6.6 SOAPHeader Methods

Method	Description
SOAPHeaderElement addHeaderElement (Name name)	Creates a new *Header* Element, initialized with the local or namespace-qualified name, and inserts it into the Header.
java.util.Iterator examineHeaderElements (java.lang.String actor)	Returns an iterator over all of the *Header* Elements that match the specified actor.

Continued

Table 6.6 Continued

Method	Description
java.util.Iterator extractHeaderElements (java.lang.String actor)	Returns an iterator over the exact same set of *Header* Elements as the above method, but additionally detaches them from the *Header*.

Similarly to *SOAPHeader*, *SOAPHeaderElement* defines certain methods in addition to those defined by *SOAPElement*, as listed in Table 6.7

Table 6.7 SOAPHeaderElement Methods

Method	Description
java.lang.String getActor()	Returns the URI representation of the actor associated with this element.
Boolean getMustUnderstand()	Returns the value of the *mustUnderstand* attribute for this element. A value of 1 represents true; a value of 0 or a non-existent attribute represents false.
void setActor(java.lang.String actorURI)	Sets the URI representation of the actor associated with this element.
void setMustUnderstand(boolean mustUnderstand)	Sets the value of the *mustUnderstand* attribute for this element. A value of 1 represents true; a value of 0 or a non-existent attribute represents false.

This is the first time we have mentioned the term *Actor*. An Actor simply describes to whom an element in a SOAP Header is addressed. It is specified as an attribute of the element (called *actor*), and its value is a URI. In an asynchronous message which is routed via multiple parties, Actors can be used to specify that certain header elements in the message are addressed to certain parties even though the message itself is ultimately being sent to another destination. For more information on Actors, refer to the SOAP specification.

In order to add content to a header Element you would generally use the JAXM DOM implementation, as defined through the *SOAPElement* interface, in combination with the specific methods in the *SOAPHeaderElement* interface for setting certain attributes (namely the *actor* and *mustUnderstand* attributes).

SOAPBody, SOAPBodyElement and *SOAPFault*

As with the interfaces described above for dealing with SOAP Headers, the *javax.xml.soap.SOAPBody* interface is intended to model the Body within a SOAP Message and the *javax.xml.soap.SOAPBodyElement* interface is designed to model elements within that SOAP Body.

In the same way as the interfaces that model the other elements of a SOAP Message, the *SOAPBody* and *SOAPBodyElement* interfaces are subtypes of *SOAPElement*, although only *SOAPBody* defines additional methods. Table 6.8 lists the methods defined by *SOAPBody*.

Table 6.8 SOAPBody Methods

Method	Description
SOAPBodyElement addBodyElement(Name name)	Creates a new *Body* Element, initialized with the local or namespace-qualified name, and inserts it into the Body.
SOAPFault addFault()	Creates a new Fault and inserts it into the Body. There should only ever be one SOAP Fault in any message.
SOAPFault getFault()	Returns the *SOAPFault* object that is attached to the Body if one exists, otherwise returns null.
boolean hasFault()	Returns true if the Body contains a SOAP Fault, otherwise returns false.

You will recall from the introductory discussion above that each SOAP Message may convey error information in the form of a Fault, and a maximum of one Fault element may exist in a particular SOAP Message. Also, if a SOAP Fault element does exist, it will exist as a direct child element of the Body.

javax.xml.soap.SOAPFault models a SOAP element. This interface is a direct subinterface of *SOAPBodyElement* and as such also extends the *SOAPElement* interface. However, unlike *SOAPBodyElement*, *SOAPFault* defines a number of additional methods, which are listed in Table 6.9.

Table 6.9 SOAPFault Methods

Method	Description
Detail addDetail()	Creates a new *Detail* object and adds it to the Fault. There may only be one *Detail* object attached to a Fault.
Detail getDetail()	Returns the Detail object attached to the Fault.
java.lang.String getFaultActor()	Returns the URI of the Actor to which the Fault is addressed.
java.lang.String getFaultCode()	Returns the Fault Code of the Fault.
java.lang.String getFaultString()	Returns the Fault String of the Fault.
void setFaultActor (java.lang.String faultActor)	Sets the URI of the Actor to which the Fault is addressed.
void setFaultCode (java.lang.String faultCode)	Sets the Fault Code.
void setFaultString (java.lang.String faultString)	Sets the Fault String.

The *Detail* object will be an instance of the *javax.xml.soap.Detail* interface, which allows any number of Detail Entries to be added through the *addDetailEntry* method, and also returns an iterator over those entries via the *getDetailEntries* method. The example code in this chapter will demonstrate how to extract information from a SOAP Fault. and You will see how to add this Fault information to a SOAP Message when we develop the SOAP Sevice in the next chapter.

Creating a SOAP Message

As well as providing the above API, JAXM also defines the concept of a *Provider*. A JAXM Provider is a type of service that can provide several tasks, including providing a store-and-forward mechanism for guaranteeing delivery of asynchronous SOAP Messages. A *Provider* is not actually part of the API; it will normally exist as a servlet or some other form of service within your J2EE container. The JAXM API provides mechanisms that enable your container-hosted application to connect to a Provider and send messages to it, and the *provider* will route incoming messages to your application. However, the actual implementation of the Provider and its capabilities are up to the specific vendor.

A JAXM Provider can only be used by applications running in a container. Does this mean that standalone Java programs cannot communicate using SOAP?

Not at all; it simply means that they are restricted to not using a Provider and therefore must communicate synchronously. This chapter focuses on these types of applications—in the next chapter we will deal with interacting with JAXM Providers in more detail.

Since the JAXM classes we have just looked at cannot be directly instantiated (*SOAPMessage* is an abstract class, *SOAPHeader*, *SOAPBody* etc. are interfaces), there is a requirement for a factory to produce the objects to build a usable SOAP message, in much the same way as factories are used with JAXP.

JAXM factories are provided by the underlying implementation to provide objects of implementation-specific classes; the interface types (Java interfaces or abstract classes) represent the specification, and what comes out of the factory is an object that conforms to that specification, though the actual implementation of that object may vary wildly from one vendor's implementation to another. We know that the object we request from the factory will implement all of the behaviors described above; exactly how it implements these and therefore how it may perform in terms of speed, memory usage, or any number of characteristics is entirely determined by the specific implementation of the JAXM API.

MessageFactory

The actual factory that will produce our *SOAPMessage* objects is called *MessageFactory*. A *MessageFactory* object is capable of producing *SOAPMessage* objects, which will each contain a certain set of objects (such as *SOAPHeader*). Additional objects are created in a hierarchical fashion, so that *SOAPHeaderElement* objects are created by *SOAPHeader* objects, for example.

The first step in constructing a JAXM SOAP message is to obtain a *MessageFactory*. This can be done a couple of ways:

- If the application is running in a container and making use of a JAXM Provider, the application will use its connection with the Provider to request a message factory. This scenario will be covered in the following chapter.

- If the application is not using a Provider, a static member of the *MessageFactory* class can be called to return a message factory instance. This is the scenario on which we will focus in this chapter.

Using the static member, we can create the factory as follows:

```
MessageFactory msgFactory = MessageFactory.newInstance();
```

A *MessageFactory* instance is used to generate SOAP messages (instances of *SOAPMessage*), and these messages will be formatted according to the properties of the *MessageFactory* itself. To create a message, the following code can be called:

```
SOAPMessage soapMsg = msgFactory.createMessage();
```

A successful call to *createMessage()* will always generate a *SOAPMessage* object with the following properties:

- A *SOAPPart* object (containing the *SOAPEnvelope* object).

- A *SOAPEnvelope* object (containing the *SOAPHeader* and *SOAPBody* objects).

- A *SOAPHeader* object, which may contain different information depending on the profile configured for the *MessageFactory*, so the header will be different for a SOAP message than for an ebXML message.

- A *SOAPBody* object.

Developing & Deploying…

Message Factories—Where can I get one?

Not only do JAXM Providers implement a store-and-forward mechanism for taking care of routing asynchronous messages to their destination and guaranteeing their delivery, but they also provide a concept known as *Profiles*—that is, they can manage the various protocols (such as ebXML) that are built on top of SOAP.

In this chapter we examine how to obtain a *MessageFactory* object by calling the *MessageFactory.newInstance* method. However, this is really only half the story. Such a factory object can only be used by JAXM applications that are communicating synchronously without the services of a JAXM Provider (such as the client application example described in this chapter).

However, if an application wishes to create messages that will be routed via a JAXM Provider, the application will have to use a different mechanism to obtain a *MessageFactory* object. The JAXM API provides a way for applications to communicate with Providers via a *ProviderConnection* object. This connection can then be used to request a *MessageFactory* instance; this is done by calling the

Continued

ProviderConnection.createMessageFactory method. In the next chapter we will examine more specifically how to create a connection to a Provider, and how to use the connection to request a factory. In this chapter we will continue to focus on applications that do not make use of a Provider.

Creating SOAP Parts, Envelopes, Headers and Bodies

For a standard SOAP profile, the *MessageFactory* will return a message object that has a skeleton body and header, as well as their enclosing envelope and *SOAPPart*. The actual SOAP XML will look like this (some carriage returns have been added for clarity):

```
<soap-env:Envelope xmlns:soap-
env="http://schemas.xmlsoap.org/soap/envelope/">
<soap-env:Header/>
<soap-env:Body/>
</soap-env:Envelope>
```

Therefore, we do not need to actually create these elements, but rather populate them with meaningful information.

Since the message factory will return messages that always create a *SOAPPart* object, we simply need to access that object through the message itself. This is done as follows:

```
SOAPPart soapPart = soapMsg.getSOAPPart();
```

Once we have accessed the *SOAPPart* object, we can use it to access the envelope as in this piece of code:

```
SOAPEnvelope soapEnvelope = soapPart.getEnvelope();
```

Likewise, the envelope can be used to access both the header and the body. To access the header:

```
SOAPHeader soapHeader = soapEnvelope.getHeader();
```

The SOAP 1.1 specification describes an example header element that specifies a transaction. The name of the element is *"Transaction"* (qualified by a namespace with a prefix of *"t"* and a URI of *"some-URI"*), it contains a *mustUnderstand* attribute of 1, and a value of 5. The XML representation of a SOAP Header containing such an element would look like this:

```
<soap-env:Header>
    <t:Transaction xmlns:t="some-URI" soap-env:mustUnderstand="1">
        5
    </t:Transaction>
</soap-env:Header>
```

To add such an element to the header object obtained above using the JAXM API we could do the following:

```
// Use the Envelope to create a new
// namespace-qualified name.
Name elementName = soapEnvelope.createName("Transaction", "t", "some-URI");


// Add a new element to the Header
// using the name we just created.
SOAPHeaderElement headerElement = soapHeader.addHeaderElement(elementName);


// The SOAPHeaderElement interface
// provides a method for manipulating
// the mustUndertsand attribute.
headerElement.setMustUnderstand(true);


// The value is added as a text node.
headerElement.addTextNode("5");
```

From this code you can see the combined usage of specialist methods such as *setMustUnderstand* alongside the generic DOM methods from the *SOAPElement* interface, such as *addTextNode*.

As previously mentioned, the Envelope is also used to access the Body:

```
SOAPBody soapBody = soapEnvelope.getBody();
```

Adding elements to the Body is very similar to adding elements to the Header, although apart from SOAP Faults (which are a specific form of SOAP Body Element), all of the manipulation of these elements must be directly done through JAXM's DOM implementation.

Adding Attachments to Messages

As discussed above, attachments are optional components of SOAP messages. They can essentially be of any format, but with some restrictions:

- They must conform to the MIME standards; refer to RFC2045 at www.ietf.org/rfc/rfc2045.txt for more details. This RFC defines, amongst other things, how binary data is to be formatted and the specification of the MIME header.

- They must contain some form of content; an empty attachment is not valid.

- Each attachment must be preceded by the correct MIME header.

In terms of the JAXM API, attachments contain *AttachmentPart* objects, which are added to the *SOAPMessage* object. When the message is sent over the network, the *AttachmentPart* objects will follow the *SOAPPart* (which is the mandatory part of the message). You can add as many *AttachmentPart* objects as you like to a message, and the attachments can be of different MIME types.

Because attachments do not come into being by default when the factory spawns a new message, they must always be specifically created. The following code will add a new attachment to an existing message:

```
AttachmentPart attachmentPart = soapMsg.createAttachmentPart();
```

As already discussed, this is not yet a valid SOAP attachment because it does not have any content or a MIME header.

Once the *AttachmentPart* object has been created, we will have to populate its content and MIME header. Both of these actions can be accomplished with a call to a single method, defined as follows:

```
setContent(java.lang.Object object,
java.lang.String contentType)
```

The *object* parameter represents the content, and the *contentType* parameter will be used to determine how the *object* parameter is interpreted and to form the variable part of the *Content-Type* MIME header. As an example, the following code could be used to add a plain text attachment:

```
String contentString
// contentString populated with some data

. . .

attachmentPart.setContent(contentString, "text/plain");
```

In the above example, the string contents of *contentString* will form the attachment's content, and it will have a single header that looks like this:

```
Content-Type: text/plain
```

For other types of content (JPEG images for example), it is a little less obvious what form the content object should take; the solution to this will be covered below.

The JAXM specification requires that a minimum set of MIME types be supported, and that these map directly to certain Java types. In the above example we passed in a *java.lang.String* content object, along with a *text/plain* content type. This was possible because *text/plain* is one of the types that is required by the JAXM specification, and also because the specification states that this type maps to the Java type of *java.lang.String*. The full set of required MIME types and their corresponding Java types is listed in Table 6.10.

Table 6.10 MIME Types Required to be Implemented by the JAXM Specification

MIME Type	Java Type
text/plain	java.lang.String
multipart/*	javax.mail.internet.MimeMultipart
text/xml	javax.xml.transform.Source
application/xml	javax.xml.transform.Source

The JavaBeans Activation Framework (JAF) was developed as a standard Java extension to enable Java programs to bind appropriate components to typed data in much the same way as a web browser does when it automatically renders JPEG data as an image. JAXM relies on parts of the JAF to provide extensible support for MIME types, potentially providing for the use of many more types than those listed above.

Each *AttachmentPart* object contains a *javax.activation.DataHandler* member, which is typically created automatically by the call to *setContent* on the attachment. It is also possible to explicitly create the *DataHandler* object and assign it using a call to *setDataHandler* on the *AttachmentPart* object. The JAF ties data handlers to *CommandMap* objects; a command map is essentially a list of the available command objects registered on the system. Through this mechanism, additional MIME types can be supported. Note that more information on the JAF can be found at http://java.sun.com/products/javabeans/glasgow/jaf.html.

It is also possible to create an attachment of any MIME type at all (assuming that the service to which you are sending the attachment knows how to interpret it) through the use of input streams. The *InputStream* class and its subclasses can be used to create objects that represent the data as bytes. Recall from the example above that we were able to pass a *String* object into the first parameter of *setContent* when the second parameter specified a MIME Type of "text/plain." It is also possible to pass an instance of *InputStream* as the first parameter and to specify an appropriate MIME Type in the second parameter. As an example, a *FileInputStream* could be used to read a JPEG image file from disk and populate an attachment:

```
try {
    FileInputStream jpegData =
        new FileInputStream("image.jpg");
    attachmentPart.setContent(FileInputStream,
                              "image/jpeg");
} catch (IOException e) {
...
}
```

It is also possible to manually set the value of an existing *Content-Type* MIME Header on an attachment by calling *setContentType*.

In terms of clearing out the contents of an *AttachmentPart* object, the *clearContent* method can be called to remove the actual data from the attachment whil retaining the MIME Headers.

Bringing it all Together—
A Complete SOAP Client

In this section we will look at a real example of a SOAP client application. In the next chapter we will cover the server side of this example, so unfortunately you will have to wait until then to test the client.

Connecting to a SOAP service

This example will be a simple program that takes a single parameter, a name for which to search, and sends this to the server as a request parameter in a SOAP message. The server example in the next chapter will perform a search against the example XML file for the name, and if found return the corresponding value. If the name is not found in the XML file it will return a SOAP fault. The client will then display the returned value or fault details.

Even though this seems like a fairly simple example, it shows how readily a web service could be implemented using JAXM to perform any number of tasks. Instead of looking up a value in an XML file, it is easy to imagine a service that registers a new subscriber or looks up and returns the time that the next bus is due at a particular bus stop. Whatever the functionality of the service itself, the sending and receiving of SOAP messages is a similar process.

One thing that should be noted at this time is that SOAP services and clients can fall into several different categories; those that use a *provider* and those that do not, and those that run within a container and those that do not.

This example client application will neither make use of a provider nor run in a container, and is thus known as a *standalone* application. This is different to many of the examples in this book in that it can be implemented in J2SE and does not require any form of servlet or EJB container. There are a couple of limitations to standalone JAXM applications (since they do not have the benefit of a provider's functionality):

- Standalone applications can only send point-to-point; a single message can only be sent directly to a single service.

- Standalone applications can only send in a request/reply model; the client will send a message and block until a reply is received.

- Standalone applications cannot function as SOAP services; they can only operate as clients.

- Standalone applications can only communicate with a running service; since they do not access a provider, there is no store and forward mechanism.

The client will format and send a SOAP message containing a single request parameter, the name against which the service will look up a value. The message will comprise several parts:

- The SOAP envelope, which is the enclosing object.

- An empty SOAP header. This is not strictly required at all in the SOAP specification if no header information is being transmitted; however the JAXM implementation always creates a header when a new message is generated.

- A SOAP body.

- Inside the body, the request parameter. The request will be called *GetValueByName*, and we will specify an arbitrary namespace URI of *www.syngress.com/JWSDP/soap-example*. A child element called *name* will enclose a text element with the name itself.

The example below requests a look up of the name *Mickey*:

```
<soap-env:Envelope xmlns:soap-
env="http://schemas.xmlsoap.org/soap/envelope/">
    <soap-env:Header/>
    <soap-env:Body>
        <myns:GetValueByName xmlns:myns="www.syngress.com/JWSDP/soap-
example">
            <name>Mickey</name>
        </myns:GetValueByName>
    </soap-env:Body>
</soap-env:Envelope>
```

The response schema is similar, with the response being called *GetValueByNameResponse*. The response to the example shown above should look like this:

```
<soap-env:Envelope xmlns:soap-
env="http://schemas.xmlsoap.org/soap/envelope/">
    <soap-env:Header/>
    <soap-env:Body>
        <myns:GetValueByNameResponse
xmlns:myns="www.syngress.com/JWSDP/soap-example">
            <value>Mouse</value>
        </myns:GetValueByNameResponse>
    </soap-env:Body>
</soap-env:Envelope>
```

This example contains five Java source files. Because it is a standalone client and does not require a container, you should be able to compile it in a J2SE environment as long as you have the required libraries, which are available in Sun's Java Web Services Developer Pack. All of the classes have been organized into a single package (com.syngress.jwsdp.soap.client), and can be accessed from the Syngress Web site.

The executable class for this example will be called *Client*, in the package *com.syngress.jwsdp.soap.client*. The example will expect one (and only one) command-line parameter, which is the name that we are requesting the service to look up. If it does not receive a single parameter, the example will report an error and abort.

Assuming that the command-line parameter was successfully passed in, the *Client* constructor will go on to create a point-to-point connection specifying the service's URL as the endpoint. This connection is created by using a *ConnectionFactory* and also by specifying a *URLEndpoint* object constructed from a URL represented as a string. In the next chapter we will examine this process more closely and also contrast this with the process for sending messages via a JAXM Provider.

The outgoing message will then be created and an attempt made to send it to the service. Remember that because this example is not using a provider, it can only send synchronously and will block until it receives a response from the service.

Once a response is received, it is tested for the presence of a SOAP Fault. If fault information is found, the specifics of the fault are extracted and displayed. If no fault information is found then the lookup has been successful and the returned value is parsed out of the message and displayed.

```
/**
 * Client.java
 *
 */


package com.syngress.jwsdp.soap.client;


import javax.xml.messaging.URLEndpoint;
import javax.xml.soap.SOAPConnectionFactory;
import javax.xml.soap.SOAPConnection;
import javax.xml.soap.SOAPMessage;
import javax.xml.transform.Transformer;
import javax.xml.transform.TransformerFactory;
import javax.xml.transform.Source;
import javax.xml.transform.stream.StreamResult;
import com.syngress.jwsdp.soap.client.Fault;
import com.syngress.jwsdp.soap.client.RequestMessage;
```

```
public class Client {

    // Define the location of the service endpoint.
    // This will be determined by where you deploy
    // the servlet that will be developed in the
    // example in the next chapter.
    static final String SERVICE_ENDPOINT =
    "http://localhost:8888/Chapter8/servlet/chapter8.ReceiverServlet";

    public static void main(String args[]) {

        // We are expecting a single
        // command line argument; the
        // name to look up.
        if (1 != args.length) {
            System.err.println(
                "Usage: java " +
                "com.syngress.jwsdp.soap.client.Client <name>");
        } else {
            new Client(args[0]);
        }

    }

    public Client(String name) {

        try {

            // For a standalone client we need
            // to specify the URL of the
            // service.
            URLEndpoint endpoint =
                new URLEndpoint(
                    SERVICE_ENDPOINT);

            // A standalone client does not
            // use a provider; create a
```

```
// connection from a connection
// factory.
SOAPConnectionFactory scf =
    SOAPConnectionFactory.
        newInstance();
SOAPConnection connection =
    scf.createConnection();

// Create the request message using
// the command line parameter as
// the name to look up.
RequestMessage reqMsg =
    new RequestMessage();
reqMsg.setName(name);

// The call method will block
// until something is returned
// from the service.
SOAPMessage replySOAP =
    connection.call(
        reqMsg.getMessage(),
        endpoint);

// Test for the presence of
// fault information in the
// response.
if (Fault.hasFault(replySOAP)) {

    // Fault information exists,
    // indicating an error
    // response from the service.
    Fault fault =
        new Fault(replySOAP);

    System.err.println(
        "Received SOAP Fault");
    System.err.println(
```

```
                                    "Fault code: " +
                                    fault.getFaultCode());
                            System.err.println(
                                    "Fault string: " +
                                    fault.getFaultString());
                            System.err.println(
                                    "Fault detail: " +
                                    fault.getFaultDetail());

                    } else {

                            ResponseMessage respMsg = new ResponseMessage(replySOAP);
                            String responseValue = null;
                            try {
                                    responseValue = respMsg.getValue();
                                    System.out.println("Response: " + responseValue);
                            } catch(SchemaException e) {
                                    System.err.println("Parsing error");
                            }

                    }

                    connection.close();

            } catch(Exception e) {
                    System.err.println(e.toString());
            }
        }
}
```

The outgoing SOAP message is constructed in the *com.syngress.jwsdp.soap* *.client.RequestMessage* class. This example is a standalone client (making use of neither a J2EE container nor a JAXM provider), and therefore it will create messages using the default message factory.

Once the SOAP message is created, we need to add the request parameter to the Body. If we were performing a lookup against the name *Mickey*, the following content needs to be added to the Body:

```
<myns:GetValueByName xmlns:myns="www.syngress.com/JWSDP/soap-example">
<name>Mickey</name>
</myns:GetValueByName>
```

To add this content to the body using the JAXM DOM implementation, perform the following steps:

1. Add a new child element to the *SOAPBody* object with a name of *GetValueByName*, a prefix of *myns*, and a URI of *www.syngress.com/JWSDP/soap-example*.

2. Add a new child element to the element just added, with a local name of "name".

3. To that child element, add a text node with a value of *Mickey*.

```java
/**
 * RequestMessage.java
 *
 */

package com.syngress.jwsdp.soap.client;

import javax.xml.soap.MessageFactory;
import javax.xml.soap.SOAPMessage;
import javax.xml.soap.SOAPPart;
import javax.xml.soap.SOAPEnvelope;
import javax.xml.soap.SOAPBody;
import javax.xml.soap.SOAPElement;
import javax.xml.soap.SOAPException;

public class RequestMessage {

    // class to represent an outgoing
    // SOAP message that will request
    // a lookup of a value by a name.

    protected SOAPMessage soapMessage = null;

    public RequestMessage()
```

```java
        throws SOAPException {

        MessageFactory mf =
            MessageFactory.newInstance();

        // Because a standalone client does not
        // use a provider, the message is created
        // from the message factory.
        soapMessage = mf.createMessage();

    }

    public void setName(String name)
        throws SOAPException {

        // Set the request paramaeter; this
        // represents the name that we will
        // be requesting the service to look up.

        // Traverse the hierarchy of SOAP
        // objects to obtain the body.
        SOAPPart soapPart =
            soapMessage.getSOAPPart();
        SOAPEnvelope envelope =
            soapPart.getEnvelope();
        SOAPBody body =
            envelope.getBody();

        // Add the request element to the body,
        // using a namespace-qualified name.
        SOAPElement requestElement;
        requestElement = body.addChildElement(
            envelope.createName(
                "GetValueByName",
                "myns",
                "www.syngress.com/JWSDP/soap-example"));
```

```
        // The value of the name to look up

        // is added as a text node as a child of the

        // request element using a local name.

        SOAPElement paramElement;

        paramElement =

            requestElement.addChildElement("name");

        paramElement.addTextNode(name);


    }


    public SOAPMessage getMessage() {


        // Get the SOAP message

        return soapMessage;

    }

}
```

A result containing a valid response is processed in the *com.syngress.jwsdp.soap* *.client.ResponseMessage* class. The *getValue* method of this class will validate that the received message adheres to the expected schema, and if it does so it will extract the value returned from the service.

```
/**

 * ResponseMessage.java

 *

 */


package com.syngress.jwsdp.soap.client;


import javax.xml.soap.SOAPMessage;

import javax.xml.soap.SOAPPart;

import javax.xml.soap.SOAPEnvelope;

import javax.xml.soap.SOAPBody;

import javax.xml.soap.SOAPException;

import javax.xml.soap.SOAPElement;

import javax.xml.soap.Name;

import java.util.Iterator;

import com.syngress.jwsdp.soap.client.SchemaException;
```

```java
public class ResponseMessage {

    // Represents a SOAP message received
    // as a response from a service.

    protected SOAPMessage soapMessage = null;

    public ResponseMessage(SOAPMessage soapMessage) {
        this.soapMessage = soapMessage;
    }

    public String getValue()
            throws SchemaException,
                    SOAPException {

        // Get the value returned for
        // the request.

        String resp = null;

        // Navigate the hierarchy
        // of SOAP objects to
        // access the body.
        SOAPPart soapPart =
            soapMessage.getSOAPPart();
        SOAPEnvelope soapEnvelope =
            soapPart.getEnvelope();
        SOAPBody soapBody =
            soapEnvelope.getBody();

        // Search for the namespace-qualified
        // response element.
        Name name;
        name = soapEnvelope.createName(
                "GetValueByNameResponse",
                "myns",
                "www.syngress.com/JWSDP/soap-example");
```

```
// Ensure there is at least one
// such element.
Iterator valueRequests =
    soapBody.getChildElements(name);
if (! valueRequests.hasNext()) {

    // Schema is not valid
    throw(new SchemaException());
}


// Retrieve the first element
// and ensure it was the only
// one.
SOAPElement soapElement =
    (SOAPElement)valueRequests.next();
if (valueRequests.hasNext()) {

    // Schema is not valid
    throw(new SchemaException());
}


// The value should be in a
// child element of this one, with
// a local name of "value".
name = soapEnvelope.createName("value");
Iterator params;
params = soapElement.getChildElements(name);
if (! params.hasNext()) {

    // Schema is not valid
    throw(new SchemaException());
}


// Ensure there is only one such element.
SOAPElement paramElement =
    (SOAPElement)params.next();
if (params.hasNext()) {
```

```
                    // Schema is not valid
                    throw(new SchemaException());
            }

            // Extract the parameter.
            resp = paramElement.
                getValue();
            if (null == resp) {

                // Schema is not valid
                throw(new SchemaException());
            }


            // Schema was successfully validated
            // and the response parameter can
            // be returned.
            return resp;
        }
}
```

The method *getResponseValue()* throws the exception *SchemaException*. This exception is used to represent an error in parsing the incoming message—the message did not comply with the expected schema:

```
/**
 * SchemaException.java
 *
 */

package com.syngress.jwsdp.soap.client;

public class SchemaException extends Exception {

    // This exception is used to
    // indicate that the XML being
    // parsed did not conform to
    // the appropriate schema.
}
```

On the other hand, messages containing a fault will be processed by the *com.syngress.jwsdp.soap.client.Fault* class. You will recall that the SOAP specification requires that error information be transmitted within a SOAP Fault, which is an optional child envelope in a SOAP Envelope. A SOAP Fault is implemented by the JAXM API as an *SOAPFault* object, which is obtained by calling the *getFault* method of the *body* object; this method will not throw an exception if there is no fault information present, but will rather return a *null*.

The *Fault* class listed below includes the static *hasFault* method that is called first with the received message as the parameter. If this returns *true* we know the message is carrying fault information and we should construct a *Fault* object, then query it using the *getFaultCode*, *getFaultString*, and *getFaultDetail* methods to return the fault code, fault string, and possibly the fault detail—if one exists. A SOAP Fault can carry a number of detail records; for the sake of this sample we can assume that the service will never return more than one. Also, a SOAP Fault will not carry a detail unless the error resulted from the processing of the message's *Body* element.

```
/**
 * Fault.java
 *
 */


package com.syngress.jwsdp.soap.client;


import javax.xml.soap.SOAPMessage;

import javax.xml.soap.SOAPPart;

import javax.xml.soap.SOAPEnvelope;

import javax.xml.soap.SOAPBody;

import javax.xml.soap.SOAPFault;

import javax.xml.soap.SOAPException;

import javax.xml.soap.Detail;

import javax.xml.soap.DetailEntry;

import java.util.Iterator;


public class Fault {


    // Fault class should usually be
    // instantiated only if the message
```

```
        // contains fault information; use
        // Fault.hasFault to test for this.


    protected SOAPFault soapFault;


    public Fault(SOAPMessage msg)
            throws SOAPException {


        // Navigate the hierarchy of
        // SOAP objects to store
        // a reference to the fault objects
        // as it is commonly used within the class.
        SOAPPart soapPart = msg.getSOAPPart();
        SOAPEnvelope soapEnvelope =
            soapPart.getEnvelope();
        SOAPBody soapBody = soapEnvelope.getBody();
        soapFault = soapBody.getFault();
    }


    public static boolean hasFault(SOAPMessage msg)
            throws SOAPException {


        // Static utility function to determine
        // whether a SOAP message contains
        // fault information.


        // Navigate the hierarchy of
        // SOAP objects.
        SOAPPart soapPart = msg.getSOAPPart();
        SOAPEnvelope soapEnvelope =
            soapPart.getEnvelope();
        SOAPBody soapBody = soapEnvelope.getBody();


        // Query whether the Body contains
        // a SOAP Fault.
        return soapBody.hasFault();
```

```
    }

public String getFaultCode() {

    // Get the SOAP fault code
    return soapFault.getFaultCode();
}

public String getFaultString() {

    // Get the SOAP fault string
    return soapFault.getFaultString();
}

public String getFaultDetail() {

    // Get the SOAP fault detail.

    String ret = null;
    Detail detail = soapFault.getDetail();

    if (null != detail) {
        Iterator it =
            detail.getDetailEntries();

        // A fault can contain
        // multiple detail entries.
        // For the sake of the example,
        // assume there is a maximum of
        // one detail entry.
        if (it.hasNext()) {
            DetailEntry detEntry =
                (DetailEntry)it.next();
            ret = detEntry.getValue();
        }

    }
```

```
        return ret;
   }
}
```

Since this example is a standalone JAXM client that adheres to the request/reply model, you will not be able to run it until the service is running. The service will be covered in the next chapter, and once it is running you can run the client by executing:

```
java com.syngress.jwsdp.soap.client.Client <name>
```

Figure 6.4 shows the output from a successful execution; the client sent a request to the service to look up *Mickey* and the service responded with *Mouse*.

Figure 6.4 A Successful Execution of the Client

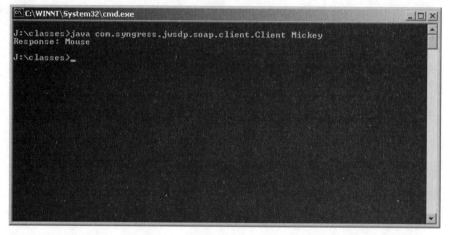

On the other hand, Figure 6.5 shows the results when a request is made to look up a name that cannot be found by the service; the client sent a request for *Donald*, and the service returned a SOAP Fault in its response.

Figure 6.5 SOAP Fault Returned from the Service

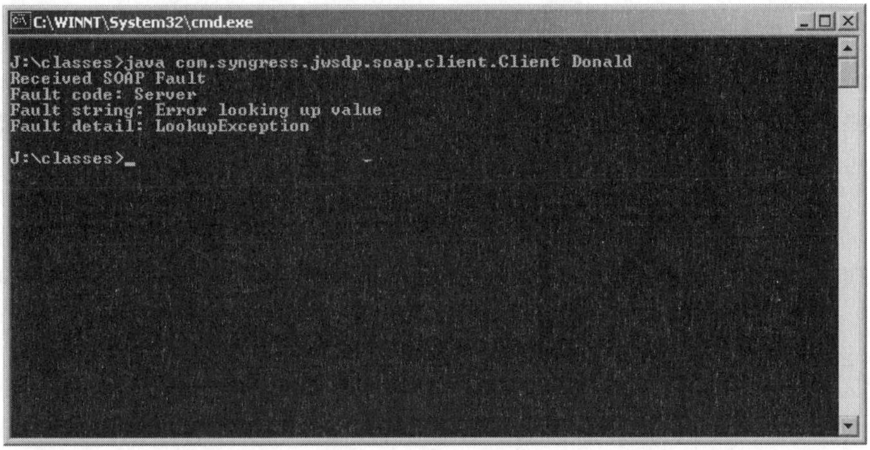

```
J:\classes>java com.syngress.jwsdp.soap.client.Client Donald
Received SOAP Fault
Fault code: Server
Fault string: Error looking up value
Fault detail: LookupException

J:\classes>_
```

Debugging...

Standalone JAXM Applications

One of the great advantages to building a standalone JAXM application, like the example developed in this chapter, is the simplicity of debugging. Because the application communicates synchronously by making a request and then waiting for a response message, issues such as trying to match up an incoming message with an outgoing request or debugging multiple threads do not need to be taken into account.

To debug the example from this chapter, you should be able to set a breakpoint at any appropriate point in Client.java and start the debugger. Just make sure that you configure the debugger to pass in the desired command-line parameter (specifying the name to send in the request), and make sure that the IDE is configured to use the libraries distributed with the Java Web Services Developer Pack.

Summary

In this chapter we covered an overview of SOAP, as well as looking in detail at how SOAP client applications can be developed using the JAXM API. We also developed a complete SOAP client application that communicates using the request–response model.

SOAP is an XML-based protocol that enjoys widespread industry support and that can enable information to be exchanged among distributed systems. Even though SOAP is XML-based, there is an additional specification that allows SOAP messages to contain attachments in a wide variety of formats including XML, plain text, or audio, picture, or video content.

JAXM, the Java API for XML Messaging, provides a unified API for creating either standard SOAP Messages or SOAP Messages with Attachments. JAXM provides an independent implementation of an XML document object model, which differs from that used by JAXP while maintaining similar capabilities. The API also provides a set of Java types that map directly to the elements of a SOAP message.

If a SOAP client does not use a container, it is known as a standalone application and it must communicate with a service synchronously (request/reply). We have explored an example of such an application, one that formats a request message and sends it to a service, then waits for a response. The response is decoded and either the returned value is displayed or any SOAP Fault information is extracted and displayed. In the next chapter we will cover an example service that can be used in conjunction with the client application.

Solutions Fast Track

Understanding SOAP

☑ SOAP is a lightweight XML-based protocol for information exchange among systems in a distributed environment.

☑ It is possible for SOAP to be used with many protocols (including TCP/IP), although its most common binding is with HTTP.

☑ Because of the lightweight nature of the SOAP protocol, it does not include a number of features found in some of the more complex distributed technologies.

☑ There is another specification known as *SOAP Messages with Attachments,* which enables SOAP messages to be carried within MIME multipart/ related messages and thus carry attachments in a similar way to email.

SOAPElement and JAXM DOM

☑ JAXM provides its own DOM implementation that is independent of the org.w3c.dom specification used by JAXP.

☑ The *SOAPElement* interface represents an XML element within a document and provides all of the methods required to manipulate such an element.

☑ All JAXM interfaces that represent elements of a SOAP message are subtypes of the *SOAPElement* interface.

JAXM SOAP Elements

☑ JAXM provides several interfaces, such as *SOAPMessage* and *SOAPPart,* to represent a SOAP Message that may or may not contain an attachment, as well as the actual SOAP part of such a message.

☑ Other elements, such as *SOAPEnvelope, SOAPHeader, SOAPBody* and the like, map directly to objects within the SOAP specification and can be manipulated via methods of the *SOAPElement* interface, as well as by some additional methods for specific functions.

☑ JAXM provides MIME functionality for adding and processing attach- ments through the use of the JavaBeans Activation Framework (JAF).

Creating a SOAP Message

☑ A *SOAPMessage* object needs to be created through a *factory* object, and the other elements can each be created by their parent elements.

☑ When an *SOAPMessage* object is created, it will contain an Envelope with an empty Header and a Body.

Bringing it all Together—A Complete SOAP Client

☑ The example client was created to run independently of a JAXM Provider or a container. Such a standalone client can only communicate using a synchronous request/reply model.

☑ The client application creates a new SOAP message requesting a value lookup against a command line-specified name, and waits to process the response from the server.

☑ The server-side of the example will be covered in the next chapter.

Frequently Asked Questions

The following Frequently Asked Questions, answered by the authors of this book, are designed to both measure your understanding of the concepts presented in this chapter and to assist you with real-life implementation of these concepts. To have your questions about this chapter answered by the author, browse to **www.syngress.com/solutions** and click on the **"Ask the Author"** form.

Q: Is SOAP specific to any particular vendor, platform, or programming language?

A: The answer to all of these is "No." SOAP enjoys the support of a very wide array of vendors, including Sun, Microsoft, IBM, Oracle, and many more. Additionally, any mainstream programming language could be used to implement SOAP communications. Implementations are available for such a diverse set of languages as Java, C++, Perl, Python, ADA, Visual Basic, and more.

Q: Does SOAP provide a security model?

A: The SOAP specification provides very little in the way of security considerations, but this does not mean that SOAP communications are inherently insecure. If SOAP is bound to HTTP, the same potential security vulnerabilities exist as with most other HTTP communications, but likewise the same security mechanisms (such as the use of Secure Sockets Layer, or SSL) can be used.

Q: Does SOAP have to operate over HTTP?

A: No, it is not mandatory for SOAP to be bound to HTTP; a SOAP message could readily be transmitted over SMTP or even a proprietary middleware protocol such as IBM's MQ Series. However, this would be dependant upon the ability for your JAXM Provider to support these bindings.

Q: Are there any SOAP mailing lists?

A: Yes, there are several; a good one is at http://discuss.develop.com/soap.html

Q: Are there any tools available to test SOAP services?

A: An organization called PushToTest publishes a free open-source framework called TestMaker, as well as a commercial product. Their website is at www.pushtotest.com

Q: Where can I find more detailed information on securing SOAP communications?

A: The IBM developerWorks site contains a very detailed article at www-106.ibm.com/developerworks/webservices/library/ws-soapsec/

Chapter 7

Writing SOAP Servers

Solutions in this chapter:

- **Message Routing**

- **Establishing a Connection to a JAXM Provider**

- **ProviderConnections**

- **Writing a SOAP Server Servlet**

- **Writing a SOAP EJB**

- **Example SOAP Servlet**

- ☑ **Summary**

- ☑ **Solutions Fast Track**

- ☑ **Frequently Asked Questions**

Introduction

Just as the last chapter looked at standalone SOAP clients, this chapter will explore hosted SOAP servers. You may recall we talked about the synchronous request–response model being the only model supported for standalone servers; this is because JAXM leverages a Java 2 Enterprise Edition (J2EE) container when routing messages for the more complicated SOAP usages. In particular, JAXM supports the routing of messages to message-driven EJBs and servlets.

In the JAXM model, the J2EE container has the additional responsibility of either being or hosting a SOAP Provider. SOAP providers form the underlying infrastructure for the routing of messages from remote clients to the message responder. They also provide for routing messages from the message responder to a different remote host; in this way J2EE-based SOAP servers can also act as SOAP clients.

In this chapter, we are going to explore the hosted SOAP environment, including connections to JAXM providers. Further, we will discuss imposing a standard set of body and header elements on a SOAP message. Known in JAXM as a *profile*, this allows for an explicit contract between a client and server without which there is no guarantee that a SOAP message would contain meaningful data in well-known locations. Profiles simplify the use of higher-level protocols such as ebXML; the profile acts to make sure that meaningful information is provided in a manner that is clear to both parties.

Message Routing

In the last chapter we focused on synchronous message routing (known as *request-response*), where the client sent a request message and blocked until some form of response came back from the service. We also saw that this request-response model was the only model supported for a standalone client (a JAXM SOAP client that did not run in an EJB or servlet container). In this section we will examine another model for SOAP communication using JAXM—*asynchronous messaging*. We will discuss the advantages of using an asynchronous message model, such as the ability to obtain guaranteed delivery and delayed responses; and we will also look at some of the complexities in the development of systems that implement this model.

Asynchronous messages

In terms of the actual SOAP specification, asynchronous SOAP messages are the more basic case; the fundamental mechanism for communicating via SOAP is one-way messaging, in which one system sends a message to another system without waiting for a response. There is nothing to say that an asynchronous system cannot include responses to messages; it is just that the sender is not reliant on an immediate response.

Figure 7.1 shows an example of a synchronous messaging system. The example shows a very familiar scenario: a web browser requesting a web page. In this scenario, the browser submits an HTTP request to the web server, requesting a specific HTML page. Once it has sent the request, the browser then waits until one of three things happens:

- It receives the HTTP response containing the HTML data.

- It receives an error, which could come from a number of sources, such as the web server or a proxy server.

- The request times out.

Figure 7.1 Example of Synchronous Messaging

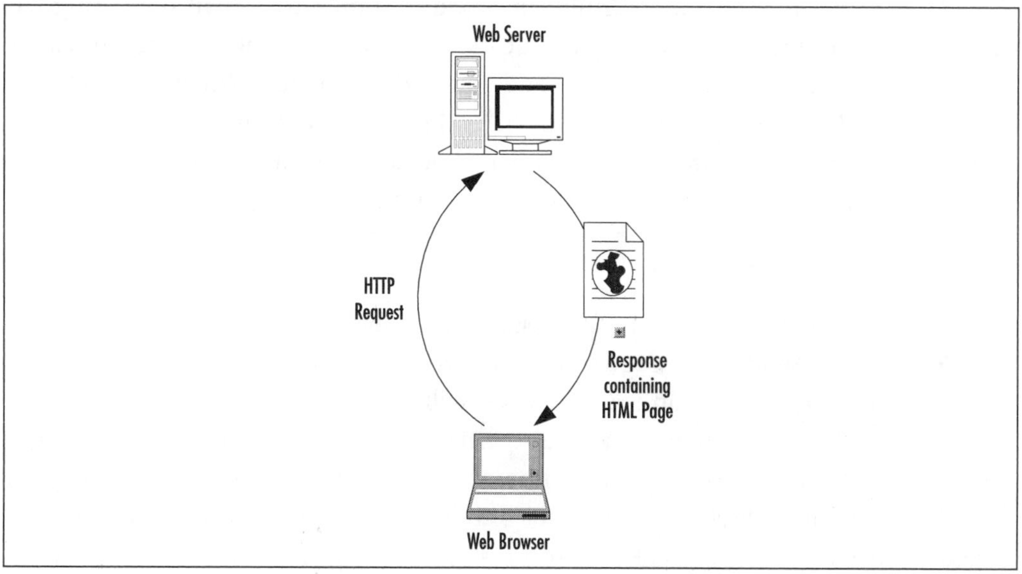

An example of an asynchronous messaging system is shown in Figure 7.2. This example should also be a very familiar scenario; Dave sends an e-mail to

Jean, asking if she'd like to meet for lunch. Jean is away from her computer for a few days and doesn't get to read the e-mail until the following week. During this time Dave (unless he is very anxious about the response to the e-mail) does not sit waiting for the response; he and his e-mail software are both free to do other things. Finally, Jean reads the e-mail and decides to send a response to Dave; yes, she would like to meet for lunch next Tuesday.

Figure 7.2 Example of Asynchronous Messaging

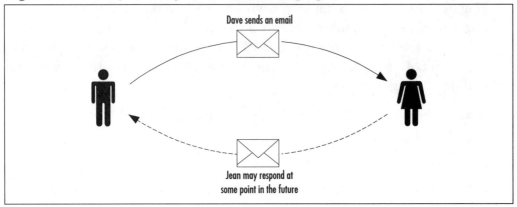

Asynchronous SOAP messaging can be quite similar to e-mail messaging (and in fact it is possible to use SMTP as a bearer for SOAP messages). The similarities are that messages are sent via a store-and-forward mechanism (such as a JAXM provider) and that the sender does not halt all other processing while it waits for a response. This clearly provides a number of advantages but also raises a few hurdles that will be discussed in the following section.

One-Way Messages

The simplest case of asynchronous messaging involves one-way messages. In this model, a system sends a message to another system—end of story. There is no expectation of a response, and no response will ever be sent.

You may wonder when a real-life scenario would work in this way. In fact, it's quite a common scenario, especially in terms of alerting and notification. Imagine a CRM (Customer Relationship Management) system that is used to collect and maintain information about the customers of an electricity company. If a customer rings up and asks for their address to be changed, we may want the CRM system to automatically notify the billing system of the change so that the customer's bills will be printed out with the correct address. This notification could certainly be done using a one-way SOAP message, and since we can rely on our JAXM provider to deliver the message, there is no need to expect any kind of response from the billing system.

This kind of example (where applications exchange data within an enterprise) is known as Enterprise Application Integration (EAI), and is increasingly becoming known as A2A (Application to Application) communication. This is definitely an area in which Web Services will be seen to play an increasing role in the near future.

Delayed Response Messages

Not all asynchronous messaging is truly one-way. There are many cases where asynchronous messaging involves sending a message and possibly receiving a response; this response may come almost immediately or after a very long delay, so under the asynchronous model we will not pause other processing while we wait for it.

Consider the case of an electronic marketplace, where a buyer submits an order to purchase 300 pencils. After a certain amount of time, the marketplace receives a message from the pencil supplier agreeing to fulfill the order, and later a message is received that says the supplier has shipped the order. At this point the marketplace may have to transfer funds between buyer and supplier and update the status of the order.

Now consider that there could be many thousands of buyers and suppliers all active in submitting and fulfilling orders, and that the delay between the submission of an order and its fulfillment could extend into weeks. It is very clear that asynchronous messaging is required; the marketplace could not afford to cease functioning for days or weeks while it waited for a response to any given message. On the other hand, the messages are clearly not one-way; a fulfillment message is a specific response to an order request message—but it is a delayed response.

A major difference in the implementation of these two models lies in how they wait for responses. In the synchronous case, the client sends a message and then waits for a response on the same connection—the understanding is that the only possible returning message will be the response to the request.

The difference with the asynchronous case is that it is essentially always expecting messages, but when a message arrives it must match it up with the corresponding sent message.

Another major difference between the implementation of the two models lies in the routing of messages. This is readily explained through an analogy with some common interpersonal communication technologies: telephone and e-mail. If you think about using a telephone, you dial somebody's number and, if they are available at the time, they will answer the phone and a conversation begins—this is similar to the synchronous case.

On the other hand, if you send your friend an e-mail, it will be delivered to a mail server; the next time your friend runs their mail client, the message will be routed to them (probably via either the POP or IMAP protocol), and they will be free to respond to the message at their leisure. It is the existence of the mail server that allows e-mail to work asynchronously; without the mail server, you could only send e-mails to your friend at times when he or she was online.

Asynchronous SOAP messages require a very similar mechanism; for messages to be truly asynchronous there must be a routing mechanism receiving messages and then routing them to the message handler when the handler becomes available. This mechanism is the J2EE container, with its implementation of a JAXM Provider.

State in Asynchronous Servers

In the e-mail example from Figure 7.2, Dave sent an e-mail and received a response after several days. In this example, when a response finally came back from Jean accepting Dave's invitation, Dave remembered that he had sent Jean an e-mail inviting her to lunch. In the interim, Dave may have received many e-mails from other people including a certain number of unsolicited advertising e-mails (or *Spam*), but when he received Jean's e-mail he knew its context—that it was a response to an earlier request he had sent her.

In this case, Dave has the ability to mentally store "state" about various messages he has sent and to which he is expecting responses, so that when he receives various responses he remembers that he was expecting them. Likewise, if he doesn't receive a message from Jean within a week he may decide to take some other action—send Jean a reminder e-mail, or perhaps try phoning her.

The developer of an asynchronous messaging system will have to implement certain abilities that are similar to what Dave is doing mentally; that is, to have a record of state so that the context of incoming messages is known, and perhaps to trigger a timeout condition (such as sending a followup message) if an expected response has not been received after a certain amount of time.

In practice, how do you go about implementing this? There are a multitude of possibilities; some are good ideas, and some are probably not. For instance, for every message that was sent out it would be possible to spawn a thread (a concurrent unit of process execution) that could wait for the corresponding reply and perhaps handle the timeout condition if it did not receive the reply within a certain timeframe. However, unless there were very few messages ever sent out, the resource overheads of so many threads being created would be prohibitively inefficient.

A better method would be to implement a session mechanism in much the same way as many web servers do. In the web server example, an identifier is passed to the server with each page request; either in the form of a cookie or embedded as a URL parameter. Either way, the web server can recognize the unique identifier and match the request to the browser instance. The web server stores the state of each current session either in memory or in a persistent database, and can tell certain things about the incoming requests. For example, a request to display a shopping cart page is coming from a user who is logged into the site and has three items in his or her shopping cart. Once a session has timed out (there have been no page requests from that browser instance for a certain amount of time), its session data may be removed from memory.

Storing session state in an asynchronous messaging system can be done in a similar manner, although the identifier would generally be associated with a message rather than a user. This identifier may be an order identifier, for example. Picture again the electronic marketplace scenario; for each order request sent to a supplier, an entry with that order number could be inserted into the database. When a fulfillment message is received, it could be matched against the appropriate request and acted on accordingly. If a fulfillment message is received that does not match any known order request, an alert is raised for manual investigation. A background task could likewise run periodically to scan the database for order requests that have not been matched with a fulfillment message within a certain timeframe, and raise alerts for appropriate action to be taken.

Message Routing

As well as having to cope with storing state, asynchronous messaging systems also need to manage the routing of messages. This effectively means delivering the messages to their final destination, possibly via a number of intermediate destinations. In this section we will discuss the main message routing scenarios and how they may be implemented in a system that uses JAXM.

Figure 7.3 shows a fairly simplistic view of the message routing scenario for a synchronous JAXM request-response scenario. It is simplistic in the sense that it does not include the container in which the server is running—this is because the container is fairly transparent to the solution. In a scenario such as this, the client directly specifies the server's URL when sending the request and the server returns the response message to the client in the same connection; the message cannot be routed elsewhere.

Figure 7.3 Message Routing for a Synchronous Message

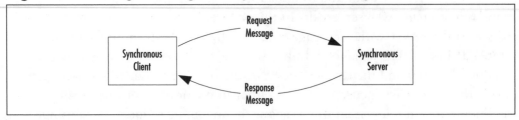

In contrast, Figure 7.4 shows a similar form of diagram, this time describing the minimum message routing required for delivery of an asynchronous message from a client to a server when both client and server are running JAXM Providers. You can see from this diagram that there are at least three levels of routing involved:

- The message must be routed from the client to its provider.

- The sending provider must know how to deliver the message to the receiving provider.

- The receiving provider must in turn know how to route the message to the server application.

Figure 7.4 Message Routing for an Asynchronous Message

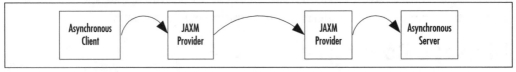

Incoming Message Routing

JAXM Servers (that is, consumers of incoming messages) may be implemented as either EJBs or servlets, although they are restricted to being implemented as servlets under the current release of the JAXM Reference Implementation and most commercial containers. As we will cover in more detail, they will still implement the same listener interfaces regardless of whether they are implemented as servlets or EJBs:

- For asynchronous servers using a Provider (EJB or servlet), they will implement *OneWayListener*.

- For synchronous servers not using a Provider (servlet only), they will implement *ReqRespListener*.

Both of these listener interfaces define an *onMessage* method; the version in *OneWayListner* has a void return value, whereas the version in *ReqRespListener* must return a message that will be routed back to the client.

In the case of the synchronous scenario (where the servlet implements *ReqRespListener*), the incoming message routing is quite straightforward: the client will address the message directly to the URL of the deployed servlet, and the servlet container will route the message to the *onMessage* method. Likewise the return value from this method will be returned directly to the calling client.

In the case of the asynchronous scenario (where either a servlet or EJB implements *OneWayListener*), things work a little differently. In this case, the sending Provider will have delivered the message to the server's JAXM Provider. This Provider has to know the servlet (or EJB) to which the message must be routed.

This routing from the incoming Provider to the actual server application is achieved because of registration information that every client of a JAXM provider must provide at deployment time. Note here that a Provider's "client" could be either a client or a server in the SOAP scenarios discussed above; whether it sends, receives or both, it is a client of the Provider.

Take for example the "Remote" sample that is deployed as part of the Java Web Services Developer Pack from Sun. This sample does a round-trip send (and asynchronous response) using the ebXML profile. If you examine the copy of *client.xml* that is deployed with this sample you should see that it looks as follows:

```
<?xml version="1.0" encoding="ISO-8859-1"?>


<!DOCTYPE ClientConfig
    PUBLIC "-//Sun Microsystems, Inc.//DTD JAXM Client//EN"
    "http://java.sun.com/xml/dtds/jaxm_client_1_0.dtd">
<ClientConfig>
    <Endpoint>
      http://www.wombats.com/remote/sender
    </Endpoint>
    <CallbackURL>
      http://localhost:8080/jaxm-remote/receiver
```

```
    </CallbackURL>
    <Provider>
        <URI>http://java.sun.com/xml/jaxm/provider</URI>
        <URL>http://127.0.0.1:8081/jaxm-provider/sender</URL>
    </Provider>
</ClientConfig>
```

Every application that makes use of a JAXM Provider must provide a *client.xml* instance in its deployment; this file may either be created manually or your development environment may automate its creation—either way, the file will contain the same content.

You can see that the client configuration provides three distinct pieces of information:

- An endpoint, expressed as a URI.
- A callback URL, which in this case is the URL of the servlet.
- Provider information as a URI and URL.

It is this information that the provider uses to route the incoming asynchronous message: the message will have been addressed to a specific URI as a destination; the Provider will then map that URI to the corresponding callback URL and ensure that the message is routed to the server's *onMessage* method.

Outgoing Message Routing

For messages outgoing via a JAXM Provider, a store-and-forward mechanism is used. This means that the message will be somehow logged (stored) and then delivered (forwarded) to the destination party. This is similar to mailing a letter; you place the letter in the post box and assume that the postal service will deliver it to its destination. In a similar way, an application can deposit the message with the Provider and trust the Provider to deliver it.

Most commercial JAXM implementations should implement the concept of *guaranteed delivery*; that is, the message will eventually be delivered to its destination, regardless of how long it takes. So if the delivery fails many times due to a serious problem with a communications link, the Provider will continue to retry delivery until it is successful. Likewise, even if the server on which the Provider is running is rebooted, the message will be stored in some form of reliable persistent storage; attempts to deliver the message will resume once the server is up and running again.

The JAXM Reference Implementation provides some of this functionality, but stops short of providing guaranteed delivery. As you can see from Figure 7.5, the reference implementation provides an application for configuring the JAXM Provider, and that the configurable parameters instantly give away several secrets about the implementation. First, you can see that there is a limited number of retries; this could be set to higher than 3, but eventually if a message cannot be delivered the Provider will give up trying. The second indication that delivery may not be guaranteed is that the messages are stored in a log file on the file system. While information stored this way will likely survive a reboot (and the Provider will continue attempting to resend messages after such an incident), files on the file system are much less reliable than using something like the Relational Database Management System (RDBMS) used in many commercial implementations.

Figure 7.5 Configuring the JAXM Provider Properties in the Reference Implementation

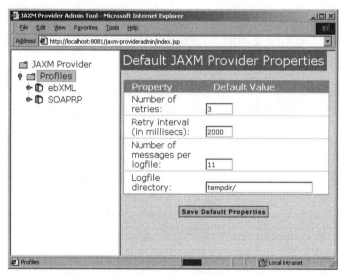

Establishing a Connection to a JAXM Provider

The JAXM Provider will typically be distributed as part of the J2EE container with which you are working; it is up to the vendor to determine how the Provider will be implemented. Generally, the JAXM Provider will be implemented as a servlet, although the implementation of the store-and-forward mechanisms will vary greatly. For example, the Provider reference implementation stores messages in a logfile directory whereas commercial implementations may well use RDBMS-based queuing mechanisms and accordingly enjoy a higher level of reliability. Regardless of the JAXM Provider implementation however, you will still use the JAXM API to establish a connection and make use of its services.

The JAXM Provider is not only responsible for routing inbound messages to your SOAP server, but is also responsible for routing outbound messages to their destinations. Your application essentially hands the message over to the Provider, which then ensures that the message is delivered, retrying the delivery until successful.

The basic steps for sending a message via a Provider are:

1. Retrieve a provider connection factory as registered with a JNDI naming service.

2. Use the factory to generate a connection with the JAXM Provider.

3. Use the connection to generate a message factory.

4. Use the message factory to generate a message, specifying a profile.

5. Populate the message.

6. Use the connection with the JAXM Provider to send the message; this will send asynchronously and will not wait for a response.

J2EE introduced the concept of the naming service based on the Java Naming and Directory Interface (JNDI) API. A naming service is a form of repository or directory that, among other things, allows various objects to be registered by name so that applications can look them up through the service and make use of them. A common use of such naming services is the registration of EJBs; this is the mechanism through which an application can access a bean.

Similar to the EJB case, JAXM Providers are registered using a unique name. Your application can then look up the Provider, using the JNDI API and providing the exact name with which the Provider was registered; thus retrieving a *ProviderConnectionFactory* object that can be used to connect to the Provider in question.

Therefore, the first requirement in this scenario is that the name of the Provider must be well known to the system that registers the Provider (probably the J2EE container) and to any applications that require connections to the Provider. The vendor may dictate this name, or it may be configurable as a property in the container's configuration files.

Developing & Deploying…

Deploying Provider Clients

In a somewhat confusing mix of terminology, a JAXM Provider's "client" may operate as either client or a server (or both) in a SOAP implementation.

Clients of Providers must not only be deployed with the usual descriptor files required by servlet containers, but also with additional deployment information contained in a file named "client.xml."

Under the JAXM Reference Implementation, this XML descriptor file must be manually created and included in the WAR file when the client is deployed. Commercial implementations will most likely include tools for automating the generation of these descriptors.

The XML file must adhere to a schema that is defined in jaxm-client.dtd and contains the following information:

- **Endpoint** A string identifying the client as a URI.

- **CallbackURL** This is used by the JAXM Provider to route received messages to the client. The received message will be addressed to a URI; the Provider will compare that URI to the registered Endpoint of each client and route the message to the CallbackURL of the matching client, retrying the delivery until successful.

- **Provider's URI and URL** Used by the client to obtain a connection to the Provider.

As mentioned above, you will need to use the JNDI API to look up the provider. This is done in two steps: a *Context* object is created, then the *lookup* method of that object is called, passing in the Provider's name. This will return a *ProviderConnectionFactory* object, as shown in the following code:

```
Context context = new InitialContext();
ProviderConnectionFactory factory;
factory = (ProviderConnectionFactory)context.lookup("MyProvider");
```

It is actually possible to obtain a *ProviderConnectionFactory* without using a naming service lookup (and therefore without using the JNDI API); this is the case where the default factory is used by calling the *ProviderConnectionFactory*'s static *newInstance* method, as shown in this code fragment:

```
ProviderConnectionFactory factory = ProviderConnectionFactory.newInstance();
```

The factory that is returned from this call will generate connections to the default Provider configuration.

Creating the connection to the JAXM Provider from the factory object is very straightforward using the factory's *createConnection* method, as the following code demonstrates:

```
ProviderConnection connection;
connection = factory.createConnection();
```

ProviderConnections

ProviderConnection objects essentially perform three different tasks:

1. Allow information (meta data) about the Provider to be queried.

2. Provide *MessageFactory* objects that can produce messages specific to a certain profile.

3. Pass messages to the Provider to be sent asynchronously.

Table 7.1 describes the four methods defined in the *ProviderConnection* interface:

Table 7.1 ProviderConnection Methods

Method	Description
void close()	Closes the connection when it is no longer required.
MessageFactory createMessageFactory (java.lang.String profile)	Creates a message factory that will produce messages according to the specified profile (for example, ebXML).
ProviderMetaData getMetaData()	Returns information about the JAXM Provider itself, including the supported profiles.
void send(SOAPMessage message)	Sends a message asynchronously via the Provider.

Using the *ProviderConnection* to Create a Message

When working with a JAXM Provider, you will create messages using a message factory generated from the provider connection. This method allows you to create a message according to any one of the specific profiles supported by your JAXM Provider. An example would be the generation of ebXML messages using a JAXM Provider that supported an ebXML profile. The following code demonstrates how such a message factory and subsequent message would be generated, having first created the provider connection object *connection* as described above:

```
MessageFactory msgFactory = connection.createMessageFactory("ebxml");
SOAPMessage myMsg = msgFactory.createMessage();
```

Using *ProviderConnection* to Send a Message

You will recall from the previous chapter that a synchronous message was sent using the *call* method of an *SOAPConnection* object:

```
SOAPMessage req;
// Populate request message
. . .
URLEndpoint endpoint = new URLEndpoint("http://destination");
SOAPMessage resp = myConnection.call(req, endpoint);
```

However, when sending an asynchronous message via a Provider, the process is a little different:

```
SOAPMessage req;
// Populate request message
. . .
myProviderConn.send(req);
```

You will immediately observe two major differences between the process of sending messages without and with a Provider:

1. The provider connection's *send* method does not return a response message (as we would expect, since this is an asynchronous model).

2. The provider connection's *send* method does not take a *URLEndpoint* parameter.

If no endpoint is passed to the *send* method, how does the Provider know where to send the message? The answer to this is specific to both the Provider and the Profile used. The Reference Implementation Provider provides two Profiles: ebXML and SOAPRP. These Profiles represent protocols built upon SOAP and each specifies a number of mandatory fields that must be provided in the SOAP Header. Specifically, both of these protocols specify that the header contain "to" elements which specify a URI for the message destination.

Figure 7.6 shows the Provider Admin application for the JAXM Reference Implementation being used to configure the ebXML/HTTP Profile. From this screenshot you can see that the profile can contain a number of *Endpoint Mappings* that are used to map URIs with destination URLs. In this case a single mapping exists: the URI *http://www.wombats.com/remote/sender* is mapped to the URL *http://127.0.0.1:8081/jaxm-provider/receiver/ebxml*.

Figure 7.6 JAXM Provider Endpoint Mappings

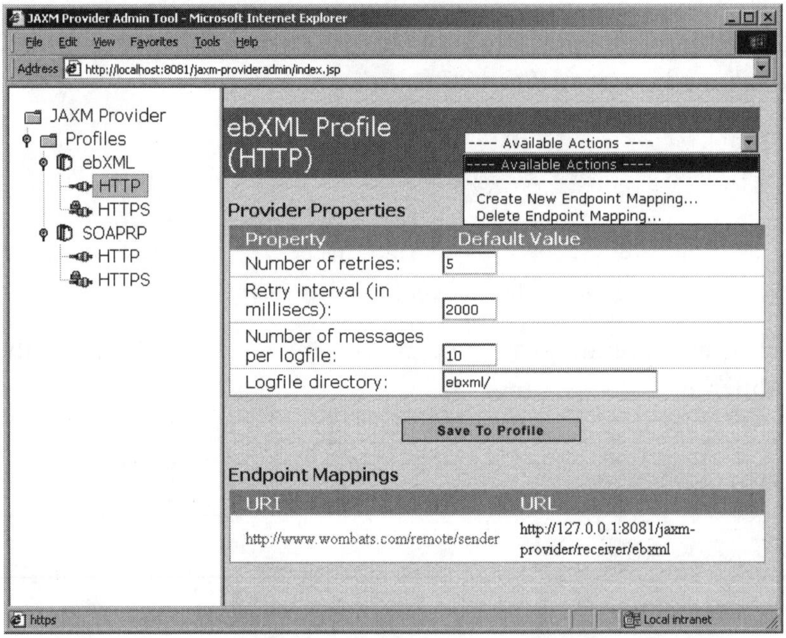

The outbound routing scenario is therefore as follows:

1. The routing of the message from the application to the JAXM Provider is implicit in the *ProviderConnection* object, as described above.

2. The routing of the message from the outgoing JAXM Provider to the destination Provider is achieved by examining the message's SOAP

Header to extract a destination URI, and then using an Endpoint Mapping to map that URI to a URL.

3. The routing of the message from the receiving JAXM Provider to the destination servlet is achieved by mapping the destination URI to a call-back URL via the deployment information provided in *client.xml*, as previously described.

Profiles

A number of protocols have already been built on top of SOAP—that is, they are protocols that comply with SOAP and specify a number of specific elements, usually with the SOAP Header. These protocols are known as *profiles*, and it is quite likely that more will be defined in the future.

In order to facilitate the use of these protocols, JAXM Providers may provide implementations of the profiles. The Provider will allow specific configuration of the properties associated with each profile (as seen in Figure 7.6), and an application may specify a particular profile (if the Provider supports it) when requesting a message factory.

An example of a profile is ebXML, which is a protocol commonly used in business-to-business (B2B) implementations, and which is built on top of SOAP. As said earlier, the following code can be used to request a message factory from a provider connection and create a message from this factory:

```
MessageFactory msgFactory = connection.createMessageFactory("ebxml");
SOAPMessage myMsg = msgFactory.createMessage();
```

As long as the Provider supports a profile named "ebxml", this code would have returned a message factory object that would in turn have created a slightly different SOAP message object than the one we created in the previous chapter. In that example we saw that a default message factory generates messages with an empty header. In the case of the ebXML profile, the message factory will actually generate pre-configured messages with a number of header elements inserted in accordance with mandatory requirements of the ebXML protocol.

If a Profile is specified, the subsequent message factory may not only produce message objects that are pre-configured with certain XML content, but these message objects may themselves be subtypes of *SOAPMessage*, and provide additional members.

Any such message class will not come from the JAXM API; they will be specific classes distributed with the JAXM Provider. As an example, the JAXM

Reference Implementation provides two distinct profiles; ebXML and SOAPRP. The Reference Implementation also ships with two corresponding messaging classes; *com.sun.xml.messaging.ebxml.EbXMLMessageImpl* and *com.sun.xml.messaging.soaprp.SOAPRPMessageImpl.* These classes are distributed in *jaxm-client..jar.*

The *EbXMLMessageImpl* class provides a number of get and set methods to support reading and writing a number of elements in an edXML message Header and Body. An example is the method:

```
void setConversationId(java.lang.String conversationId)
```

The *setConversationId* method (as its name implies) allows the conversation ID parameter to be set in the message header; this is a mandatory element in an ebXML message.

Similarly, the *SOAPRPMessageImpl* class provides a number of methods for reading and writing various elements within a SOAPRP message, such as the following method, which retrieves the "reverse path" from the SOAPRP message header:

```
java.util.Vector getSOAPRPRevMessagePath()
```

Writing a SOAP Server Servlet

Using JAXM, there are a couple of ways that you can implement a SOAP service that runs in a container and makes use of a JAXM provider; either as a servlet (running in a servlet container), or as a message-driven bean (running in an EJB container).

Figure 7.7 shows how a servlet may be used to implement a SOAP Server. You can see that even within a container, the use of a JAXMProvider can be optional depending upon the model of SOAP communication used and the features required. For example, a SOAP Server that communicates with a standalone client via the request-response model and which does not need features such as an ebXML profile, does not need to use a JAXM Provider; the servlet will receive the request message from the client (via the servlet container), process the message, and return the response message to the client. On the other hand, more complex message routing and the use of JAXM profiles will require the use of the JAXM Provider.

Figure 7.7 The Use of a Servlet as a SOAP Server

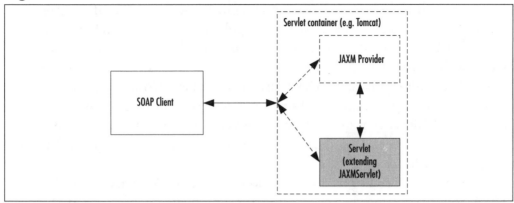

JAXMServlet

The superclass provided by the JAXM API for implementing SOAP Servers using servlets is *javax.xml.messaging.JAXMServlet*. This is an abstract class, meaning that you cannot directly instantiate objects of this type; you must first create a base class that extends *JAXMServlet* and that implements either the *javax.xml.messaging.OnewayListener* or *javax.xml.messaging.ReqRespListener* interface. Note also that there is no actual requirement to extend *JAXMServlet*; you could create your own servlet class that provided similar functionality as long as it implemented *OnewayListener* or *ReqRespListener*, however *JAXMServlet* offers a certain convenience. As an example of a situation where you may not wish to use the *JAXMServlet* class, imagine that you wanted to implement SOAP communications bound to a protocol other than HTTP; since *JAXMServlet* extends *HTTPServlet*, it can only be used for SOAP bound to HTTP. Note that the *dispatch* method of *JAXMServlet* checks that the *this* object implements either *OnewayListener* or *ReqRespListener* in order to correctly route the message. For this reason, your *JAXMServlet* subclass must implement one of these two possible interfaces.

The *OnewayListener* interface is implemented by servlets that are designed to perform asynchronous SOAP communication; that is, they will receive a message with no response required. Such a servlet may never send a response message, it may send one immediately, or it may send one in a few days' time.

On the other hand, the *ReqRespListener* interface should be implemented by servlets that will participate in synchronous SOAP communication; the servlet will receive a message, perform some processing of it, and make a response of some sort.

We have already established that the *JAXMServlet* class extends *HTTPServlet*; furthermore, it provides an overridden implementation of *doPost*. If you are familiar with writing HTTP servlets for regular browser-based web pages and the like, you may be tempted to override the *doPost* method and attempt to work with the *HttpServletRequest* and *HttpServletResponse* objects directly. However, this is usually not a good idea; the JAXM listener interfaces (*ReqRespListener* and *OnewayListener*) are designed to abstract the processing of JAXM messages to a level that is independent of whether the server is implemented as a servlet or an EJB. As we shall shortly see, these interfaces provide the appropriate mechanism for handling messages.

Another best-practice recommendation is that a servlet derived from *JAXMServlet* should not be used for functionality that is unrelated to SOAP processing; the *JAXMServlet* class is specifically designed for consuming and possibly sending SOAP messages. If, for example, you wished to provide a browser-based web page with parallel functionality to a web service, it would be best to create two independent servlets of appropriate types, and perhaps move common business logic into the EJB layer. The architecture for this kind of approach is shown in Figure 7.8.

Figure 7.8 Using the JAXMServlet Subclass Only for SOAP Processing

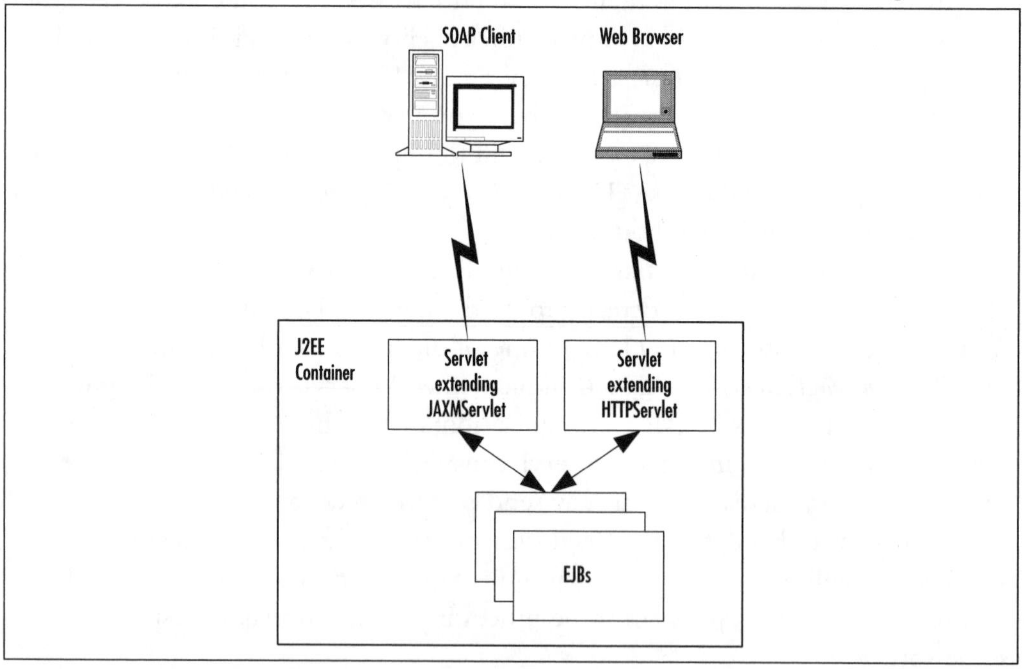

Required Overrides

The *JAXMServlet* class does not require you to override any specific methods. The most likely method for overriding within this superclass is the *init* method, which allows you to perform some processing when the servlet is first initialized—this could be very useful in performing any resource-hungry processing that only needs to be run once. To override this method you would do the following:

```
public class MyServlet
        extends JAXMServlet
        implements OnewayListener {

    public void init(ServletConfig servletConfig)
            throws ServletException {

        // Be sure to call the superclass method
        super.init(servletConfig);

        // Perform once-off initialization
        // processing here
        . . .

    }


    . . .

}
```

Even though the *JAXMServlet* class does not require you to override specific methods, you will have to implement either the *OnewayListener* or *ReqRespListener* interface, both of which have a single *onMessage* method, although these methods differ in their return types.

If you develop an asynchronous SOAP server using a servlet that implements *OnewayListener*, you will have to provide an *onMessage* method implementation that looks like this:

```
public void onMessage(SOAPMessage message) {
    // Process the incoming message
    . . .

}
```

However, if you develop a synchronous SOAP server using a servlet that implements *ReqRespListener*, you will need to provide a slightly different implementation of *onMessage*:

```
public SOAPMessage onMessage(SOAPMessage soapMsg) {
    // Process the request message

    . . .


    SOAPMessage myResponse;


    // Create and populate the response message

    . . .


    return myResponse;
}
```

Notice that the two versions of *onMessage* differ in their return types: a *OnewayListener* implementation does not need to return a value from the *onMessage* method, whereas an implementation of *ReqRespListener* requires that a *SOAPMessage* is returned from *onMessage*; this returned message is the response message in the synchronous request-response model and will be routed back to the client.

Handling Messages

As discussed above, regardless of the chosen listener interface it is the *onMessage* method that will be implemented to handle messages; in the case of the *OnewayListener* this will apply purely to inbound messages, whereas the *ReqRespListener* will handle both the inbound (request) and outbound (response) messages.

This is not to say that a servlet that implements *OnewayListener* cannot send outgoing messages; it certainly can. The situation is just that these outgoing messages will be asynchronous; they are not sent back as responses to the incoming messages, but rather as unsolicited messages sent either to the originating SOAP client or to another destination altogether.

Later on in this chapter we will complete the example started in the previous chapter and implement a service to look up the requested name and return the value. Because our example follows the synchronous model (standalone JAXM clients can only communicate this way), we will create a servlet that implements *ReqRespListener*.

Writing a SOAP EJB

The other method for creating a SOAP server using JAXM is with an EJB. This relies on the EJB 2.1 specification, which provides for message-driven beans that can be bound to a JAXM provider.

The EJB 2.0 specification first introduced the concept of *message-driven beans*. These are a variant of the Enterprise Java Beans (EJBs) that are in turn similar to stateless session beans, but with the following major differences:

- Message driven beans do not have a home, local or remote interface.
- The container passes messages to the bean and the bean processes them.

Prior to the concept of message-driven beans, the task of receiving messages, invoking a bean and passing the messages to the bean had to be handled by a custom-developed process (or *daemon*) which would be responsible for receiving messages and then creating a stateless session bean, then communicating via the bean's remote interface, generally using RMI over IIOP (as shown in Figure 7.9). The obvious disadvantages of this are the need to develop a custom daemon and the fact that the daemon runs outside of the EJB container and must communicate with the bean using RMI.

Figure 7.9 Traditional Method of Passing Messages to EJBs

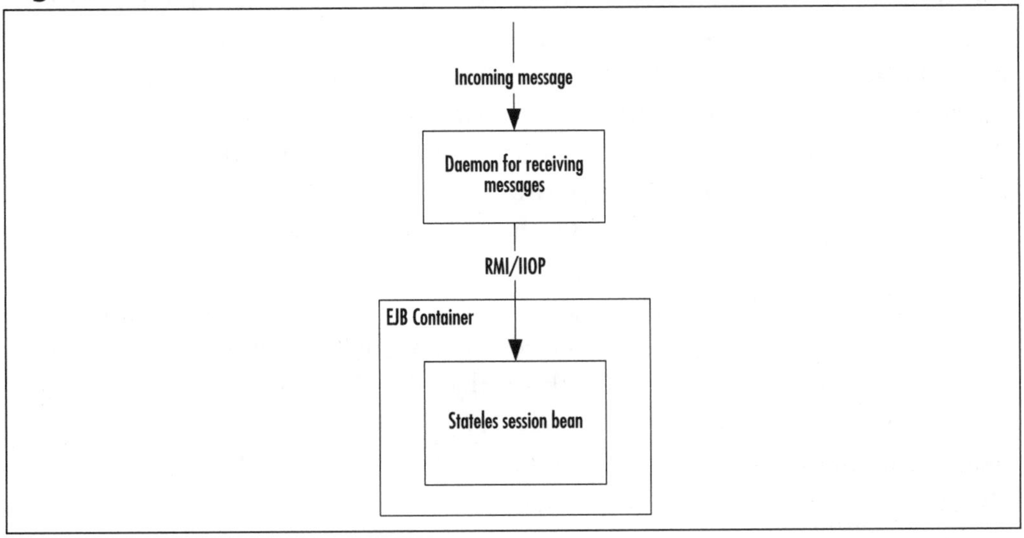

Figure 7.10 shows a simplified view of a scenario that is similar but that makes use of a message-driven bean. In this case there is no requirement for a

process to stand outside of the container and remotely invoke the EJB; instead the container will ensure that the messages are delivered to the bean. In fact, since the bean has neither a remote interface nor a home interface, it cannot be accessed by another application. Note however that there must be some form of asynchronous messaging technology involved; in EJB 2.0 the messages can only be JMS messages; in EJB 2.1 implementations the messages could be asynchronous SOAP messages passing through a JAXM provider.

Figure 7.10 The Use of Message-driven Beans

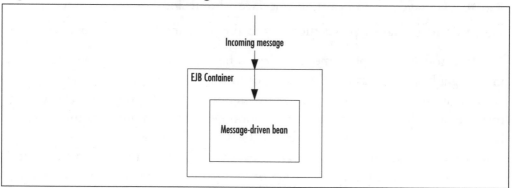

The EJB 2.0 message-driven beans are based on the Java Message Service (JMS) API. When a JMS message is received, the container routes the message directly to the bean. This provides a very useful mechanism for decoupling the EJB from applications; an application can send a JMS message that will be processed asynchronously by the message-driven bean at some point. It is the EJB 2.0 version of message-driven beans that is implemented by most commercial J2EE containers at the time of this writing.

The EJB 2.1 specification extends the concept of the message-driven bean to cater for beans that are bound to JAXM providers. This means that an EJB can be invoked directly by the container and passed an incoming asynchronous SOAP message, similar to the way that a servlet implementing *OnewayListener* receives SOAP messages. The implication of this is that it enables EJBs to be directly exposed as web services across the internet, and through the functionality provided by the JAXM provider and the EJB container, such features as asynchronous and guaranteed delivery of the messages to the bean are enabled.

Overriding *MessageDrivenBean* and *OnewayListener*

A message-driven bean should always implement the *MessageDrivenBean* interface. This interface contains two methods that must be implemented, as listed in Table 7.2.

Table 7.2 Methods that Must be Implemented in *MessageDrivenBean*

Method	Description
void ejbRemove()	The container will invoke this before the bean is removed; perform any required clean-up action within this method.
void setMessageDrivenContext (MessageDrivenContext ctx)	This method will be invoked after the instance of the bean has been created, to provide the bean with its context object. The implementation of this method should usually store a copy of the context object in an instance variable.

Message-driven beans that will be SOAP message handlers must also implement *OnewayListener*. In doing so, they become similar in their implementation to the JAXM servlets that implement this same interface.

You may be wondering why message-driven beans can implement *OnewayListener* but do not have the option of implementing *ReqRespListener*; the answer is that message-driven beans can only operate asynchronously via a provider—a message-driven bean does not listen on a URL in the way a servlet does and so cannot receive messages directly; all messages are routed to it by the JAXM Provider.

For further information on the specifics of implementing message-driven beans that respond to JAXM messages, refer to the documentation provided by the vendor of the container to be used. Remember that this form of message-driven bean requires a container that complies with EJB 2.1, and that most of the commercially-available containers at the time of writing comply with EJB 2.0.

Example SOAP Servlet

In this section we will develop a functioning SOAP service that will complete the example begun with the previous chapter's standalone SOAP client. You will recall that the client application sent a SOAP message to a service requesting a value to be looked up by a name; this service will do the lookup and return the value to the client. If there are any errors in this process, whether from parsing the incoming message or looking up the value, the error information will be returned to the client in the form of a SOAP Fault.

Receiving and Processing SOAP Messages

This example will be implemented as a servlet; it will override both *JAXMServlet* and *ReqRespListener*. Why does it override *ReqRespListener* and not *OnewayListener*? Because our client, developed in the previous chapter, is a standalone application sending messages synchronously, so we are bound to the request-response model.

The schema of the request and response messages was outlined in the previous chapter. You will remember that the client sends a name in a request, and that the server is expected to look up a value against that name and return the matching value (if found).

The actual lookup will be done against the sample XML that will be read in from a file during the servlet's initialization. You will recall that our sample XML file looks like this:

```
<entries>
    <entry>
        <name>foo</name>
        <value>bar</value>
    </entry>
    <entry>
        <name>Mickey</name>
        <value>Mouse</value>
    </entry>
</entries>
```

So if the client requested a lookup of the name *Mickey*, we would return the value *Mouse*, whereas a lookup of *Peter* (or even *mickey* without the capital *M*) would need to generate a SOAP fault in the response.

Our example will be based on a servlet that extends *JAXMServlet*, so it obviously needs to run in a container. Since we are using a standalone client we are bound to the request-response model; the client sends a request and blocks, waiting until we send some kind of response back. For this reason we will implement *ReqResponseListener*.

Our servlet will only override two methods: *init*, which allows us to perform a couple of one-off tasks (including reading the sample XML file from disk), and *onMessage*, which is called by the container each time a SOAP message is sent to our servlet. The version of *onMessage* that is defined in the *ReqResponseListener* interface is passed a *SOAPMessage* object when it is called by the container; this is the request message that was sent from the client. It must also return a *SOAPMessage* object, which will be sent back to the client as the response.

```java
/**
 * ReceiverServlet.java
 *
 */

package com.syngress.jwsdp.soap.server;

import javax.xml.messaging.JAXMServlet;
import javax.xml.messaging.ReqRespListener;
import javax.xml.messaging.JAXMException;
import javax.xml.soap.MessageFactory;
import javax.xml.soap.SOAPMessage;
import javax.xml.soap.SOAPException;
import javax.servlet.ServletConfig;
import javax.servlet.ServletException;
import com.syngress.jwsdp.soap.server.ReceivedMessage;
import com.syngress.jwsdp.soap.server.LoadXMLException;
import com.syngress.jwsdp.soap.server.LookupException;
import com.syngress.jwsdp.soap.server.FaultMessage;
import com.syngress.jwsdp.soap.server.SchemaException;
import com.syngress.jwsdp.soap.server.NameValueLookup;
import com.syngress.jwsdp.soap.server.ReplyMessage;

public class ReceiverServlet
        extends JAXMServlet
        implements ReqRespListener {

    // Instance variables that will be populated
    // by the init method.
```

```java
protected MessageFactory messageFactory = null;
protected NameValueLookup lookUpper = null;

// All SOAP messages are routed to the onMessage
// method.
public SOAPMessage onMessage(SOAPMessage soapMsg) {

    SOAPMessage retMsg = null;
    ReceivedMessage recMsg = null;
    ReplyMessage replyMsg = null;

    String name = null;
    String value = null;

    try {

        // Initialize the ReceivedMessage object
        // with the incoming request message.
        recMsg = new ReceivedMessage(soapMsg);

        // Parse the message to extract the
        // requested name parameter.
        name = recMsg.getRequestedName();

        // Attempt to retrieve the value
        // that matches the name from the
        // sample XML.
        value = lookUpper.lookup(name);

        // Construct the response message.
        replyMsg = new ReplyMessage(
            messageFactory);

        // Set the response parameter
        // in the outgoing message.
        replyMsg.setValue(value);
```

```
        retMsg = replyMsg.getMessage();
} catch(SchemaException e) {

    // There was an error parsing the
    // request message.
    try {
        FaultMessage faultMsg =
            new FaultMessage(
                messageFactory);

        faultMsg.setFaultCode(
            "Server");
        faultMsg.setFaultString(
            "Invalid Schema");
        faultMsg.setFaultDetail(
            "SchemaException");

        retMsg = faultMsg.getMessage();
    } catch(Exception ex) {
        // Ignore errors generating
        // fault and allow a
        // null return.
    }
} catch(SOAPException e) {

    try {
        FaultMessage faultMsg =
            new FaultMessage(
                messageFactory);

        faultMsg.setFaultCode(
            "Server");
        faultMsg.setFaultString(
            "SOAP Exception");
        faultMsg.setFaultDetail(
            "SOAPException");
```

```
                retMsg = faultMsg.getMessage();
        } catch(Exception ex) {
                // Ignore errors generating
                // fault and allow a
                // null return.
        }
} catch(LookupException e) {

        // This should indicate that the
        // requested name was not found
        // in the XML.
        try {
                FaultMessage faultMsg =
                    new FaultMessage(
                        messageFactory);

                faultMsg.setFaultString(
                    "");
                faultMsg.setFaultCode(
                    "Server");
                faultMsg.setFaultString(
                    "Error looking up value");
                faultMsg.setFaultDetail(
                    "LookupException");

                retMsg = faultMsg.getMessage();
        } catch(Exception ex) {
                // Ignore errors generating
                // fault and allow a
                // null return.
        }
} catch(Exception e) {

        // All other errors.
        try {
                FaultMessage faultMsg =
                    new FaultMessage(
```

```
            messageFactory);

        faultMsg.setFaultString(
            "");
        faultMsg.setFaultCode(
            "Server");
        faultMsg.setFaultString(
            "General server error");

        retMsg = faultMsg.getMessage();
    } catch(Exception ex) {
        // Ignore errors generating
        // fault and allow a
        // null return.
    }
} finally {

    // Since this is called synchronously,
    // the message will be sent directly as
    // a response to the original request.
    return retMsg;
}
}


public void init(ServletConfig servletConfig)
        throws ServletException {

    // Method performs once-off initialization.

    // Be sure to call the superclass
    // implementation.
    super.init(servletConfig);

    // Attempt to create a new message factory.
    try {
        messageFactory =
            MessageFactory.newInstance();
```

```
        } catch(JAXMException e) {
            e.printStackTrace();
        } catch(SOAPException e) {
            e.printStackTrace();
        }


        // Attempt to create an object that will
        // look up values by name in the XML.
        try {
            lookUpper = new NameValueLookup();
        } catch(LoadXMLException e) {
            e.printStackTrace();
            System.exit(1);
        }
    }
}
```

The incoming message is represented by the class *ReceivedMessage*, which uses the JAXM DOM implementation to parse the request and extract the appropriate parameter.

```
/**
 * ReceivedMessage.java
 *
 */


package com.syngress.jwsdp.soap.server;


import javax.xml.soap.SOAPMessage;
import javax.xml.soap.SOAPPart;
import javax.xml.soap.SOAPEnvelope;
import javax.xml.soap.SOAPBody;
import javax.xml.soap.SOAPException;
import javax.xml.soap.SOAPElement;
import javax.xml.soap.Name;
import java.util.Iterator;
import com.syngress.jwsdp.soap.server.SchemaException;
```

```java
public class ReceivedMessage {

    // Class represents a SOAP message received from
    // a client, which should contain
    // a valid request to look up a name.

    protected SOAPMessage soapMessage = null;

    public ReceivedMessage(SOAPMessage soapMessage) {
        this.soapMessage = soapMessage;
    }

    public String getRequestedName()
            throws SchemaException, SOAPException {

        // Get the name parameter that was
        // reuested for lookup. This will perform
        // some validation of the XML.

        String resp = null;

        SOAPPart soapPart;
        SOAPEnvelope soapEnvelope;
        SOAPBody soapBody;
        Name name;

        // Traverse the hierarchy of SOAP
        // objects to obtain the body.
        soapPart = soapMessage.getSOAPPart();
        soapEnvelope = soapPart.getEnvelope();
        soapBody = soapEnvelope.getBody();

        // Search for an element
        // with the correct
        // namespace-qualified name.
        name = soapEnvelope.createName(
                "GetValueByName",
```

```
                    "myns",
                    "www.syngress.com/JWSDP/soap-example");


        // Check there's at least one such
        // element.
        Iterator valueRequests =
            soapBody.getChildElements(name);


        if (! valueRequests.hasNext()) {


            // Schema is not valid
            throw(new SchemaException());
        };


        // Check there's no more than one
        // such element.
        SOAPElement soapElement =
            (SOAPElement)valueRequests.next();


        if (valueRequests.hasNext()) {


            // Schema is not valid
            throw(new SchemaException());
        }


        // Look for the appropriate child
        // element containing the name parameter.
        name = soapEnvelope.createName(
            "name");


        Iterator params =
            soapElement.getChildElements(
                name);


        if (! params.hasNext()) {


            // Schema is not valid
```

```
            throw(new SchemaException());
        }


        // Ensure there's only one such element.
        SOAPElement paramElement =
            (SOAPElement)params.next();

        if (params.hasNext()) {

            // Schema is not valid
            throw(new SchemaException());
        }


        // Attempt to read out the value of the
        // name parameter.
        resp = paramElement.getValue();

        if (null == resp) {

            // Schema is not valid
            throw(new SchemaException());
        }


        // Schema is valid.
        return resp;
    }
}
```

The *NameValueLookup* class provides the functionality to load the XML file from disk into a DOM document and to search that document for a value matching a requested name. Note that this class makes use of the JAXP DOM implementation, which adheres to the org.w3c.dom specification.

```
/**
 * NameValueLookup.java
 *
 */
```

```java
package com.syngress.jwsdp.soap.server;

import org.w3c.dom.Document;
import org.w3c.dom.NodeList;
import org.w3c.dom.Node;
import org.xml.sax.InputSource;
import org.xml.sax.SAXException;
import javax.xml.parsers.DocumentBuilder;
import javax.xml.parsers.DocumentBuilderFactory;
import javax.xml.parsers.ParserConfigurationException;
import java.io.FileReader;
import java.io.FileNotFoundException;
import java.io.IOException;
import com.syngress.jwsdp.soap.server.LookupException;
import com.syngress.jwsdp.soap.server.LoadXMLException;

public class NameValueLookup {

    // Class represents an in-memory instance
    // of the sample XML file and
    // can perform a name/value lookup.
    // Uses the DOM for parsing.

    // Assumes that the XML file is stored
    // in the root directory of the primary
    // HDD on a Windows system; adjust for
    // different systems.
    protected static final String docSource =
        "c:\\sample.xml";

    protected Document domDoc = null;

    public NameValueLookup()
            throws LoadXMLException {

        // Create a document builder
        // for loading the file into the
```

```
                    // DOM document.
            DocumentBuilderFactory dbFactory =
                    DocumentBuilderFactory.newInstance();


            DocumentBuilder docBuilder = null;


            try {
                    docBuilder =
                            dbFactory.newDocumentBuilder();
            } catch(ParserConfigurationException e) {
                    throw new LoadXMLException();
            }


            // Use a FileReader to access the
            // file from disk.
            FileReader reader = null;


            try {
                    reader = new FileReader(docSource);
            } catch(FileNotFoundException e) {
                    throw new LoadXMLException();
            }


            // Attempt to parse the XML
            // file into the DOM document.
            InputSource source = new InputSource(reader);


            try {
                    domDoc = docBuilder.parse(source);
            } catch(IOException e) {
                    throw new LoadXMLException();
            } catch(SAXException e) {
                    throw new LoadXMLException();
            }
    }


public String lookup(String name)
```

```
            throws LookupException {

        // Looks up the value corresponding
        // to the name parameter.

    String value = null;

    try {
        NodeList nameNodes;

            // Retrieve all of the elements
            // named "name".
            nameNodes =
                domDoc.getElementsByTagName(
                    "name");

            int len = nameNodes.getLength();

            // Iterate through the matching
            // elements.
            for (int ix=0;
                ix < nameNodes.getLength();
                ix++) {

                // Compare the name with the
                // value of the first child
                // node.
                if (nameNodes.
                    item(ix).
                    getChildNodes().
                    item(0).
                    getNodeValue().
                    equals(name)) {

                    // We have a match on
                    // the name; need to
                    // retrieve the value.
```

```java
NodeList childNodes;

Node parent =
    nameNodes.
    item(ix).
    getParentNode();

childNodes =
    parent.getChildNodes();

for (int iy = 0;
    iy < childNodes.getLength();
    iy++) {

    // Look for a child node
    // with a name of "value".
    if (childNodes.
        item(iy).
        getNodeName().
        equals("value")
    ) {

        // Retrieve the value
        // of the first child
        // node.
        value =
            childNodes.
            item(iy).
            getChildNodes().
            item(0).
            getNodeValue();

        // We have now
        // successfully looked
        // up the value.
        break;
    }
```

```
                }
                break;
            }
        }
    } catch(Exception e) {
        throw new LookupException();
    }

    // Throw an exception if we didn't find
    // a value.
    if (null == value) {
        throw new LookupException();
    }

    return value;
    }

}
```

The *ReplyMessage* class is used to model a response message to be returned to the client. This class contains the functionality to insert the value that was found in the lookup into the correct schema.

```
/**
 * ReplyMessage.java
 *
 */

package com.syngress.jwsdp.soap.server;

import javax.xml.soap.MessageFactory;
import javax.xml.soap.SOAPMessage;
import javax.xml.soap.SOAPPart;
import javax.xml.soap.SOAPEnvelope;
import javax.xml.soap.SOAPBody;
import javax.xml.soap.SOAPException;
import javax.xml.soap.SOAPElement;
```

```
public class ReplyMessage {

    // Class represents a SOAP message
    // to be returned back to the client.

    protected SOAPMessage soapMessage = null;

    public ReplyMessage(MessageFactory messageFactory)
            throws SOAPException {

        // Create a new message from the
        // message factory passed in.
        soapMessage = messageFactory.createMessage();
    }

    public void setValue(String value)
            throws SOAPException {

        // Set the response value
        // to be returned.

        SOAPPart soapPart;
        SOAPEnvelope soapEnvelope;
        SOAPBody soapBody;

        // Traverse the hierarchy of
        // SOAP objects to obtain the
        // body.
        soapPart = soapMessage.getSOAPPart();
        soapEnvelope = soapPart.getEnvelope();
        soapBody = soapEnvelope.getBody();

        // Add the response element to the body,
        // using a namespace-qualified name.
        SOAPElement responseElement =
            soapBody.addChildElement(
                soapEnvelope.createName(
```

```
                    "GetValueByNameResponse",

                    "myns",

                    "www.syngress.com/JWSDP/soap-example"));


            // The value to be returned

            // is added as a text node as a child of the

            // response element using a local name.

            SOAPElement paramElement = null;


            paramElement = responseElement.
                addChildElement("value");


            paramElement.addTextNode(value);


            soapMessage.saveChanges();

        }


    public SOAPMessage getMessage() {


            // Get the SOAP Message.


            return soapMessage;

        }

    }
```

Several exception classes are used in the example. *SchemaException* is used to indicate that the request message did not adhere to the agreed schema.

```
/**

 * SchemaException.java

 *

 */


package com.syngress.jwsdp.soap.server;


public class SchemaException extends Exception {


    // This exception is used to
```

```
        // indicate that the XML being
        // parsed did not conform to
        // the appropriate schema.
}
```

The *LoadXMLException* is used to indicate that an error occurred in loading the sample XML file from disk into the DOM document.

```
/**
 *  LoadXMLException.java
 *
 */


package com.syngress.jwsdp.soap.server;


public class LoadXMLException extends Exception {


        // This exception is used to
        // indicate any error in loading
        // the sample XML data from the
        // file.
}
```

The *LookupException* is used to indicate that the requested name could not be found in the sample XML.

```
/**
 *  LookupException.java
 *
 */


package com.syngress.jwsdp.soap.server;


public class LookupException extends Exception {


        // This exception is used to
        // indicate that no value could
        // be found corresponding to the
        // requested name.
}
```

As you will remember from the previous chapter, errors transported in SOAP Messages take the form of a SOAP Fault. The *FaultMessage* class is used to model a response to return fault information to the client.

```java
/**
 * FaultMessage.java
 *
 */

package com.syngress.jwsdp.soap.server;

import javax.xml.soap.MessageFactory;
import javax.xml.soap.SOAPMessage;
import javax.xml.soap.SOAPPart;
import javax.xml.soap.SOAPEnvelope;
import javax.xml.soap.SOAPBody;
import javax.xml.soap.SOAPException;
import javax.xml.soap.SOAPElement;
import javax.xml.soap.SOAPFault;
import javax.xml.soap.Name;
import javax.xml.soap.Detail;
import javax.xml.soap.DetailEntry;
import java.util.Iterator;

public class FaultMessage {

    // Class represents a message containing
    // fault information to be returned
    // to the client.

    SOAPMessage message;
    SOAPFault fault;

    public FaultMessage(MessageFactory messageFactory)
            throws SOAPException {

        // Create a new message from the
```

```
        // message factory passed in.
        message = messageFactory.createMessage();


        SOAPPart soapPart;
        SOAPEnvelope soapEnvelope;
        SOAPBody soapBody;


        // Traverse the hierarchy of
        // SOAP objects to obtain the
        // body.
        soapPart = message.getSOAPPart();
        soapEnvelope = soapPart.getEnvelope();
        soapBody = soapEnvelope.getBody();


        // Add a SOAP Fault to the
        // body.
        fault = soapBody.addFault();
}


public void setFaultCode(String faultCode)
        throws SOAPException {


    // Set the fault code in the SOAP Fault.
    fault.setFaultCode(faultCode);
}


public void setFaultString(String faultString)
        throws SOAPException {


    // Set the fault string in the SOAP Fault.
    fault.setFaultString(faultString);
}


public void setFaultDetail(String faultDetail)
        throws SOAPException {


    // Set the fault detail in the SOAP Fault.
```

```
        // This will be added as a single
        // detail entry under a
        // namespace-qualified name.
        SOAPEnvelope soapEnvelope =
            message.getSOAPPart().getEnvelope();


        Detail detail = fault.addDetail();


        Name name = soapEnvelope.createName(
            "FaultDetail",
            "myns",
            "www.syngress.com/JWSDP/soap-example");


        DetailEntry entry =
            detail.addDetailEntry(name);


        entry.addTextNode(faultDetail);
    }


    public SOAPMessage getMessage() {


        // Retrieve the underlying
        // SOAPMEssage object.
        return message;

    }

}
```

Once the servlet is compiled, you will need to deploy it in a servlet container. This is done exactly as you have deployed servlets in the past: because the servlet does not make use of a JAXM Provider, there is no need for any JAXM-specific deployment information (that is, you do not need to provide a client.xml file).

You should be able to test the servlet with the client developed in the previous chapter. Ensure that you recompile Client.java with the URL of your newly-deployed servlet assigned to the *SERVICE_ENDPOINT* variable and there should be little else to do; run the client with an appropriate name as a command-line parameter and observe the results.

Debugging…

End-to-End Debugging

The examples developed in this chapter and the previous one form an end-to-end system. In the previous chapter we developed a SOAP client application, and in this chapter we developed a matching server application as a servlet.

It should be perfectly feasible to debug the entire system as an end-to-end solution, by using two instances of the debugger. In order to do this you would start up a debugger instance on the machine that will run the SOAP client, and catch the execution at a breakpoint somewhere prior to the request message being sent out. Then you would use another debugger instance on the machine running the server in the servlet container—you may require information provided by the vendor of your servlet container on how to do this. The idea is to set a breakpoint within the *ReceiverServlet* class' *onMessage* method. You should be able to place a breakpoint at the first line of code within the method.

From this point on, you can continue to step line-by-line through the client's code execution until the request message is sent out. Once that happens you should be able to move back over to the server debugger instance; the servlet should have received the message and the breakpoint should have interrupted execution. You can then step through the server code until a response message is returned from the *onMessage* method, when execution will resume on the client.

Summary

In this chapter we examined in more detail what a JAXM Provider is, and how an application can work with a JAXM Provider to send and receive messages asynchronously. Such an application must be hosted within a container, either as a servlet or as a message-driven bean. For outgoing messages the Provider will be responsible for routing the message to its destination and ensuring it is delivered using a store and forward mechanism. For incoming messages the JAXM Provider will be responsible for receiving the messages and then routing them to the appropriate servlet or EJB.

We also developed a SOAP server (as a servlet) that will respond to requests made by the client from the previous chapter, look up a value from the sample XML file, and return either the value or a SOAP Fault error message. Because the client was developed as a standalone application, the server will operate synchronously (and the servlet will implement *ReqRespListener*).

Solutions Fast Track

Message Routing

☑ Applications that use a JAXM Provider can communicate using asynchronous communications.

☑ The use of a JAXM Provider means that messages' delivery can be guaranteed, even if the receiver is inactive at the time a given message is sent. This is achieved using a store and forward mechanism.

☑ An asynchronous model using JAXM Providers requires that outgoing messages be routed to their destination, and that incoming messages received by a JAXM Provider be routed to the appropriate service.

Establishing a Connection to a JAXM Provider

☑ A JAXM Provider is registered with a naming service.

☑ An application that wishes to make use of a JAXM Provider uses the JNDI API to look up the Provider in much the same way as an EJB lookup is performed.

ProviderConnections

☑ The *ProviderConnection* object is used to obtain a MessageFactory.

☑ An application sends asynchronous messages via the *ProviderConnection*. Such a request does not specify a destination URL, nor does it wait for a response.

☑ The JAXM Provider will determine the destination from a URI in the message header, in combination with endpoint mappings configured within the JAXM Provider which map URIs to URLs.

Writing a SOAP Server Servlet

☑ JAXM SOAP servers can be implemented either as servlets or as EJBs, although currently only servlets are supported by most vendors.

☑ A SOAP Server servlet can either receive synchronous messages (request-reply) or asynchronous messages.

☑ A servlet that will operate synchronously (without a JAXM Provider) should implement *ReqRespListener*.

☑ A servlet that will operate asynchronously (with a JAXM Provider) should implement *OnewayListener*.

Writing a SOAP EJB

☑ A SOAP EJB is a form of message-driven bean, and should implement the *MessageDrivenBean* interface.

☑ A SOAP message-driven bean cannot operate synchronously; it must implement *OnewayListener*.

☑ The processing of *OnewayListener.onMessage* in a message-driven bean is very similar to that within an asynchronous SOAP servlet.

Example SOAP Servlet

☑ We covered the development of a service that can be called by the client described in the previous chapter. Because that client is a standalone application operating synchronously, the service must also operate without a JAXM Provider.

☑ The service uses the sample XML that we use throughout this book to look up a value against a name specified in the request.

☑ If there is a failure in decoding the request or looking up the name, the service returns SOAP Fault information in the response message.

Frequently Asked Questions

The following Frequently Asked Questions, answered by the authors of this book, are designed to both measure your understanding of the concepts presented in this chapter and to assist you with real-life implementation of these concepts. To have your questions about this chapter answered by the author, browse to **www.syngress.com/solutions** and click on the **"Ask the Author"** form.

Q: What is ebXML?

A: ebXML is a set of B2B specifications for enabling enterprises to conduct business over the Internet. ebXML is a set of B2B specifications for enabling enterprises to conduct business over the Internet. ebXML is backed by OASIS (the Organization for the Advancement of Structured Information Standards) and UN/CEFACT (the United Nations Center for Trade Facilitation and Electronic Business).

Q: How do I configure the Reference Implementation JAXM Provider?

A: If you have installed the Java Web Services Developer Pack, the Provider Admin tool will by default be installed to http://servername:8081/jaxm-provider admin. You will need to ensure that Tomcat is already running (through the startup.bat or startup.sh scripts). The admin tool is password-protected; you will need to modify the tomcat-users.xml file to remove the comments around the entry with the username "jaxm-provideradmin;" it would also be a good idea to change the password from "changeme" to something more unique.

Q: Why are SOAP Server EJBs restricted to implementing *OnewayListener* when servlets may implement either *OnewayListener* or *ReqRespListener*?

A: A servlet has the option of operating with or without a JAXM Provider; if it operates without a Provider, client sending the request accesses it directly by its URL. On the other hand, an EJB cannot be directly addressed by a URL—it has no URL, and can only operate in an asynchronous mode where a JAXM Provider receives the messages and routes them to the EJB.

Chapter 8

Using XML-based RPC

Solutions in this chapter:

- **JAX-RPC Summary**

- **Mapping Java Data Types**

- **Conversion Between Java Classes and WSDL**

- **Creating a JAX-RPC Client**

- **Creating a JAX-RPC Server**

- **Creating a Simple XML-RPC Server and Client**

- ☑ **Summary**

- ☑ **Solutions Fast Track**

- ☑ **Frequently Asked Questions**

Introduction

You might think that the last thing the world needs is another remote procedure call protocol; after all, there are dozens already in existence. That's largely a true statement, and for many situations, XML-based RPC offers few advantages over existing remote procedure call interfaces. Further, encoding the request into XML makes the calls less efficient than direct (binary) interfaces.

However, there are times when XML-based RPC solves a business problem. You might have to communicate via an RPC mechanism across organizational boundaries through firewalls, for instance. Alternately, you might be communicating with wildly disparate systems—a mainframe speaking PL/1 and a desktop speaking Java. You might even be creating a server system where you have no way of knowing the remote client, let alone controlling it. XML-based RPC also provides some resilience in the face of change. Since the published interfaces are XML-based instead of binary, elements can sometimes be added or removed without breaking the connection between the server and existing clients.

JAX-RPC uses two industry standards surrounding XML-based RPC: SOAP and WSDL. SOAP (covered in chapters 6 & 7) is used for the transfer of data between end points. Web Service Description Language (WSDL) is the functional analog of IDL files in other remote procedure systems: it provides a common language for describing the inputs, outputs and semantics of remote client services.

JAX-RPC Summary

The Java API for XML-based RPC (JAX-RPC) is an API used to facilitate remote procedure calls. Remote procedure calls are nothing new; the technology has been around for years, but the difference between JAX-RPC and older RPC mechanisms is the data exchange format. Unlike with older implementations, method calls and subsequent return values in JAX-RPC are passed back and forth as SOAP messages. The SOAP specification contains provisions for representing remote procedure calls and the subsequent responses of those calls. These SOAP messages usually use HTTP as the transport layer. The combination of these technologies opens new doors in the area of interoperability and EAI. Since both the data exchange format and the transport mechanism are both built upon platform-neutral standards, clients and servers deployed on disparate platforms and operating systems can now use the same set of services.

JAX-RPC manifests itself as specialized XML messages; the clients invoking the RPC and the servers hosting the RPC's functionality operate in a synchronous manner. Execution of the client is delayed until such time that the RPC has returned a response.

NOTE

It is important to note that while most other XML messages request a service in a decoupled manner, XML-RPC defines function call semantics. These function call semantics define the name of the method to invoke, the number and type of parameters to pass to the method, and the return value type.

Understanding Stubs and Ties

The process of taking method calls and translating them into the appropriate format for transmission, then translating them back on the server end is implemented by *stubs and ties* . This process is officially known as *marshaling* and *unmarshaling*. Figure 8.1 illustrates where these stubs and ties fit into the XML-RPC architecture.

Figure 8.1 XML-RPC using JAX-RPC Overview

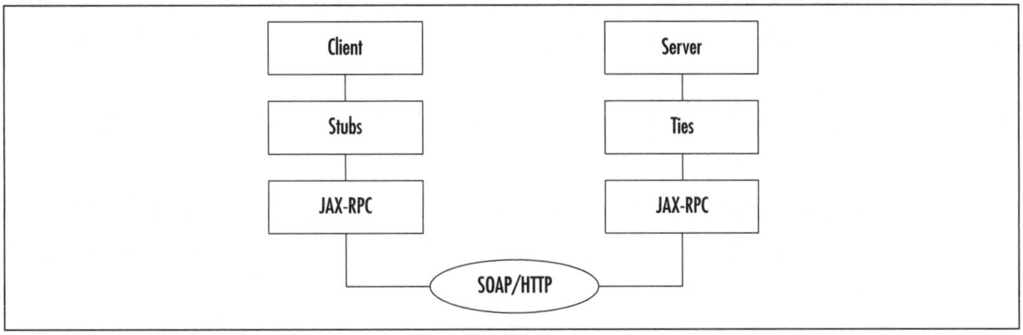

Both the stubs and ties work with the core JAX-RPC APIs to transmit SOAP encoded XML using standard HTTP.

If you use the JWSDP to create a web service application then the stubs and ties are created by the *xrpc* tool. This tool can take either the Service Definition Interface (SDI) or a WSDL configuration file and generate the appropriate stubs and ties. xtpcc is discussed in greater detail later in this chapter.

When you create your client, you will use the generated stub class(es) to invoke your web service on the server side. The stub then acts as a service proxy, masking the marshalling and remote procedure call from the client.

When you create your service definition and implementation you do not need to explicitly work with the tie class(es). The JAX-RPC framework will use behind-the-scenes ties to unmarshall the data and invoke the appropriate method in your service.

Sending a XML-RPC Message

The sending and receiving of XML-RPC messages involves some fairly complex functionality. The JAX-RPC API shields us from those complexities and leaves us to focus on business needs. The process of sending these XML-RPC messages involves the following steps. Since XML-RPC is a synchronous process, each of these steps will be executed in turn. Granted, there is more going on behind the scenes than the list suggests, but it does cover the high-level milestones in the RPC process.

1. **Client—Creation** The client application will create an instance of the stub class that serves a proxy for the desired functionality.

2. **Client—Invocation** The client will then invoke the business methods through this proxy by specifying the method, its parameters and the service endpoint.

3. **Client—Conversion to SOAP Message** The stub class will take the method name and specified parameters, and create a SOAP message that embodies that data.

4. **Client—Message Transport** This SOAP message is then sent over HTTP by virtue of a POST request to the service endpoint.

5. **Server—Remote Listener** The HTTP web server located at the URL defined by the endpoint receives the request and passes it on to an XML-RPC listener.

6. **Server—Message Parsing** This listener parses the SOAP message to retrieve the method name and parameters of that method. Once parsed, the listener calls that method, passing in those parameters.

7. **Server—Method Response** The method returns a value to the listener. This listener will package the response as an XML document. A SOAP message is created from this XML document.

8. **Server—Response Transmission** The HTTP server will return the SOAP message, encapsulating the method call's response in its response to the original HTTP POST request.

9. **Client—Message Receipt** The originating client receives the response

JAX-RPC offers distinct advantages over other RPC technologies. By virtue of using HTTP to transmit XML-based remote procedure calls, the invoking platform and the service-hosting platform need not be of the same type. Windows-based clients written in Visual Basic can invoke procedure calls on services written in Perl running on Solaris machines.

JAX-RPC places no restrictions on the physical location of the client and server boxes, so a great distance could separate clients and servers, provided the server is reachable by the client and that the network latency associated with the established connection does not adversely affect client performance.

The use of JAX-RPC enables you to use a truly distributed heterogeneous enterprise platform. You as the developer or architect of a system can choose best-of-breed solutions without being necessarily limited due to platform-compatibility issues when choosing your products. Admittedly, this is oversimplifying the matter a bit, but the truth remains that XML is becoming the standard for data exchange. Since data exchanges are using a standard format and being transmitted using a common protocol (HTTP), you can achieve platform independence when designing and implementing your system.

Mapping Java Data Types

The JAX-RPC specification spells out the mapping that occurs when translating Java data types to the appropriate XML representation. Support presently exists for most of the data types in Java, as well as the facilities to create your own wrappers for unsupported types.

Supported Java Data Types

The JAX-RPC specification mandates support for most of the Java primitive data types. The sole exception is the *char* type. All others, including *boolean, byte, short, int, long, float* and *double* are supported. JAX-RPC also supports the wrapper classes for this list of primitives (*java.lang.Integer*, for example).

The JAX-RPC specification also provides support of a small set of classes from the standard JRE class library. This set consists of:

- *java.lang.String*

- *java.util.Date*

- *java.util.Calendar*

- *java.math.BigInteger*

- *java.math.BigDecimal*

There is also support for arrays. Supported arrays must consist of a previously defined supported Java data type or class. The specification also calls for support of arrays of type *java.lang.Object*.

Data Type to XML/WSDL Definition Tables

This section covers the mapping of Java data types to their corresponding types for the XML/WSDL definition. In the current version of the JWSDP there is support for the mapping of both primitive and object data types.

Primitives

Table 8.1 illustrates the mapping of supported primitive Java data types to the corresponding XML data type.

Table 8.1 Primitive Type Mapping

Primitive Data Type	XML Data Type
boolean	xsd:boolean
byte	xsd:byte
double	xsd:double
float	xsd:float
int	xsd:int
long	xsd:long
short	xsd:short

Object Types

The JAX-RPC also supports the following Java classes shown in Table 8.2. Note that the Java wrapper classes are mapped to their corresponding SOAP encoded type.

Table 8.2 Object Type Mapping

Object Data Type	XML Data Type
java.lang.String	xsd:String
java.lang.Boolean	xsd:boolean
java.lang.Byte	xsd:byte
java.lang.Double	xsd:double
java.lang.Float	xsd:float
java.lang.Integer	xsd:int
java.lang.Long	xsd:long
java.lang.Short	xsd:short
java.math.BigDecimal	xsd:decimal
java.math.BigInteger	xsd:integer
java.util.Calendar	xsd:dateTime
java.util.Date	xsd:dateTime

Arrays

The JAX-RPC specification supports arrays, provided they are of a type already supported by JAX-RPC. For example, the following code represents a perfectly valid service definition interface. Both the *String* Object type and the *int* primitive data type are supported, so an array of those types is likewise supported.

```
import java.rmi.Remote;
import java.rmi.RemoteException;

public interface LoanApplicationIF extends Remote
{
    public String[] getCreditRating( int[] ids )
    throws RemoteException;
}
```

The JAX-RPC also provides support for multi-dimensional arrays. Again the constraint is that the data type of the array must be of a supported type.

```
import java.rmi.Remote;
import java.rmi.RemoteException;
```

```
public interface WorkingHoursCalculateIF extends Remote
{
      public int[][] getWorkingHours( int year )
      throws RemoteException;

}
```

Application Classes

Typically, when you design an OO application you create custom classes that represent objects. These objects can be *Customers, Orders, Trouble Tickets, Employees,* or whatever you need. These classes encapsulate the state of each instance of those objects. An *Employee* class might hold a first name, last name, social security number, hire date and so on.

JAX-RPC provides support for these types of classes. In the JAX-RPC specification these classes are referred to as *Value Types.* That name was assigned because the class passes its state (values) from the client to the server and back.

The application class can be treated as a value type under the following conditions.

- The application class must have a public *no-argument* (default) constructor.

- Neither the application class nor any of its super classes may implement the *java.rmi.Remote* interface.

- All members of the application class must be of one of the supported types.

Assuming that these requirements are satisfied, the application class may have any of the following characteristics:

- The members of the application can have any of the defined scope modifiers; public, private, protected, and the default (package).

- The application class is free to implement any interface except for *java.rmi.Remote.*

- The application class may extend any other class, so long as it does not derive from a class that implements *java.rmi.Remote.*

- The application class may contain transient members.

- The application class may contain static members.

If your application class has been created as a JavaBean, the JAX-RPC API can still support it. The requirements for JavaBean support are that the bean follows the standard naming convention for its accessors and mutators. JAX-RPC adds the restriction that the properties of that bean must be of one of the supported types.

> **NOTE**
>
> The use of the *java.rmi.Remote* interface when creating your service interfaces marks them as remote objects that may be invoked from a remote virtual machine.

Arbitrary Java Classes

The JAX-RPC specification provides an extensible type-mapping framework that allows developers to add support for mapping between XML types and Java types that are not supported in the default configuration. This mapping framework is implemented by *serializers* and *deserializers*. These serializers and deserializers are plugged into the framework and provide the mapping between any arbitrary Java type and XML type.

Serializers

A serializer is a Java class that can transform a Java data type to SOAP-encoded XML. This serializer implements a method called *serialize* which is invoked by a container (stub or tie) when a Java data type needs to be converted to its XML representation.

There are several requirements that a serializer must satisfy in order to be used within the JAX-RPC framework. The following list highlights those requirements:

- The serializer must implement the *SOAPSerializer* interface.
- The serializer must be stateless.
- The serializer must be thread-safe.

Deserializers

A deserializer is a Java class that can recreate instances of a Java data type that were SOAP-encoded during serialiazation. A deserializer performs the following steps.

1 The object represented by an XML element is opened.

2. Each of that object's members are deserialized.

3. The appropriate Java data type is created and initialized with the deserialized members.

4. The new object instance is passed back as the return value of the *deserialize* method.

There are several requirements that a deserializer must satisfy in order to be used within the JAX-RPC framework. The following list highlights those requirements.

■ The deserializer must implement the *SOAPDeserializer* interface.

■ The deserializer must be stateless.

■ The deserializer must be thread-safe.

These requirements are basically the same as those of the serializers, except that deserializers implement a different interface.

Holder Classes

Holder classes are used to enable the Java to WSDL mapping to preserve the wsdl:operation signature and parameters.

Each holder class has the same characteristics. These characteristics are as follows.

■ The holder class will be defined as implementing the *javax.xml.rpc .holders.Holder* interface.

■ A public member named *value* that is of a type consistent with a valid mapped Java type.

■ A default *no-argument* constructor. This constructor will initialize the *value* member.

■ A constructor that has a single parameter of the same type as the *value* member. This constructor should set the value member to the specified value. The JAX-RPC specification provides holder classes for the primitive data types in the *javax.xml.rpc.holders* package. The name of these pre-defined holder classes is derived by taking the name of the primitive type and adding a *Holder* suffix.

Conversion Between Java Classes and WSDL

A WSDL file is an XML document used to describe a Web Service. It contains the definitions of all methods available, the parameters' data types and the data type of the return value. These WSDL files can get complex in a hurry. Fortunately the JWSDP has provided a tool to facilitate the creation of these files.

WSDL Generator

The JWSDP comes with a command-line tool called *xrpcc* that automates the tasks of creating client stubs, server ties and WSDL files. This tool is located at *<JWSDP_HOME>/bin*. The tool accepts several command-line options that affect what it generates. It can create RMI Interfaces or a WSDL Document, depending on what is specified in its config file. The xrpcc tool has the following syntax.

```
xrpcc.extension [options] config_filename
```

Here, *extension* will be *bat* for Windows and *sh* for UNIX.

Command Line Options

The xrpcc command-line tool has several options. These options determine its runtime behavior. Table 8.3 list the command-line options.

Table 8.3 xrpcc tool command line options

Option	Description
-server	Generates all server artifacts. This includes Ties, Server Configuration File, and WSDL file or a Service Definition Interface (whichever of the two is not defined)
-client	Generates all client artifacts. This includes stubs, the Service Interface, Implementation Classes and possibly the Remote Interface.
-both	Instructs the xrpcc tool to generate both the server and the client artifacts listed above.
-classpath *classpath*	Explicitly sets the classpath that the tool will use during execution.
-d *directory*	Denotes the directory where the output of the tool should go.
-keep	Instructs the tool to keep the Java source files generated after they have been compiled. The default behavior is to remove these source files after compilation.
-version	Instructs the tool to display the version number of the JAX-RPC API.

Tool Configuration File

The following example illustrates one of the two general structures of the xrpcc config file. In this case we are assuming that we have the RMI interfaces and wish to generate the WSDL file (along with the stubs and ties).

```
<configuration xmlns="http://java.sun.com/jax-rpc-ri/xrpcc-config">
    <rmi name="..." targetNamespace="..."
         typeNamespace="...">
        <service name="..." packageName="...">
            <interface name="..." servantName="..."
                       soapAction="..."
                       soapActionBase=""/>
        </service>
        <typeMappingRegistry>
        ...
        </typeMappingRegistry>
    </rmi>
</configuration>
```

Table 8.4 shows the config file elements for RMI-based generation.

Table 8.4 config file elements for RMI based generation

Element	Attribute	Description
rmi	name	This attribute denotes the name you have given this model.
	targetNamespace	This attribute denotes the target namespace for the generated WSDL file.
	typeNamespace	This attribute denotes the target namespace for the schema section of the generated WSDL file.
service	name	This attribute denotes the name you have given this service.
	packageName	This attribute denotes the full package name to give the generated classes.
interface	name	The fully qualified package name of the Service Definition Interface.
	servantName	The fully qualified package name of the Service Implementation class.
	soapAction	This optional attribute allows you to specify a String to be used as the *SOAPAction* for all actions.
	soapActionBase	This optional attribute allows you to specify a String value that will be used as a prefix for the *SOAPAction* strings.
typeMappingRegistry	N/A	This elements body is where you would place optional type mapping information.

The DTD that defines this document dictates that there only be one *rmi* element. Multiple *service* elements containing one or more *interface* child element(s) are permissible, however.

The following is the general structure of the xrpcc config file for those instances where you have the WSDL file and wish to generate the RMI interfaces (along with the stubs and ties).

```
<configuration xmlns="http://java.sun.com/jax-rpc-ri/xrpcc-config">

    <wsdl name="..." location="..." packageName="...">
```

```
<typeMappingRegistry>


</typeMappingRegistry>
    </wsdl>
</configuration>
```

Table 8.5 shows the config file elements for WSDL-based generation.

Table 8.5 config file elements for WSDL based generation

Element	Attribute	Description
wsdl	name	This attribute denotes the name you have given this model.
	location	This attribute denotes a URL that points to a WSDL document.
	packageName	This attribute denotes the fully quali-fied package name for the generated classes and interfaces.
typeMappingRegistry	N/A	This element's body is where you would place optional type mapping information.

For this document the DTD specifies that one and only one *wsdl* element may exist.

Server Configuration File

The xrpcc tool also generates a properties file, which is used to configure the server web application during its initialization. A reference is placed to this prop-erties file within the initialization parameters for the service endpoint servlet, which is in turn within the server web application's *web.xml* deployment descriptor.

```
<init-param>
    <param-name>configuration.file</param-name>
    <param-value>/WEB-INF/ServiceName_Config.properties</param-value>
</init-param>
```

The name of the generated properties file is derived by applying the Service Name found in the Tool Configuration file to the following formula.

```
<Service Name>_Config.properties.
```

A typical properties file will contain information similar to the following example.

```
port0.tie=websvc.accounting.IAccountsPayable_Tie
port0.servant=websvc.accounting.AccountsPayableImpl
port0.name=IAccountsPayable
port0.wsdl.targetNamespace=http://mybusiness.org/wsdl
port0.wsdl.serviceName=AccountPayable
port0.wsdl.portName=AccountPayablePort
port1.tie=websvc.accounting.IAccountsReceivable_Tie
port1.servant=websvc.accounting.AccountsReceivableImpl
port1.name=IAccountsReceivable
port1.wsdl.targetNamespace=http://mybusiness.org/wsdl
port1.wsdl.serviceName=AccountsReceivable
port1.wsdl.portName=AccountsReceivablePort
portcount=2
```

NOTE

The config file used to define the runtime behavior of the xrpcc command-line tool, as well as the tool itself, are not actually part of the JAX-RPC specification. Therefore it is safe to assume that the syntax of the tool may change by the final release of the specification.

Using Classes Generated by the Stub Generator

The server-specific classes generated by the tool must be packaged into the WAR file containing the service implementation. For the client to use the classes generated by the xrpcc tool, they only need to be in the CLASSPATH environment variable that is accessible by your client application.

Creating a JAX-RPC Client

A JAX-RPC Client is an application that invokes methods through a proxy hosted at a service endpoint. Using the tools provided by the JWSDP, the creation of a JAX-RPC client is not that complicated. You will most certainly possess or have access to the WSDL file that describes the services available, or you may have the stubs that were generated using the WSDL (or xrpcc config file).

Your client CLASSPATH will have to contain the service stub classes generated by the xrpcc tool described earlier.

Before the client can invoke service methods it will have to get an instance of the service stub. This service stub acts as a proxy to the service implementation. Once an instance of this stub is created, calls can be made on this stub as if the service was a local object.

Once the client has been coded, you can simply compile it and run. If all works correctly your client application will be able to invoke methods on remote service objects and return the results.

Creating a Connection to a Remote Server

The client starts the process of invoking a remote method by first instantiating the appropriate stub class. The name of the required stub class will conform to the following naming convention: *<Service Definition Interface Name>_Stub.class.*

This class is generated automatically by the xrpcc tool. If you use the *–keep* option on this tool when you generate the stubs the source file will remain on your file system. If you examine this source file, you will see that it is defined as implementing the SDI methods. The generated implementations of those methods contain the code necessary to establish a connection, send a SOAP message, and retrieve a result (if necessary).

Once a stub instance has been created it needs to be directed as to where to locate the remote service. This is accomplished by calling the *_setProperty (String, String)* method of the stub instance. The first String parameter should denote the name of the property for the endpoint, in this case accessible as the class member *javax.xml.rpc.Stub.ENDPOINT_ADDRESS_PROPERTY*, and the second String parameter should contain the service endpoint, or location, that is hosting the functionality desired.

Invoking Methods on a Remote Server

The stub class contains the same methods as the SDI. Once the stub has been instantiated you may invoke the same methods defined in that interface. The parameters are passed to the service endpoint, the target method is executed and the resulting data (if any) is returned to the client that invoked the method in the first place. From the client's perspective, the process looks the same as a local method call.

There are other issues that need to be considered here. Since you are making a call over the network, latency needs to be addressed. The remote procedure calls are synchronous, so it is imperative that you design your application with this in mind. You may want to consider passing as much data as you can back and forth over the wire with as few calls as possible.

Creating a JAX-RPC Server

The JAX-RPC Server provides business logic that is accessible as a remote procedure call. This server is hosted by a web server and is invoked by the client as a URL passing SOAP messages back and forth.

Creating the Service Definition Interface

The creation of a JAX-RPC Server starts with the design and development of the SDI. It is through this interface that all business functions are called. The following are examples of what these interfaces might look like.

```
import java.rmi.Remote;
import java.rmi.RemoteException;

public interface ISchoolAdministration extends Remote
{
    public String[] studentList( String class )
                    throws RemoteException;
    public double gpa( String student )
                throws RemoteException;
    public boolean enroll( String student )
                throws RemoteException;
    public boolean graduate( String student )
                throws RemoteException;
}
```

Here we have defined several business methods that a school administrator might want to invoke.

Creating the xrpcc Config File

The xrpcc command-line tool is used to generate files for the JAX-RPC API. Given a WSDL file, it can create a set of RMI classes, and vice-versa. A config file called *config.xml* is used to determine the various parameters that dictate the tool's output.

Developing the Service Implementation

The next step is to create the actual service implementation. This class will be defined as implementing the service interface defined above. The implementation will also need the services of ties and other classes to communicate with the client. These classes are generated by xrpcc passing in the *-server* argument. Xrpcc will use the config file created in the previous step to generate the necessary classes.

Building the Server WAR File

The service definition is packaged as a Web Archive (WAR) file. This WAR file is a specialized JAR package whose directory structure and mandatory contents are defined in the Java Servlet Specification version 2.3. By packaging a service definition in this manner it becomes possible to deploy the Service across a wide variety of platforms.

The Service Definition WAR package contains the following mandatory items:

- All service definition interfaces, each with exactly one interface to describe the methods available.

- All implementing classes of these service definition interfaces.

- All resources of the service implementations. A resource may include graphics, static content (such as HTML), XML documents and so on.

- the web.xml deployment descriptor, whose content conforms with that specified in the Java Servlet Specification version 2.3. This deployment descriptor must be within the /WEB-INF folder relative to the package root.

The Service Definition WAR package may also contain the following optional items:

- Any Serializers or De-serializers to be used for custom data type mapping.

- A WSDL file that describes the service to be deployed.

Once packaged into a WAR file the web application can be deployed to any Servlet 2.3-compliant web server.

Developing & Deploying…

Developing and Deploying a Web Service made with the JAX-RPC API

The development and deployment of a Web Service that is built upon the JAX-RPC API can be summarized in the following steps.

1. Define your service provider interface.
2. Create an implementation based on that interface.
3. Create a config file that describes your web service to xrpcc.
4. Generate the server ties and related classes using xrpcc.
5. Package the server into a WAR file as per the Servlet 2.3 Specification.
6. Deploy the WAR file to your web server.

Creating a Simple XML-RPC Server and Client

Now we will go through the entire process of creating a web service with a client application to call it. The first step will be to design and create the SDI. As described earlier in this chapter, this interface will define those business methods we will want to make accessible via an RPC from a remote client.

In this example we will use an on-line library. This library will offer the ability to search for books that contain keywords in the titles and return a list of books that match. This service should also offer the ability to check books in and out.

The following is an SDI that satisfies our business requirements.

```
import java.rmi.Remote;
import java.rmi.RemoteException;
```

```
public interface ILibrary extends Remote
{
    /**
     * Performs a search for a book (or books) whose title
     * contains the key specified. Returns a String array
     * containing the ISBN numbers of books that matched.
     */
    public String[] searchForBook( String key )
                    throws RemoteException;


    /**
     * Performs a checkout of a book denoted by the ISBN
     * parameter and using the library card number
     * provided.
     * Returns true the book was checked out successfully.
     */
    public Boolean checkOutBook( String ISBN,
                                    String cardNumber )
                    throws RemoteException;


    /**
     * Performs a checkin of a book denoted by the ISBN
     * parameter.
     * Returns true the book was checked in successfully.
     */
    public Boolean checkInBook( String ISBN )
                    throws RemoteException;
}
```

Having completed our service definition, you need to make the actual service implementation. This example does not go into detail as to how to perform the lookup of the books. Presumably you will have some sort of data store (probably a relational database) that this class will search for the library book information.

```
public class LibraryImpl implements ILibrary
{
    /**
     * Performs a search for a book (or books) whose
```

```
    * title contains the key specified.
    * Returns a String array containing the
    * ISBN numbers of books that matched.
    */
   public String[] searchForBook(String key)
   {
       /*
        * Perform the lookup an return the results.
        */
   }


   /**
    * Performs a checkout of a book denoted by the
    * ISBN parameter and using the library card number
    * provided.
    * Returns true the book was checked out successfully.
    */
   public Boolean checkOutBook(String ISBN,
                                   String cardNumber)
   {
       /*
        * Checkout the book and return status.
        */
   }


   /**
    * Performs a checkout of a book denoted by the ISBN
    * parameter.
    * Returns true the book was checked in successfully.
    */
   public Boolean checkInBook(String ISBN)
   {
       /*
        * Check in the book and return status.
        */
   }
}
```

We will use the xrpcc command-line tool that comes with the JWSDP to generate the stubs, ties and the WSDL file that will describe our library Web service. To configure xrpcc's runtime behavior, we will need to create a config.xml file that describes the service and what the tool needs to generate.

In our example we will need to create the following XML file:

```xml
<?xml version="1.0" encoding="UTF-8"?>
<configuration xmlns="http://java.sun.com/jax-rpc-ri/xrpcc-config">
    <rmi name="LibraryService" targetNamespace="http://210-ch08.org/wsdl"
        typeNamespace="http://210-ch08.org/types">
        <service name="Library" packageName="websvc">
            <interface name="websvc.ILibrary" servantName="websvc.
                LibraryImpl"/>
        </service>
    </rmi>
</configuration>
```

By virtue of including a child *<rmi>* element, we have effectively told xrpcc that we have the RMI class (service definition interface) and we wish it to generate the WSDL file (as well as the usual client stubs and server ties).

Use xrpcc's *-server* option to generate only those ties and classes necessary for the server implementation. Once this is complete, you should have a list of generated classes that look like this:

```
ILibrary_Tie.class

Library_SerializerRegistry.class

CheckInBook_RequestStruct.class

CheckInBook_RequestStruct_SOAPSerializer.class

CheckInBook_ResponseStruct.class

CheckInBook_ResponseStruct_SOAPSerializer.class

CheckOutBook_RequestStruct.class

CheckOutBook_RequestStruct_SOAPSerializer.class

CheckOutBook_ResponseStruct.class

CheckOutBook_ResponseStruct_SOAPSerializer.class

SearchForBook_RequestStruct.class

SearchForBook_RequestStruct_SOAPSerializer.class

SearchForBook_ResponseStruct.class

SearchForBook_ResponseStruct_SOAPBuilder.class

SearchForBook_ResponseStruct_SOAPSerializer.class
```

Finally, you will want to create a client capable of invoking the service. The following is an example of a client application that serves an access point to the library service. Since the client will reference the stubs for this service, you have to generate them using xrpcc's *-client* option. This will give you a list of generated classes that looks like this:

```
ILibrary_Stub.class

Library.class

Library_Impl.class

Library_SerializerRegistry.class

CheckInBook_RequestStruct.class

CheckInBook_RequestStruct_SOAPSerializer.class

CheckInBook_ResponseStruct.class

CheckInBook_ResponseStruct_SOAPSerializer.class

CheckOutBook_RequestStruct.class

CheckOutBook_RequestStruct_SOAPSerializer.class

CheckOutBook_ResponseStruct.class

CheckOutBook_ResponseStruct_SOAPSerializer.class

SearchForBook_RequestStruct.class

SearchForBook_RequestStruct_SOAPSerializer.class

SearchForBook_ResponseStruct.class

SearchForBook_ResponseStruct_SOAPBuilder.class

SearchForBook_ResponseStruct_SOAPSerializer.class
```

The stub class, conspicuously named with the *_Stub* suffix, will be the proxy class through which the client will invoke library functions.

```
package websvc;

public class LibraryClient
{
    private ILibrary_Stub stub;

    public LibraryClient( String endpoint ) throws Exception
    {
        stub = (ILibrary_Stub)( new Library_Impl().getILibrary() );
        stub._setProperty( javax.xml.rpc.Stub.ENDPOINT_ADDRESS_PROPERTY,
            endpoint );
    }
```

```java
public String[] searchForBook( String Key )
{
    String[] result = null;

    try
    {
        result = stub.searchForBook( Key );
    }
    catch( Exception e )
    {
        e.printStackTrace();
    }

    return result;
}

public boolean checkOutBook( String ISBN,
                             String cardNumber )
{
    try
    {
        stub.checkOutBook( ISBN, cardNumber );
    }
    catch( Exception e )
    {
        e.printStackTrace();
    }
}

public boolean checkInBook( String ISBN,
                            String cardNumber )
{
    try
    {
        stub.checkInBook( ISBN, cardNumber );
    }
```

```
        catch( Exception e )
        {
            e.printStackTrace();
        }
    }
}
```

Once the client has been compiled and packaged it may be deployed any-where that it can access the web server hosting the web service we created earlier.

NOTE

These examples were developed against the JAX-RPC specification version 0.8 PFD.

Summary

The JAX-RPC API offers a fast way to incorporate remote procedure calls into your distributed heterogeneous application. This functionality is realized via a framework that creates remote procedure calls using synchronous XML messages, which contain function-call semantics. These web services are built on the Java language and can be deployed on multiple platforms.

The interface that defines the methods to be made available as a web service is called the *service definition*. This interface must extend *java.rmi.Remote*, and each method must be declared to throw *java.rmi.RemoteException*.

The client that wishes to invoke methods on the server and receive execution results does so through a stub. A stub is a class that serves as a service proxy for the client. The server that wishes to be enabled for remote procedure calls must have a tie class. This tie class acts as a client proxy for the server. Both the stubs and ties translate method calls and return values to SOAP-encoded XML for transmission over HTTP.

A Web Service Description Language (WSDL) file describes a Web Service. This description includes the service methods and their associated semantics, as well as the location of the service provider. A client that wishes to use a Web Service can then use this WSDL file to determine the service offerings and the syntax to invoke them.

The JWSDP provides a command-line driven tool called xrpcc that facilitates the creation of stubs, ties and the other artifacts necessary to develop web services. This tool is configured using an XML file. Given the SDI or the WSDL file, xrpcc can generate all necessary files.

The SDI, ties and other generated server artifacts are packaged together in a Web Archive (WAR) file with an internal directory structure and including a deployment descriptor as defined by the Java Servlet Specification version 2.3. This WAR file, which effectively contains the entire Web Service, may be deployed on a web server that has been prepared so as to include the necessary libraries from the JWSDP.

Once deployed, your Web Service may be invoked by any client, including (but not limited to) Java based clients. This interoperability is possible due to the support for SOAP over HTTP and WSDL in the JAX-RPC.

Solutions Fast Track

JAX-RPC Summary

- ☑ JAX-RPC API is an API for building web services.
- ☑ JAX-RPC is facilitated by using synchronous XML messages using SOAP over HTTP.

Mapping Java Data Types

- ☑ All Java primitive types (except *char*) are supported.
- ☑ Java classes that are not supported out of the box can be supported using custom serializers and deserializers.
- ☑ JavaBeans are supported by the JAX-RPC API.

Conversion Between Java Classes and WSDL

- ☑ The xrpcc command-line tool can create the WSDL service definition file from a proprietary config file and a service definition interface.
- ☑ Xrpcc and the config file that supports it are not part of the JAX-RPC specification and are subject to change in future releases.
- ☑ If the WSDL file already exists, then the RMI class can be generated from it.
- ☑ If the RMI classes already exist, then the WSDL file can be generated from them.

Creating a JAX-RPC Client

- ☑ JAX-RPC Clients use stubs to communicate with the server.
- ☑ The stubs needed for communication can be generated using xrpcc with the optional *-client* argument.

Creating a JAX-RPC Server

☑ JAX-RPC Servers use ties created by xrpcc to communicate with the client.

☑ The SDI is that interface which defines the methods to be published by the web service.

☑ A server defines an endpoint to access the desired service. This endpoint is basically a URL that gets mapped to the service implementation.

Creating a Simple XML-RPC Server and Client

☑ We created a web service with an asociated client application. The first step was to design and create the SDI, which defined those business methods we wanted to make accessible via an RPC from a remote client.

☑ We used the xrpcc command-line tool that comes with the JWSDP to generate the stubs, ties and the WSDL file to describe our Library Web Service. To configure xrpcc's runtime behavior, we had to create a config.xml file to describe the service and what the tool needed to generate.

☑ We included a child *<rmi>* element to tell the xrpcc tool that we had the RMI class (SDI) and we wished it to generate the WSDL file (as well as the usual client stubs and server ties).

☑ Once the client was compiled and packaged, it could be deployed anywhere that it could access the web server hosting the web service we created earlier.

Frequently Asked Questions

The following Frequently Asked Questions, answered by the authors of this book, are designed to both measure your understanding of the concepts presented in this chapter and to assist you with real-life implementation of these concepts. To have your questions about this chapter answered by the author, browse to **www.syngress.com/solutions** and click on the **"Ask the Author"** form.

Q: What are some of the JAX-RPC API-related concerns that I might need to address in the design of my application?

A: XML-RPC is a synchronous communication framework. Therefore, your remote method calls will block until the result of the method invocation comes back over the wire. Architecture considerations include designing your remote method calls to pass as much data as possible in order to minimize the number of connections you'll need to make. Another consideration is to make those classes that perform the actual remote method invocation threaded and/or pooled so as to provide some measure of decoupling with the rest of the client application.

Q: How can I improve the speed or efficiency of my client's remote procedure calls?

A: A common technique for improving efficiency is to design your SDI to perform several functions with one method call. By bundling functionality over a single HTTP request you can improve your client's overall performance of. Another approach would be to pool instances that call the service.

Q: Can I obtain the source code for the generated ties and stubs?

A: The xrpcc command-line tool will normally remove any generated Java source files after successful compilation. You can override this behavior by using the -*keep* argument. This will instruct the tool to leave the source files where it compiled the class files.

Q: How can I use web services built with the JAX-RPC API if I do not know the signatures of the methods I want to call until runtime?

A: The use of Dynamic Invocation Interfaces (DII) would solve your problem. Due to the complexity and difficulty in debugging such clients, it is not generally recommended to use DII unless there is no other alternative. The JAX-RPC specification covers this functionality in greater detail.

Q: What are the differences between stubs and ties?

A: Both deal with the marshalling and unmarshalling of data. They both take data in the form of XML containing method call semantics and convert the data to and from network transport formats. The stubs perform this function on the Client side and the ties perform this function on the Server side.

Chapter 9

Locating Web Services

Solutions in this chapter:

- **Registries**
- **Categorizing Web Services**
- **Connecting to a Registry**
- **Querying the Registry**
- **WSDL Documents**
- **Storing Information in a Registry**

- ☑ **Summary**
- ☑ **Solutions Fast Track**
- ☑ **Frequently Asked Questions**

Introduction

To call a Web service, several pieces of information are required. In particular, the location (URL) of the service and the schema to pass requests in are critical for a message to be understood by the right remote service.

The simplest means of deriving this information is by hand. You can, for instance, communicate with a fellow programmer or use Web sites such as www.xmethods.com to find out the relevant information. However, the problem with this method is that with the Web being a fluid environment, new services are added and old ones removed continually. Consequently, evaluating the connection protocol for a Web service by hand calls for a lot of maintenance work to ensure the system continues to run smoothly.

To solve this problem, Web services can be published to registries. A *registry* is a collection of meta-information about Web services such as their location, the protocol used to contact them and so forth. While registries were originally seen as a global mechanism—where companies published Web services for anonymous business partners to find—more commonly, registries are being used internally by organizations to render service-based architectures more resilient and reliable.

In this chapter, we will explore JAXR, the Web Services Developer Pack component employed for communicating with registries. Additionally, we will introduce WSDL, the standard mechanism for describing the schema with which to call a remote service.

Registries

As mentioned in the introductory paragraph, a Web service registry contains information about Web services and their providers. The utility of registries lies in the fact that they can be searched by Web service clients to obtain data on available Web services. In this section, we discuss how the metadata about services is stored and also the standards upon which the registries are built.

Storage of Metadata about Services

A registry entry stores information about an organization such as:

- The name of the organization
- The description of the organization
- A collection of services offered by the organization

- The name of the person who is the primary contact for the organization

- The postal address of the organization

- A key object that represents the ID through which an organization entry is uniquely identified by the registry and so on

In most cases, a service seeker or client would be looking for services pertaining to a specific industry sector. Thus, the client is less likely to search for a specific organization by name; instead, he is more likely to choose an industry sector to search for organizations that offer the desired services in that sector. In view of this, the registry uses classifications to categorize the information in the registry database. We now discuss how information in the registry is categorized.

Categories

The NAICS (North American Industry Classification System) is used for categorizing various businesses/ services, classifying business establishments on the basis of their major economic activity. The classification is production-oriented in the sense that it groups similar services or production processes.

NAICS groups services into 20 broad economic activity categories such as Manufacturing, Wholesale Trade, Information, Finance, Insurance, and so on. These economic activity categories are subdivided into subsectors. For example, Manufacturing has Food Manufacturing as a subsector. Each subsector is divided into industry groups. For example, Bakery and Tortilla Manufacturing is an industry group under the Food Manufacturing subsector. An industry group is finally divided into various NAICS industries. Though there are no further subclassifications beyond this level, the NAICS industries may be further divided to accommodate variations in U.S., Canadian, and Mexican industry nomenclatures. Figure 9.1 illustrates this classification of services concept.

Thus, categories are subdivided and organized in a tree hierarchy until they can be subdivided no further. (Categorizing concepts will be clarified further when we choose a classification for our organization in the section, "Using the Default Registry." See Figure 9.4 later in the chapter for an illustration of this).

There are a total of 1,170 NAICS categories, out of which 474 lie in the Manufacturing sector. NAICS uses a standard coding structure for assigning codes to the categories. Each industry is assigned a six-digit code. The first two digits of this code specify the economic activity category, the third digit specifies the subsector, the fourth digit the industry group, the fifth digit the NAICS industry, and the sixth digit is for U.S., Canadian, and Mexican industries.

We shall now discuss categorizing of services on the basis of location.

Figure 9.1 Categorizing Business Services in a Registry

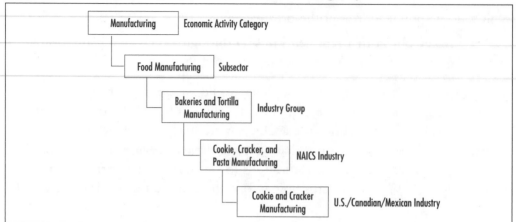

Locations

The geographical location of the service provider is an important criterion for the service seeker. This is especially true in the case of business transactions that will eventually involve transportation of physical goods from the manufacturer to the buyer because, the geographical location will determine to a great extent the transportation cost as well as the delivery schedules in terms of time required for transportation.

The *iso-ch:3166:1999* taxonomy for geographical regions is followed for classifying the location for a service. This taxonomy divides the physical locations on the basis of continents such as Asia, Europe, North America, and so on, or major continent-regions such as the Caribbean, the Middle East, and so on. These continents/continent-regions are subdivided into countries. For example, North America is subcategorized into the following North American countries: the U.S.A., Canada, and Mexico.

Major Registry Standards

In order to understand JAXR, you must first understand that it provides a standardized interface to common registry standards. JAXR simplifies the utilization of these registries, and ensures that code written for one registry can be moved transparently to another. In particular, JAXR provides interfaces for the most commonly used registry standards for Web services: UDDI and ebXML RegRep.

UDDI

Universal Description, Discovery, and Integration (UDDI) is an open specification that strives to implement a universal business registry capable of integrating electronic commerce sites. UDDI is a project initiated by the concerned industry sectors and businesses. The aim of UDDI is to create a platform-independent, global, and open specification for the following purposes:

- To enable vendors to offer/describe their services and businesses

- To enable potential buyers to search for these services and businesses

- To integrate these services and businesses over the Web

In short, UDDI aims at propelling the growth of business-to-business (B2B) e-commerce. UDDI does not concentrate on the listing and finding of services alone. It also addresses the problem of the lack of a standard mechanism to conduct business, once a buyer has found a suitable service provider. UDDI tackles this issue by enabling vendors to programmatically specify their preferred business practices and procedures.

The UDDI specification is implemented as the public UDDI Business Registry that is elemental to the infrastructure that supports e-commerce. The UDDI Business Registry is implemented as a set of distributed registries on Web-enabled media. Vendors can register their services and businesses with these registries and buyers can browse them to search for vendors and/or services. The distributed UDDI registries are maintained as registry nodes, where each node is managed by an operator who is bound by an agreement to follow the policy and quality of service guidelines formulated by an Operator's Council (IBM and Microsoft are two such operators who are currently operating registry nodes). Each registry node contains a complete set of the records registered with all the registry nodes taken together. This is achieved by regularly replicating the registrations across all the nodes. The operators use a common set of APIs to ensure that all the nodes can exchange information with one another.

Though the original intent of UDDI was to have global registries accessible over the Internet, organizations are implementing private registries, compliant with the UDDI specification, on their intranets, extranets, or private networks on the Internet. These private registries may offer functionality and services tailored for specific authorized users. For example, a private registry may catalog an organization's services that can be located over the organization's private networks with trading partners, or be used for internal reference purposes.

The UDDI Business Registry structure categorizes information under the following headings:

- **Business-Entity** A business entity is a unique identifier for an entry in the registry. Besides this, it contains the following information:

  - The name of the business.

  - A short description of the service/business.

  - Basic contact information regarding the vendor.

  - A list of categories that describe the service/business.

  - A URL that provides more information about the service/business.

- **Business Service** The business service lists the services/businesses offered by an entity. Each of these service/business entries contain the following information:

  - A description of the service/business.

  - A list of categories that describe the service/business.

  - A list of pointers pointing to locations where related information about the service/business can be found.

- **Specification Pointers** Each business service entry contains a list of specification pointers. These specification pointers serve a dual purpose.

  - They point to those URLs where information related to a business service can be found. These URLs, in turn, may contain information on how to invoke a service.

  - They associate a business service entry with a particular service type.

- **Service Types** A service type defines the nature of a business service, and can include multiple categories. It is defined by a tModel, which contains the following information:

  - The name of the tModel.

  - The name of the organization that published the tModel.

  - A list of categories that describe the service type.

  - Technical specifications for the service type such as protocols, interface definitions, message formats and so on.

UDDI uses the Simple Object Access Protocol (SOAP). However, a service registered with UDDI can use any Internet protocol such as SOAP, COM+, ebXML Message Service, CORBA, Java RMI, and so on for its service interface (The interface that is used to invoke the service).

NOTE

A UDDI registry, though searchable, is very different from a search engine. Search engines are meant to search unstructured and random data related to any field, such as education, industry, society, and so on. A UDDI registry, however, is highly structured and is specifically meant for offering services and businesses. Instead of a random search, it supports one focused on industry, product category, and geographical location. A search engine, however, can use the UDDI registry as a source while producing search results.

ebXML

ebXML is a suite of specifications that defines standard methods to enable business transactions over the Web. It details methods for defining and registering business processes, exchanging business data and messages and conducting business relationships, and includes searchable public repositories (like the UDDI Registry) where services/ businesses can be registered. ebXML is designed to be platform-independent so that any system that supports XML, the standard Internet protocols, and, of course, ebXML, can transact e-business using ebXML.

ebXML is an initiative backed by UN/CEFACT (United Nations Centre for Trade Facilitation and Electronic Business) and OASIS (Organization for the Advancement of Structured Information Standards). (UN/CEFACT is a United Nations body whose mission is to facilitate international transactions by standardizing business procedures and harmonizing information flow. OASIS, on the other hand, is a global consortium that develops standards for Web services, electronic publishing, business transactions on the Internet and elsewhere, and encourages adoption of e-business standards.)

Extensible Markup Language (XML) is at the core of ebXML, and was chosen for ebXML because it allows exchange of structured data like the data stored in databases and is a freely available standard for information exchange widely supported by the industry. Another advantage is that XML supports Unicode that can display most of the world's languages.

The ebXML architecture is composed of two parts:

1. **Product Architecture** The product architecture constitutes the technical infrastructure of the software. It consists of the following elements:

   ■ **Messaging Service** This is a protocol-neutral service that standardizes the way business messages are exchanged between trading organizations. This messaging service is secure and reliable and also allows for routing a message to an internal application once an organization has received it. Any standard protocol such as FTP, HTTP, SMTP and so on can be employed for file transfer while using the messaging service. Additionally, all communications with the Registry are possible only through the use of the ebXML messaging service.

   ■ **Registry** An ebXML Registry is akin to the user interface of a repository. The registry stores information about items that are actually stored in the repository. The repository items can be created, modified or deleted through requests made to the registry. ebXML specifies a minimum information model (that defines the types of information stored in the registry) and the manner in which other applications interact with the registry, but it does not specify the implementation of the registry or repository. The registry contains information such as business documents or agreements, component-definition for business process modeling, and so on. The ebXML Registry is a single one as against the distributed registry network of UDDI (which can be used to locate an ebXML registry).

   ■ **Trading Partner Information** The Collaboration Profile Protocol (CPP) is used to define an XML document that details the manner in which an organization can conduct e-business. These details include information about the organization such as the types of protocol used by it, security implementations, network addresses, and business procedures. The Collaboration Protocol Agreement (CPA) specifies how two trading partners have agreed to conduct business electronically. The ebXML specification includes issues involved in creating a CPA from the CPPs of the two parties that intend to conduct business, though it does not specify the algorithm for generating the CPA.

- **Business Process Specification Schema (BPSS)** This schema defines an XML document (as an XML DTD) to describe how an organization conducts its business. Note that CPP or CPA deals with *how* an organization conducts e-business while BPSS deals with the actual business process. This includes the business transactions, document flow, business level acknowledgements, legal and security aspects, and so on. The BPSS can be used by an application to configure the details of conducting e-business with a chosen business partner.

2. **Process Architecture** The process architecture is meant for analysis and development. This architecture provides the following contributions:

  - **Business Process Analysis Worksheet and Guidelines** The Business process Analysis worksheets and the guidelines for using them assist in collecting the information necessary to describe a business process. This information can be used to create a BPSS XML document. Business Process Editors can be developed on the basis of the worksheets. These editors can guide the user in collecting information and automatically generating the XML business process specification.

  - **Catalog of Common Business Processes** This catalog contains description of common business processes being used by various organizations.

  - **E-Commerce Patterns** The e-commerce patterns contain descriptions and examples of the common business patterns. To date, only one pattern has been listed, which is for simple contract formation.

  - **Core Components** The core components are the basic information elements used in business messages. The type of information for these core elements may vary with industry, geographical location, and so on. The core components are developed from existing or new business documents and analyzed so as to standardize them for use in specific industries or regions. These business messages and documents exchanged in a business process are composed of the core components that are also known as "business information objects."

The product and process architecture are linked through the BPSS that is a machine or software application interpretable encoding of a business process.

Thus, ebXML provides a standard structure and syntax on which developers can build packaged applications for the smooth exchange of business data.

Readers should note that though UDDI and ebXML RegRep address the same issue, UDDI is a specification backed by an industry-led consortium, whereas ebXML is an open standard.

Categorizing Web Services

Web services receive, process (if required), and respond to requests from Web-clients. They encompass any self-contained software component/application or piece of code that can be deployed on a Web server, and subsequently be invoked over the Web by Web-clients. The realm of Web services varies from simple acknowledgement of a client's request to complex business processes. If Web services are to cater to businesses, it is imperative that data on Web services should be categorized to create a semblance of order to make them searchable. In this section, we discuss how Web services can be categorized.

Category Hierarchies

As mentioned in the section, "Storage of Metadata about Services," categorization is crucial for proper organization and maintenance of a business registry. Since JAXR APIs are specifically meant for use with business registries, they obviously contain provisions to categorize registry objects.

The *ClassificationScheme* interface in the *javax.xml.registry.infomodel* package is a subinterface of the *RegistryObject* interface and is used to represent a taxonomy that may be used to categorize *RegistryObject* instances. The *RegistryObject* class is an abstract class that provides the minimal metadata for various registry objects. For example, in Figure 9.1, *Industry* is the classification scheme that has been used to categorize the services. If we categorize services or organizations on the basis of their geographical location, then *Geography* would be the classification scheme. A *ClassificationScheme* instance can be used to obtain, add, or remove child concepts from a classification scheme. (A *concept*, meanwhile, is used in JAXR to hold the information about a specification.) The *ClassificationScheme* interface provides numerous methods to set or retrieve information about classification schemes. Some of these methods, whose names are self-explanatory, are *addChildConcepts()*, *getChildConcepts()*, *addClassifications()*, *removeClassifcations()*, and so on.

While the *ClassificationScheme* interface refers to a classification scheme, the *Classification* interface is used for actual classification of *RegistryObject* instances. Adding *Classification* instances to the *RegistryObject* classifies the *RegistryObject* along multiple dimensions. These dimensions could be the industry, the products, and the geographical location.

The *Classification* interface allows the classification of *RegistryObjects* using a *ClassificationScheme*. This *ClassificationScheme* may represent an internal taxonomy (in which the taxonomy elements and their structural relationship with one another is represented within the registry provider) or an external taxonomy (in which the taxonomy elements and their structural relationship with one another is represented outside the registry provider). A *Classification* instance that uses a *ClassificationScheme* representing an internal taxonomy is known as an internal classification. Whereas, a *Classification* instance that uses a *ClassificationScheme* representing an external taxonomy is known as an external classification. The Classification interface provides a number of methods to set or retrieve classification schemes and information related to a registry object. These methods include *getClassificationScheme()*, *setClassificationScheme()*, *getConcept()*, *setConcept()*, *getClassifiedObject()*, and so on.

Example Hierarchies

The most common and widely-known example of a classification scheme is the classification of the world into living and non-living objects. Living things are further classified into plants and animals, animals are classified into mammals, and so on. Thus, living things are classified under a tree-like structure.

Another example, more appropriate to the current discussion, is that of the NAICS (North American Industry Classification System) used to classify businesses and services on the basis of the industry to which they belong. As explained in the subsection, "Categories," under the section, "Storing Metadata about Services," the NAICS breaks up a broad industry sector into subsectors, in a hierarchical pattern, right up to the point where the industry narrows down to its smallest logical unit.

Organization, User

An organization is the physical entity that represents an entry in a business registry. The Web services being offered and searched for in a registry are eventually offered by an organization that makes it possible for the requested service to be executed.

The *javax.xml.registry.infomodel* provides the *Organization* interface to encompass this physical entity (the organization). As mentioned in the section, "Storing Metadata about Services," an organization has distinguished parameters such as the name of the organization, its description, its postal address, the primary contact person in the organization, telephone number, e-mail address for the contact, services offered by the organization, and so on. Thus, the Organization interface that represents an organization provides methods to retrieve this organizational information when a registry is searched. These methods include *getName()*, *getDescription()*, *getServices()*, *getPrimaryContact()*, and so on.

A vendor who uses a business registry to offer services, submits the relevant information to the registry in the form of an *Organization* instance. Hence, the *Organization* interface also encompasses methods to create an organization and set its data such as name, description (*setDescription()*), services (*addServices()*), and so on.

Though an organization is a physical entity, it remains abstract in nature. It is the people working in the organization that give it a definitive structure and a tangible physical form. Therefore, a primary contact person, his/her telephone number/e-mail address, and so forth are a part of the organizational data stored in a business registry. To add the primary contact person information to an organization, the *javax.xml.registry.infomodel* package provides the *User* interface. The *User* interface supplies methods to set the primary contact information, such as the person's name (*setPersonName()*), his/her telephone number (*setTelephoneNumbers()*), e-mail ID (*setEmailAddresses()*), and so on. On the querying side, the *User* interface provides methods to retrieve information about the primary contact using methods such as *getPersonName()*, *getTelephoneNumbers()*, *getEmailAddresses()*, and so on.

Note that the *User* interface is closely connected to the *Organization* interface and the contact person information is automatically retrieved within the *Organization* instances returned upon searching a registry. Similarly, after a *User* instance is created and relevant information is added to it, the *setPrimaryContact()* method of the *Organization* interface is used to set the *User* instance information within the current *Organization* instance. When the *Organization* instance is submitted to the registry, the *User* information is also submitted.

Connecting to a Registry

The first step in searching a business registry is connecting to it. In this section, we discuss how various interfaces/classes in the Java API for XML Registries, JAXR can be used to programmatically connect to a business registry.

To connect to a registry, we create a client program using JAXR. The client program begins by setting properties that define the URL for the registry being accessed and the class that implements the connection factory for the registry. For example, the following lines of code set the URL for IBM's test query registry (UDDI registry) that we shall be using for the examples in this chapter:

```
Properties props = new Properties();
String curl = "http://www-3.ibm.com/services/uddi/v2beta/inquiryapi";
props.setProperty("javax.xml.registry.queryManagerURL", curl);
```

We now set the class for the connection factory implementation of the UDDI registry through the following line of code:

```
props.setProperty("javax.xml.registry.factoryClass",
                "com.sun.xml.registry.uddi.ConnectionFactoryImpl");
```

The next step is to instantiate the factory class and set its property as follows:

```
ConnectionFactory factory = ConnectionFactory.newInstance();
factory.setProperties(props);
```

The *javax.xml.registry* package in JAXR provides the Connection interface that actually initiates a connection or session with the registry provider. We use the connection factory instance to create the connection as in the following line of code:

```
Connection connection = factory.createConnection();
```

If the client is behind a firewall, then to access the registry, you must specify the proxy host address and port on which the proxy service is running. This can be achieved by setting the proxy host and proxy port properties as shown in the following lines of code:

```
String httpProxyHost = "HostIPAddress";
String httpProxyPort = "ProxyPortOnHost";

props.setProperty("javax.xml.registry.http.proxyHost", httpProxyHost);
props.setProperty("javax.xml.registry.http.proxyPort", httpProxyPort);
```

All the preceding steps performed by the client to connect to the registry have been combined into the method *connection()* that has been included in the class *Doconnect* that returns a *Connection* object. The code for the *Doconnect* class is listed in Figure 9.2.

Figure 9.2 Connecting to a Registry Using the *Doconnect* Class

```
import javax.xml.registry.*;
import javax.xml.registry.infomodel.*;
import java.net.*;
import java.util.*;

public class Doconnect
{
Connection connection1;
public Doconnect()
{}
/* This method will make a connection to the Registry server. This will
    use the IBM UDDI registry server*/

public Connection connection()
{
 /* Use these two string values to provide the ProxyHost and Proxyport*/
 String httpProxyHost = "";
 String httpProxyPort = "";

 String curl = "http://www-3.ibm.com/services/uddi/v2beta/inquiryapi";
 String purl =
     "https://www-3.ibm.com/services/uddi/v2beta/protect/publishapi";

 Properties props = new Properties();
 props.setProperty("javax.xml.registry.queryManagerURL", curl);
 props.setProperty("javax.xml.registry.lifeCycleManagerURL", purl);
 props.setProperty("javax.xml.registry.factoryClass",
                   "com.sun.xml.registry.uddi.ConnectionFactoryImpl");
 props.setProperty("javax.xml.registry.http.proxyHost", httpProxyHost);
 props.setProperty("javax.xml.registry.http.proxyPort", httpProxyPort);

 try
 {
     // Create the connection, passing it the
     // configuration properties
     ConnectionFactory factory = ConnectionFactory.newInstance();
```

Continued

Figure 9.2 Continued

```
        factory.setProperties(props);

        connection1 = factory.createConnection();

        System.out.println("Created connection to registry" +

                           connection1);

  }

  catch (Exception e)

  {

        e.printStackTrace();

  }

  return connection1;

  }


}
```

The class *Doconnect* has been used in the *SimpleQuery* class listed later in the chapter in Figure 9.9 (and also in subsequent classes) to connect to the registry. The confirmation line that the *connection()* method in the *Doconnect* class outputs upon successfully connecting to the registry can be seen in Figure 9.10 that shows the output for the *SimpleQuery* class. (Note the line *Created Connection to registrycom.sun.xml.registry.uddi.ConnectionImpl@e83912* in Figure 9.10.)

Using the Default Registry

The Java WSDP package comes complete with a WSDP Registry Server that defines the default Registry. To use this default registry, you need to perform the following steps:

1. Place the bin directory of your JWSDP installation in your PATH variable, or, go to this directory at the command prompt.

2. Start Tomcat using the command **startup** for Windows and **startup.sh** for a Unix system. Start the Xindice database using **xindice-start** on Windows and **xindice-start.sh** on Unix.

3. Start the JAXR Registry Browser (the Registry Browser acts as a JAXR client that can be used to search registries and submit data to the registries) using the command **jaxr-browser** on Windows and **jaxr-browser.sh** on Unix. Note that if you are using the default registry,

you need not specify the proxy host and proxy port as command-line arguments.

4. In the Registry Location drop-down list on the browser, choose the URL: **http://localhost:8080/registry-server/RegistryServerServlet**. You need not change the localhost setting for the default registry server running on your computer.

You can now add an organization to the default registry, delete an organization from it, or query it.

> **NOTE**
>
> As of the time of writing this chapter, a bug in the Default Registry prevents the username and password from being authenticated. A fatal error is reported when you try to submit the authentication information. Therefore, we are using the IBM registry to explain the process of adding an organization to the registry and querying the registry.

Adding an Organization

We use the IBM test registry to show how you can add an organization to the IBM registry using the Registry Browser. Choose the URL **https://www-3.ibm.com/services/uddi/v2beta/protect/publishapi** from the **Registry Location drop-down list**. This will bring up a user interface (as shown in Figure 9.3) that seeks information about the organization (chiefly, the name, description, primary contact, phone, e-mail, and so on).

Leave the **Id** field blank, the ID will be allocated to you by the registry upon successful submission. Click the **Add** button under the *Classifications* label to add classifications. This prompts a pop-up window, as shown in Figure 9.4.

The classifications follow the NAICS (North American Industry Classification System) that classifies various industry/service sectors. The classifications window also allows classification on the basis of location. Click the label **ntis-gov:naics:1997** in the classifications window and choose the sector that best describes your company services. You can choose only one industry sector for classification. If, however, your company activities lie in multiple sectors, you need to create a separate entry for each sector. Click the label **iso-ch:3166:1999** in the classifications window to specify the location. Just as for the industry sector, you can choose only one location for an entry. If your company is active at more than one geographical location, you have to make an entry for each of the locations separately. Clicking the **Add** button in the classifications window will include your organization in the chosen industry sector/location as can be seen from the two text fields under the *Classifications* Add/Remove button in Figure 9.3 (The number *51121* given against the text *Software Publishers* is a value that uniquely identifies an industry sector in the NAICS taxonomy). Now click the **Submit** button (see Figure 9.3) to submit your organization information to the registry. This will result in a pop-up window that asks for a username and password, as shown in Figure 9.5.

Figure 9.3 The Registry Browser's User Interface

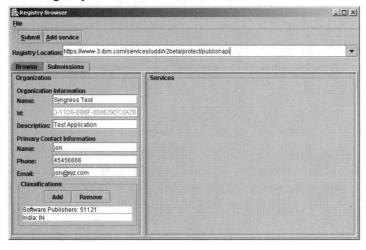

Figure 9.4 Choosing an Industry Sector for Classification

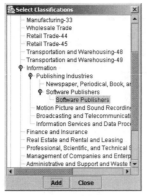

Figure 9.5 The Authentication Window

> **NOTE**
>
> To publish to the IBM registry, you are required to first obtain a username and password. To obtain the username and password, go to the URL **https://www-3.ibm.com/services/uddi/v2beta/protect/registry.html** and click the **Get An IBM ID And Password link**. The resulting page provides you with the option of registering for an IBM UDDI Account. Follow the guidelines provided on this page and obtain an IBM ID and password. As in the case of a mail account, your username should be unique to the registry.

Enter the username and password for your IBM UDDI Account. Once the registry accepts your submission, you will be required to provide this username and password for authentication every time you seek to modify your organization's information in the registry. Clicking the **OK** button in the authentication window will submit your registration information to the registry and you will receive a confirmation of successful registration along with a unique ID as shown in Figure 9.6.

Figure 9.6 The Confirmation Message When an Organization Is Added to the Registry

This key uniquely identifies your organization's entry in the registry. To check that your organization has been added to the registry, you can query the registry by entering your organization's name in the query interface (See the next section, "Querying the Registry" to find out how you can query the registry). For example, when we entered *Syngress Test* (this was the organization name we gave to the submission we made to the IBM registry) as the search criterion in the organization-name field, we obtained query results as shown in Figure 9.7.

Figure 9.7 Searching for Your Organization in the Registry

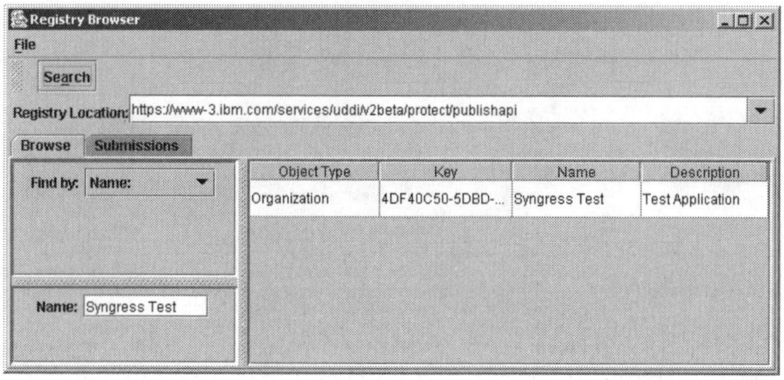

Note that the *Name* and *Description* column (see Figure 9.7) contain the name and description of our organization as entered by us while registering our organization with the registry. Also, the key value under the Key column is the one that the message box (Figure 9.6) had displayed on successful submission of our entry.

NOTE

The Registry Browser allows you to add or delete organizations, but does not support modifying organizations. If you try to modify an organization, a new organization is created when you submit the modified data.

Querying the Registry

To query the IBM test registry, choose the URL **http://www-3.ibm.com/ services/uddi/v2beta/inquiryapi** from the **Registry Location drop-down list**. This brings up a search interface that allows you to query the registry based on the name of an organization or on a classification (see the Find By option in Figure 9.8). Let us assume that we search for organizations by name and enter the letter *I* as the search criterion. Enter *I* in the text field labeled *Name* (see Figure 9.8). The query returns organizations whose name begins with the letter *I* (as shown in the same figure).

The Registry Browser displays the name and description for the organizations returned in the query results. The *Key* column in Figure 9.8 lists the key that uniquely identifies an entry of an organization in the registry.

Figure 9.8 Querying the Registry

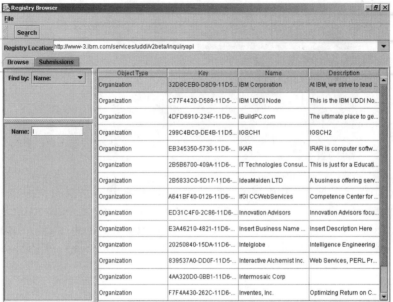

To query the registry on the basis of Classifications, choose the **Classifications** option from the options against the *Find by* label in Figure 9.8. You may choose a classification on the basis of an industry sector or on the basis of location (just as we had done while adding an organization). Clicking the **Search** button displays results based on the classification you choose.

NOTE

The default registry uses a single URL http://localhost:8080/registry-server/ RegistryServerServlet for both adding an organization, as well as querying the registry. You can switch between the two options by clicking the **Submissions** and **Browse** buttons, respectively (see Figure 9.3). The procedure for adding an organization or querying the default registry is the same as what we used in the case of the IBM test registry.

However, note that the default registry does not allow wild card pattern matching for the search criterion. For example, if you specify *%software%* in the case of the IBM test registry, it will search for organizations in whose name *software* occurs anywhere. The default registry, however, does not allow the use of the percent (%) sign for pattern matching.

Querying the Registry

Upon successful connection with a registry, the next step is to query the registry to locate specific vendors and/or services. The *ServiceRegistry* interface in the *javax.xml.registry* package enables the client program to obtain the interfaces being used by the *Connection* class to connect to the registry. The *BusinessQueryManager* interface in the *javax.xml.registry* package supports various methods to search for data in a registry using the JAXR information model. In this section, we discuss how these interfaces can be used to query a registry.

Finding a Service Using a Simple Query

We begin with a simple query that tries to search for organizations in the IBM registry whose name begins with the letter *A*. First of all, we obtain the *ServiceRegistry* object and use it to create a *BusinessQueryManager* object as shown in the following lines of code:

```
RegistryService myservice = connection.getRegistryService();
BusinessQueryManager bqmanager = myservice.getBusinessQueryManager();
```

Here, *connection* is the connection object used to connect to the registry. We now create two *Collection* objects, the first one storing the sorting order for the search results, and the second one the pattern that we want to search for in an organization's name:

```
Collection findQualifier = new ArrayList();
findQualifier.add(FindQualifier.SORT_BY_NAME_DESC);


Collection namePattern = new ArrayList();
namePattern.add("A");
```

The preceding code specifies that the results be sorted alphabetically and designates *A* as the string pattern we are searching for. Next, we use the *findOrganizations()* method of the *BusinessQueryManager* object to search the registry. The *findOrganizations()* method returns a *BulkResponse* object (which is a collection of objects) as shown next:

```
BulkResponse response = bqmanager.findOrganizations(
                          findQualifier, namePattern,
                          null, null,
                          null, null);
```

The *findOrganization()* method accepts the collections, *findQualifier* and *namePattern*, that respectively specify the qualifiers for the search and pattern to be matched. The remaining four parameters (specified as null) are also collections that may specify classifications, specifications, external identifiers, and external links for the organizations. The method searches for organizations that satisfy all the search conditions specified by the collections passed to it as parameter values. Since the BulkResponse received is a collection of objects, we retrieve it in a *Collection* variable as follows:

```
Collection orgs = response.getCollection();
```

Using an *Iterator* object, we loop through the collection, obtaining names of organizations and the services offered by them as shown in the following code snippet:

```
Iterator orgIter = orgs.iterator();
while (orgIter.hasNext())
{
  Organization org = (Organization) orgIter.next();
  String name = (org.getName()).getValue();
}
```

The services offered by an organization are obtained using the *getServices()* method that returns a collection of services. The following code snippet iterates through the services for an organization:

```
Collection services = org.getServices();
Iterator svcIter = services.iterator();
while (svcIter.hasNext())
{
  Service svc = (Service)svcIter.next();
  String sname = (svc.getName()).getValue();
}
```

Figure 9.9 lists the code for the class *SimpleQuery* that executes a simple query using its *query()* method. Note that the *SimpleQuery* class instantiates the *Doconnect* class to connect to the registry using the following lines of code:

```
Doconnect myconnection = new Doconnect();
connection = myconnection.connection();
```

If the connection is successful, the *Doconnect* class (Figure 9.2) returns a *Connection* object that is subsequently used to create a *ServiceRegistry* object.

Figure 9.9 Using a Simple Query to Search the Registry

```
import javax.xml.registry.*;
import javax.xml.registry.infomodel.*;
import java.net.*;
import java.util.*;

public class SimpleQuery
{
  static Connection connection = null;

  public SimpleQuery()
  {}

  public static void main(String[] args)
  {
    SimpleQuery squery = new SimpleQuery();

    //This part of Code will make a connection to the Registry Server
    Doconnect myconnection = new Doconnect();
    connection = myconnection.connection();

    squery.query();
  }

  /*This method will make a query to the Registry Server*/
  public void query()
  {
    try
    {
      RegistryService myservice = connection.getRegistryService();
      BusinessQueryManager bqmanager;
      Bqmanager = myservice.getBusinessQueryManager();
```

Continued

Figure 9.9 Continued

```
Collection findQualifier = new ArrayList();
findQualifier.add(FindQualifier.SORT_BY_NAME_DESC);
Collection namePattern = new ArrayList();
namePattern.add("A");

BulkResponse response;
response = bqmanager.findOrganizations( findQualifier,
                                        namePattern, null,
                                        null, null, null);
Collection orgs = response.getCollection();
Iterator orgIter = orgs.iterator();
while (orgIter.hasNext())
{
   Organization org = (Organization) orgIter.next();
   String name = (org.getName()).getValue();
   System.out.println("This is the organisation name   :" +
                       name + '\n');


   String key = (org.getKey()).getId();
   System.out.println("This is the organisation Key   :" +
                       key + '\n');
   Collection services = org.getServices();
   Iterator svcIter = services.iterator();
   while (svcIter.hasNext())
    {
      Service svc = (Service)svcIter.next();
      String sname = (svc.getName()).getValue();
      System.out.println(
         "This is the organisation service name   :" +
         sname + '\n');
    }
  }
}
catch(Exception ex)
 {
```

Continued

Figure 9.9 Continued

```
        ex.printStackTrace();
    }
  }
}
```

Querying the registry using the *query()* method of the code listing in Figure 9.9 produces the output shown in Figure 9.10.

Figure 9.10 The Results of a Simple Query

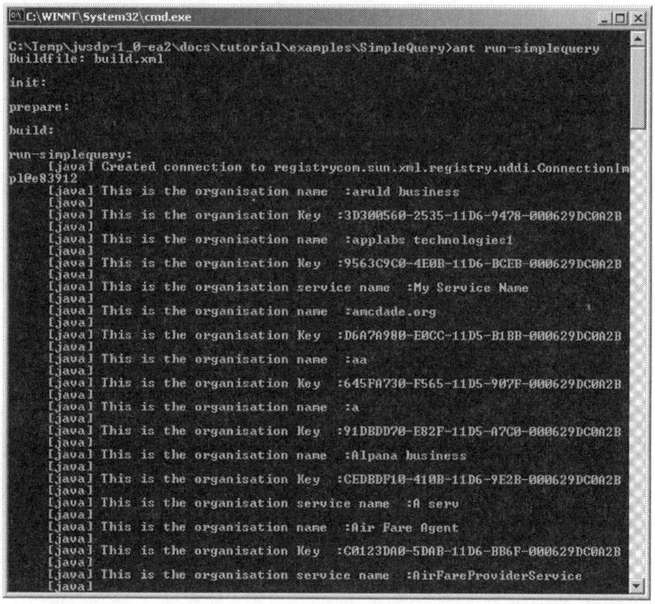

The output prints the names of organizations that begin with the letter *A*, their respective key values and the services offered by them.

Finding a Service Using a Complex Query

We now use a complex query to find organizations in the registry on the basis of classification. For complex queries, we need to implement both the *BusinessQueryManager* and the *BusinessLifeCycleManager*. In our example of a complex query, we use the *BusinessLifecycleManager* to create a classification on the basis of a specified classification scheme as shown in the code snippet that follows:

```
BusinessLifeCycleManager blcm = rs.getBusinessLifeCycleManager();
String schemeName = "uddi-org:types";
ClassificationScheme uddiOrgTypes;
UddiOrgTypse = bqm.findClassificationSchemeByName(schemeName);


Classification wsdlSpecClassification;
wsdlSpecClassification = blcm.createClassification(uddiOrgTypes,
                                                   "wsdlSpec",
                                                   "wsdlSpec");
```

The first argument *uddiOrgTypes* is the classification scheme, while the second and third arguments, *wsdlSpec*, are the taxonomy name and value, respectively, defined by the UDDI specification for a WSDL (Web Services Description Language) document. We assign the classification to a collection and use the *findConcepts()* method of the business query manager:

```
Collection classifications = new ArrayList();
classifications.add(wsdlSpecClassification);
BulkResponse br;
br = bqm.findConcepts(null, null, classifications, null, null);
```

When we pass the classification created by the business life cycle manager to the *findConcepts()* method, it ensures that only those concepts are returned for which the services offered are based on WSDL or whose technical specifications conform to WSDL. The *findConcepts()* method returns a collection of concepts (a concept is used in JAXR to hold the information about a specification). We can now iterate through the concept collection to obtain the search results as given in the following code snippet:

```
Collection specConcepts = br.getCollection();
Iterator iter = specConcepts.iterator();
while (iter.hasNext())
{
  Concept concept = (Concept) iter.next();
  String name = (concept.getName()).getValue();
  Collection links = concept.getExternalLinks();
  System.out.println( "\nSpecification Concept:\n\tName: " + name +
                      "\n\tKey: " + concept.getKey().getId() +
                      "\n\tDescription: " +
                      (concept.getDescription()).getValue());
```

```
   if (links.size() > 0)
   {
     ExternalLink link = (ExternalLink) links.iterator().next();
     System.out.println("\tURL of WSDL document: '" +
                       link.getExternalURI() + "'");
   }
}
```

The *getValue()* method returns a taxonomy code associated with the concept. The *getKey()* method returns a key that represents the universally unique ID (UUID) for the concept. The *getID()* method returns this UUID. The *getDescription()* method returns a text that describes the concept. The *getExternalLinks()* method returns a collection of links outside the registry that contain additional information about the concept.

The organizations that satisfy a concept specification can be found using the *findOrganizations()* method as shown next:

```
Collection specConcepts1 = new ArrayList();
specConcepts1.add(concept);
br = bqm.findOrganizations(null, null, null, specConcepts1, null, null);
```

As in the previous example of a simple query, we can iterate through the collection of organizations returned by the *findOrganizations()* method and retrieve information pertaining to these organizations. The code listing of Figure 9.11 uses the *ComplexQuery* class that contains the method *wsdlQuery()* for querying a registry based on a classification. The *ComplexQuery* class also instantiates the *Doconnect* class (Figure 9.2) to obtain a connection with the registry.

Figure 9.11 Using Classifications to Query the Registry

```
import javax.xml.registry.*;
import javax.xml.registry.infomodel.*;
import java.net.*;
import java.util.*;
public class ComplexQuery
{
  static Connection connection = null;
  public ComplexQuery()
  {}
```

Continued

Figure 9.11 Continued

```
public static void main(String[] args)
{
  ComplexQuery cquery = new ComplexQuery();

  // This part of Code will make a connection to the Registry Server
  Doconnect myconnection = new Doconnect();
  connection = myconnection.connection();

  cquery.query();
}

public void query()
{
  try
  {
    RegistryService myservice;
    BusinessQueryManager bqmanager;
    BusinessLifeCycleManager blmanager;
    ClassificationScheme uddiOrgTypes;
    Classification wsdlSpecClassification;
    BulkResponse br;

    myservice = connection.getRegistryService();
    bqmanager = myservice.getBusinessQueryManager();
    blmanager = myservice.getBusinessLifeCycleManager();
    System.out.println("Got registry service, query " +
                       "manager, and lifecycle manager");

    String sName = "uddi-org:types";
    uddiOrgTypes = bqmanager.findClassificationSchemeByName(sName);

    wsdlSpecClassification = blmanager.createClassification(
                                       uddiOrgTypes,
                                       "wsdlSpec",
                                       "wsdlSpec");
```

Continued

Figure 9.11 Continued

```
Collection classifications = new ArrayList();
classifications.add(wsdlSpecClassification);


br = bqmanager.findConcepts( null, null, classifications,
                                 null, null);
Collection specConcepts = br.getCollection();


Iterator iter = specConcepts.iterator();
if (!iter.hasNext())
{
   System.out.println("No WSDL specification concepts found");
}
else
{
   while (iter.hasNext())
   {
     Concept concept = (Concept) iter.next();
     String name = (concept.getName()).getValue();
     Collection links = concept.getExternalLinks();
     System.out.println("\nSpecification Concept:\n\tName: " +
                         name + "\n\tKey: " +
                         concept.getKey().getId() +
                         "\n\tDescription: " +
                         (concept.getDescription()).getValue());
     if (links.size() > 0)
     {
       ExternalLink link = (ExternalLink) links.iterator().next();
       System.out.println("\tURL of WSDL document: '" +
                           link.getExternalURI() + "'");
     }

     // Find organizations using this concept
     Collection specConcepts1 = new ArrayList();
     specConcepts1.add(concept);
```

Continued

Figure 9.11 Continued

```
            br = bqmanager.findOrganizations( null, null, null,
                                            specConcepts1, null, null);


            Collection orgs = br.getCollection();

            // Display information about organizations
            Iterator orgIter = orgs.iterator();
            if (orgIter.hasNext())
            {
               System.out.println("Organizations using the '" +
                            name + "' WSDL Specification:");
            }
            else
            {
               System.out.println("No Organizations using the '" +
                            name + "' WSDL Specification");
            }

            while (orgIter.hasNext())
            {
               Organization org = (Organization) orgIter.next();
               System.out.println("\tName: " + (org.getName()).getValue() +
                            "\n\tKey: " + org.getKey().getId() +
                            "\n\tDescription: " +
                            (org.getDescription()).getValue());
            }
          }
        }
      }
      catch (Exception e)
      {
         e.printStackTrace();
      }
    }
  }
}
```

The output of the *ComplexQuery* class is as shown in Figure 9.12.

Figure 9.12 Results from the Complex Query

Understanding the Query Results

In this section, we use the query results of the simple and complex queries discussed in the previous sections to highlight the information that can be obtained by querying a business registry.

Metadata Returned

The Metadata returned by the query is in the form of details about the organization that are contained in the registry database. This information includes:

- A Name object that contains the name of the organization. Note that the organization name in the preceding queries was obtained by type-casting an *Iterator* object into an organization object and using the code *org.getName().getValue()*, where *org* is the Organization object.

- A Description object that gives the description of the organization *org.getDescription().getValue()*.

- A collection of Service objects that contain the services offered by the organizations; this collection being obtained using the *getServices()* method.

Additionally, you can also obtain the following information from the query results using the respective method of the Organization Interface:

- A Key object that represents the ID through which an organization entry is uniquely identified by the registry.

- A Primary Contact object that can be used to obtain the name of the person who is the primary contact for an organization. This can be done using the *getPrimaryContact()* method—namely, *org.getPrimaryContact() .getPersonName()*.

- Postal Address of the organization by using the *getPostalAdress()* method.

- A Collection object for the users affiliated to the organization by using the *getUsers()* method.

- A collection of child organizations of an organization by using the *getChildOrganizations()* method, and so on.

External Data

The external data derived from the preceding queries is in the form of external links obtained using the code *concept.getExternalLinks()*. These external links are URLs from where the services offered by an organization can be accessed. The URL obtained as an external link may also contain content outside a registry—for example, an organization may put its home page link in the registry information. Additionally, these external links may point to WSDL documents that define the XML format for transacting business with the company (see the links against the URL of the WSDL document label in Figure 9.12).

WSDL Documents

Web Services Description Language (WSDL) is a part of UDDI's initiative to provide business directories and service descriptions for online services. Akin to XML grammar for Web services, WDSL is a specification frequently used to describe networked XML-based services, allowing service providers to describe the basic format of requests that can be sent to their systems irrespective of the protocol (such as SOAP) or encoding (such as Multipurpose Internet Messaging Extensions) being used. In this section, we discuss the structure of a WSDL document and create an example document.

Structure of a WSDL Document

In essence, WSDL defines a standardized format for data exchange to facilitate e-business. Structurally, a WSDL document has a *<definitions>* element as the root, like that shown next:

```
<definitions name="nmtoken" targetNamespace="uri">


<-- put definitions here -->
</definitions>
```

The *<definitions>* element defines the name of the Web service. It also declares multiple namespaces used in other elements in the document. The *<definitions>* element contains a set of related services. WSDL defines these services using the following six main elements:

- **Types** The *<types>* element specifies the low-level data types used for the procedure contents or the messages being transmitted between the client and the server. W3C XML Schema specification is WSDL's default choice for the type-system. Thus, if a service uses only the simple built-in type of the XML schema (strings, integers, and so on), the *<types>* element is not required. The format for the *<types>* element is as follows:

```
<types>
    <schema targetNamespace="http://namespaces.myURL.com"
        xmlns="http://www.w3.org/1999/XMLSchema">
    ...........................................
    ...........................................
</types>
```

- **Message** The *<message>* element defines the data format for a message. The message could be a client request message or a server response message. The message element defines the name of the message and may contain one or more *<part>* elements which can refer to message parameters or to message return values. The syntax for defining a message is as follows:

```
<message name="msgName">
        <part name="myPart" element="myElement?" type=
"myns:partNS "?/>
</message>
```

- **PortType** The *<portType>* element is used to group messages that form a single logical operation. A single logical operation is a complete client-server communication that encloses both a client request to the server and the server response to this request. For example, a request may trigger a response, or in case of error or exception, an error or exception. This request–response or request–exception exchange can be grouped together into a WSDL port type. This is equivalent to saying that the *<portType>* element defines what operations or functions the service described by the WSDL document will support. A single *<portType>* element can define more than one operation. The syntax for the *<portType>* element is as follows:

```
<portType name="myPort">
        <operation name="myOperation">
            <input message= "inputMSG" name="myInput"/>
            <output message = "outputMSG" name="myOutput"/>
            <fault message = "errorMSGs" name="myError"/>
        </operation>
</portType>
```

NOTE

WSDL supports four basic types of operations. These are:

- **One-way** The service receives a message. This would mean that only the *<input>* element shown earlier will be present.
- **Request-Response** The service receives a message and sends a response. Thus the operation will have an *<input>* element, followed by an *<output>* element as given in the *<portType>* syntax. The *<fault>* element is optional. The request-response pattern is most commonly used in SOAP services.
- **Solicit-Response** The service (*not* the client) initiates communication by sending a message and receives a response. Hence, this operation will have an *<output>* element followed by an *<input>* element. The *<fault>* element is optional.
- **Notification** The service sends a message and seeks no response. The operation will therefore, have a single *<output>* element only.

Figure 9.13 shows these four operations.

Figure 9.13 The Basic Operations Supported by WSDL

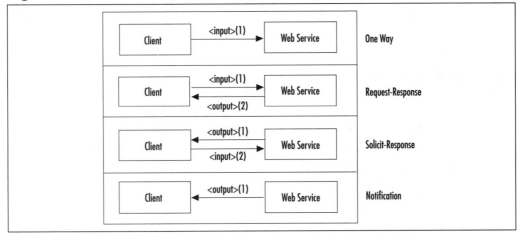

The number in brackets (1 or 2) at the end of the *<input>/ <output>* tag indicates the order in which the operation occurs.

- **Binding** The *<binding>* element describes the concrete specifics of how the service will be practically implemented. It defines the message format and the protocol details (say, SOAP-specific information) for the operations and messages defined by a particular *portType*. A given portType may have any number of bindings. The syntax is as follows:

```
<binding name="myBinding" type="myPort">
    <operation name="myOperation">
        <input name="myInput">
            .............................. .
        </input>
        <output name="myOutput">
            .............................. .
        </output>
        <fault name="myError">
            .............................. .
        </fault>
    </operation>
</binding>
```

- **Port** A *<port>* element defines a single address for a binding. A port must not specify more than one binding and should contain only the address information for the binding. The syntax of this element is as follows:

```
<port name="myPort" binding="myBinding">
    .......................... .
</port>
```

- **Service** The *<service>* element provides the location of the service (in other words, the URL from which the service may be invoked). This normally is the Web address or the URI for a provider of the described service. The *<service>* element uses a port and its specified binding to define a physical location for a communication end point. The syntax of this element is as follows:

```
<service name="nmtoken">
        <port name="myPort" .... />
</service>
```

Example WSDL Document

We now use the elements described in the "Structure of a WSDL Document" section to develop a sample WSDL document, shown in Figure 9.14.

Figure 9.14 Example of a WSDL Document

```
<?xml version="1.0" encoding="UTF-8"?>
<definitions name="TestService"
    targetNamespace="http://www.syngress.com/wsdlDocs/TestService.wsdl"
    xmlns="http://schemas.xmlsoap.org/wsdl/"
    xmlns:soap="http://schemas.xmlsoap.org/wsdl/soap/"
    xmlns:tns="http://www.syngress.com/wsdl/TestService.wsdl"
    xmlns:xsd="http://www.w3.org/2001/XMLSchema">

    <message name="clientRequest">
        <part name="firstName" type="xsd:string"/>
    </message>
    <message name="ServerResponse">
        <part name="welcomeMessage" type="xsd:string"/>
    </message>
```

Continued

Figure 9.14 Continued

```
<portType name="testPortType">
    <operation name="welcomeClient">
        <input message="tns:clientRequest"/>
        <output message="tns:ServerResponse"/>
    </operation>
</portType>


<binding name="testBinding" type="tns:testPortType">
    <soap:binding style="rpc"
        transport="http://schemas.xmlsoap.org/soap/http"/>
    <operation name="welcomeClient">
        <soap:operation soapAction="welcomeClient"/>
        <input>
            <soap:body
                encodingStyle="http://schemas.xmlsoap.org/soap/encoding/"
                namespace="urn:examples:testservice"
                use="encoded"/>
        </input>
        <output>
            <soap:body
                encodingStyle="http://schemas.xmlsoap.org/soap/encoding/"
                namespace="urn:examples:testservice"
                use="encoded"/>
        </output>
    </operation>
</binding>


<service name="testService">
    <port binding="tns:testBinding" name="testPort">
        <soap:address
            location="http://localhost:8080/soap/servlet/rpcrouter"/>
    </port>
</service>
</definitions>
```

Let us now analyze the sample WSDL document of Figure 9.14 on the basis of our discussion in the section, "Structure of a WSDL Document."

The *<definitions>* Element

The *<definitions>* element in the listing of Figure 9.14 specifies that this Web service is called the *TestService*. The *<definitions>* element also specifies a number of namespaces that have been used in further elements of the WSDL document. The use of namespaces enables the WSDL document to reference multiple external specifications such as the WSDL specification, the SOAP specification, the XML Schema specification, and so on.

Note the *targetNamespace* attribute in the *<definitions>* element:

```
<definitions name="SyngressTestService"
targetNamespace="http://www.syngress.com/wsdlDocs/TestService.wsdl" ...>
```

The *targetNamespace* is an XML Schema convention that enables the WSDL document to refer to itself.

The definitions element also specifies a default namespace as follows: *xmlns="http://schemas.xmlsoap.org/wsdl/"*. Elements such as *<message>* that do not have a namespace prefix are therefore assumed to be part of the default WSDL namespace.

The *<message>* Element

The listing of Figure 9.14 defines two message elements, a request message named *clientRequest* from the client, and a response message named *serverResponse* from the server. Note the *<part>* element within the *<message>* element:

```
<message name="clientRequest">
    <part name="firstName" type="xsd:string"/>
</message>
<message name="serverResponse">
    <part name="welcomeMessages" type="xsd:string"/>
</message>
```

The *<part>* element for the client request specifies a single request (message) parameter—that is, a *firstName* parameter. The *<part>* element for the response specifies a return value that happens to be a welcome message for the client in our case. The *type* attribute of the *<part>* element specifies an XML Schema data type. Note that the value of the *type* attribute must be namespace-qualified, hence the use of *xsd* as a prefix (*xsd* references the namespace for XML Schema).

The *<portType>* Element

The *<portType>* element defines a single operation named *welcomeClient*. This operation consists of the client's request message, named *clientRequest* and the server's response message named *serverResponse*. Note that the message attribute in the code snippet that follows should also be specified with reference to a namespace:

```
<portType name="testPortType">
    <operation name="welcomeClient">
        <input message="tns:clientRequest"/>
        <output message="tns:ServerResponse"/>
    </operation>
</portType>
```

For example, the message attribute of the *<input>* element has the prefix *tns* that references the *targetNamespace* defined in the definitions element. Thus, as already mentioned while describing the *<definitions>* element of the sample WSDL document, the *targetNamespace* attribute is used for self-referencing.

The *<binding>* Element

The *<binding>* element specifies how the portType operation (*welcomeClient*) will actually be transmitted over the wire. HTTP GET, HTTP POST, and SOAP are some of the protocols that can be used for transporting the Bindings over the network.

The *<binding>* element itself specifies the binding name and a *type* attribute that refers to the portType named *testPortType*, using the self-referencing targetNamespace:

```
<binding name="Hello_Binding" type="tns:Hello_PortType">
```

The *<soap:binding>* element indicates that the binding will be made available via SOAP (WSDL has built-in extensions for SOAP that enables you to specify SOAP-specific details such as SOAP headers, SOAP encoding styles, and the *SOAPAction* HTTP header). The value rpc for the style attribute of the *<soap:binding>* element specifies an RPC format. This means that the function parameters will be embedded inside a wrapper XML element. This wrapper XML element will indicate the function name and will be included within the body of the SOAP request. Similarly, the body of the SOAP response will contain a wrapper element within which the function parameters will be embedded.

The value of the transport attribute, *http://schemas.xmlsoap.org/soap/http*, indicates the SOAP HTTP transport, whereas *http://schemas.xmlsoap.org/soap/smtp* indicates the SOAP SMTP transport.

The *<soap:operation>* element indicates the binding of a particular operation to a specific SOAP implementation. The *soapAction* attribute specifies that the *SOAPAction* HTTP header be used for identifying the service.

The *<soap:body>* element is used to specify the details of the input and output messages such as the SOAP encoding style, the namespace associated with the specified service, and so on.

The *<service>* Element

The *<service>* element specifies the location of the service. Since our WSDL document specifies a SOAP service, we have used the *<soap:address>* element and specified the local host address for the Apache SOAP rpcrouter servlet—that is, http://localhost:8080/soap/servlet/rpcrouter.

This concludes our discussion on WSDL documents. We'll now talk about how we can add data to, delete data from, or modify data in the registry using JWSDP.

Storing Information in a Registry

In the section, "Using the Default Registry," we explained how the Registry Browser can be used for adding an organization to the registry. In this section, we perform the tasks of adding/deleting an organization to/from the registry and modifying existing records using JWSDP classes. We use IBM's test registry in the examples given in this section.

Adding New Registry Records

We again begin by making a connection to the registry using the *connection()* method. (Please refer to the section, "Connecting to a Registry," to review how the *connection()* method works.) The first step in creating an organization is providing a username and password to the registry for authentication. The authentication information is used to set the credentials for the connection object as shown in the following code snippet:

```
String username = "Yash1";
String password = "yashraj1";
```

```
PasswordAuthentication userdetail;
userdetail = new PasswordAuthentication (username, passw.toCharArray());
Set user = new HashSet();
user.add(userdetail);
connection.setCredentials(user);
```

Recollect from the discussions in the "Using the Default Registry" section that you need to create an IBM UDDI Account to obtain the username and password.

Next, we create a business life cycle manager to create an organization that we can submit to the registry:

```
BusinessLifeCycleManager blmanager;
blmanager = myservice.getBusinessLifeCycleManager();
```

We use a *BusinessLifeCycleManager* object since it provides methods that are required to set the necessary information pertaining to an organization, as will be clear from the following discussions.

We use the *createOrganization()* method of the business life cycle manager to create an Organization object as shown in the following line of code:

```
Organization org;
org = blmanager.createOrganization("Dreamtech Software India Inc.");
```

This sets "Dreamtech Software India Inc." as the name of the organization. To add a description for the organization, we use the following code:

```
InternationalString s;
s = blmanager.createInternationalString(
                        "Where Dreams Become Technology");
org.setDescription(s);
```

To create a primary contact for the organization, we use the *createUser()* method of the business life cycle manager as shown next:

```
User primaryContact = blmanager.createUser();
PersonName pName = blmanager.createPersonName("Yash");
primaryContact.setPersonName(pName);
```

The *setPersonName()* method sets the name of the primary contact. In a similar manner, we can set the telephone number for the primary contact as shown in the following:

```
TelephoneNumber tNum = blmanager.createTelephoneNumber();
```

```
tNum.setNumber("(91) 011-3243077");
Collection phoneNums = new ArrayList();
phoneNums.add(tNum);
primaryContact.setTelephoneNumbers(phoneNums);
```

The *createEmailAddress()* and *setEmailAddress()* methods are used in a similar fashion to set the e-mail for the primary contact:

```
EmailAddress emailAddr;
emailAddr = blmanager.createEmailAddress("yash@dreamtechsoftware.com");
Collection emailAddresses = new ArrayList();
emailAddresses.add(emailAddr);
primaryContact.setEmailAddresses(emailAddresses);
```

We now add the primary contact to the organization ("org," created earlier) using the following line of code:

```
org.setPrimaryContact(primaryContact);
```

After providing organizational information, we turn to the classifications that we need to choose for the organization. We use the *ntis-gov:naics* scheme to add classification to our organization, as shown in the following lines of code:

```
Classification classification;
classification = (Classification) blmanager.createClassification(
                                    cScheme,
                                    "Software Publishers",
                                    "51121");
Collection classifications = new ArrayList();
classifications.add(classification);
org.addClassifications(classifications);
```

Recollect from the discussions in the using the Default Registry section that the NAICS taxonomy classifies various industry sectors such as Agriculture, Food Processing, and so on (see Figure 9.4). Notice that in the *createClassifications()* method, we have passed "Software Publishers" as the classification name and *51121* as the value that uniquely identifies this sector (these values are the same as were obtained using the Registry Browser in Figure 9.3).

After classification, we add services and service descriptions to our organization, once again using the methods of the business life cycle manager as shown in the code snippet that follows:

```
Collection services = new ArrayList();
Service service = blmanager.createService("My Service Name");
InternationalString is;
is = blmanager.createInternationalString("My Service Description");
service.setDescription(is);
```

The next step is to create service bindings that bind the service to a URL from where that service can be accessed, as shown here:

```
Collection serviceBindings = new ArrayList();
ServiceBinding binding = blmanager.createServiceBinding();
is = blmanager.createInternationalString(
                    "My Service Binding Description");
binding.setDescription(is);
binding.setAccessURI("http://dreamtechsoftware.com");
serviceBindings.add(binding);
service.addServiceBindings(serviceBindings);
```

We now add these services to the organization:

```
services.add(service);
org.addServices(services);
```

We are now ready to submit our organization to the registry. We do this by using the following lines of code:

```
Collection orgs = new ArrayList();
orgs.add(org);
BulkResponse response = blmanager.saveOrganizations(orgs);
```

The *saveOrganizations()* method will return an exception if the organization cannot be submitted, else the response contains the unique ID key that is assigned to the organization upon successful submission (see Figure 9.6).

This key can be retrieved by iterating through the response collection. Figure 9.15 lists the code for the *PublishEntry* class that submits an organization to the registry and prints the ID if the organization is successfully submitted; otherwise, it prints out the exceptions that caused the submission process to fail.

Figure 9.15 Using the *PublishEntry* Class to Add an Organization to the Registry

```
import javax.xml.registry.*;
import javax.xml.registry.infomodel.*;
import java.net.*;
import java.security.*;
import java.util.*;


public class PublishEntry
{
  static Connection connection = null;

  public PublishEntry()
  {}

  public static void main(String[] args)
  {
    String username = "Yash1";
    String password = "yashraj1";

    PublishEntry publishdoc = new PublishEntry();

    //This part of Code will make a connection to the Registry Server
    Doconnect myconnection = new Doconnect();
    connection = myconnection.connection();

    publishdoc.publishentry(username, password);
  }

  public void publishentry(String username, String passw)
  {
    RegistryService myservice = null;
    BusinessLifeCycleManager blmanager = null;
    BusinessQueryManager bqmanager = null;

    try
    {
```

Continued

Figure 9.15 Continued

```
myservice = connection.getRegistryService();
blmanager = myservice.getBusinessLifeCycleManager();
bqmanager = myservice.getBusinessQueryManager();
System.out.println(
    "Got registry service, query manager, and life cycle manager");


PasswordAuthentication userdetail;
userdetail = new PasswordAuthentication(username,
                                        passw.toCharArray());
Set user = new HashSet();
user.add(userdetail);


connection.setCredentials(user);
System.out.println("Checked Security Issues User Logged ON");


// Create organization name and description
Organization org;
org = blmanager.createOrganization(
                        "Dreamtech Software India Inc.");
InternationalString s;
s = blmanager.createInternationalString(
                        "Where Dreams Become Technology");
org.setDescription(s);


// Create primary contact, set name
User primaryContact = blmanager.createUser();
PersonName pName = blmanager.createPersonName("Yash");
primaryContact.setPersonName(pName);


// Set primary contact phone number
TelephoneNumber tNum = blmanager.createTelephoneNumber();
tNum.setNumber("(91) 011-3243077");
Collection phoneNums = new ArrayList();
phoneNums.add(tNum);
primaryContact.setTelephoneNumbers(phoneNums);
```

Continued

Figure 9.15 Continued

```
// Set primary contact email address
EmailAddress emailAddr;
emailAddr =blmanager.createEmailAddress(
                        "yash@dreamtechsoftware.com");
Collection emailAddresses = new ArrayList();
emailAddresses.add(emailAddr);
primaryContact.setEmailAddresses(emailAddresses);

// Set primary contact for organization
org.setPrimaryContact(primaryContact);

// Set classification scheme to NAICS
ClassificationScheme cScheme;
cScheme = bqmanager.findClassificationSchemeByName(
                        "ntis-gov:naics");

// Create and add classification
Classification classification;
classification = (Classification) blmanager.createClassification(
                        cScheme,
                        "A Software Development Company",
                        "722213");
Collection classifications = new ArrayList();
classifications.add(classification);
org.addClassifications(classifications);

// Create services and service
Collection services = new ArrayList();
Service service = blmanager.createService("My Service Name");
InternationalString is;
is = blmanager.createInternationalString("My Service Description");
service.setDescription(is);

// Create service bindings
```

Continued

Figure 9.15 Continued

```
Collection serviceBindings = new ArrayList();
ServiceBinding binding = blmanager.createServiceBinding();
is = blmanager.createInternationalString(
                        "My Service Binding Description");
binding.setDescription(is);
binding.setAccessURI("http://dreamtechsoftware.com");
serviceBindings.add(binding);

// Add service bindings to service
service.addServiceBindings(serviceBindings);

// Add service to services, then add services to organization
services.add(service);
org.addServices(services);

// Add organization and submit to registry
// Retrieve key if successful
Collection orgs = new ArrayList();
orgs.add(org);
BulkResponse response = blmanager.saveOrganizations(orgs);
Collection exceptions = response.getException();
if (exceptions == null)
{
  System.out.println("Organization saved");

  Collection keys = response.getCollection();
  Iterator keyIter = keys.iterator();
  if (keyIter.hasNext())
  {
    javax.xml.registry.infomodel.Key orgKey;
    orgKey = (javax.xml.registry.infomodel.Key) keyIter.next();
    String id = orgKey.getId();
    System.out.println("Organization key is " + id);
    org.setKey(orgKey);
  }
```

Continued

Figure 9.15 Continued

```
        }
      else
      {
          Iterator excIter = exceptions.iterator();
          Exception exception = null;
          while (excIter.hasNext())
          {
            exception = (Exception) excIter.next();
            System.err.println("Exception on save: " +
                                exception.toString());
          }
        }
      }
    }
  catch (Exception e)
  {
    e.printStackTrace();
    if (connection != null)
    {
      try
      {
        connection.close();
      }
      catch (JAXRException je)
      {
        System.err.println("Connection close failed");
      }
    }
  }
  }
}
```

The output for the *PublishEntry* class is shown in Figure 9.16.

Note that the output in Figure 9.16 shows a successful operation that prints out the organization key.

Figure 9.16 Output of an Add-Organization Request

Updating Records

Once we add our organization to the registry, it is also possible to update the information to reflect any changes made to the organization's general information, such as the primary contact, telephone numbers, and so on, or changes in the services offered by the organization.

As an example, let's delete the service we added in the *PublishEntry* class and instead add a new service to our organization. We begin by querying the registry to search for our organization. For this, we set the name of our organization as the name pattern to be searched, as shown in the code fragment that follows:

```
String businessname = "Dreamtech Software India Inc.";
Collection namePatterns = new ArrayList();
namePatterns.add(businessname);
```

We now use the business query manager's *getOrganizations()* method to search for our organization, as in the following code:

```
BulkResponse response;
response = bqm.findOrganizations(findQualifiers, namePatterns, null,
                                 null, null, null);
```

Here, *bqm* is the business query manager.

We iterate through the bulk response (see the explanation in the section, "Querying the Registry") and obtain the services offered by our organization using the *getServices()* method:

```
services = org.getServices();
```

Here, *org* is the organization object that refers to our organization. We loop through the services to obtain the key associated with the services by using the following *while* loop:

```
while(serIter.hasNext())
{
   Service serve = (Service)serIter.next();
   System.out.println("This is the service name to be deleted " +
                      (serve.getName()).getValue() + '\n');
   mykey = serve.getKey();
   System.out.println("This is the service key to be deleted " +
                      mykey.getId() + '\n');
}
```

We now delete the service specified by the key value in the variable, *mykey*. Since we added only one service, we shall have only one record for services. If more than one service was added, at the end of the *while* loop, the *mykey* variable would contain the key for the last service listed for our organization. We use the business life cycle manager, *blmanager*, to delete the service, as shown in the following code snippet:

```
Collection keys = new ArrayList();
keys.add(mykey);
BulkResponse response1 = blmanager.deleteServices(keys);
System.out.println("Deleted Service" + '\n');
```

Note that while the querying process requires no authentication, deleting a service requires authentication. Therefore, we authenticate ourselves with our username and password, just as we had done while adding our organization to the registry (see the code listing in Figure 9.16).

After deleting the service, we add a new service using the *createService()* method to create the service, as in the following code:

```
Collection newservices = new ArrayList();
Service service = blmanager.createService("Test Service Name");
InternationalString is;
is = blmanager.createInternationalString("This is Service Description");
service.setDescription(is);
```

We now set this service to our organization and save it using the *saveServices()* method of the business life cycle manager:

```
service.setOrganization(org);
newservices.add(service);
BulkResponse response2 = blmanager.saveServices(newservices);
```

This completes our updates. The entire code for the *Update* class is listed in Figure 9.17.

Figure 9.17 Using the *Update* Class to Update Registry Records

```java
import javax.xml.registry.*;
import javax.xml.registry.infomodel.*;
import java.net.*;
import java.security.*;
import java.util.*;


public class Update
{
  static Connection connection = null;

  public Update()
  {}

  public static void main(String[] args)
  {
    String username = "Yash1";
    String passw = "yashraj1";
    String businessname = "Dreamtech Software India Inc.";
    Update updatedata = new Update();

    //This part of Code will make a connection to the Registry Server
    Doconnect myconnection = new Doconnect();
    connection = myconnection.connection();

    updatedata.update(username, passw, businessname);
  }

  public void update(String username, String pass, String businessname)
  {
```

Continued

Figure 9.17 Continued

```
Collection services = null;
javax.xml.registry.infomodel.Key mykey = null;
javax.xml.registry.infomodel.Key depkey = null;
Organization org = null;

try
{
  RegistryService rs = connection.getRegistryService();
  BusinessQueryManager bqm = rs.getBusinessQueryManager();
  BusinessLifeCycleManager blmanager;
  blmanager = rs. getBusinessLifeCycleManager();
  System.out.println("Got registry service and query manager");

  // Define find qualifiers and name patterns
  Collection findQualifiers = new ArrayList();
  findQualifiers.add(FindQualifier.SORT_BY_NAME_DESC);
  Collection namePatterns = new ArrayList();
  namePatterns.add(businessname);

  BulkResponse response;
  response = bqm.findOrganizations(findQualifiers, namePatterns,
                                   null, null, null, null);
  Collection orgs = response.getCollection();
  Iterator orgIter = orgs.iterator();
  while (orgIter.hasNext())
  {
    org = (Organization)orgIter.next();
    System.out.println((org.getKey()).getId() + '\n');
    String name = (org.getName()).getValue();
    System.out.println("This is the organisation name   :" +
                       name + '\n');
    services = org.getServices();
  }

    //This part of code will authenticate the user
```

Continued

Figure 9.17 Continued

```
PasswordAuthentication userdetail;
userdetail = new PasswordAuthentication(username,
                                         pass.toCharArray());
Set user = new HashSet();
user.add(userdetail);
connection.setCredentials(user);
System.out.println("Checked Security Issues User Logged ON");

//This part of code will delete a service
Iterator serIter = services.iterator();
while(serIter.hasNext())
{
  Service serve = (Service)serIter.next();
  System.out.println("This is the service name to be deleted " +
                     (serve.getName()).getValue() + '\n');
  mykey = serve.getKey();
  System.out.println("This is the service key to be deleted " +
                     mykey.getId() + '\n');
}
Collection keys = new ArrayList();
keys.add(mykey);
BulkResponse response1 = blmanager.deleteServices(keys);
System.out.println("Deleted Service" + '\n');

//This part of code will add a service
Collection newservices = new ArrayList();
Service service = blmanager.createService("Test Service Name");
InternationalString is;
is = blmanager.createInternationalString(
                     "This is Service Description");
service.setDescription(is);
service.setOrganization(org);
newservices.add(service);
BulkResponse response2 = blmanager.saveServices(newservices);
System.out.println("Service Added" + '\n');
```

Continued

Figure 9.17 Continued

```
        }

    catch(Exception e)

    {

        e.printStackTrace();

    }

  }

}
```

The output from the *Update* class is shown in Figure 9.18. The *Update* class also calls the *Doconnect* class (Figure 9.2) to connect to the registry.

Figure 9.18 The Output from the *Update* Class

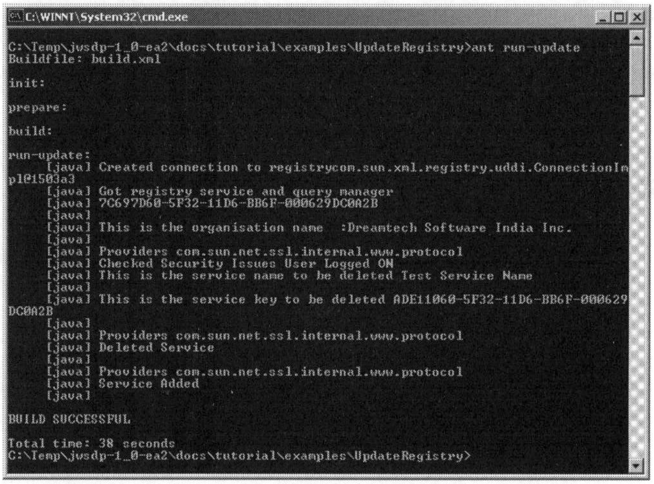

The output from the *Update* class (as shown in Figure 9.18) prints status messages that confirm that the service named *Test Service Name* has been deleted and a new service has been added. The organization records thus stand updated.

Deprecating and Deleting Existing Records

We have seen how to add an organization to the registry and how to modify and update registry records. We now discuss how these records can be deprecated or deleted.

Deprecation is equivalent to saying that the services of an organization are no longer available. The difference between deprecating an organization record and deleting an organization record is that, when you delete an organization, you permanently remove access to its services, until you re-create and resubmit the organization. Deprecating, on the other hand, is temporary in nature, since you can un-deprecate a deprecated organization at any time to put it back in business. A deprecated organization, however, will not be listed in the query results of a registry until it is un-deprecated.

We now build a class, the *DeleteEntry* class that contains methods both to deprecate and delete an organization (see the methods *deprecateEntry()* and *deleteEntry()*, respectively, in the code listing of Figure 9.19).

Just as for updating records, we begin by querying the registry using our organization's name as follows:

```
Collection namePatterns = new ArrayList();

namePatterns.add(busName);

BulkResponse response;

response = bqmanager.findOrganizations(findQualifiers, namePatterns, null,
                                    null, null, null);
```

Here the variable *busName* contains the string "Dreamtech Software India Inc."

Once again, we authenticate the user information by furnishing our username and password, as shown in the following code:

```
PasswordAuthentication userdetail;

userdetail = new PasswordAuthentication(username,
                                    password.toCharArray());

Set user = new HashSet();

user.add(userdetail);

connection.setCredentials(user);
```

We obtain the organization key by iterating through the bulk response returned by the query results. We now pass this key to the *deprecateObjects()* method of the business life cycle manager to deprecate the organization as shown in the following lines of code:

```
String keyname = key.getId();

Collection keys = new ArrayList();

keys.add(key);

BulkResponse response = blmanager.deprecateObjects(keys);
```

Here *key* is the organization key that is passed to the method *deprecateEntry()* as a parameter.

Similarly, we pass this key to the *deleteEntry()* method as a parameter and use the *deleteOrganizations()* method to delete the organization as in the following lines of code:

```
String keyname = key.getId();
Collection keys = new ArrayList();
keys.add(key);
BulkResponse response = blmanager.deleteOrganizations(keys);
```

The complete code for the *DeleteEntry* class is listed in Figure 9.19. Again, we use the *Doconnect* class (Figure 9.2) to connect to the registry.

Figure 9.19 Using the *DeleteEntry* Class for Deprecating and Deleting Existing Records

```
import javax.xml.registry.*;
import javax.xml.registry.infomodel.*;
import java.net.*;
import java.security.*;
import java.util.*;

public class DeleteEntry
{
  static Connection connection = null;

  RegistryService rs = null;
  public DeleteEntry()
  {}

  public static void main(String[] args)
  {
    String username = "Yash1";
    String password = "yashraj1";
    String bname = "Dreamtech Software";

    javax.xml.registry.infomodel.Key key1 = null;
    DeleteEntry myentry = new DeleteEntry();

    //This part of Code will make a connection to the Registry Server
```

Continued

Figure 9.19 Continued

```
   Doconnect myconnection = new Doconnect();
   connection = myconnection.connection();
   key1 = myentry.query(bname);

   myentry.deleteEntry(key1,username,password);
}

public javax.xml.registry.infomodel.Key query(String busName)
{
   BusinessQueryManager bqmanager = null;
   javax.xml.registry.infomodel.Key organisationKey = null;
   try
   {
      rs = connection.getRegistryService();
      bqmanager = rs.getBusinessQueryManager();
      System.out.println("Got registry service and " + "query manager");

      // Define find qualifiers and name patterns
      Collection findQualifiers = new ArrayList();
      findQualifiers.add(FindQualifier.SORT_BY_NAME_DESC);
      Collection namePatterns = new ArrayList();
      namePatterns.add(busName);

      // Find using the name
      BulkResponse response;
      response = bqmanager.findOrganizations(findQualifiers,
                                             namePatterns, null,
                                             null, null, null);
      Collection organisation = response.getCollection();
      Iterator organisationIT = organisation.iterator();
      while(organisationIT.hasNext())
      {
         Organization myorg = (Organization)organisationIT.next();
         System.out.println(" Found Organisation " + '\n');
         organisationKey = myorg.getKey();
```

Continued

Figure 9.19 Continued

```
        String id = organisationKey.getId();
        System.out.println(" This is the organisation ID " + id + '\n');
    }
  }
  catch(Exception e)
  {
    e.printStackTrace();
  }
  return organisationKey;
}


public void deprecateEntry( String username,
                            String password,
                            String bname)
{
  javax.xml.registry.infomodel.Key mykey = null;
  BusinessQueryManager bqmanager = null;
  BusinessLifeCycleManager blmanager = null;
  Collection Services = null;
  String keyname = null;
  try
  {
    bqmanager = rs.getBusinessQueryManager();

    Collection findQualifiers = new ArrayList();
    findQualifiers.add(FindQualifier.SORT_BY_NAME_DESC);
    Collection namePatterns = new ArrayList();
    namePatterns.add(bname);

    BulkResponse response;
    response = bqmanager.findOrganizations(findQualifiers,
                                    namePatterns, null,
                                    null, null, null);
    Collection organisation = response.getCollection();
    Iterator organisationIT = organisation.iterator();
```

Continued

Figure 9.19 Continued

```
while(organisationIT.hasNext())
{
  Organization myorg = (Organization)organisationIT.next();
  System.out.println(" Found Organisation " + '\n');
  Services = myorg.getServices();
}


blmanager = rs.getBusinessLifeCycleManager();
PasswordAuthentication userdetail;
userdetail = new PasswordAuthentication(username,
                                        password.toCharArray());
Set user = new HashSet();
user.add(userdetail);
connection.setCredentials(user);
System.out.println("Checked Security Issues User Logged ON");


Iterator serIter = Services.iterator();
while(serIter.hasNext())
{
  Service serve = (Service)serIter.next();
  System.out.println("This is the service name to be deleted " +
                     (serve.getName()).getValue() + '\n');
  mykey = serve.getKey();
  System.out.println("This is the service key to be deleted " +
                     mykey.getId() + '\n');
}


keyname = mykey.getId();
System.out.println("Deprecating Organisation with ID " +
                   keyname + '\n');
Collection keys = new ArrayList();
keys.add(mykey);
BulkResponse response1 = blmanager.deprecateObjects(keys);
System.out.println("Depricated service" + '\n');
}
```

Continued

Figure 9.19 Continued

```
        catch(Exception ex)
        {
          ex.printStackTrace();
        }
    }


    public void deleteEntry(javax.xml.registry.infomodel.Key key,
                            String username,
                            String password)
    {
      BusinessLifeCycleManager blmanager = null;
      try
      {
        blmanager = rs.getBusinessLifeCycleManager();
        PasswordAuthentication userdetail;
        userdetail = new PasswordAuthentication(username,
                                               password.toCharArray());
        Set user = new HashSet();
        user.add(userdetail);
        connection.setCredentials(user);
        System.out.println("Checked Security Issues User Logged ON");


        String keyname = key.getId();
        Collection keys = new ArrayList();
        keys.add(key);
        BulkResponse response = blmanager.deleteOrganizations(keys);
        System.out.println("Deleted service of the following Key " +
                           keyname + '\n');
      }
      catch(Exception ex)
      {
        ex.printStackTrace();
      }
    }
}
```

The output for the *DeleteEntry* class is shown in Figure 9.20. It lists the key for the organization that has been deleted.

Figure 9.20 The Output for the *DeleteEntry* Class

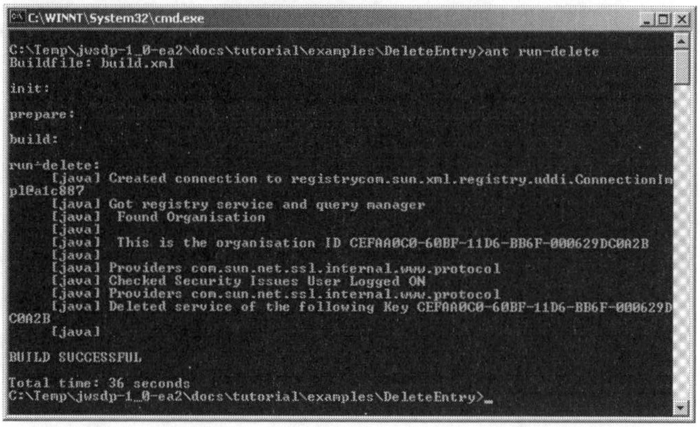

> **NOTE**
>
> As of the time of writing this book, the *deprecateObjects()* method (see code listing of Figure 9.19) generates an *UnsupportedCapabilityException*, perhaps due to some unresolved compatibility issues between the registry and the JAXR pack.

Security Requirements

In each of the classes listed earlier, *PublishEntry*, *UpdateRegistry*, and *DeleteEntry*, we have supplied a username and password to authenticate ourselves before we can add, modify, or delete our organization's information in the registry. Each of the code listings in Figure 9.15, Figure 9.17, and Figure 9.19 contain the following code snippet:

```
PasswordAuthentication userdetail;
userdetail = new PasswordAuthentication(username,
                                    password.toCharArray());
Set user = new HashSet();
user.add(userdetail);
connection.setCredentials(user);
```

This code snippet is a must since without verifying the user's credentials, the registry does not allow addition, modification, or deletion of data. In the "Using the Default Registry" section too, where we had used the Registry Browser, we were asked for our username and password when trying to submit our organization to the registry (see Figure 9.5). This ensures that the information in the registry is secure and no one can change the registry information without proper authorization.

Summary

This chapter focused on business registries, their classification, and methods to access and search business registries. We discussed the categorization of services in business registries on the basis of industry sectors and on the basis of location that makes them easily searchable. We also explained protocols such as SOAP and the major registry standards such as UDDI and ebXML RegRep. After reviewing the structure of registries, we explored the default registry that comes with the JWSDP pack and is used for testing and development purposes. We explained how the Registry Browser, also a part of the JWSDP pack, is used to access a registry and search it, as well as add an organization to it.

Querying techniques were elaborated at length since the major purpose of business registries is to let vendors register themselves and let buyers search them. To clarify the process of querying, we used an example of a simple query that matches a name string pattern and a complex query that searches the registry on the basis of classification. In the process, we described the major JAXR interfaces, classes, and methods that make querying the registry possible. Towards the end of the chapter, we took up JWSDP interfaces, classes, and so on that allow you to programmatically add/delete an organization to/from a registry, and update existing information in the registry. In a nutshell, this chapter covered all aspects relevant to business registries.

Solutions Fast Track

Registries

☑ A registry is a collection of meta-information about Web services and their providers.

☑ Information in a registry is categorized on the basis of industry sector and geographical location.

☑ SOAP is the major protocol used for accessing and communicating with registries.

☑ UDDI and ebXML are two industry initiatives that seek to standardize the way business is conducted over the Internet.

Categorizing Web Services

☑ Web services are those that receive, process (if required), and respond to requests from Web-clients. Web services encompass any self-contained software component/application or piece of code that can be deployed on a Web server, and subsequently be invoked over the Web by Web-clients.

☑ Categorization is crucial for proper organization and maintenance of a business registry.

Connecting to a Registry

☑ The *ConnectionFactory* class in the JAXR API is used to establish a connection with the registry.

☑ Connecting to the registry entails setting the appropriate query URL for querying the registry, or publish URL for submitting an organization to the registry.

☑ The proxy host and proxy port needs to be appropriately set if you are connecting to the registry from behind a firewall.

Querying the Registry

☑ The registry can be queried on the basis of organization name-pattern, or on the basis of classification (industrywise or locationwise).

☑ The business query manager and business life cycle manager provide methods to query the registry based on name patterns and classification schemes.

☑ The *javax.xml.registry* package provides various methods, such as *findOrganizations()*, *findServices()*, *findConcepts()*, and so on, to query a registry.

☑ Querying the registry returns a collection of objects that provide information about the organizations that match the search criteria such as organization name, primary contact, services offered, and so on.

WSDL Documents

☑ WSDL is UDDI's initiative to provide XML grammar for Web services so that the format for data and message exchange for e-business are standardized.

☑ A WSDL document defines the XML grammar within a *<definitions>* tag and the services are defined using the six major elements, *<types>*, *<message>*, *<portType>*, *<binding>*, *<port>*, and *<service>*.

☑ An example was shown of a WSDL document that defines a business message process involving receipt of a first name in the client request and which sends back a welcome message to the client using SOAP.

Storing Information in a Registry

☑ The *BusinessLifeCycleManager* interface in the *javax.xml.registry* package provides various methods required to create an organization and add to it information such as the organization name, contact person, telephone numbers, services offered, and so on.

☑ A username and password are required for authentication to store information in the registry or to modify existing information.

☑ Existing records in the registry can be updated—for example, the *deleteServices()* method can be used to delete a service or the *saveServices()* method can be used to save a new service created. Updating requires proper authentication using the username and password submitted for the organization being updated.

☑ An existing organization in the registry can be deleted using the *deleteObjects()* method, or deprecated using the *deprecateObjects()* method. Both operations require proper authentication (username and password).

Frequently Asked Questions

The following Frequently Asked Questions, answered by the authors of this book, are designed to both measure your understanding of the concepts presented in this chapter and to assist you with real-life implementation of these concepts. To have your questions about this chapter answered by the author, browse to **www.syngress.com/solutions** and click on the **"Ask the Author"** form.

Q: Why do we need business registries when so many search engines are available on the Web?

A: Search engines are meant to search unstructured and random data related to a variety of fields such as education, industry, society, and so on that is available at any URL on the World Wide Web. By contrast, a business registry is highly structured and is specifically meant for offering services and businesses. A registry enables a focused search on the basis of industry, product category, and geographical location. Additionally, registries provide links to URLs from where services being offered over the Web can be invoked.

Q: What is the purpose of standards like UDDI and ebXML?

A: Standards such as UDDI and ebXML strive to standardize the format of business messages and business data exchanged between clients and service providers over the Internet. Such globally accepted standards will make e-business simpler for trading parties by eliminating incompatibility between their various data and message formats.

Q: How can I invoke a desired service after I have found a vendor for it while searching the registry?

A: More often than not, the organization information in the registry contains links in the form of URLs that can be used to invoke a particular service. These links usually refer to a WSDL document that provides the request format for calling the service.

Q: What is JAXR?

A: JAXR is a pack that comes clubbed with the JWSDP pack and provides an API to access a variety of XML registries. Programs written using the JAXR API are portable across different registries.

Q: What is the Java WSDP Registry Server?

A: The JWSDP Registry Server serves the same purpose as an actual business registry does, except that it contains no actual data on service providers and cannot be searched by actual clients over the Internet. This is a test registry server that can be used by developers to test their programs that use JAXR classes to access and query business registries.

Q: What is the purpose of WSDL?

A: Web Services Description Language (or WSDL) is an attempt at standardizing the request-response messages transmitted between trading parties over the Internet. WSDL allows service providers to specify formats that can be used to send requests to their services irrespective of the underlying protocol.

Chapter 10

Java Secure Sockets Layer

Solutions in this chapter:

- **Configuring JSSE**
- **Using HTTPS URL Handlers**
- **Using SocketFactories**
- **Using Secure Server Sockets**
- **Using Secure Client Sockets**
- **Using JSSE Applications with WSDP**

- ☑ **Summary**
- ☑ **Solutions Fast Track**
- ☑ **Frequently Asked Questions**

Introduction

The Java Secure Sockets Extension (JSSE) is an odd addition to the Web Services Developer Pack; it was added on somewhat late, and was made available as a Java platform extension. However, JSSE is a standard component of J2SE as of version 1.4. So you only need to include JSSE in an environment that uses a JVM release prior to 1.4 provided that the version is 1.2.1 or later.

JSSE provides a standard mechanism for establishing secure communication among TCP/IP sockets. It supports the Secure Socket Layer (SSL) and Transport Layer Security (TLS) security protocols. JSSE is designed to provide a standard, royalty-free implementation of these protocols for commercial applications.

What is interesting about JSSE is its approach: JSSE introduces the concept of a *socket factory* (and a *server socket factory*). Socket factories are helper classes that return socket instances; the socket instances in turn depend upon the socket factory used. The default socket factory, for example, returns insecure sockets; the default *SSLFactory* returns *SSLSockets*. Using *SSLSocket* automatically handles the handshaking required by the SSL protocol.

The user subsequently has to update the code to use socket factories instead of creating sockets directly. Once this is done, the application is ready for secure communication.

The use of SSL for transferring secure content over a network entails the use of private and public keys and their associated security certificates. This introduces the concept of a *keystore,* which is used to store the key and information regarding the certificates. JSSE retrievs this information from the keystore for relevant purposes. We'll discuss the *keytool* utility (that is used to create and manage a keystore) below. But first, let us discuss the process of configuring JSSE.

Configuring JSSE

This book deals specifically with JSSE version 1.0.2, which is available as an extension to the Java platform. JSSE must be configured before you can use it. The Java Cryptography Architecture security provider class, *SunJSSE,* is used to implement JSSE. Installation of JSSE requires the prior installation of Java 2 SDK version 1.2.1 or later and Java Runtime Environment (JRE) version 1.2.1 or later. The steps for installing and configuring JSSE are discussed below.

Download JSSE and Extract the Files

Download the JSSE package and save it in any directory on your system. Extracting the downloaded file will create a directory named jsse1.0.2 in which you will find two subdirectories: doc and lib. Note that the JSSE packages and properties can also be used with the WSDP, as we shall see in the "Using JSSE Applications with WSDP" section.

Install the .jar Files

The lib subdirectory contains the following extension files:

- jsse.jar
- jcert.jar
- jnet.jar

Place these three in the java-home/lib/ext directory.

Register the SunJSSE Provider

You need to explicitly register the SunJSSE provider before accessing its services. This registration can be done in two possible ways: static or dynamic.

Static Registration

Edit the security property file. for WIN32, this file is as follows:

```
<java-home>\lib\security\java.security
```

For any Unix-based system (Solaris, Linux and so on), this file is as follows:

```
<java-home>/lib/security/java.security
```

The java.security file contains one property of the type:

```
security.provider.n=providerClassName
```

This property declares a provider and sets its preference order (n). If no specific provider is requested, the preference order determines the order in which providers will be searched. Set this property as follows:

```
security.provider.1=com.sun.net.ssl.internal.ssl.Provider
security.provider.2=sun.security.provider.Sun
```

SunJSSE will now be the first preferred provider.

Dynamic Registration

Programmatically, dynamic registration is done by adding the following line of code to the program seeking to use JSSE services:

```
Security.addProvider(new com.sun.net.ssl.internal.ssl.Provider());
```

This line of code should be added to a program before using JSSE, preferably in the application or servlet's initialization method. The provider is now added dynamically at runtime using the *java.net.Security* class.

Readers should note that when the provider is set statically, it is available to any JSSE program on the system. On the other hand, if the property is not set statically, every program using JSSE classes will have to essentially include code to configure the provider.

Configure The URL Handler

Configuring the URL handler enables JSSE programs to access URLs working on the HTTPS (Secure HTTP) protocol. Like the provider, the URL handler can be configured either statically or dynamically at runtime.

Static Configuration

The URL handler can be statically configured via the *java.protocol.handler.pkgs* property. To set this property, execute the following command at the command line:

```
java -D java.protocol.handler.pkgs=\com.sun.net.ssl.internal.
    www.protocol.
```

Once the property is set statically, you need not configure it in JSSE code again. Instead, URLs that use HTTPS can directly be accessed using the *URLConnection* class.

Dynamic Configuration

To set the URL handler programmatically, use the *java.lang.System* class as follows:

```
System.setProperty("java.protocol.handler.pkgs", "com.sun.net.ssl.
    internal.www.protocol");
```

Note that the first parameter (*java.protocol.handler.pkgs*) refers to the property, while the second parameter (*com.sun.net.ssl.internal.www.protocol*) is the value assigned to this property. This is the same as in static configuration, except that here we use the *java.lang.System* class instead of executing a command on the command line.

Readers should be aware that configuring the URL handler programmatically at runtime does not set the corresponding system property. This means that if you have not configured the URL handler statically, every JSSE program seeking to use the URL handler will have to necessarily use the above line of code in order to connect to HTTPS URLs. On the other hand, when this property is set statically through the command line, any JSSE program on the system can use it to access HTTPS URLs with no need to set the property through code.

Install a JSSE-Specific cacerts file (Optional Configuration Step)

The Java2 SDK contains a default security certificate. However, if required, you can provide a JSSE-specific set of trusted root certificates. When JSSE implementation creates a default TrustManager, it checks for alternate cacert files before resorting to the standard cacerts file. If a file is specified by *javax.net.ssl.trustStore*, it is used as the trust store, otherwise the implementation looks for <java-home>/lib/security/ jssecacerts and <java-home>/lib/security/cacerts in that order.

Introduction to Keys and Certificates

A key is an algorithmically-generated number that is associated with a particular entity, say a company or an individual. A key uniquely identifies an entity, and hence provides a mechanism to verify that entity. A key can be private or public; a private key is supposed to be known only to the entity to whom it belongs. On the other hand, a public key is meant to be made available to anyone who intends to have authenticated/trusted interaction with the entity that owns it. Public and private keys exist in pairs, with a private key corresponding to exactly one public key. A key is what uniquely identifies each entry made in a keystore (This will be discussed in the next section).

A certificate is what certifies a key; it is a digital entity that is used by its issuer to vouch for certain information being provided from another party (the *owner* of the certificate). For example, the issuer confirms that an entity's public key as given by the certificate has a certain specified value. The first party (the issuer) is generally a Certification Authority (CA) who is bound by legal agreements to create and issue valid and reliable certificates. Examples of CAs are VeriSign and Thawte.

A certificate contains information on the its issuer and the digital signature of the entity referred to by the certificate. Apart from this, a certificate contains additional information, such as:

- The certificate serial number (that uniquely identifies the certificate and is assigned by the entity that created the certificate).

- The X.509 version (v1, v2 and v3). X.509 is a standard that defines what information can be stored in a certificate and its data format.

- The issuer of the certificate.

- The certificate's validity period.

- The algorithm used by the CA to sign the certificate.

- The subject name (the name of the entity whose public key is specified by the certificate).

- Public key information of the subject, and so on.

For all practical purposes, a key is certified, not by one certificate alone, but by a chain of certificates. A certificate chain consists of say, a certificate from authority *B*, certifying the key of entity *A*, followed by a certificate from authority *C*, vouching for the integrity of information from authority *B*, followed by a certificate from authority *D*, that certifies the certificate from authority *C* and so on.

When a new key is added to the keystore using the *-genkey* command (which is explained in the next section), a self-signed certificate is added to form the first element of the certification chain. In a self-signed certificate, the issuer is the same as the subject name (the name of the entity whose public key is specified by the certificate). After a certificate signing request is sent to a CA and the certificate is received, it replaces the self-signed certificate. The certificate for the CA's public key is also appended to the key's certificate chain. Apart from the original, there could be more certificates in the chain from different CAs, with each authority certifying the certificate of the authority right above it in the chain. The certificate chain thus grows until a self-signed *root* certificate is reached.

NOTE

It is worth mentioning the fact that most chains end in a certificate self-signed by a well-known and trusted CA. Chains that end in unknown CAs are the genesis of some IE security warning messages.

Using keytool to Create a Keystore

The *keytool* is a key and certificate management utility that allows users to administer their own public or private key pairs and associated certificates. The keytool facilitates use of digital signatures for authentication services like self-authentication. In other words, the user authenticates himself/herself to other users. The keytool stores the keys and certificates in a keystore. By default, this keystore is implemented as a file (the private keys are protected with a password). Information from this keystore is used by the jarsigner tool to generate or verify digital signatures for Java Archive (JAR) files.

NOTE

The keytool and jarsigner together replace the javakey tool in JDK 1.1. The keystore architecture replaces the identity database created and managed by javakey. It also provides more features than javakey, password protection for private keys and verification of digital signatures, for example.

A keystore contains two types of entries:

- **key entries** A key entry typically consists of a secret or private key with associated certificate chain information. Since such a key contains sensitive information, it is saved in a protected format. The keytool and jarsigner handle private keys only.

- **trusted certificate entries** A trusted certificate entry is a public key certificate that contains the identity of the owner of the certificate. It is called "trusted" because the keystore owner *trusts* that it conforms to the identity prescribed by the certificate.

The keystore entries are accessed using aliases. Each keystore entry has a unique, case-insensitive alias. An alias is specified when making an entry to the keystore. Subsequent keytool commands must use the same alias when referring to the entry being considered. (Aliases will be clarified by the subsequent discussions on generating keystore entries.)

Creating a Keystore

The default location for the keystore is the .keystore file in the user's home directory. The home directory is determined by the *user.home* system property. This property varies with operating system configuration. For example, on a multi-user Windows 95 system, *user.home* defaults to C:\Windows\Profiles\ username. However, for a single-user Windows 95, system *user.home* defaults to C:\Windows.

A keystore is created when any of the following commands are used to make an entry to a keystore that does not as yet exist:

- **-genkey** The *-genkey* command generates a key pair. Consider the following command:

```
keytool –genkey –alias myKey -keypass mykeyPassword
```

This command generates a key with the alias *myKey* and the password *mykeyPassword* that is subsequently required to access the key. As mentioned earlier, the alias is used when referring to the key. For example, if the password for this key is to be changed to, say, *newPassword*, the following command might be used:

```
keytool –keypasswd –alias myKey –keypass newPassword
```

Note that the alias *myKey* or *mykey* will both refer to the same key since aliases are case-insensitive. The keystore location can be specified using the *-keystore* option. If this option is not specified, it defaults to the .keystore file in the user's home directory as given by the *user.home* system property.

WARNING

A password should not be specified on the command line unless you are on a secure system. When you do not specify the password option on the command line, you are prompted for it. The password typed at this prompt is echoed as it is; displayed in plain alphanumeric characters, exactly as typed (no "*" characters are used!). Hence, care should be exercised to ensure privacy while typing the password.

- **-import** The *-import* command imports an entry from a specified certificate file, into the keystore and stores it against the specified alias. The data to be imported should either be binary encoded or Base64 encoded.

- **-identitydb** This command reads all the entries from a JDK1.1 identity database (as created by the javakey tool) and adds these entries into the keystore. If the keystore does not exist, it creates one.

Apart from using the above commands, a keystore can also be created by specifying a new one using the *-keystore* option.

Using Keytool to Create/Install a Certificate

Using keytool, it is possible to create or import a certificate to the keystore. keytool currently handles X.509 certificates. All X509 certificates contain the signature of the entity referred to by the certificate, the certificate serial number, the signature algorithm identifier, the issuer's name, the certificate's validity period, the subject name, the subject's public key information and the X509 version.

As mentioned earlier, the keytool can create and manage key entries in the keystore, each of which contains a private key and its associated certificate chain. The public key corresponding to the private key entry in the keystore forms the first certificate in the chain. We now discuss how certificates can be generated and/or imported into the keystore.

Importing a Certificate

The *keytool* is used to import certificates associated with a key using the *-import* command. As mentioned in the previous section, the *-import* command uses a certificate file name to identify the certificate's source and an alias name to identify the destination key. The imported certificates are added to the destination key's certificate chain. Consider the following command:

```
keytool -import -alias destinationKeyName -file certificateFileName.cer
```

This command will import the certificate specified by the certificateFileName file and add it to the certificate chain of the key known by the *destinationKeyName* alias. The keytool can import certificates with X.509 versions 1, 2, or 3. The general form of an *-import* command is as follows:

```
-import {-alias aliasName} {-file certificateFile} [-keypass keyPassword]
    {-noprompt} {-tustcacerts} {-storetype storetype} {-keystore keystore}
```

```
[-storepass storePassword] [-provider providerClassName] {-v}
    {-Jjavaoption option}
```

Lets take a look at the code parts involved here:

- *-storetype* defines the type of store that is given by the *keystore.type* property. The default keystore type is *jks*, which is proprietary to Sun Microsystems. You may choose any other type for the keystore, say a type like *SyngressKS,* which is descriptive of a keystore type created by Syngress.

- *-provider* specifies the name of the service provider's master file, if that name is not already listed in the securities property file.

- *-v* indicates verbose mode, whereby detailed information regarding the certificate is output.

- *-Jjavaoption* passes the *<javaoption>* to the Java interpreter. This can be used for changing JVM parameters; for example, you could ask the JVM to allocate additional memory for more efficient execution.

The rest of the options are self-explanatory or have been explained earlier. Note that when a new trusted certificate is being imported, the key identified by the alias name should not exist in the keystore. If the alias name already exists in the keystore, the new certificate chain will replace the old one associated with the alias. However, this requires that the password being used to protect the already existing alias entry in the keystore be supplied to the *-keypass* option when importing. If you have not supplied the password, you will be prompted for it; without supplying the valid password, you cannot change the certificate chain of the previous alias entry. Also, you cannot create a duplicate alias entry in the keystore while importing certificates. If you are determined to use the same alias for your entry, first delete the existing alias using the *-delete* option ("*keytool -delete -alias IwantThisAlias*") and then import the certificate.

Generating a Self-Signed Certificate

A self-signed certificate can be generated using the *-selfcert* keytool:

```
keytool -selfcert {-alias aliasName} {-sigalg signatureAlgorith}
    {-dname distinguishedName} {-validity validityDays} [-keypass
        keyPassword] {-storetype storetype} {-keystore keystore}
            [-storepass storePassword] [-provider providerClassName] {-v}
                {-Jjavaoption option}
```

- *-sigalg* denotes the algorithm used to sign the certificate.
- *-dname* is the X.500 distinguished name for the CA.

For example, the following command replaces the certificate chain entry for the myAlias key with a self-signed certificate from an authority with a specified X.500 distinguished name:

```
keytool -selfcert -alias myAlias -keypass myPassword -dname "CN=myName,
    OU=myUnit, O=muOrganization, L= myCity, S=myState, C=US"
```

Note the values for the *-dname* option:

- *CN* denotes common name of a person
- *OU* denotes the department, division or unit
- *O* denotes the name of the organization
- *L* denotes the city
- *S* denotes the state or province
- *C* denotes the two-letter country code

Importing a Certificate From an Identity Database

The *-identitydb* keytool option is used to import keys and certificates from a JDK1.1 identity database managed by the javakey tool:

```
keytool -identitydb {-file idbFile} {-storetype storetype} {-keystore
    keystore} [-storepass storePassword][-provider providerClassName]
        {-v} {-Jjavaoption option}
```

Here, the *-file* option specifies the identity database file. An identity in the identity database may have more than one certificate. However, while importing, only an identity's first certificate is imported into the keystore.

Referring to Keystores with JSSE Properties

The Java API's *KeyStore* class can be used to refer to the information kept in the keystore. This class allows information about keys and certificates to be accessed and used in a program. Let us examine this class in detail.

The *KeyStore* Class

The *KeyStore* class is a part of the java.security package. This class represents the collection of keys and certificates contained in the keystore. Since the keystore contains the two types of entries (keys and certificates), this class is capable of managing both. The *KeyStore* class' *getInstance()* method is used to instantiate it. This method has two forms:

```
getInstance(String keystoreType)
```

The first form is:

```
KeyStore ksInstance = KeyStore.getInstance("JKS");
```

Note that we are providing the default keystore type (*jks*). The above code will check for a *jks* keystore implementation in the environment.

The second form is:

```
getInstance(String keystoreType, Provider provider)
```

The provider can also be provided with the keystore type when instantiating the *KeyStore* class as in the following code:

```
KeyStore ksInstance = KeyStore.getInstance("JKS", "SUN");
```

The system will now determine whether the keystore implementation of the specified type exists in the provider package.

Before a keystore can be accessed, the keystore must be loaded; an input stream is passed to the *load()* method, which loads the keystore. This can be achieved with the following line of code:

```
ksInstance.load(new FileInputStream(fileName), password);
```

The parameter password causes the keystore integrity to be verified before it is loaded. If a *null* is passed as the input stream parameter, it creates an empty keystore.

Upon a successful loading, the keystore information can be accessed using various methods provided by the *KeyStore* class. Methods are also available to modify or delete keystore entries. We discuss some of these methods below:

- **size()** This method returns an integer that gives the number of entries in the keystore.

- **aliases()** This method returns an *Enumeration* object that contains all the aliases listed in the keystore. These aliases can further be used to obtain individual information about them.

- **getCertificate(String aliasName)** This method returns the certificate associated with the given alias.

- **getCertificateChain(String aliasName)** This returns the certificate chain associated with the key entry as recognized by the specified alias name.

- **getKey(String aliasName, char[] password)** This method returns the key that is identified by the given alias. The password is required to retrieve the key.

- **containsAlias(String aliasName)** This method returns a Boolean value that indicates whether the given name exists in the keystore.

- **deleteEntry(String aliasName)** This method deletes the entry corresponding to the given alias.

- **setKeyEntry(String aliasName, Key key, char[] password, Certificate[] certChain)** This method assigns the key specified by *key* to the alias given by *aliasName*. This key entry is protected by the password given by *password* while *certChain* provides the certificate chain associated with the key.

- **setCertificateEntry(String aliasName, Certificate cert)** This method assigns the certificate given by *cert* to the key entry recognized by the alias, *aliasName*.

- **getProvider()** This method returns the provider of the keystore.

- **getType()** This method returns the type of the keystore.

The Certificate Class

Apart from the *KeyStore* class, the *Certificate* class in the java.security.cert package can also be used for getting specific information on the certificate entries in the keystore. For example, when the *KeyStore* class' *getCertificateChain()* method is called, it returns an array of certificate objects. The information and properties associated with each of these certificate objects can then be obtained using the methods given in the *Certificate* class.

The constructor of the Certificate class can be used to create a certificate by specifying the type of certificate.

```
Certificate(String certType);
```

Here are some methods of the *Certificate* class:

- **getPublicKey()** This method returns the public key for the certificate.
- **getType()** This method returns the type of the certificate.
- **verify(PublicKey key)** This method verifies that the certificate was signed using the private key for the public key specified by `key`.
- **getEncoded()** This method returns the encoded certificate.

Let us conclude our discussion by examining some sample code that uses these JSSE properties to keystore entries.

Using JSSE Properties to Refer to the keystore

We call our class *TestKeys.java*. This class obtains information stored in a keystore and prints out the information it reads. The code for *TestKeys.java* is given in Figure 10.1.

Figure 10.1 The TestKeys Class

```
import java.net.*;
import javax.net.ssl.*;
import java.security.*;
import javax.security.cert.X509Certificate;
import com.sun.net.ssl.*;
import java.io.*;
import java.util.*;
import java.security.cert.*;
public class TestKeys
{
 public static void main(String[] args) throws Exception
  {
   Security.addProvider(new com.sun.net.ssl.internal.ssl.Provider());
   char[] passphrase = "passphrase".toCharArray();
   KeyManagerFactory kmf = KeyManagerFactory.getInstance
        (KeyManagerFactory.getDefaultAlgorithm());
   KeyStore ks = KeyStore.getInstance("JKS");
   ks.load(new FileInputStream("keys"), passphrase);

   System.out.println(ks.getType());
```

Continued

Figure 10.1 Continued

```
Enumeration enum = ks.aliases();

while(enum.hasMoreElements())

{

 System.out.println("This is the allias " + (String)

    enum.nextElement());

}

System.out.println((ks.getProvider()).toString());

System.out.println((ks.getKey("duke", passphrase)).getAlgorithm());

System.out.println((ks.getKey("duke", passphrase)).getFormat());

java.security.cert.Certificate[] cera = ks.getCertificateChain("duke");

for (int i = 0; i < cera.length; i++)

{

 System.out.println((cera[i]).getType());

}


 }

}
```

Note that the code uses the *getInstance()* method, which receives only the store type parameter. The *KeyStore* instance thus created is loaded using the file input stream that points to the file named "keys". The keystore is validated since the load method is supplied with a password given by *passphrase*. The code begins by obtaining the keystore's type. It then obtains the *Enumeration* array for all the entries in the keystore, and prints them to the console. Note the code fragments:

```
ks.getKey("duke", passphrase)).getAlgorithm();
ks.getKey("duke", passphrase)).getFormat()
```

The first fragment uses the *getAlgorithm()* method to obtain the algorithm used for the key entry identified by its alias, "duke." The second fragment obtains the associated format using the *getFormat()* method. The following code obtains the certificate chain associated with the key identified by the alias "duke" in a certificate array:

You might be wondering why the key is named duke? Duke is the name of the java triangle guy!

```
ks.getCertificateChain("duke");
```

The type of each certificate in this certificate chain is then printed to the console using the following line of code:

```
System.out.println((cera[i]).getType());
```

Here *cera[i]* gives the element at the ith position of the certificate array. The output of the *TestKeys* class is as given in Figure 10.2.

Figure 10.2 Output from TestKeys Class

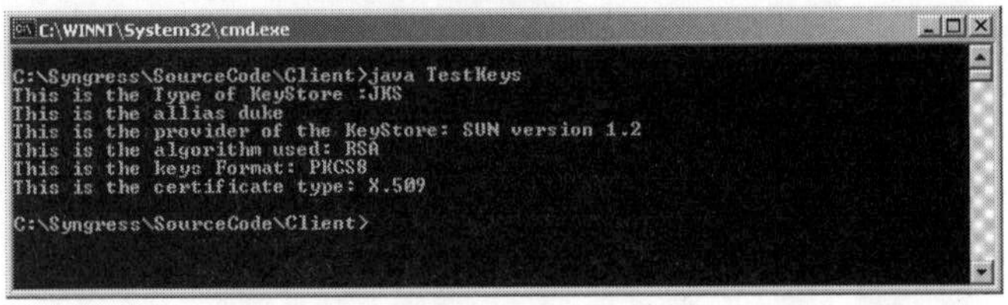

Using HTTPS URL Handlers

As mentioned in the section on configuring JSSE, the JSSE implementation contains a URL handler for URL requests that use the HTTPS protocol. This handler can be used only after its implementation package name has been added to the list of packages searched by the *java.net.URL* class. This can be done statically by setting the *java.protocol.handler.pkgs* system property, or dynamically at runtime.

When using the HTTPS protocol through proxy servers, you need to set the *https.proxyHost* and *https.proxyPort* system properties to point them to the proxy server's host name and port, respectively. This can be achieved by executing the following code:

```
java -Dhttp.proxySet=true -Dhttps.proxyHost=proxyMachineName
-Dhttps.proxyPort=8000
```

proxyMachineName is the name of the host that is serving as the proxy server.

Configuring URL Handler for JSSE

The *java.protocol.handler.pkgs* property can be set by specifying the following java command option at the command line:

```
java -Djava.
java.protocol.handler.pkgs=\com.sun.net.ssl.internal.www.protocol.
```

To set the property programmatically, first check for any previously configured protocol handlers. If none are found, just set the *java.protocol.handler.pkgs* property. If a previously configured protocol handler exists, append the URL handler to the existing handlers as shown in the code snippet below:

```
String prop = System.getProperty("java.protocol.handler.pkgs");
if (prop != null)
  prop += "com.sun.net.ssl.internal.www.protocol";
else
 prop = "com.sun.net.ssl.internal.www.protocol";
System.setProperty("java.protocol.handler.pkgs",prop);
```

NOTE

The code listings in this chapter do not check for previously configured URL providers since we did not have any other protocol handlers configured on our system. The code listings directly configure the URL handler using the following code line:

```
System.setProperty("java.protocol.handler.pkgs","com.sun.net.ssl.
    internal.www.protocol");
```

However, it is advisable to make a check as given in the above code snippet.

Let us now consider a sample code that configures the URL handler for JSSE. It uses the class *Addproperty.java* as in Figure 10.3.

Figure 10.3 Configuring the URL Handler

```
import java.security.*;
public class Addproperty
{
 public static void main(String[] args)
 {
  try
  {
   //This line of code Configures the HTTPS URL handler
   System.setProperty("java.protocol.handler.pkgs", "com.sun.net.ssl.
       internal.www.protocol");
   //This property registers the SunJSSE provider.
```

Continued

Figure 10.3 Continued

```
      Security.addProvider(new com.sun.net.ssl.internal.ssl.Provider());

    }

   catch(Exception ex)

   {

    ex.printStackTrace();

   }

  }

 }
```

This is evidently a two-line code that sets the URL handler and sets the provider (See the section on configuring JSSE for details)

Creating a HTTPS Connection

We'll now examine an example that illustrates configuring the URL handler for JSSE and using it to connect to a URL using HTTPS.

Using the URL Handler

We use the *URLHandler* class to implement the JSSE URL handler dynamically at runtime. It then connects to a URL using HTTPS and creates a *BufferedReader* instance to read data from the URL. The data so read is then echoed as output. Code for the *URLHandler* class is shown in Figure 10.4.

Figure 10.4 The URLHandler Class

```
import java.net.*;

import java.io.*;

import javax.net.ssl.*;

import java.security.*;


public class URLHandler {

    public static void main(String[] args) throws Exception {

  System.setProperty("java.protocol.handler.pkgs", "com.sun.net.ssl.
      internal.www.protocol");


  URL verisign = new URL("https://netbanking");
```

Continued

Figure 10.4 Continued

```
Security.addProvider(new com.sun.net.ssl.internal.ssl.Provider());

BufferedReader in = new BufferedReader(new InputStreamReader
    (verisign.openStream()));
System.out.println("Testing the code");
String inputLine;

while ((inputLine = in.readLine()) != null)
    System.out.println(inputLine);

in.close();
    }
}
```

The output from the *URLHandler* class is as shown in Figure 10.5. Note that this output represents the HTML content returned by the URL.

Figure 10.5 Output from the URLHandler Class

Figure 10.4 clearly shows that once the URL handler has been implemented, the *java.net.URL* class can be used to create a URL that uses the HTTPS.

```
URL verisign = new URL("https://netbanking");
```

This URL can then be used to open an input stream from the URL, just as is done when creating an HTTP connection. Data can be read using any of the methods available to the reader instance associated with the input stream. The *URLHandler* class in Figure 10.4 uses the *readLine()* method to read one line at a time from the HTTPS connection.

Thus, with the exception of setting the JSSE URL handler, the process involved in securing an HTTPS connection is the same as for an HTTP URL connection.

Using SocketFactories

The URLs discussed in the previous section provide a high-level mechanism for connections over a network. Sockets on the other hand, provide a lower-level interface for making connections and accessing resources over a network. Let us discuss the various classes available for creating sockets. Sockets are mainly used for client-server applications where multiple clients connect to a single server over a network. The server implements the socket-server, which is capable of accepting multiple client connections. Let us explore the concept of sockets.

Creating Sockets and ServerSockets (By Hand)

The java.net package provides two classes: the *Socket* class and the *ServerSocket* class implement the client side and server side of the sockets, respectively.

The *ServerSocket* Class

Another class from the java.net package, the *ServerSocket* class implements the listener service on the server. The *ServerSocket* class listens at a specified port for client requests and accepts them. Since a request is always initiated by a client, the server needs to be a listening program, hence the need for a server socket. The following line of code creates a server socket that listens at the port 5555:

```
ServerSocket serverSocket = new ServerSocket (5555);
```

> **WARNING**
>
> Before implementing a server socket, ensure that the port at which the listener listens is not being used by any other application on the server machine. Also, socket numbers 1-1024 are reserved for system functions and should generally not be used by applications.

In the code line above, port 5555, becomes dedicated to the listener program implementing the server socket. This server socket can be used to accept client connections:

```
Socket clientConnection = serverSocket.accept();
```

The above code would open a new socket on the server machine to send data to the client or receive data from the client. Readers should note that if a class fails to create a socket, it throws an *IOException* error.

The *Socket* Class

The *Socket* class in the java.net package is used to create the client socket. The communication is through the input and output streams associated with the socket. A socket can be created as follows:

```
Socket clientSocket = new Socket(localhost, 5555);
```

This creates a socket on the local machine by connecting to the listening port (in this case, 5555) on the server machine (localhost). Readers should replace *localhost* with the name of their computer. To read from a socket, an input stream can be opened using the socket instance:

```
BufferedInputStream clientIPStream = new
BufferedInputStream(clientSocket.getInputStream());
```

Similarly, output streams can be created to use the socket for writing:

```
BufferedOutputStream clientOPStream = new
BufferedOutputStream(clientSocket.getOutputStream());
```

These streams can now be used by the client to read or write data using the *clientSocket* instance.

Using SocketFactories and ServerSocketFactories

Another method of creating sockets and server sockets is by using the factory classes, *SocketFactory* and *ServerSocketFactory*, respectively.

The *SocketFactory* Class

The *SocketFactory* class is an abstract class that extends the *java.lang.Object* class:

```
public abstract class SocketFactory extends Object
```

This class provides the *createSocket()* method to create sockets:

```
public abstract Socket createSocket(String hostMachine, int port) throws
    IOException,                                UnknownHostException
```

If the host computer referred by *hostMachine* is unreachable, an *IOException* is thrown, and if the name given by *hostMachine* cannot be resolved, an *UnknownHostException* is thrown. Now, suppose we want to create a socket at port 2022 using the *Socket* class. The following line of code may be used:

```
Socket factorySocket = SocketFactory.createSocket(localhost, 2022);
```

The *ServerSocketFactory* Class

This class is also an abstract class that extends the *java.lang.Object* class as follows:

```
public abstract class ServerSocketFactory extends Object
```

It can be used to create server sockets using the *createServerSocket()* method, which returns a server socket bound to the specified port on the server machine.

```
public abstract ServerSocket createServerSocket(int port)
        throws IOException
```

To create a server socket at port 5555, the following line of code may be used:

```
ServerSocket factoryServerSocket = ServerSocketFactory.
        createServerSocket(5555);
```

Advantages of SocketFactories

Socket factories offer the following advantages:

- Both factories and sockets show polymorphism. This enables an application to use different types of sockets by passing different kinds of factories.

- The parameters used in socket construction can be used to customize factories. Practical use of such customization could be to obtain sockets with different networking timeouts

- The sockets created by using factory classes can expose features like statistics collection, compression, and so on.

Determining Default and Installed Cipher Suites

Connecting to a URL using HTTPS requires a handshaking mechanism. Handshaking ensures that the two connecting machines support compatible cipher suites, which are required to transmit and receive data over a secure connection. The cipher suites installed on a machine may differ from the cipher suits it supports. (This is equivalent to a feature being supported by a machine but not being installed on it.) During the handshaking process, the two connecting machines exchange cipher suite information to determine if they can connect using a secure connection. The cipher suites installed on a machine can be obtained using the *getCipherSuites()* method, which returns the available cipher suits in the form of an array of string values. Let us illustrate this concept with an example.

Determining the Installed Cipher Suites

We create a class called *JSSE_install_check.java*, which prints out the installed cipher suites. The code for this class is given in Figure 10.6.

Figure 10.6 The JSSE_install_check.java Class

```
import java.net.*;
import javax.net.ssl.*;
import java.security.*;
public class JSSE_install_check
{

    public static void main(String[] args) throws Exception
  {

  Security.addProvider(new com.sun.net.ssl.internal.ssl.Provider());

  SSLServerSocketFactory myfactory = (SSLServerSocketFactory)
      SSLServerSocketFactory.getDefault();

  SSLServerSocket mysslSocket = (SSLServerSocket)
          myfactory.createServerSocket( 5757 );

  String [] cipherSuites = mysslSocket.getEnabledCipherSuites();

  for (int i = 0; i < cipherSuites.length; i++)
  {
   System.out.println(cipherSuites[i]);
  }
    }
}
```

Note that since cipher suites constitute an SSL concept, the SunJSSE provider is being configured at runtime. The *SSLServerSocketFactory* class is being instantiated using its *getDefault()* method. This instance is then being used to create a *ServerSocket* at port 5757. The *getEnabledCipherSuites()* method is used by the instance of the server socket (*mysslSocket*) to obtain the installed cipher suites. The output for this class is shown in Figure 10.7.

Figure 10.7 Printing the Available Cipher Suites

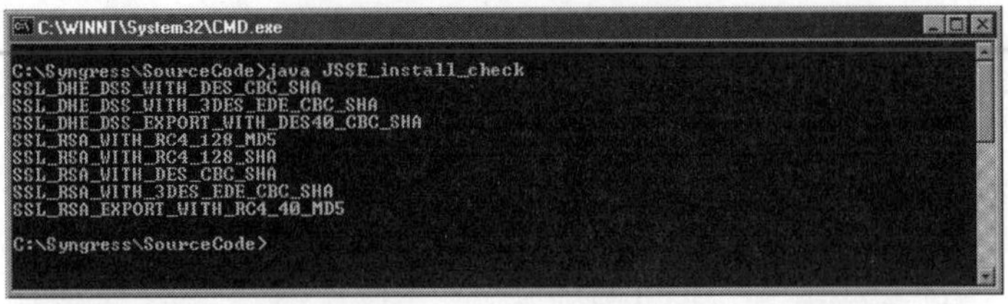

Using Secure Server Sockets

We have already seen how server sockets are created and what purpose they serve. Now let us examine the process of securing server sockets. A secure socket is one that supports data transmission between a client and server over SSL. Secure sockets behave like normal sockets, except that they add a security layer to the underlying transport protocol (TCP) being used on the client-server network. This security layer provides protection as entailed in the SSL protocol. The protection provided covers the following:

- **Data Integrity** SSL protects against the modification of messages during transmission.

- **Authentication** SSL provides for server authentication as well as client authentication (if requested by the server). This ensures that data is being sent to or received from a bonafide resource that is authorized to receive or send the data.

- **Confidentiality/Privacy** SSL encrypts the data being exchanged over the network. This ensures that wiretapping measures cannot access sensitive/confidential data, such as a user's personal information.

We will now describe the process of creating secure server sockets; and explain how secure server sockets accept connections and how secure content can be read or written using them. These concepts will then be consolidated with the help of an example.

Getting the Secure Socket Factory

The *SSLServerSocketFactory* class in the *javax.net.ssl* package acts as the factory that creates secure server sockets. This is an abstract class that extends the *ServerSocketFactory* class.

```
public abstract class SSLServerSocketFactory extends ServerSocketFactory
```

The fact that the *SSLServerSocketFactory* class extends the *ServerSocketFatory* class should come as no surprise. The basic purpose and working of a secure socket remain the same as for an ordinary socket, except that secure content can be transmitted through it. The secure server factory encompasses the details of creating and configuring secure sockets. These details, in turn, include information on authentication keys, cipher suites, certificate validation etc.

The secure server socket factory can be obtained as follows:

- By calling the *getDefault()* method, which returns the default implementation of the *SSLServerSocketFactory*.

```
SSLServerSocketFactory.getDefault();
```

  The value of the *SSL.ServerSocketFactory.provider* security property in the Java security properties file determines the default factory implementation; this property can be set to a desired class. Finally, an instantiation exception is thrown if SSL has not been properly configured for a virtual machine.

- By using an instance of the *SSLContext* class. The *SSLContext* class encapsulates state information (session state information, for example) that is shared by all sockets created under that context. The *SSLContext* can be instantiated as follows:

```
SSLContext SSLContextInstance = SSLContext.getInstance("SSL");
```

  Information on configuring the context instance and associated methods shall be discussed later with reference to Figure 10.8. For the time being, we use this context instance to obtain a factory instance using the following code.

```
SSLServerSocketFactory factoryInstance =  SSLContextInstance.
    getServerSocketFactory();
```

We will now use this factory instance to create a secure server socket.

Registering a Secure Server Socket

The *SSLServerSocket* class in the javax.net.ssl package creates a server socket that is protected using the SSL protocol.

```
public abstract class SSLServerSocket extends ServerSocket
```

As expected, this class provides methods that are specific to secure sockets. A secure server socket can be created by using an instance of the factory class.

```
SSLServerSocket mysslSocket = (SSLServerSocket)factoryInstance.
    createServerSocket(5757);
```

The above code creates a secure socket server on port 5757 of the host machine, using the instance of SSL server socket factory class, *factoryInstance*.

Accepting Connections

Just as with server sockets, a secure server socket can be used to accept secure connections from clients. The *SSLServerSocket* class uses the *accept()* method of its super class (the *ServerSocket* class) to accept client connections. The secure server socket listens for communication from clients and accepts a connection when requested by a client.

```
Socket mySocket = mysslSocket.accept();
```

Accepting a connection returns a socket on the client machine. If the connection cannot be accepted, the *accept()* method throws an *IOException* or a *SecurityException*. The *SecurityException* is thrown when an existing security manager disallows connections from the requesting client machine.

Reading Data

The secure server socket is similar to a server socket, except for the additional security it provides. Thus, it uses the same reader and input stream classes for reading client data as are used by the server sockets. For example, let us create a *BufferedReader* using the *InputStream* associated with the *mySocket* socket created above.

```
BufferedReader readdata = new BufferedReader(new
InputStreamReader(mySocket.getInputStream()));
```

This *BufferedReader* can now be used to read data from the client, using any of the available methods of the *BufferedReader* class.

Writing Data

In a manner similar to that for reading data, we can write data back to the client using an output stream. All methods associated with output streams will be available to the server socket. A print stream is created for the secure server socket in the following line of code:

```
PrintStream send = new PrintStream(mysocket.getOutputStream());
```

The *send* object of the *PrintStream* type can now be used to write data to a client as follows:

```
send.println("This text is response from server");
send.flush();
```

The *flush()* method commits the response.

Closing Connections

The input and output streams associated with a secure server socket can be closed using their respective *close()* methods. The secure server socket also inherits the *close()* method from any *ServerSocket* class that closes a socket. Each of these *close* methods close their respective streams/sockets and free up the system resources being utilized by them.

```
send.close(); // closes the output stream
readdata.close(); // closes the input stream
mysocket.close(); // closes the socket
```

We will now consider an example in which a secure server socket is created and used to accept a connection from a client, read data from that client, and write data back to it in Figure 10.8.

Figure 10.8 The *SecureServer* Class

```
import java.net.*;
import javax.net.ssl.*;
import java.security.*;
import java.io.*;
import javax.security.cert.X509Certificate;
import com.sun.net.ssl.*;
public class SecureServer
{
```

Continued

Figure 10.8 Continued

```
    public static void main(String[] args) throws Exception
{

  Security.addProvider(new com.sun.net.ssl.internal.ssl.Provider());

  char[] passphrase = "passphrase".toCharArray();
  SSLContext ctx = SSLContext.getInstance("SSL");
  KeyManagerFactory kmf = KeyManagerFactory.getInstance("SunX509");
  KeyStore ks = KeyStore.getInstance("JKS");

  ks.load(new FileInputStream("keys"), passphrase);
  kmf.init(ks, passphrase);
  ctx.init(kmf.getKeyManagers(), null, null);

  SSLServerSocketFactory myfactory = ctx.getServerSocketFactory();
  SSLServerSocket mysslSocket = SSLServerSocket)
       myfactory.createServerSocket(5757);
  System.out.println("Server Started");
  SSLSocket mysocket = (SSLSocket)mysslSocket.accept();

  PrintStream send = new PrintStream(mysocket.getOutputStream());
  BufferedReader readdata = new BufferedReader(
       new InputStreamReader(mysocket.getInputStream()));
  String myrequest = readdata.readLine();
  System.out.println(myrequest);

  send.println("This text is response from server");
  send.flush();
  send.close();
  readdata.close();

  mysocket.close();
  }
}
```

Figure 10.8 introduces another concept, that of the *KeyManagerFactory* class. This class acts as a factory for creating key managers, depending upon a source of key material. Each key manager manages a specific type of key material that is provider-specific or based on a keystore. Here the line of code *KeyManagerFactory .getInstance("SunX509");* generates an instance of the *KeyManagerFactory* class by passing the name of the algorithm, "SunX509" to its *getInstance()* method. The code fragment, *kmf.getKeyManagers(),* generates one key manager for each type of key material.

The *KeyStore* class is instantiated and the keystore is loaded (These steps have already been discussed in the "Referring to keystores with JSSE properties" section).

The *SSLContext* class is invoked by passing the protocol *SSL* as a parameter. This creates an SSL context object that implements the SSL protocol; the *init()* method initializes the SSL context. The array of key managers generated using the *getKeyManagers()* method is passed to the *SSLContext* object to initialize it. Note that we are using the SSL context instance to instantiate the *SSLServerSocketFactory* class. The secure server socket created using the factory class is then used to print out the enabled cipher suites on the server. This socket, *mysslSocket,* is also used to read data from the client. The text "This text is response from server" is written back to the client.

Using Secure Client Sockets

A secure client socket can be created in two ways.

- By using the *SSLSocketFactory* class. The factory class is first instantiated using its *getDefault()* method:

```
SSLSocketFactory.getDefault();
```

This returns the default implementation of the factory class. The factory class' *createSocket()* method can be used to create a secure socket using the following code:

```
FactoryInstance.createSocket(Socket s, Sting hostname, int
portNumber);
```

This returns a secure socket on the port of the host specified by hostname.

- Through the *accept()* method of the *SSLServerSocket*. When a secure server socket accepts a client connection, it returns a secure socket on the client machine using the following code:

```
SSLSocket secureSocket = mysslSocket.accept();
```

Here, *mysslSocket* is the server socket instance.

Connecting to a Remote Secure Server

First, a secure server is created on the client machine using the factory instance. This secure socket is then used to obtain the set of supported cipher suites. Note that this is important because the creation of a secure connection requires the use of these cipher suites during the handshake process.

```
SSLSocket socket = (SSLSocket)factory.createSocket("localhost", 5757);
String [] cipherSuites = socket.getSupportedCipherSuites();
socket.setEnabledCipherSuites(cipherSuites);
```

The actual connection is created when the socket's *startHandshake()* method is called. This method starts an SSL handshake between the client and server machines, including the exchange of information pertaining to the cipher suites, encryption keys, and so on.

```
socket.startHandshake();
```

If a network error is encountered, the method throws an *IOException*.

Writing Data

Data can be written from the client to the server by using the *getOutputStream()* method associated with a secure client socket. Note that this method is inherited from *SSLSockets*'s super class, the *Socket* class, and hence the returned stream behaves exactly as an output stream would. Consequently, all methods associated with output streams (*write()*, *flush()*, *close()*) are available to the secure socket.

The following lines of code write the text "This text is sent by the client as request to the server" to the server:

```
String str1 = "This text is sent by the client as request to the server";
PrintStream send = new PrintStream(socket.getOutputStream());
send.println(str1);
send.flush();
```

Reading Data

As with writing data, a secure socket uses the *Socket* class's *getInputStream()* method for reading data from the server. Consequently, all methods associated with input streams (*read(), close(), skip()*) are available to the secure socket.

The following lines of code read data from the server and print it to the console:

```
BufferedReader readdata = new BufferedReader(new InputStreamReader
    (socket.getInputStream()));
String str = readdata.readLine();
System.out.println(str);
```

Closing the Connection

The input/output streams associated with the socket can be closed using their respective *close()* methods. The secure socket also inherits the *close()* method from the *Socket* class. The *close()* method frees the system resources being used by the object (input/output stream or socket) on which it is called.

```
send.close(); // closes the output stream
readdata.close(); // closes the input stream
mysslsocket.close(); // closes the socket
```

We now create the client side for the secure server socket. The code for the *SecureClient* class is given in Figure 10.9.

Figure 10.9 Code for SecureClient

```
import java.net.*;
import java.io.*;
import javax.net.ssl.*;
import java.security.*;
import javax.security.cert.X509Certificate;
import com.sun.net.ssl.*;

public class SecureClient
{
 public static void main(String[] args) throws Exception
 {
```

Continued

Figure 10.9 Continued

```
Security.addProvider(new com.sun.net.ssl.internal.ssl.Provider());
try
{
 char[] passphrase = "passphrase".toCharArray();
 SSLContext ctx = SSLContext.getInstance("SSL");
 KeyManagerFactory kmf = KeyManagerFactory.getInstance("SunX509");
 KeyStore ks = KeyStore.getInstance("JKS");

 ks.load(new FileInputStream("keys"), passphrase);
 kmf.init(ks, passphrase);
 ctx.init(kmf.getKeyManagers(), null, null);

 SSLSocketFactory factory = ctx.getSocketFactory();
 SSLSocket socket = (SSLSocket)factory.createSocket("localhost", 5757);
 String [] cipherSuites = socket.getSupportedCipherSuites();
 socket.setEnabledCipherSuites(cipherSuites);
 socket.startHandshake();

 String str1 =
   "This text is sent by the client as request to the server";
 PrintStream send = new PrintStream(socket.getOutputStream());
 send.println(str1);
 send.flush();

 BufferedReader readdata = new BufferedReader(
        new InputStreamReader(socket.getInputStream()));
 String str = readdata.readLine();
 System.out.println(str);
 }
catch(Exception ex)
 {
 ex.printStackTrace();
 }
 }
}
```

Developing & Deploying…

Configuring the Cacerts File

To ensure that the client-server programs in Figure 10.8 and Figure 10.9 work properly, the following procedure may be adopted:

1. Locate the file titled "samplecacerts" in your JSSE directory. It is likely to be found in the JSSE/Samples directory.

2. Copy the "samplecacerts" file into the Program Files/JavaSoft/JRE 1.2.1/Security/ directory.

3. Rename the "samplecacerts" file to "jssecacerts."

When the server/client is run, the program tries to locate this file to obtain certificate information. Not performing this step may result in the code not working properly.

Run the secure server socket and the secure client socket from Figure10.8 and Figure 10.9, respectively. Start by running the server first. Use the *java SecureServer* java command, at the command prompt to run the server. When you see the "Server Started" string message (See Figure 10.10) on the server console, run the client using the *SecureClient* java command in another command-line window. The client will now try to connect to the server. Upon accepting the client connection, the server console will show the message "This text is sent by the client as request to the server" as shown in Figure 10.10. This is the message that the client sends to the server. The server will now send the string message "This text is response from server" to the client. The client, upon reading this message, will print it to the client console as shown in Figure 10.11.

Figure 10.10 The Server Console

Figure 10.11 The Client Console

Debugging…

Using the Debug Mode

The output for the client-server classes, *SecureServer* and *SecureClient* are as shown in Figure 10.10 and Figure 10.11, respectively. The message that is read by the client/server gets printed to the console aswould have happened if the client and server were connected without using SSL. Yet there is a difference, which will become apparent when these two programs are run in the debug mode as explained below.

To enable debugging, compile and run the following code (just as you run a java program in the normal mode):

```
import com.sun.net.ssl.*;
public class DebugHelp
{
public static void main(String[] args)
{
  com.sun.net.ssl.internal.ssl.Debug.Help() ;
}
}
```

After you have run this program, use the following command to run the server:

```
java -Djavax.net.debug=all SecureServer
```

When you run this command, you will find a huge amount of data scrolling up the server console. This information includes information on the truststore location, truststore type, key information from the truststore, associated certificate information from the "jssecacert" file, and so on. To obtain details of the information being printed on the server console, you may save this information as a text file using the following command:

Continued

```
java -Djavax.net.debug=all SecureServer>server.txt
```

This will create the file "server.txt" in the same directory that contains the *SecureServer* class file.

While going through the "server.txt" file you will come across information on the key known as "duke", and that happens to be the only key entry in our keystore. This will be followed by the key's certificate chain. Details of each certificate, like the signature algorithm, validity period, the issuer of the certificate, and the serial number. will be enumerated. (If the keystore had contained any other keys, information on their certificates would also have been printed). After all the certificates are read, the server is ready to service client requests. The text message "Server Started" will appear at the end of the information on the certificates in the certificate chain of the keystore entry known as "duke".

Now run the client using the following command:

```
java -Djavax.net.debug=all SecureClient.
```

The client output will also begin with the listing of certificates as in the case of the server. This output can be saved in a text file using the following command:

```
java -Djavax.net.debug=all SecureClient>client.txt
```

client.txt will now contain the complete output from the client console.

Going beyond the line "Server Started" in server.txt, you will find phrases like "ClientHello" and "ServerHello" followed by information on cipher suites and compression methods. Interspersed with the certificate information being exchanged between the client and the server, you may find text information like "ServerHelloDone," "Handshake," "ClientKeyExchange," "SESSION KEYGEN," "CONNECTION KEYGEN" and so on that gives an idea about the process followed during the handshake.

The console outputs for the server and client are shown in Figure 10.12 and Figure 10.13 respectively. Since these images do not list the complete console output, it is recommended that you refer to server.txt and client.txt.

Note that data sent from the client to the server and back is encrypted. This data is decrypted at the receiving end and thet resprective text messages are displayed. The server file will contain phrases such as "Plaintext after DECRYPTION: len = 77" and "Plaintext before ENCRYPTION: len = 54," followed by the encrypted/ decrypted message. The client request will appear as a string message.

Continued

The client file will also contain similar information regarding client/server hello and handshaking, except that it will be listed in the order that is appropriate for the client side.

Figure 10.12 Server Output in Debug Mode

Figure 10.13 Client Output in Debug Mode

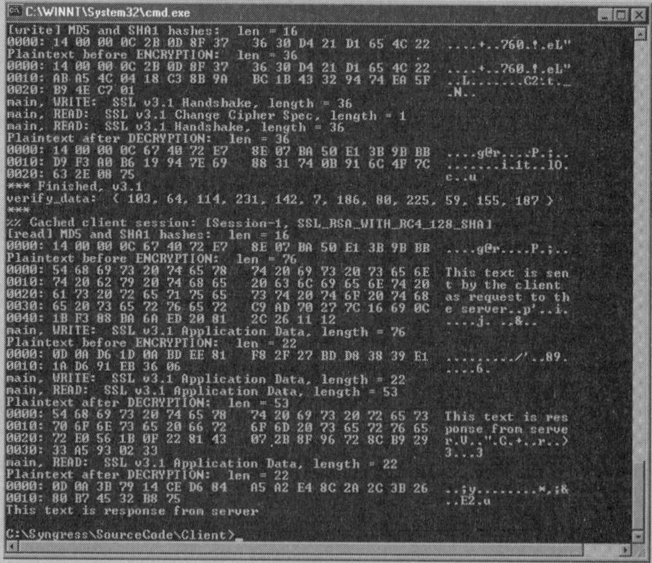

Using JSSE Applications with WSDP

The JSSE examples covered in previous sections run as Java programs using the command line. However, JSSE can also be used to create secure Web services. Therefore, in this section we present modified codes from previous examples and their associated Java Server Pages (JSP) to run them as Web services. These Web services are compatible with the latest Java Web Service Developers Pack (WSDP) release (WSDP/1.0-ea2).

We begin with the *TestKeys.java* class from Figure 10.1, which appears in a modified version in Figure 10.14. Code modification is imperative since the code of Figure 10.1 (and subsequent examples given in this chapter) use the *main()* method to print the output to the console. However, a Web service requires that the output be displayed in a browser/web-client. Thus, the code should be modified so that it may be called in a JSP page (whose output is sent to the browser) as a Java Bean.

The modified version of *TestKeys.java* uses JSSE properties in a manner similar to the listing in Figure 10.1. The difference is that we have removed the *main()* method and its *System.out.println()* statements. Instead, we retrieve all the key and certificate properties within a method, named *getValues()*, that returns a string buffer. This string buffer contains the key, keystore, and certificate information retrieved using JSSE. The modified code is as follows:

Figure 10.14 Modified Version of TestKeys.java

```
import java.net.*;

import javax.net.ssl.*;

import java.security.*;

import javax.security.cert.X509Certificate;

import java.io.*;

import java.util.*;

import java.security.cert.*;
public class TestKeys
{
 public StringBuffer getValues() throws Exception
 {
  //Security.addProvider(new com.sun.net.ssl.internal.ssl.Provider());
  StringBuffer str = new StringBuffer();
  char[] passphrase = "passphrase".toCharArray();
```

Continued

Figure 10.14 Continued

```
KeyManagerFactory kmf = KeyManagerFactory.getInstance(
    KeyManagerFactory.getDefaultAlgorithm();
KeyStore ks = KeyStore.getInstance("JKS");

ks.load(new FileInputStream("keys"), passphrase);

str = str.append("This is the Type of KeyStore :" + ks.getType() + "|");
Enumeration enum = ks.aliases();
while(enum.hasMoreElements())
{
 str = str.append("This is the allias " + (String)enum.
     nextElement() + "|" );
}
str = str.append("This is the provider of the KeyStore: " +
     (ks.getProvider()).toString() + "|");
str = str.append("This is the algorithm used: " +
     (ks.getKey( "duke", passphrase )).getAlgorithm() + "|");
str = str.append("This is the keys Format: " +
     (ks.getKey("duke", passphrase)).getFormat() + "|");
java.security.cert.Certificate[] cera = ks.getCertificateChain("duke");
for (int i = 0; i < cera.length; i++)
{
 str = str.append("This is the certificate type: " +
         (cera[i]).getType() + "|");
}
 return str;
}
}
```

The *getValues()* method appends the retrieved information to the string buffer variable (*str*) with each entry separated by the pipe (|) character. This enables the calling JSP page to split the returned string buffer into individual properties. Figure 10.15 lists the testKeys.jsp, which makes use of the *TestKeys* class from Figure 10.14.

Figure 10.15 Calling the *TestKeys* Class in the testKeys.jsp page

```
<%@ page import="java.util.*" %>
<%@ page import="TestKeys" %>
<%@ page contentType="text/html; charset=ISO-8859-5" %>
<html>
<head>

 <title>Socket Server Application</title>
</head>
<body bgcolor="white">
<jsp:useBean id="mykeys" scope="application" class="TestKeys"/>
<h1><FONT FACE="ARIAL" SIZE=12>TestKeys Application JSP page</FONT></h1>
<hr>
<%
   StringBuffer str1 = mykeys.getValues();
   String mystring = str1.toString();
   StringTokenizer token = new StringTokenizer(mystring,"|");
   while(token.hasMoreTokens())
   {
%>
<p><FONT FACE="ARIAL" SIZE=6><%=token.nextToken()%>
<% } %>
</body>
</html>
```

testKeys.jsp imports the *TestKeys* class and uses it as a bean with the ID *mykeys*. The following code line calls the *getValues()* method of the *TestKeys* class and stores the string buffer returned by it in the *str1:*variable.

```
StringBuffer str1 = mykeys.getValues();
```

The string buffer variable is converted to a string using the *toString()* method. This string is broken into tokens using the *StringTokenizer* class as given in the following code line:

```
StringTokenizer token = new StringTokenizer(mystring,"|");
```

A *while* loop is then run to display all these tokens in the browser using the output directive <%=token.nextToken()%>. The testKeys.jsp page when run in the browser displays the output as shown in Figure 10.16.

Figure 10.16 Output of testKeys.jsp

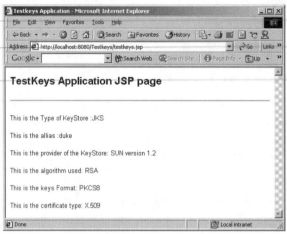

Note that this output is similar to the console output shown in Figure 10.2, except that it contains a description string prefixed to each property value.

Using the URLHandler in a Web Service

Once again, we modify the code listing of Figure 10.4 to add a *pdata()* method to the *URLHandler.java* class to return a string buffer. The *pdata()* method is as follows (It is left to the readers to incorporate this method into a *URLHandler.java* class in order to run the JSP from Figure 10.17):

```java
public StringBuffer pdata()
 {
  StringBuffer str = new StringBuffer();
  try
  {
  URL verisign = new URL("https://www.verisign.com");
  BufferedReader in = new BufferedReader(
      new InputStreamReader(verisign.openStream()));
  String inputLine;
  while ((inputLine = in.readLine()) != null)
  {
   str = str.append(inputLine);
  }
  in.close();
  }
  catch(Exception ex)
```

```
  {
    System.out.println(ex);
  }
  return str;
}
```

The code, for urlhandler.jsp, that calls the modified *URLHandler.java* class is given in Figure 10.17.

Figure 10.17 The urlhandler.jsp page

```
<%@ page import="java.util.*" %>
<%@ page import="URLHandler" %>
<%@ page contentType="text/html; charset=ISO-8859-5" %>
<jsp:useBean id="myURLHandler" scope="application" class="URLHandler"/>
<%
  StringBuffer str1 = myURLHandler.pdata();
%>
<%=str1.toString()%>
```

Akin to the *URLHandler* class from Figure 10.4, urlhandler.jsp shows the HTML content from the invoked site (www.verisign.com). Since the output here appears not on the console but on the browser, the HTML is decoded by the browser and the content of the HTML page is displayed as shown in Figure 10.18.

Figure 10.18 Output from the urlhandler.jsp page

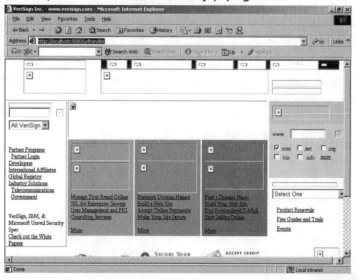

NOTE

The output of urlhandler.jsp, when displayed in the browser, does not show most of the images. This is because most of the image tags in the source HTML contain relative URLs for the *src* (image source) property. If you use the browser's **View-Source** menu to see the source HTML, you will come across image tags in the following format:

<img src="/images/.../abc.gif">

The *src* property in the above tag does not give the physical path of the images directory in whose subfolder(s) the images reside. Instead, it defines the path of images directory relative to the root of the web site. When you read the HTML content as a stream and display it using a JSP output directive, the browser tends to look for the images directory in the default JSP root folder on the local machine. Since the actual images are on the verisign web server and not on the local machine, the browser fails to locate them. If the *src* property of an <img> tag contains a complete URL of the form http://www.verisign.com/images/.../abc.gif, then the browser will retrieve the image from the verisign server (provided you are online) and display it.

Displaying the Installed Cipher Suites through a Web Service

To display the cipher suites in a browser using a Web service, we create a JSP called security.jsp. Instead of modifying the existing java class *install_check.java* of Figure 10.6 and calling it as a bean in security.jsp, we include the actual code fragments within the JSP page to obtain the enabled cipher suites and to output them. (The same methodology of including java code in JSP pages can also be used in the code listings of Figure 10.15 and Figure 10.17). Figure 10.19 contains code listing for *security.jsp*.

Figure 10.19 Code for security.jsp

```
<%@ page import="java.net.*" %>
<%@ page import="javax.net.ssl.*" %>
<%@ page import="java.security.*" %>
<%@ page contentType="text/html; charset=ISO-8859-5" %>

<html>
```

Continued

Figure 10.19 Continued

```
<head>
 <title>Security Check Application</title>
</head>

<body bgcolor="white">
<h1><FONT FACE="ARIAL" SIZE=6>
    Security Check Application JSP page
    </FONT></h1>
<%
    SSLServerSocketFactory myfactory =
      (SSLServerSocketFactory)
        SSLServerSocketFactory.getDefault();
    SSLServerSocket mysslSocket =
        (SSLServerSocket)myfactory.createServerSocket(5757);
    String [] cipherSuites = mysslSocket.getEnabledCipherSuites();
    for (int i = 0; i < cipherSuites.length; i++)
    {
%>
<p><FONT FACE="ARIAL" SIZE=2><%=cipherSuites[i]%>
<%
    }
%>

</body>
</html>
```

This code needs no explanation since it contains fragments from the *install_check.java* class that have already been explained (See code listing in Figure 10.6). The output directive <%=cipherSuites[i]%> displays the cipher suites on the browser as shown in Figure 10.20.

Client-Server Web Service

Once again we use the modified forms of *SecureServer.java* and *SecureClient.java* as beans in their respective JSPs. The modified version of *SecureServer.java* is listed in Figure 10.21 and encloses the working code (previously within the *main()* method) in a user defined method named *startServer()*.

Figure 10.20 Output of security.jsp

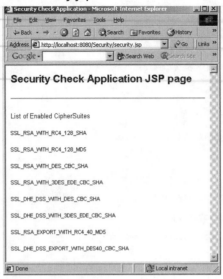

Figure 10.21 Modified Version of SecureServer.java

```java
import java.net.*;
import javax.net.ssl.*;
import java.security.*;
import java.io.*;
import javax.security.cert.X509Certificate;
//import com.sun.net.ssl.*;
import java.util.*;
public class SecureServer
{
    public StringBuffer startServer() throws Exception
    {
  StringBuffer str = new StringBuffer();
  char[] passphrase = "passphrase".toCharArray();
  SSLContext ctx = SSLContext.getInstance("SSL");
  KeyManagerFactory kmf = KeyManagerFactory.getInstance("SunX509");
  KeyStore ks = KeyStore.getInstance("JKS");

  ks.load(new FileInputStream("keys"), passphrase);
  kmf.init(ks, passphrase);
  ctx.init(kmf.getKeyManagers(), null, null);
```

Continued

Figure 10.21 Continued

```
SSLServerSocketFactory myfactory = ctx.getServerSocketFactory();
SSLServerSocket mysslSocket =
   (SSLServerSocket)myfactory.createServerSocket(5757);
str = str.append("Server Started" + "|");
SSLSocket mysocket = (SSLSocket)mysslSocket.accept();

PrintStream send = new PrintStream(mysocket.getOutputStream());
BufferedReader readdata = new BufferedReader(
   new InputStreamReader(mysocket.getInputStream()));
String myrequest = readdata.readLine();
str = str.append(myrequest);

send.println("This text is response from server\n");
send.flush();
send.close();
readdata.close();

mysocket.close();
return str;
}
```

The *startServer()* method returns a string buffer containing the message that was received from the client. This method is called in the server.jsp page as shown in Figure 10.22.

Figure 10.22 Calling SecureServer.java from server.jsp

```
<%@ page import="java.util.*" %>
<%@ page import="SecureServer" %>
<%@ page contentType="text/html; charset=ISO-8859-5" %>
<html>
<head>
 <title>Socket Server Application</title>
</head>
```

Continued

Figure 10.22 Continued

```
<body bgcolor="white">
<jsp:useBean id="myServer" scope="application" class="SecureServer"/>
<h1><FONT FACE="ARIAL" SIZE=12>Server Application JSP page</FONT></h1>
<hr>
<%
   StringBuffer str1 = myServer.startServer();
   String mystring = str1.toString();
   StringTokenizer token = new StringTokenizer(mystring,"|");
   while(token.hasMoreTokens())
   {
%>
<p><FONT FACE="ARIAL" SIZE=6><%=token.nextToken()%>
<% } %>
</body>
</html>
```

The server.jsp program obtains the string buffer returned by *SecureServer.java* in the *str1* variable, converts it into a string and breaks the string into tokens using the pipe (|) character as delimiter. The tokens so obtained are displayed in the browser using the output directive, <%=token.nextToken()%>. The output appears in Figure 10.23.

Figure 10.23 Output of server.jsp

A similar client.jsp uses the *SecureClient.java*'s *startClient()* method to output messages received by the client to the browser window. We leave it to the reader to modify the *SecureClient.java* class from Figure 10.9 and replace its *main()* method with the *startClient()* method. Code for client.jsp is given in Figure 10.24.

Figure 10.24 Calling the *SecureClient* Class in client.jsp

```
<%@ page import="java.util.*" %>
<%@ page import="SecureClient" %>
<%@ page contentType="text/html; charset=ISO-8859-5" %>
<html>
<head>
 <title>Socket Client Application</title>
</head>

<body bgcolor="white">
<jsp:useBean id="myClient" scope="application" class="SecureClient"/>
<h1><FONT FACE="ARIAL" SIZE=12>Client Application JSP page</FONT></h1>
<hr>
<%
  String str1 = myClient.startClient();
%>

<p><FONT FACE="ARIAL" SIZE=6><%=str1.toString()%>
</body>
</html>
```

The output of client.jsp is shown in Figure 10.25. Note that this is the message that the client receives back from the server.

Figure 10.25 Output of client.jsp

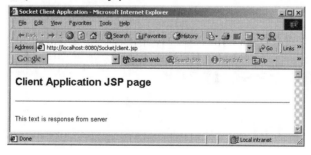

Summary

In this chapter we introduced the concept of a *keystore* containing the keys and associated certificates that are used in secure communications over a network using SSL. We also explained at length the structure of certificates and the role they play in certifying information in a secure-communication environment. We then discussed the keytool utility that can be used to create a keystore and administer its keys and associated certificate chains. We explained the *-import*, *-selfcert* and *-identitydb* commands as provided by the keytool utility to create certificates in the keystore.

The rest of the chapter was devoted to JSSE and various classes in the java.security, java.security.cert, javax.net.ssl and other JSSE packages that are used to secure information from a keystore or add information to one. We began with a discussion on how JSSE can be installed and configured, was followed by a discussion on using JSSE properties to obtain information about the keystore, such as the number of aliases in the keystore, their associated certificate chains, the keystore type and so on. We then showed how to configure a URL handler for communication using HTTPS by setting the *java.protocol.handler.pkgs* property.

Thereafter, we briefly discussed the basic classes such as *Socket*, *ServerSocket*, *ServerSocketFactory*, *SocketFactory* and the subclasses that are used for secure communications, such as *SSLServerSocketFactory*, *SSLSocketFactory*, *SSLServerSocket* and *SSLSocket*. In the remainder of the chapter we used examples and working code listings to explain how these sockets and socket factories can be used to develop a client-server application using SSL. We also included in the chapter a complete description of how you can see the list of certificates being exchanged between a client and server during a secure communication cycle, and how data is encrypted at the transmitting end and decrypted at the receiving end. In essence, this chapter provided a basic guide to secure communications using JSSE.

Solutions Fast Track

Configuring JSSE

- ☑ The JSSE can be configured by setting the SunJSSE provider and configuring the URL handler for JSSE.

- ☑ The keytool utility is used to create and manage keystore aliases and their associated certificate chains, for example, the *-genkey* command can be used to create a key entry in a keystore while the *-import*, *-selfcert* and *-identitydb* commands can be used to generate or import certificates.

☑ The java.security and java.security.cert packages provide various methods such as *getKey()*, *getCertificateChain()*, *getProvider()*, *getType()* and so on that can be used to retrieve information about a keystore.

Using HTTPS URL Handlers

☑ The URL handler for JSSE can be configured by setting the *java.protocol.handler.pkgs* property.

☑ The URL handler for JSSE can be used to connect to a URL using HTTPS; and data can then be read over this secure connection using a buffered input stream.

Using SocketFactories

☑ Socket factory classes are used to create sockets on both the server (*ServerSocketFactory*) and client (*SocketFactory*) sides.

☑ The *getCipherSuites()* method of an *SSLServerSocket* object can be used to read the cipher suites installed on a machine.

Using Secure Server Sockets

☑ The *SSLServerSocket* class plays the same role in secure communications as is played by the *ServerSocket* class in traditional programming: creating secure server sockets. The *SSLServerSocketFactory* class provides the *createServerSocket()* method to create server sockets.

☑ The secure server socket can be used to read and/or write data using input and/or output streams. However, the data being read or written will remain secure.

Using Secure Client Sockets

☑ The *SSLSocketFactory* class' *createSocket()* method is used to create secure client sockets.

☑ The *SSLSocket* class' *startHandshake()* method begins the process of exchanging certificates and establishing a connection with a server upon verification of the certificate information.

☑ Input and output streams can be used to read/write data using a secure socket.

☑ The *SSLSocket* class' *close()* method is used to close the socket that automatically closes the connection with the server.

Using JSSE Applications with WSDP

☑ While using WSDP, JSSE classes and properties can be used in servlets/ JSPs in exactly the same manner as they are used in a traditional java program.

☑ A traditional java program that uses JSSE can be converted into a Java Bean with minimal modification by removing the *main()* method and incorporating the code in a user-defined method that returns values retrieved using JSSE to the calling JSP page.

Frequently Asked Questions

The following Frequently Asked Questions, answered by the authors of this book, are designed to both measure your understanding of the concepts presented in this chapter and to assist you with real-life implementation of these concepts. To have your questions about this chapter answered by the author, browse to **www.syngress.com/solutions** and click on the **"Ask the Author"** form.

Q: What versions of the JDK does JSSE 1.0.2 support?

A: It supports Java 2 SDK, Standard Edition, version 1.2.1 or later. The JSSE API can be implemented on either JDK 1.1.x or JavaTM 2 Platform, Standard Edition.

Q: What version of SSL does JSSE support?

A: JSSE 1.0.2 supports SSL version 3.

Q: Can JSSE perform RSA encryption?

A: Yes, JSSE 1.0.2 performs RSA encryption

Q: When I compile my JSSE program, I get the following error: Package javax.net.ssl not found in import. What could be the possible reason?

A: If you install JSSE in accordance to the installation instructions in this chapter, its JAR files are automatically installed. However, if you are using JSSE as a bundled extension with an application, you need to point your CLASSPATH variable to the JSSE JAR files. Otherwise you'll get the above error.

Q: When I run my JSSE program, I get the following exception:

```
Exception in thread "main":
SSL implementation not available.
```

Do you know of any remedies?

A: The following could be the possible reasons:

- You may not have registered the SunJSSE provider. (See the section on configuring JSSE.)

- The keystore may be corrupted or invalid. (The keytool may be used to check for a valid keystore.)

Chapter 11

Using JWSDP Tools

Solutions in this chapter:

- **JWSDP UDDI Registry**

- **Tomcat**

- **Ant**

☑ **Summary**

☑ **Solutions Fast Track**

☑ **Frequently Asked Questions**

Introduction

Included in the JWSDP are a set of tools that can be used in the development or deployment of Web services. These tools can be employed to support a development server, and can even be used for some production releases. The tools include a UDDI registry (Java WSDP registry server), a servlet/JSP container (Tomcat), and a build tool (Ant).

The Java WSDP registry server is least likely to be used in production environments—at least in its current form. It has limitations in the scope of UDDI supported, its capability to provide highly available services, and in its performance. These will likely be addressed in future releases, so it will be interesting to see if it eventually evolves into a production-level tool.

Tomcat is a much more capable tool. Behind IBM's WebSphere and BEA's WebLogic, it represents one of the most accomplished and up-to-date servlet engines. It may even be suitable for small production environments. This depends on your overall willingness to assume risk, of course. Tomcat is generally supported by open-source volunteers, and does not provide high-availability features.

If used in development, Ant is the tool you would likely continue to use as you moved toward production. As a build tool, the issues of high availability are moot. Ant is as capable a tool for Web services as any other make utility—perhaps even more so. Keep in mind that it's a very different tool than standard make utilities, and does take some getting used to.

JWSDP UDDI Registry

The Universal Description Discovery and Integration Protocol (UDDI) is an infrastructure that allows Web services to register, or become publicly known by, a registry. The registry used by Java WSDP is known as the UDDI Registry. Once these Web services are known to the registry, they are then made available to any client request. The UDDI Registry contents are XML-based and are accessed in a directory tree-style.

In order to deploy your Web services, you will need to set up the UDDI Registry, enabling you to add your Web services to the registry. To begin, download the Java Web Services Developer Pack, containing the Registry Server, from the following URL: http://java.sun.com/webservices/downloads/webservicespack.html. This link will prompt you to download the following executable for Microsoft Windows: jwsdp-1_0-ea2-win.exe. For Unix or Linux users, you will download this executable: jwsdp-1_0-ea2-unix.sh.

Developing & Deploying...

UDDI Registry

The UDDI Registry Server is automatically installed along with Tomcat and some additional administrative tools to assist you in deploying your Web services.

Installing

Prior to installing the JWSDP, you must have the Java 2 SDK or Runtime Environment of version 1.3.1 or later already installed on your computer.

Microsoft Windows Installation Instructions

JWSDP is supported on Microsoft Windows 2000 and XP only. Microsoft Windows 95, 98, ME, and NT 4.0 are unsupported. Double-click the self-extracting executable **jwsdp-1_0-ea2-win.exe**.

Unix, Linux Installation Instructions

JWSDP is supported on Solaris and Linux, but is not supported on Mac OS X and other Unix platforms. Execute the following command against the self-installing executable **% /bin/sh jwsdp-1_0-ea2-Unix.sh**.

Both these methods will bring up the InstallShield Wizard shown in Figure 11.1 to assist in installing JWSDP to your computer. Once you have reached this screen, perform the following steps:

1. From the InstallShield Wizard screen (Figure 11.1) click **Next**.

2. This will bring up the Evaluation Agreement screen shown in Figure 11.2. You must agree with it to proceed, so check **Approve**, then click **Next**.

3. The InstallShield Wizard will automatically detect the JDK1.3.1 installation on your computer (Figure 11.3). Click **Next**.

Figure 11.1 Welcome Screen of the InstallShield Wizard

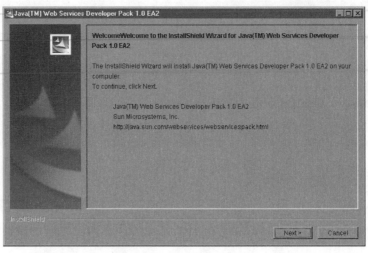

Figure 11.2 Evaluation Agreement Screen

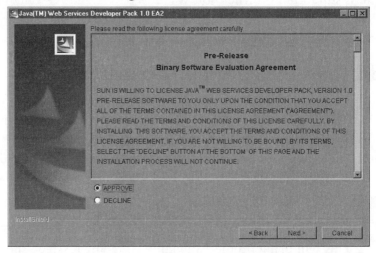

Figure 11.3 JDK Version Selection Screen

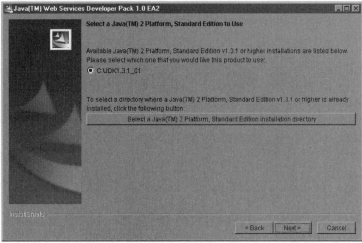

4. Fill in a username and password to administer Tomcat, as shown in Figure 11.4. Click **Next**.

Figure 11.4 Creation of Tomcat Administrative User Screen

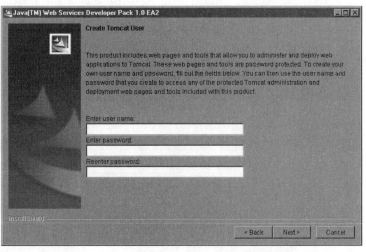

5. You now must specify which directory to install in, as shown in Figure 11.5. Use the default directory setting and click **Next**.

Figure 11.5 Destination Directory Screen

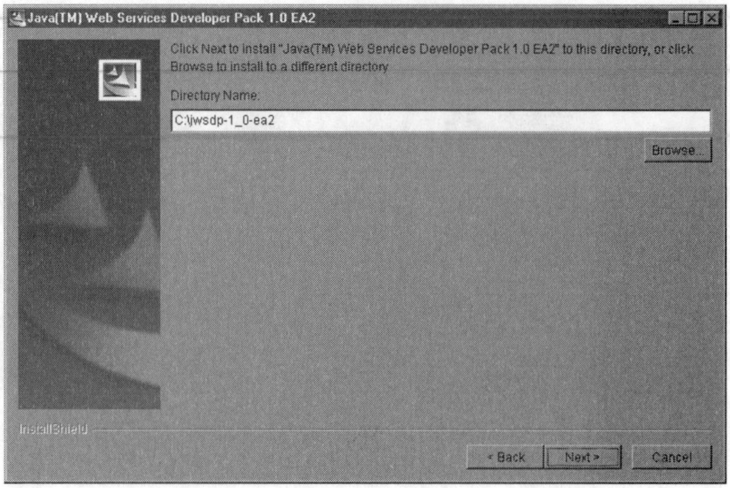

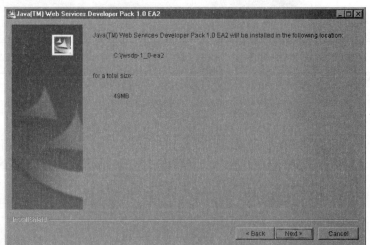

NOTE

The rest of this chapter will assume you have installed in c:\jwsdp-1_0-ea2 (Windows) or /home/myuserid/jwsdp-1_0-ea2 (Linux/Unix). If you install into different directories, you will have to adjust the paths given in this chapter accordingly.

6. This will bring you to the Confirmation screen prior to installation (Figure 11.6). Click **Next**.

Figure 11.6 Location Confirmation and Size Screen

7. Now the actual installation begins. You should see the screen displayed in Figure 11.7, which shows the progress of the install.

Figure 11.7 Installing JWDP Screen

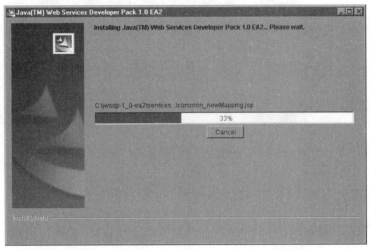

8. Once the install has completed, you will see the screen (shown in Figure 11.8) telling you that the install has completed successfully. Click **Next**.

Figure 11.8 Successful Installation Screen

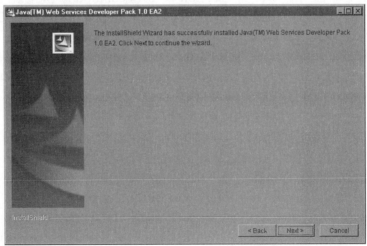

9. You will now be brought to the final install screen, shown in Figure 11.9. Select **Yes, restart my system** and click **Finish**.

Figure 11.9 Restart Computer Screen

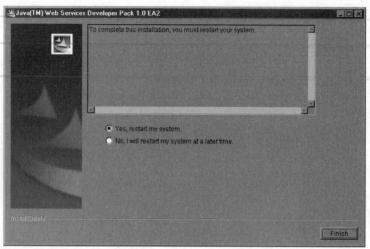

Configuring

You need to add the /bin directory of the JWSDP to the PATH variable in your environment. This will then allow you to run any of the JWSDP executables from any directory. For Microsoft Windows users, modify your PATH variable through the **Control Panel | System | Advanced | Environmental Variables** section. Once this section is accessed, modify the existing PATH setting by appending the following directory path: c:\jwsdp-1_0-ea2\bin. Check your Microsoft Windows manual on instructions for configuring environmental variables for your version of Windows. For Unix and Linux users, modify your PATH variable by appending the following directory to the existing PATH: /home/myuserid/jwsdp-1_0-ea2/bin.

Activating

Once the JWSDP is installed and configured, the JAXR Registry Server can be easily launched in Windows by executing the startup script for the Tomcat server, which is located under the /bin directory. Or, it can be launched from the **Start | Programs | Java Web Services Developer Pack | Startup Tomcat** menu as shown in Figure 11.10. Unix and Linux users execute the startup.sh script, whereas the Microsoft Windows users execute the startup.bat batch file. Likewise, the Server can be shut down in the same manner using the shutdown xindice script for both platforms.

Figure 11.10 Activation of the Tomcat Server

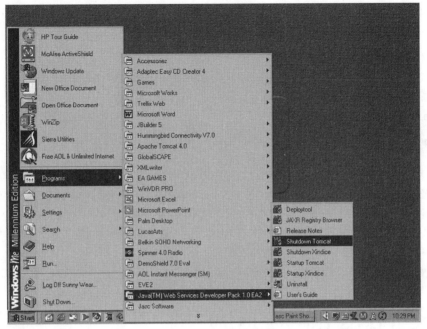

Limitations

JWSDP does not support the following versions of Microsoft Windows: Windows 95, 98, ME, and NT 4.0. In addition, JWSDP does not support the following versions of Unix: Mac OS X and other Unix platforms. Please see the README text of the JWSDP Registry for the latest limitations if you are using a version later than EA2.

Also, the following messages are not yet supported within the Registry Server:

- *add_publisherAssertions*
- *delete_publisherAssertions*
- *get_assertionStatusReport*
- *get_publisherAssertions*
- *find_relatedBusiness*

Likewise, the *uploadRegisters* argument is not supported within the *save_business* and *save_tModel* messages.

Limitations exist regarding the *find_** messages. The following arguments are not supported when attempting a search:

- *findQualifiers*
- *identifierBag*
- *categoryBag*
- *tModelBag*
- *discoveryURLs*

After creating an organization, you can search for the organization name; however, the query of the Registry is case-sensitive. In addition, when searching for organization names, the percent sign (%), indicating the string can occur anywhere in the name, does not work. You cannot use multiple *<name>* values in searches, as this is not supported.

No connection pooling or indexing are available for performance optimizations in this release.

Selecting as the Registry

The Registry Server has a browser-based tool used to administer the server. Prior to activating the Registry Browser, make sure Tomcat is running. See the Tomcat section in this chapter for instructions on starting your Tomcat server. You can activate the Registry Browser by one of two methods. The first is to execute the jaxr-browser.bat (or jaxr-browser.sh) program at a DOS prompt. This program is located under $JWSDP_HOME\bin directory. The second method is to launch the Registry Browser from the **Start | Programs | Java Web Services Developer Pack | JAXR Registry Browser** menu. The dialog box shown in Figure 11.11 will appear.

Select a registry using the dialog box drop-down list. You will be able to access the last registry in the list, provided that Tomcat is currently running. The last registry in the list provides UDDI Registry samples. If Tomcat is running, you will be able to access these samples from the drop-down list using this URL: http://localhost:8080/registry-server/RegistryServerServlet. Several other registries are listed in the drop-down list as well, which Sun Microsystems makes available as test registries. Administration of any Registry Server requires some level of authentication. If you are interested in adding Web services to these registries, you must go to one (or both) of these sites and become a registered user with a username and password: http://uddi.microsoft.com or http://www-3.ibm .com/services. Figure 11.12 shows a listing of the test registries.

Figure 11.11 The JAXR (UDDI) Registry Browser

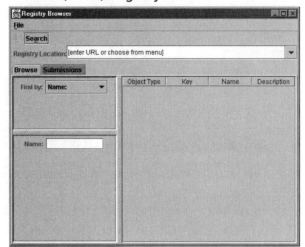

Figure 11.12 Selection of Registry Locations from the Drop-down List

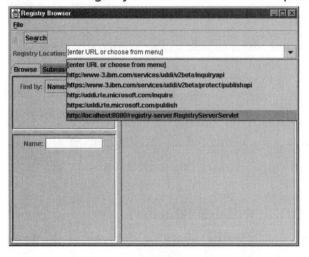

Using this browser menu, you can select the **Submissions** tab (Figure 11.13) to add, modify, edit, or delete Web services to within your Registry Server.

Clients attempting to connect to your Web services will query the Registry Server to find the names of registered objects. The properties associated with each Web service are collectively known as the organization. After you enter the specific information pertaining to a particular organization, click **Add service** to activate the next menu which allows you to add your organization name to the list of registered objects. This list of registered objects is collectively known as Services.

Figure 11.13 The Submissions Input Area in the Registry Browser

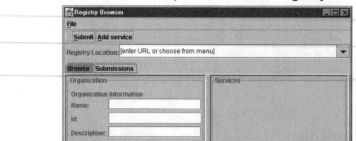

Next is an overview of the field names and their definitions.

Organization

There are three properties available in the registry that provide identification for your Web services object. They include the following: name, ID, and description.

- **Name** Any name you would like to associate with this object

- **Id** This becomes the unique key the registry uses to find your object; this is internally generated by the server itself

- **Description** Here you can provide any text describing your object

Primary Contact Information

Each Web Service object registered within the registry needs to be administered by an authorized user. The Registry Browser provides properties to identify and associate the authorized user with the organization. The three pieces of contact information that need to be supplied are:

- **Name** The name of the user authorized to use this registry

- **Phone** The phone number of the authorized user

- **Email** The e-mail address of the authorized user

Classifications

If you want to group your organization with other organizations under the same general heading, you can use what is known as a classification. Multiple organizations that have some relationship to each other are collected under a classification name. To add your organization to a classification, select the classification you want to add your organization to and click **Add** as shown in Figure 11.14. This is only possible if classifications are already available within your Registry Server. When you first install your Registry Server, no classifications are listed. If you wish to add a new classification, you can do so within the **Add Service** textboxes. Adding your organization to a classification group is an optional feature.

Figure 11.14 Adding an Organization to a Classification Grouping

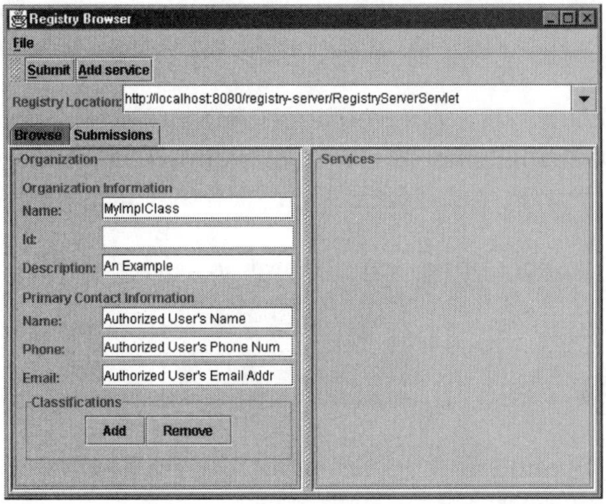

The next step is to add your organization to the registry in order to make it available to client requests. This is known as adding Service objects to the registry. To begin the process, click **Add Service**. A new set of textboxes appear, as shown in Figure 11.15. The following are the field names and their definitions:

- **Name** The Service object name
- **Id** The unique key that identifies the Service object; it's generated by the Registry Server
- **Description** Any text describing the Service object

Figure 11.15 Adding Your Web Service to the Registry

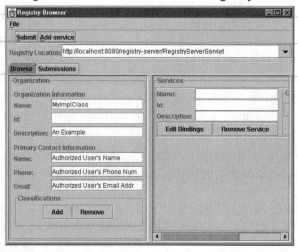

Once you identify the Service object's name and description, click **Edit Bindings** to have the Registry Server bind your object within its registry. A small dialog box appears, as shown in Figure 11.16. Click **Add Binding**.

Figure 11.16 Adding/Editing Service Bindings Listed within the Registry

Each Service Binding must be made publicly available to clients through a URI. A description can also be provided. This information is entered in the appropriate textboxes of the dialog box shown in Figure 11.17.

Figure 11.17 Adding/Removing a Service Binding within the Registry

When finished, click **Done**. You will be prompted for authorization information. Enter your username and password, then click **OK**. You have successfully added a Web Service object to your registry. You can now return to the **Browse** tab (see Figure 11.18) to see your newly created object. From this Browse tab, you can query for Web services based on organization name or classification name. To do so, enter the name to search for in the textbox, then click **Search**.

Figure 11.18 Browsing/Searching Web Services within the Registry

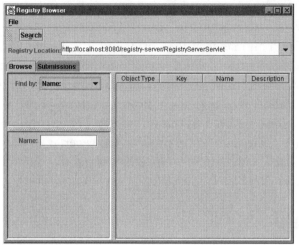

Tomcat

Tomcat is an open-source Web server freely available through the Jakarta Project (http://jakarta.apache.org). The Tomcat Web server can serve HTML pages, Java Server Pages, and Java Servlets. This is made possible by the inclusion of a servlet/JSP container (or engine) within the Web server itself.

Installing

Bundled within the JWSDP is a fully-working Tomcat Web server with the servlet/JSP container. By following the instructions for installing the JWSDP (under **Section JWSDP UDDI Registry | Installing**), Tomcat is automatically installed to your computer. No additional installation is required.

Windows

See the installation instructions for Microsoft Windows users under the section entitled **JWSDP UDDI Registry | Installing**.

Linux

Installation instructions for Unix and Linux users can be found under the section entitled **JWSDP UDDI Registry | Installing**.

Environmental Variables

The following environmental variables need to be set up on your computer: *JAVA_HOME, CATALINA_HOME*. Create a *JAVA_HOME* environmental variable to point to the location of your JDK installation. Make sure the *$JAVA_HOME*/*bin* path is added to your *PATH* environmental variable, so you can run Java commands at the command line. Finally, create a *CATALINA_HOME* environmental variable to point to the location of your Tomcat installation. Since JWSDP bundles Tomcat within it, this variable will point to a location similar to the following: *c:\jwsdp-1_0*.

Any modifications required to the *CLASSPATH* environmental variable are done for you during the installation process. However, if you are setting your variables up manually, add *$JAVA_HOME\lib\tools.jar* to your *CLASSPATH* environmental variable.

Configuring

All configurations required for the running of Tomcat are automatically set during the installation process. No additional configurations are necessary.

Server.xml

The server.xml file is the main file that Tomcat provides to allow server configurations. These configurations can modify the behavior of the servlet/JSP container. The server.xml file is located under the $JWSDP_HOME\conf directory. The structure of the file is nested tags, beginning with the top-level parent tag of *Server* representing the entire JVM. Multiple service instances can be contained within the Server tag. A Service instance is denoted with the nested tag called Service. A service represents a group of connectors associated with an engine. Within a service tag, Web applications and other services are made available to clients on specified port numbers. Such services are known as *connectors* and are denoted by a tag of the same name. These connectors act as interfaces between external clients and the services themselves, providing the ability to receive and respond to those client requests. It is within these connector tags that you can set up various port numbers to listen for particular client requests and subsequently invoke the appropriate Java class at runtime.

An example of a connector within a service tag shows how you can enable SSL to run on port 8443. The following entry defines the connector class that Tomcat provides to support an SSL connection. Various details are configured within this tag, including port number, the minimum and maximum number of processors, the scheme, and the toggling of the secure value.

```
<!-- Define an SSL HTTP/1.1 Connector on port 8443 -->
<Connector className="org.apache.catalina.connector.http.HttpConnector"
port="8443" minProcessors="5" maxProcessors="75" scheme="https"
        secure="true">
</Connector>
```

The Engine or Container tag specifies various listeners that can be configured to handle numerous client requests. For example, the standard engine for handling HTTP requests runs on port 8080 under the engine name of "localhost." Within the configuration of this engine, a host tag is configured for the webapps directory used as the document root directory.

```
<!-- Default Virtual Host -->
<Host     name="localhost" appBase="Webapps" debug="0" unpackWARs="false">
</Host>
```

The webapps Directory and WAR files

The default document root directory for the Tomcat Web server is the webapps directory. The Web server serves up HTML pages from this directory, therefore any new Web applications can easily be added to the server thru the creation of new subdirectories under webapps. Such subdirectories are known as *context paths* to your application. Additionally, you can invoke Java classes from your Web application which require the creation of another directory called WEB-INF and a subdirectory of classes.

Web ARchive (WAR) files are files that contain a packed version of an entire tree directory structure and all nested file types contained within the tree. Such file types can include HTML, JSP, CLASS, and CSS. WAR files are used for ease of deployment.

Structure of a webapps Directory

In order to create a correctly-formatted WAR file, a particular structure is required. You will need to "pack up" or arrange your WAR file in the same order that Tomcat will later use to execute that WAR file. Therefore, starting with your document root directory (also known as *context path*), you will have the structure shown in Figure 11.19 when constructing your WAR file.

Figure 11.19 Structure When Constructing Your WAR File

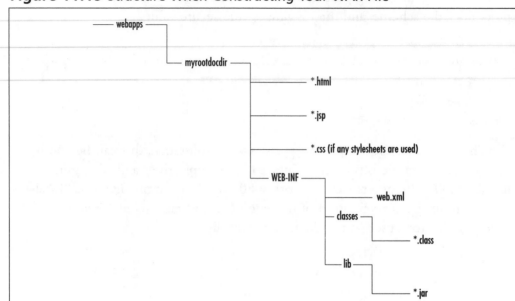

The complete syntax and semantics for the deployment descriptor is defined in Chapter 13 of the Servlet API Specification, version 2.2. Over time, it is expected that development tools will be provided that create and edit the deployment descriptor for you. In the meantime, to provide a starting point, a basic web.xml file is provided. This file includes comments that describe the purpose of each included element.

Where to Put WAR Files

In order for Tomcat to unpack a WAR file, it must be placed within the webapps directory. Tomcat automatically unpacks the WAR file upon startup making the application available for client requests.

When to Use Each

If you require your application to be deployed on multiple servers, it is recommended you pack up your tree directory within a WAR file. It will be portable and easily deployable to other Web servers. However, if your application resides on the same server and same flavor of Web server (for instance, Tomcat), then use the server.xml configuration.

The web.xml Configuration File

The web.xml file is located under the webapps\mydocumentrootdirectory\
WEB-INF\web.xml (for Linux and Unix users this is the webapps/
mydocumentrootdirectory/WEB-INF/web.xml). This file is used to assist in
the installation of a WAR file. It contains a deployment descriptor that defines
all aspects of your application that Tomcat needs to know for executing purposes.
Such details described within this file include all servlet names, servlet mappings,
servlet session configurations, and general application information such as the
application name.

Debugging…

WAR File Redeployment

If you decide to modify the WAR file and redeploy to Tomcat, make sure
you delete the old WAR file and the old unpacked directory, then stop
and restart Tomcat.

Activating

Tomcat can be started manually or automatically under either platform.
Instructions for setting up and activating the Tomcat server are described next.

Starting Tomcat under Windows NT Manually

To start the Tomcat server, open a DOS-prompt and change to the following
directory: $JWSDP_HOME\bin. Execute the following batch file: **startup.bat.**

Starting Tomcat under Windows NT as a Service

To have Tomcat start up as an NT service, open the **Control Panel | Services**
menu. Then, add **$JWSDP_HOME\bin\startup.bat** as a service. Do the same
for the shutdown.

Starting Tomcat under Linux Manually

To start the Tomcat server at the command line, change to the following directory: **$JWSDP_HOME/bin**. Then execute the following batch file: **startup.sh**

Starting Tomcat under Linux at Startup Time

The Tomcat server can automatically start up on Linux platforms by placing the startup.sh script within the /etc/rcN/init directory which is owned by root.

Relationship to Apache Servers

Apache servers can be used in conjunction with Tomcat servers for delegating services and load-balancing needs. You can configure an Apache Web server, used to handle static content of HTML, and images to delegate all JSP and Servlet requests to Tomcat that contain a servlet/JSP container. By establishing multiple Tomcat servers between the Apache server, an application can perform load balancing of client requests among the multiple resources available.

Acting Standalone

Tomcat contains an HTTP Web server along with a servlet/JSP container. Although the Web server can serve up HTML and other static content, it's lacking in speed. However, the setup of a Tomcat server is relatively simple.

Proxied behind Apache Servers

Tomcat server can be proxied behind multiple Apache servers for scalability, security and performance reasons. The Apache 1.3 server provides the ability to proxy client requests through to the Tomcat 4 servers. This is useful in masking the hostname and IP address of the actual server that contains the content. Likewise, SSL can be configured to provide an encrypted session between the proxy server and Tomcat.

Ant

Ant is an open-source build tool developed by Jakarta (http://jakarta.apache.org) that uses XML-based files to configure target directories. Written in Java, it uses classes for the actual compilation and execution of a variety of build-related commands.

Structure of an Ant Input File

The structure of an Ant input file contains a project definition, target directories, and any tasks that need to be performed during the build.

Projects

Each XML-based Ant build file contains one project.

Project Definition

Projects have three attributes: name, default, and basedir.

Required Elements

At a minimum, you must specify a default directory that will be used in cases where no target directory is provided.

Optional Elements

The attributes of name and basedir are optional.

Defining Project Properties

A project can contain a set of properties which can be used as a source in path-names or configuration files. A property is set up as a name/value pair and can be sourced within the Ant file using the dollar sign and opening and closing curly braces with the name of the property contained between the braces. For instance, *${file.separator}* will evaluate out to a "\" or "/" depending upon the platform where the build file is run.

Targets

A project can be set up to contain one or more targets which have five attributes: name, depends, if, unless, and description. Only the name attribute is required.

Dependencies between Tasks

Each target defines one or more tasks you can set to be executed. Upon the startup of Ant, you can specify which targets you wish executed.

Ordering of Dependencies

Targets can be dependent upon other targets. For instance, if you plan on distributing your code in a WAR file after compilation, then the construction of that distribution file is dependent upon the first target of compilation. This dependency is set up within the build file using the attribute called *depends*.

Specifying Target Locations

When specifying target locations, it is possible to check for the setting of a property value prior to execution of the target. This provides you with more control over the build in regards to external variables. This conditional check is done with the use of the *if* attribute within the target declaration tag (for instance, *<target name="my-build-example" if="property-A-is-set" />*). Execution of the target is guaranteed in the absence of an *if* attribute.

Tasks

Tasks are defined within the target tags and direct some piece of code to execute. The type of code could be of a variety of languages. For example, the task could be the DOS command of **echo**, done to display a message to the user screen, or it could be the execution of a Java class using the **java** command.

Structure of a Task Entry

The structure of the task entry begins with an opening tag followed by the name of the task (which really could be a command) immediately followed by an attribute name which will equal the value of that attribute. For example, *<echo message="-- Running CLI client to process request: ${request} --" />*
    Ant provides many built-in and optional tasks described next.

Built-in Tasks

Some of the built-in tasks provided by Ant that might be of interest to you include javac, jar, and war. The javac task is used to compile Java source code or ★.java files. The jar and war tasks are available to pack up files in either a JAR or WAR file.

Optional Tasks

Many other tasks are provided by Ant as optional tasks to be used with other technologies. Please consult the list of optional tasks located at the following URL: http://jakarta.apache.org/ant/manual/index.html.

Defining Tasks

Ant also provides the capability for you to write your own tasks. See the section entitled "Developing with Ant" for more information on this at the following URL: http://jakarta.apache.org/ant/manual/index.html.

Invoking ANT

The following section describes how to invoke the Ant script from the command-line. There are a variety of options that can be added as additional arguments to the invocation of the program.

Invoking from the Command Line

Once you are ready to compile, all you need to do is invoke the **ant** command at the command line from the project source directory. Make sure the following files are added to your CLASSPATH: ant.jar, crimson.jar, and jaxp.jar. When you execute this command and do not use the *-buildfile* option, Ant will look in the current directory for a build.xml file. Here is a summary of the usage statement along with all available options:

```
ant [options] [target [target2 [target3] ...]]
Options:
-help                   print this message
-projecthelp            print project help information
-version                print the version information and exit
-quiet                  be extra quiet
-verbose                be extra verbose
-debug                  print debugging information
-emacs                  produce logging information without adornments
-logfile file       use given file for log output
-logger classname     the class that is to perform logging
-listener classname    add an instance of class as a project listener
-buildfile file     use specified buildfile
-find file           search for buildfile towards the root of the
    filesystem and use the first one found
-Dproperty=value       set property to value
```

Specifying or Defaulting a Build File

By default, Ant will look for a build.xml file in the current directory. If no file is found and the *-find* option is turned on, Ant will continue looking up the directory tree until it reaches the root of your filesystem. If you would like to override the default behavior, specify a buildfile using the –buildfile *file* option where *file* is the name of your build file.

Invoking Specific Targets

Ant provides the capability to invoke several targets within a project. However, if no targets are specified, then Ant will default to use the target defined within the *default* attribute of the *<project>* tag.

Setting Properties

If you would like to override the properties that are sourced in from the build.properties file, simply use the *-Dproperty=value* as an option to the **ant** command.

Integrating with IDEs

There are several open-source projects available that provide the ability to incorporate Ant inside of an IDE. If you are interested in exploring this further, go to the following Web site: http://jakarta.apache.org/ant/manual/index.html.

An Ant Example

We will now demonstrate an example of a simple Ant file that compiles a servlet, builds a WAR, and deploys that WAR file to the Tomcat container.

In order to run this example successfully, you will first need to create a file called *build.properties* which contains variables to be sourced into the *build.xml* file. Here is a sample:

```
appname=samplebuildfile
wars.dir=../../warfiles
appname.home=../newhome
```

For this example, in order to create a WAR file, you need to generate a file called web.xml which contains information about your servlet code. Here is a sample:

```
<?xml version="1.0" encoding="ISO-8859-1"?>

<!DOCTYPE web-app
    PUBLIC "-//Sun Microsystems, Inc.//DTD Web Application 2.2//EN"
    "http://java.sun.com/j2ee/dtds/web-app_2_2.dtd">

<web-app>
  <display-name>Sample Build File</display-name>
```

```
<description>no description</description>
<servlet>
  <servlet-name>HelloWorldServlet</servlet-name>
  <display-name>HelloWorldServlet</display-name>
  <description>no description</description>
  <servlet-class>HelloWorldServlet</servlet-class>
 </servlet>


<servlet-mapping>
  <servlet-name>HelloWorldServlet</servlet-name>
  <url-pattern>/servlet/HelloWorldServlet</url-pattern>
</servlet-mapping>
</web-app>
```

Finally, you will need to create your build.xml file which is what Ant will initially look to find when invoked. The following shows how your build.xml file should look:

```
<project name="samplebuildfile" default="unwar" basedir=".">


<!-- Lookup all of the webapps currently configured on Tomcat -->
<property file="../../build.properties"/>          <!-- For all webapps -->


<!-- Classpath:  need to have servlet.jar to compile a servlet -->
  <path id="samples.classpath">
    <fileset dir="../../common/lib" includes="servlet.jar"/>
  </path>
  <target name="compile">
      <echo message="Compiling the servlet source code..."/>
      <javac classpathref="samples.classpath"
             srcdir="${basedir}/WEB-INF/src"
             destdir="${basedir}/WEB-INF/classes">
      </javac>
  </target>


<!-- Create a WAR file -->
<target name="war"
  description="Creating the WAR file"
```

```
    if="wars.dir"
  depends="compile">
    <echo message="Creating WAR file..."/>
   <mkdir dir="${wars.dir}" />
   <war warfile="${wars.dir}/${appname}.war" webxml="WEB-INF/web.xml">
        <zipfileset dir="."/>
   </war>
</target>


<!-- Deploy WAR to Tomcat container -->
<target name="unwar" depends="war">
<unwar src="${wars.dir}/${appname}.war" dest="${appname.home}" />
  <echo message="Deploying WAR file..."/>
</target>
</project>
```

Running the Sample

To run the sample, turn the verbose option on to see messages to the console:

```
$ant  -v
```

Summary

After installing the JWSDP from the self-extracting executable, you will have the following tools available on your computer: the UDDI Registry Server, the Tomcat Web server, samples, and services. Installation instructs are carefully detailed in this chapter for ease of use. The JWSDP contains several tools that assist you in deploying your Web services. An integral piece to deploying Web services is registering your Web services within a registry. JWSDP provides a UDDI Registry Server as well as an easy-to-use browser tool for administration of the server. Within this registry browser, you can set up your Web services by identifying them as organizations. Those organizations can be stand-alone or associated with a classification. Then you can easily add your service to the registry with the click of a button. Browsing your available Web services is made easy within the Browse tab of the tool. In addition to the registry server, a full version of Tomcat is provided, enabling you to deploy your WAR files to this server which can execute them. Tomcat also provides a fully-functioning Web server to serve HTML pages, and a servlet/JSP container for the handling of servlet or Java Server Pages requests. Finally, the pack includes several Ant build file samples which you can use to easily compile and build your WAR or JAR files for distribution of your Web applications to the Tomcat Web server or other flavors of Web servers. Ant is easy to use and provides many capabilities in the creation of build files for your Web applications. Many options are available to be added as arguments to the command-line invocation of Ant in order to provide extra functionality.

Solutions Fast Track

The JWSDP UDDI Registry

☑ The UDDI Registry requires the startup of the Tomcat server first.

☑ The UDDI Registry can be administered through the command line or through a browser-based tool.

☑ There are sample registries available within the Registry Browser for more practice.

Tomcat

- ☑ The Tomcat Server can be started or stopped through the command line or from a menu.

- ☑ The Tomcat Server is relatively easy to install and includes a quick environmental setup.

- ☑ Tomcat enables the deployment and redeployment of WAR files.

- ☑ Tomcat executes WAR files by unpacking them into the Tomcat Web applications structure.

Ant

- ☑ Ant uses XML-based files to configure target directories. Written in Java, it uses classes for the actual compilation and execution of a variety of build-related commands.

- ☑ Ant enables multiple targets to be built within one project or build file.

- ☑ The Ant build tool provides many useful built-in tasks offering a multitude of options within the build file.

Frequently Asked Questions

The following Frequently Asked Questions, answered by the authors of this book, are designed to both measure your understanding of the concepts presented in this chapter and to assist you with real-life implementation of these concepts. To have your questions about this chapter answered by the author, browse to **www.syngress.com/solutions** and click on the **"Ask the Author"** form.

Q: What version of Ant should I be using?

A: The JWSDP recommends you use Ant 1.4 or later.

Q: Why isn't there a separate startup command for the UDDI Registry Server?

A: The UDDI Registry Server is actually a special servlet that is run as a Web application within Tomcat. Thus, you must start Tomcat in order to use the registry.

Q: Can Tomcat be used in a production environment?

A: No. Since Tomcat is open-source, there is no support provided for the product in the traditional vendor support manner. However, it could be used in a small production environment so long as the risk is assumed.

Q: I'm new to servlets and Java Server Pages. Where can I go to learn more about them?

A: Go to the Sun Microsystems Trail Maps Web site at http://java.sun.com/docs/books/tutorial.

Q: How does Ant know how to compile my source code just by using the *<javac></javac>* tag?

A: Ant is actually written in Java so all the tags you use actually invoke Java classes that take in your value between the tags as arguments. You can learn more about how Ant works at the Jakarta–Ant Web site at http://jakarta.apache.org/ant/index.html.

Index